The
American
Record

Images of the Nation's Past

Volume Two: Since 1865

The
American
Record

Images of the Nation's Past

Second Edition

Volume Two: Since 1865

Edited by

William Graebner
State University of New York, College at Fredonia

Leonard Richards
University of Massachusetts, Amherst

Alfred A. Knopf   New York

Library of Congress Cataloging-in-Publication Data

The American record.

    Contents: v. 1. To 1877 — v. 2. Since 1865.
    1. United States—History. 2. United States—
History—Sources. I. Graebner, William.
II. Richards, Leonard L.
E178.6.A4145 1987   973   87–3523
ISBN 0–394–35620–9 (v. 1)
ISBN 0–394–35621–7 (v. 2)

Second Edition
987654321
Text design: Leon Bolognese
Cover design: Nadja Furlan-Lorbek

Cover illustration: "Soldier home on furlough, Brown Summit, North Carolina, May 1944."
Photograph by Sol Libsohn. Photographic Archives, University of Louisville, Louisville,
Kentucky.

Preface

During the past two or three decades, the study of history in the United States has become in many ways more sophisticated and, we think, more interesting. Until the 1950s the dominant tradition among American historians was to regard the historian's domain as one that centered on politics, diplomacy, and war. Now, in the late 1980s, historians are eager to address new kinds of subjects, and to include whole sections of the population that were neglected in the traditional preoccupation with presidential administrations, legislation, and treaties. Women and children, the poor and economically marginal, have moved nearer the center of the historians' stage. And we have become almost as eager to know how our ancestors dressed, ate, reared their children, made love, and buried their dead as we are to know how they voted in a particular presidential election. The result is a collective version of our national past that is more inclusive, more complicated, and less settled.

The second edition of *The American Record* continues the effort begun in the first. We have attempted to bridge the gap between the old history and the new, to graft the excitement and variety of modern approaches to history on an existing chronological and topical framework with which most of us feel comfortable. Most of the familiar topics are here. We have included essays on the early colonial settlements, the Revolutionary War, the Founding Fathers, immigration, Progressivism, and the civil rights movement. But by joining these essays to primary sources, we have tried to make it possible for teachers and students to see links between the early settlements and European poverty; between the Revolutionary War and the colonial class structure; between the Founding Fathers and the physical layout of the nation's capital; between immigration and the prairie houses of Frank Lloyd Wright; between Progressivism and the proclamation of Mother's Day; between the civil rights movement and rock 'n' roll. This is a book that teaches the skill of making sense out of one's whole world.

Throughout, we have attempted to incorporate materials with *texture:* documents that are not only striking but that can be given more than one interpretation; photographs that invite real examination and discussion; tables and maps that have something new and interesting to contribute; and essays, such as Allen Matusow's treatment of the New Left and Laurel Thatcher Ulrich's examination of Puritan women, that are at once superb examples of recent historical scholarship and accessible to undergraduates.

From the beginning, we realized that our approach to American history would require adjustment for many students and teachers. It was one thing to expect a student to place an address by Teddy Roosevelt in the context of turn-of-the-century imperialism, yet quite another to expect students to do the same with Edgar Rice Burroughs's *Tarzan of the Apes*. For this reason, we have offered a good deal of guidance. Introductions to primary and second-ary materials are designed not just to provide basic background information, but to suggest productive avenues of interpretation. Interpretive essays and questions are intended to create a kind of mental chemistry in which students will have enough information to experience the excitement of putting things together, and yet not so much guidance that conclusions become obvious.

We remain indebted to R. Jackson Wilson, who inspired the first edition of this book. We also wish to thank our editors at Alfred A. Knopf—first David Follmer and then Chris Rogers—for their patient supervision of a difficult project. And we are especially grateful to the teachers and students who used the first edition of *The American Record* and showed us how to make the book better.

William Graebner
State University of New York, College at Fredonia

Leonard Richards
University of Massachusetts, Amherst

Contents

Chapter 6 Progressivism: The Age of Reform *125*

Chapter 7 From War to Normalcy *149*

Chapter 8 The Great Depression and the New Deal *180*

Chapter 13   America Under Siege   335

The American Record

Record

Images of the Nation's Past

Volume Two: Since 1865

1

Reconstruction

When it was first coined in the crisis months between the election of Lincoln and the beginnings of the Civil War, the term "Reconstruction" meant simply the reunification of the nation. By the time the war ended in 1865, the idea of Reconstruction was more complicated: it now meant more than simple political re-establishment of the Union; it meant reconstructing the South, refashioning its social and economic life to some degree or other. For the freedmen—many only days removed from slavery—Reconstruction would soon come to represent freedom itself. Even in 1865, most Southern blacks realized that without thoroughgoing Reconstruction, in which freedmen obtained land as well as the right to vote, freedom would mean only a new kind of economic oppression.

Twelve years later, in 1877, many people, North and South, realized that Reconstruction had ended. But by then the term had taken on intense moral meanings. To most white Southerners, it was a term of resentment, the name of a bleak period during which vindictive Yankee politicians had tried to force "black rule" on a "prostrate South." Tried and finally failed, for the South had in the end been "redeemed" by its own leaders. Slavery had ended, but at least white supremacy had been firmly re-established. To perhaps a majority of whites in the North, Reconstruction had over the years become a nuisance, and they were glad to let go of it, to reaffirm the value of the Union, and to let the bitter past die. There were other Northerners, however, who looked back from 1877 to twelve years of moral failure, of lost opportunities to force freedom and equality on an unrepentant South.

There were hundreds of thousands of freedmen who experienced this "moral failure" in very real ways. Instead of farming their own land, they farmed the lands of whites as tenants and sharecroppers. Far from benefiting from meaningful voting rights, most blacks were denied the franchise, and those who continued to exercise it did so in a climate of hostility hardly conducive to political freedom. Nonetheless, it was possible for blacks to look back positively at the Reconstruction experience. The 1866 Civil Rights Act granted blacks both citizenship and all the civil rights possessed by whites. When the constitutionality of that statute seemed in doubt, Congress made ratification of the Fourteenth Amendment (accomplished in 1868) a precondition for Southern restoration to the Union. In theory, that amendment made the federal government the protector of rights that might be invaded by the states. Under "Radical" reconstruction, carried out by Congress after 1867, hundreds of thousands of Southern blacks voted, and many held high elective office. And in 1875, when whites had re-established their authority throughout most of the region, a new civil rights act "guaranteed" blacks equal rights in theaters, inns, and other public places. If in the end it proved impossible to maintain these gains, Reconstruction still remained the bright spot in the lives of many former slaves.

Interpretive Essay

Elizabeth Rauh Bethel

Promised Land

Most accounts of the Reconstruction period have been written largely from the perspective of powerful white men such as presidents, Northern congressmen, or Southern "redeemers." As a result, students often get the impression that all decisions were made by whites, and blacks were idly sitting on their hands, just the beneficiaries or victims of white actions. That was not the case. Throughout the South black men and women, even though they were just months away from slavery, actively shaped their own futures and challenged the power and prejudices of their white neighbors. Most wanted to own land and become family farmers. The odds against them were immense, and many struggled valiantly only to see their hopes dashed by their lack of money, or by political decisions made in distant Washington, or by white terrorists such as the Ku Klux Klan. But some, as Elizabeth Rauh Bethel documents in the following selection, overcame great obstacles and established tightly-knit communities. What do you think accounts for the courage and determination of the families Bethel describes? Do you think the course of

American history would have been changed if most black families during Reconstruction had obtained a forty-acre farm? In what respect?

The opportunity to acquire land was a potent attraction for a people just emerging from bondage, and one commonly pursued by freedmen throughout the South. Cooperative agrarian communities, instigated in some cases by the invading Union Army and in other cases by the freedmen themselves, were scattered across the plantation lands of the South as early as 1863. Collective land purchases and cooperative farming ventures developed in the Tidewater area of Virginia, the Sea Islands of South Carolina and Georgia, and along the Mississippi River as refugees at the earliest contraband camps struggled to establish economic and social stability.

These initial land tenure arrangements, always temporary, stimulated high levels of industrious labor among both those fortunate enough to obtain land and those whose expectations were raised by their neighbors' good fortunes. Although for most freedmen the initial promise of landownership was never realized, heightened expectations resulted in "entire families laboring together, improving their material conditions, laying aside money that might hopefully be used to purchase a farm or a few acres for a homestead of their own" during the final years of the war.

The desire for a plot of land dominated public expressions among the freedmen as well as their day-to-day activities and behaviors. In 1864 Secretary of War Stanton met with Negro leaders in Savannah to discuss the problems of resettlement. During that meeting sixty-seven-year-old freedman Garrison Frazier responded to an inquiry regarding living arrangements by telling Stanton that "we would prefer to 'live by ourselves' rather than 'scattered among the whites.' " These arrangements, he added, should include self-sufficiency established on Negro-owned lands. The sentiments Frazier expressed were not unusual. They were repeated by other freedmen across the South. Tunis Campbell, also recently emancipated, testified before the congressional committee investigating the Ku Klux Klan that "the great cry of our people is to have land." A delegate to the Tennessee Colored Citizens' Convention of 1866 stated that "what is needed for the colored people is land which they own." A recently emancipated Negro representative to the 1868 South Carolina Constitutional Convention, speaking in support of that state's land redistribution program, which eventually gave birth to the Promised Land community, said of the relationship between landownership and the state's Negro population: "Night and day they dream" of owning their own land. "It is their all in all."

At Davis Bend, Mississippi and Port Royal, South Carolina, as well as similar settlements in Louisiana, North Carolina, and Virginia, this dream

From Elizabeth Rauh Bethel, *Promiseland: A Century of Life in a Negro Community* (Philadelphia: Temple University Press, 1981), pp. 3, 5–8, 17–21, 23, 25–33, 39–40. © 1981 by Temple University. Reprinted by permission of Temple University Press.

was in fact realized for a time. Freedmen worked "with commendable zeal
. . . out in the morning before it is light and at work 'til darkness drives
them to their homes" whenever they farmed land which was their own.
John Eaton, who supervised the Davis Bend project, observed that the most
successful land experiments among the freedmen were those in which planta-
tions were subdivided into individually owned and farmed tracts. These small
farms, rather than the larger cooperative ventures, "appeared to hold the
greatest chance for success." The contraband camps and federally directed
farm projects afforded newly emancipated freedmen an opportunity to "redis-
cover and redefine themselves, and to establish communities." Within the
various settlements a stability and social order developed that combined economic self-sufficiency with locally directed and controlled schools, churches,
and mutual aid societies. In the years before the Freedmen's Bureau or the
northern missionary societies penetrated the interior of the South, the freedmen, through their own resourcefulness, erected and supported such community institutions at every opportunity. In obscure settlements with names
like Slabtown and Acreville, Hampton, Alexandria, Saxtonville, and Mitchel-
ville, "status, experience, history, and ideology were potent forces operating
toward cohesiveness and community.". . .

. . . In South Carolina, perhaps more intensely than any of the other
southern states, the thirst for land was acute. It was a possibility sparked
first by General William T. Sherman's military actions along the Sea Islands,
then dashed as quickly as it was born in the distant arena of Washington
politics. Still, the desire for land remained a goal not readily abandoned by
the state's freedpeople, and they implemented a plan to achieve that goal at
the first opportunity. Their chance came at the 1868 South Carolina Constitutional Convention.

South Carolina was among the southern states which refused to ratify
the Fourteenth Amendment to the Constitution, the amendment which established the citizenship of the freedmen. Like her recalcitrant neighbors, the
state was then placed under military government, as outlined by the Military
Reconstruction Act of 1867. Among the mandates of that federal legislation
was a requirement that each of the states in question draft a new state constitution which incorporated the principles of the Fourteenth Amendment. Only
after such new constitutions were completed and implemented were the separate states of the defeated Confederacy eligible for readmission to the Union.

The representatives to these constitutional conventions were selected by
a revolutionary electorate, one which included all adult male Negroes. Registration for the elections was handled by the Army with some informal assistance by "that God-forsaken institution, the Freedman's Bureau." Only South
Carolina among the ten states of the former Confederacy elected a Negro
majority to its convention. The instrument those representatives drafted called
for four major social and political reforms in state government: a state-wide
system of free common schools; universal manhood suffrage; a jury law which
included the Negro electorate in county pools of qualified jurors; and a land

redistribution system designed to benefit the state's landless population, primarily the freedmen.

White response to the new constitution and the social reforms which it outlined was predictably vitriolic. It was condemned by one white newspaper as "the work of sixty-odd Negroes, many of them ignorant and depraved." The authors were publicly ridiculed as representing "the maddest, most unscrupulous, and infamous revolution in history." Despite this and similar vilification, the constitution was ratified in the 1868 referendum, an election boycotted by many white voters and dominated by South Carolina's 81,000 newly enfranchised Negroes, who cast their votes overwhelmingly with the Republicans and for the new constitution.

That same election selected representatives to the state legislature charged with implementing the constitutional reforms. That body, like the constitutional convention, was constituted with a Negro majority; and it moved immediately to establish a common school system and land redistribution program. The freedmen were already registered, and the new jury pools remained the prerogative of the individual counties. The 1868 election also was notable for the numerous attacks and "outrages" which occurred against the more politically active freedmen. Among those Negroes assaulted, beaten, shot, and lynched during the pre-election campaign months were four men who subsequently bought small farms from the Land Commission and settled at Promised Land. Like other freedmen in South Carolina, their open involvement in the state's Republican political machinery led to personal violence.

Wilson Nash was the first of the future Promised Land residents to encounter white brutality and retaliation for his political activities. Nash was nominated by the Republicans as their candidate for Abbeville County's seat in the state legislature at the August 1868 county convention. In October of that year, less than two weeks before the general election, Nash was attacked and shot in the leg by two unidentified white assailants. The "outrage" took place in the barn on his rented farm, not far from Dr. Marshall's farm on Curltail Creek. Wilson Nash was thirty-three years old in 1868, married, and the father of three small children. He had moved from "up around Cokesbury" within Abbeville County, shortly after emancipation to the rented land further west. Within months after the Nash family was settled on their farm, Wilson Nash joined the many Negroes who affiliated with the Republicans, an alliance probably instigated and encouraged by Republican promises of land to the freedmen. The extent of Nash's involvement with local politics was apparent in his nomination for public office; and this same nomination brought him to the forefront of county Negro leadership and to the attention of local whites.

After the attack Nash sent his wife and young children to a neighbor's home, where he probably believed they would be safe. He then mounted his mule and fled his farm, leaving behind thirty bushels of recently harvested corn. Whether Nash also left behind a cotton crop is unknown. It was the unprotected corn crop that worried him as much as his concern for his own safety. He rode his mule into Abbeville and there sought refuge at the local

Freedman's Bureau office where he reported the attack to the local bureau agent and requested military protection for his family and his corn crop. Captain W. F. DeKnight was sympathetic to Nash's plight but was powerless to assist or protect him. DeKnight had no authority in civil matters such as this, and the men who held that power generally ignored such assaults on Negroes. The Nash incident was typical and followed a familiar pattern. The assailants remained unidentified, unapprehended, and unpunished. The attack achieved the desired end, however, for Nash withdrew his name from the slate of legislative candidates. For him there were other considerations which took priority over politics.

Violence against the freedmen of Abbeville County, as elsewhere in the state, continued that fall and escalated as the 1868 election day neared. The victims had in common an involvement with the Republicans, and there was little distinction made between direct and indirect partisan activity. Politically visible Negroes were open targets. Shortly after the Nash shooting young Willis Smith was assaulted, yet another victim of Reconstruction violence. Smith was still a teenager and too young to vote in the elections, but his age afforded him no immunity. He was a known member of the Union League, the most radical and secret of the political organizations which attracted freedmen. While attending a dance one evening, Smith and four other League members were dragged outside the dance hall and brutally beaten by four white men whose identities were hidden by hoods. This attack, too, was an act of political vengeance. It was, as well, one of the earliest Ku Klux Klan appearances in Abbeville. Like other crimes committed against politically active Negroes, this one remained unsolved.

On election day freedmen Washington Green and Allen Goode were precinct managers at the White Hall polling place, near the southern edge of the Marshall land. Their position was a political appointment of some prestige, their reward for affiliation with and loyalty to the Republican cause. The appointment brought them, like Wilson Nash and Willis Smith, to the attention of local whites. On election day the voting proceeded without incident until midday, when two white men attempted to block Negroes from entering the polling site. A scuffle ensued as Green and Goode, acting in their capacity as voting officials, tried to bring the matter to a halt and were shot by the white men. One freedman was killed, two others injured, in the incident which also went unsolved. In none of the attacks were the assailants ever apprehended. Within twenty-four months all four men—Wilson Nash, Willis Smith, Washington Green, and Allen Goode—bought farms at Promised Land.

Despite the violence which surrounded the 1868 elections, the Republicans carried the whole of the state. White Democrats refused to support an election they deemed illegal, and they intimidated the newly enfranchised Negro electorate at every opportunity. The freedmen, nevertheless, flocked to the polls in an unprecedented exercise of their new franchise and sent a body of legislative representatives to the state capitol of Columbia who were wholly committed to the mandates and reforms of the new constitution. Among the first legislative acts was one which formalized the land redistribution program through the creation of the South Carolina Land Commission.

The Land Commission program, as designed by the legislature, was financed through the public sale of state bonds. The capital generated from the bond sales was used to purchase privately owned plantation tracts which were then subdivided and resold to freedmen through long-term (ten years), low-interest (7 percent per annum) loans. The bulk of the commission's trans-actions occurred along the coastal areas of the state where land was readily available. The labor and financial problems of the rice planters of the low-country were generally more acute than those of the up-country cotton plant-ers. As a result, they were more eager to dispose of a portion of the landhold-ings at a reasonable price, and their motives for their dealings with the Land Commission were primarily pecuniary.

Piedmont planters were not so motivated. Many were able to salvage their production by negotiating sharecropping and tenant arrangements. Most operated on a smaller scale than the low-country planters and were less depen-dent on gang labor arrangements. As a consequence, few were as financially pressed as their low-country counterparts, and land was less available for purchase by the Land Commission in the Piedmont region. With only 9 percent of the commission purchases lying in the up-country, the Marshall lands were the exception rather than the rule.

The Marshall sons first advertised the land for sale in 1865. These lands, like others at the eastern edge of the Cotton Belt, were exhausted from genera-tions of cultivation and attendant soil erosion; and for such worn out land the price was greatly inflated. Additionally, two successive years of crop failures, low cotton prices, and a general lack of capital discouraged serious planters from purchasing the lands. The sons then advertised the tract for rent, but the land stood idle. The family wanted to dispose of the land in a single transaction rather than subdivide it, and Dr. Marshall's farm was no competition for the less expensive and more fertile land to the west that was opened for settlement after the war. In 1869 the two sons once again advertised the land for sale, but conditions in Abbeville County were not improved for farmers, and no private buyer came forth.

Having exhausted the possibilities for negotiating a private sale, the family considered alternative prospects for the disposition of a farm that was of little use to them. James L. Orr, a moderate Democrat, former governor (1865 to 1868), and family son-in-law, served as negotiator when the tract was offered to the Land Commission at the grossly inflated price of ten dollars an acre. Equivalent land in Abbeville County was selling for as little as two dollars an acre, and the commission rejected the offer. Political promises took precedence over financial considerations when the commission's regional agent wrote the Land Commission's Advisory Board that "if the land is not bought the (Republican) party is lost in this district." Upon receipt of his advice the commission immediately met the Marshall family's ten dollar an acre price. By January 1870 the land was subdivided into fifty small farms, averaging slightly less than fifty acres each, which were publicly offered for sale to Negro as well as white buyers.

The Marshall Tract was located in the central sector of old Abbeville County and was easily accessible to most of the freedmen who were to make the lands their home. . . .

The farms on the Marshall Tract were no bargain for the Negroes who bought them. The land was only partially cleared and ready for cultivation, and that which was free of pine trees and underbrush was badly eroded. There was little to recommend the land to cotton farming. Crop failures in 1868 and 1869 severely limited the local economy, which further reduced the possibilities for small farmers working on badly depleted soil. There was little credit available to Abbeville farmers, white or black; and farming lacked not only an unqualified promise of financial gain but even the possibility of breaking even at harvest. Still, it was not the fertility of the soil or the possibility of economic profit that attracted the freedmen to those farms. The single opportunity for landownership, a status which for most Negroes in 1870 symbolized the essence of their freedom, was the prime attraction for the freedmen who bought farms from the subdivided Marshall Tract.

Most of the Negroes who settled the farms knew the area and local conditions well. Many were native to Abbeville County. In addition to Wilson Nash, the Moragne family and their in-laws, the Turners, the Pinckneys, the Letmans, and the Williamses were also natives of Abbeville, from "down over by Bordeaux" in the southwestern rim of the county which borders Georgia. Others came to their new farms from "Dark Corner, over by McCormick," and another nearby Negro settlement, Pettigrew Station—both in Abbeville County. The Redd family lived in Newberry, South Carolina before they bought their farm; and James and Hannah Fields came to Promised Land from the state capitol, Columbia, eighty miles to the east.

Many of the settlers from Abbeville County shared their names with prominent white families—Moragne, Burt, Marshall, Pressley, Frazier, and Pinckney. Their claims to heritage were diverse. One recalled "my grand-daddy was a white man from England," and others remembered slavery times to their children in terms of white fathers who "didn't allow nobody to mess with the colored boys of his." Others dismissed the past and told their grandchildren that "some things is best forgot." A few were so fair skinned that "they could have passed for white if they wanted to," while others who bought farms from the Land Commission "was so black there wasn't no doubt about who their daddy was."

After emancipation many of these former bondsmen stayed in their old neighborhoods, farming in much the same way as they had during slavery times. Some "worked for the marsters at daytime and for theyselves at night" in an early Piedmont version of sharecropping. Old Samuel Marshall was one former slave owner who retained many of his bondsmen as laborers by assuring them that they would receive some land of their own—promising them that "if you clean two acres you get two acres; if you clean ten acres you get ten acres" of farmland. It was this promise which kept some freedmen on the Marshall land until it was sold to the Land Commission. They cut and cleared part of the tract of the native pines and readied it for planting in anticipation of ownership. But the promise proved empty, and Marshall's death and the subsequent sale of his lands to the state deprived many of those who labored day and night on the land of the free farms they hoped would be theirs. "After they had cleaned it up they still had to pay for it." Other freedmen in the county "moved off after slavery ended but couldn't get no place" of their own to farm. Unable to negotiate labor or lease arrangements, they faced a time of homelessness with few resources and limited options until the farms became available to them. A few entered into labor contracts supervised by the Freedman's Bureau or settled on rented farms in the county for a time.

The details of the various postemancipation economic arrangements made by the freedmen who settled on the small tracts at Dr. Marshall's farm, whatever the form they assumed, were dominated by three conscious choices all had in common. The first was their decision to stay in Abbeville County following emancipation. For most of the people who eventually settled in Promised Land, Abbeville was their home as well as the site of their enslavement. There they were surrounded by friends, family and a familiar environment. The second choice this group of freedmen shared was occupational. They had been Piedmont farmers throughout their enslavement, and they chose to remain farmers in their freedom.

Local Negroes made a third conscious decision that for many had long-range importance in their lives and those of their descendents. Through the influence of the Union League, the Freedman's Bureau, the African Methodist Church, and each other, many of the Negroes in Abbeville aligned politically with the Republicans between 1865 and 1870. In Abbeville as elsewhere in the state, this alliance was established enthusiastically. The Republicans promised land as well as suffrage to those who supported them. If their political activities became public knowledge, the freedmen "were safe nowhere"; and men like Wilson Nash, Willis Smith, Washington Green, and Allen Goode who were highly visible Negro politicians took great risks in this exercise of freedom. Those risks were not without justification. It was probably not a coincidence that loyalty to the Republican cause was followed by a chance to own land.

. . . The Land Commission first advertised the farms on the Marshall Tract in January and February 1870. Eleven freedmen and their families established conditional ownership of their farms before spring planting that year. They were among a vanguard of some 14,000 Negro families who acquired small farms in South Carolina through the Land Commission program between 1868 and 1879. With a ten-dollar down payment they acquired the right to settle on and till the thin soil. They were also obliged to place at least half of their land under cultivation within three years and to pay all taxes due annually in order to retain their ownership rights.

Among the earliest settlers to the newly created farms was Allen Goode, the precinct manager at White Hall, who bought land in January 1870, almost immediately after it was put on the market. Two brothers-in-law, J. H. Turner and Primus Letman, also bought farms in the early spring that year. Turner was married to LeAnna Moragne and Letman to LeAnna's sister Francis. Elias Harris, a widower with six young children to raise, also came to his lands that spring, as did George Hearst, his son Robert, and their families. Another father-son partnership, Carson and Will Donnelly, settled on adjacent tracts. Willis Smith's father Daniel also bought a farm in 1870.

Allen Goode was the wealthiest of these early settlers. He owned a horse, two oxen, four milk cows, and six hogs. For the other families, both material resources and farm production were modest. Few of the homesteaders produced more than a single bale of cotton on their new farms that first year; but all, like Wilson Nash two years earlier, had respectable corn harvests, a crop essential to "both us and the animals." Most households also had sizable pea, bean, and sweet potato crops and produced their own butter. All but the cotton crops were destined for household consumption, as these earliest settlers established a pattern of subsistence farming that would prevail as a community economic strategy in the coming decades.

This decision by the Promised Land farmers to intensify food production and minimize cotton cultivation, whether intentional or the result of other conditions, was an important initial step toward their attainment of economic self-sufficiency. Small scale cotton farmers in the Black Belt were rarely free agents. Most were quickly trapped in a web of chronic indebtedness and marketing restrictions. Diversification of cash crops was inhibited during the 1870's and 1880's not only by custom and these economic entanglements but also by an absence of local markets, adequate roads, and methods of transportation to move crops other than cotton to larger markets. The Promised Land farmers, generally unwilling to incur debts with the local lien men if they could avoid it, turned to a modified form of subsistence farming as their only realistic land-use option. Through this strategy many of them avoided the "economic nightmare" which fixed the status of other small-scale cotton growers at a level of permanent peonage well into the twentieth century.

The following year, 1871, twenty-five more families scratched up their ten-dollar down payment; and upon presenting it to Hollinshead obtained conditional titles to farms on the Marshall Tract. The Williams family, Amanda and her four adult sons—William, Henry, James, and Moses—purchased farms together that year, probably withdrawing their money from their accounts at the Freedman's Savings and Trust Company Augusta Branch for their separate down payments. Three of the Moragne brothers—Eli, Calvin, and Moses—joined the Turners and the Letmans, their sisters and brothers-in-law, making five households in that corner of the tract soon designated "Moragne Town." John Valentine, whose family was involved in A.M.E. organizational work in Abbeville County, also obtained a conditional title to a farm, although he did not settle there permanently. Henry Redd, like the Williamses, withdrew his savings from the Freedman's Bank and moved to his farm from Newberry, a small town about thirty miles to the east. Moses Wideman, Wells Gray, Frank Hutchison, Samuel Bulow, and Samuel Burt also settled on their farms before spring planting.

As the cluster of Negro-owned farms grew more densely populated, it gradually assumed a unique identity; and this identity, in turn, gave rise to a name, Promised Land. Some remember their grandparents telling them that "the Governor in Columbia [South Carolina] named this place when he sold it to the Negroes." Others contend that the governor had no part in the naming. They argue that these earliest settlers derived the name Promised Land from the conditions of their purchase. "They only promised to pay for it, but they never did!" Indeed, there is some truth in that statement. For although the initial buyers agreed to pay between nine and ten dollars per acre for their land in the original promissory notes, few fulfilled the conditions of those contracts. Final purchase prices were greatly reduced, from ten dollars to $3.25 per acre, a price more in line with prevailing land prices in the Piedmont.

By the end of 1873 forty-four of the fifty farms on the Marshall Tract had been sold. The remaining land, less than seven hundred acres, was the poorest in the tract, badly eroded and at the perimeter of the community. Some of those farms remained unsold until the early 1880's, but even so the land did not go unused. Families too poor to consider buying the farms lived on the state-owned property throughout the 1870's. They were squatters, living there illegally and rent-free, perhaps working a small cotton patch, always a garden. Their condition contrasted sharply with that of the landown- ers who, like other Negroes who purchased farmland during the 1870's, were considered the most prosperous of the rural freedmen. The freeholders in the community were among the pioneers in a movement to acquire land, a movement that stretched across geographical and temporal limits. Even in the absence of state or federal assistance in other regions, and despite the difficulties Negroes faced in negotiating land purchases directly from white landowners during Reconstruction, by 1875 Negroes across the South owned five million acres of farmland. The promises of emancipation were fulfilled for a few, among them the families at Promised Land.

Settlement of the community coincided with the establishment of a public school, another of the revolutionary social reforms mandated by the 1868 constitution. It was the first of several public facilities to serve community residents and was built on land still described officially as "Dr. Marshall's farm." J. H. Turner, Larkin Reynolds, Iverson Reynolds and Hutson Lomax, all Negroes, were the first school trustees. The families established on their new farms sent more than ninety children to the one-room school. Everyone who could be spared from the fields was in the classroom for the short 1870 school term. Although few of the children in the landless families attended school regularly, the landowning families early established a tradition of school attendance for their children consonant with their new status. With limited resources the school began the task of educating local children.

The violence and terror experienced by some of the men of Promised Land during 1868 recurred three years later when Eli and Wade Moragne were attacked and viciously beaten with a wagon whip by a band of Klansmen. Wade was twenty-three that year, Eli two years older. Both were married and had small children. It was rumored that the Moragne brothers were among the most prominent and influential of the Negro Republicans in Abbeville County. Their political activity, compounded by an unusual degree of self-assurance, pride, and dignity, infuriated local whites. Like Wilson Nash, Willis Smith, Washington Green, and Allen Goode, the Moragne brothers were victims of insidious political reprisals. Involvement in Reconstruction politics for Negroes was a dangerous enterprise and one which addressed the past as well as the future. It was an activity suited to young men and those who faced the future bravely. It was not for the timid.

The Republican influence on the freedmen at Promised Land was unmistakable, and there was no evidence that the "outrages" and terrorizations against them slowed their participation in local partisan activities. In addition to the risks, there were benefits to be accrued from their alliance with the Republicans. They enjoyed appointments as precinct managers and school trustees. As candidates for various public offices, they experienced a degree of prestige and public recognition which offset the element of danger they faced. These men, born slaves, rose to positions of prominence as landowners, as political figures, and as makers of a community. Few probably had dared to dream of such possibilities a decade earlier.

During the violent years of Reconstruction there was at least one official attempt to end the anarchy in Abbeville County. The representative to the state legislature, J. Hollinshead—the former regional agent for the Land Commission—stated publicly what many local Negroes already knew privately, that "numerous outrages occur in the county and the laws cannot be enforced by civil authorities." From the floor of the General Assembly of South Carolina Hollinshead called for martial law in Abbeville, a request which did not pass unnoticed locally. The Editor of the *Press* commented on Hollinshead's request for martial law by declaring that such outrages against the freedmen "exist only in the imagination of the legislator." His response was probably typical of the cavalier attitude of southern whites toward the problems of their former bondsmen. Indeed, there were no further reports of violence and attacks against freedmen carried by the *Press,* which failed to note the murder of County Commissioner Henry Nash in February 1871. Like other victims of white terrorists, Nash was a Negro.

While settlement of Dr. Marshall's Farm by the freedmen proceeded, three community residents were arrested for the theft of "some oxen from Dr. H. Drennan who lives near the 'Promiseland.'" Authorities found the heads, tails, and feet of the slaughtered animals near the homes of Ezekiel and Moses Williams and Colbert Jordan. The circumstantial evidence against them seemed convincing; and the three were arrested and then released without bond, pending trial. Colonel Cothran, a former Confederate officer and respected barrister in Abbeville, represented the trio at their trial. Although freedmen in Abbeville courts were generally convicted of whatever crime they were charged with, the Williamses and Jordan were acquitted. Justice for Negroes was always a tenuous affair; but it was especially so before black, as well as white, qualified electors were included in the jury pool. The trial of the Williams brothers and Jordan signaled a temporary truce in the racial war, a truce which at least applied to those Negroes settling the farms at Promised Land.

In 1872, the third year of settlement, Promised Land gained nine more households as families moved to land that they "bought for a dollar an acre." There they "plow old oxen, build log cabin houses" as they settled the land they bought "from the Governor in Columbia." Colbert Jordan and Ezekiel Williams, cleared of the oxen stealing charges, both purchased farms that year. Family and kinship ties drew some of the new migrants to the community. Joshuway Wilson, married to Moses Wideman's sister Delphia, bought a farm near his brother-in-law. Two more Moragne brothers, William and Wade, settled near the other family members in "Moragne Town." Whitfield Hutchison, a jack-leg preacher, bought the farm adjacent to his brother Frank. "Old Whit Hutchison could sing about let's go down to the water and be baptized. He didn't have no education, and he didn't know exactly how to put his words, but when he got to singing he could make your hair rise up. He was a number one preacher." Hutchison was not the only preacher among those first settlers. Isaac Y. Moragne, who moved to Promised Land the following year, and several men in the Turner family all combined preaching and farming.

Not all of the settlers came to their new farms as members of such extensive kinship networks as the Moragnes, who counted nine brothers, four sisters, and an assortment of spouses and children among the first Promised Land residents. Even those who joined the community in relative isolation, however, were seldom long in establishing kinship alliances with their neighbors. One such couple was James and Hannah Fields who lived in Columbia before emancipation. While still a slave, James Fields owned property in the state capitol, which was held in trust for him by his master. After emancipation Fields worked for a time as a porter on the Columbia and Greenville Railroad and heard about the up-country land for sale to Negroes as he carried carpet bags and listened to political gossip on the train. Fields went to Abbeville County to inspect the land before he purchased a farm there. While he was visiting, he "run up on Mr. Nathan Redd," old Henry Redd's son. The Fieldses' granddaughter Emily and Nathan were about the same age, and Fields proposed a match to young Redd. "You marry my granddaughter, and I'll will all this land to you and her." The marriage was arranged before the farm was purchased, and eventually the land was transferred to the young couple.

By the conclusion of 1872 forty-eight families were settled on farms in Promised Land. Most of the land was under cultivation, as required by law; but the farmers were also busy with other activities. In addition to the houses and barns which had to be raised as each new family arrived with their few possessions, the men continued their political activities. Iverson Reynolds, J. H. Turner, John and Elias Tolbert, Judson Reynolds, Oscar Pressley, and Washington Green, all community residents, were delegates to the county Republican convention in August 1872. Three of the group were landowners. Their political activities were still not received with much enthusiasm by local whites, but reaction to Negro involvement in politics was lessening in hostility. The *Press* mildly observed that the fall cotton crop was being gathered with good speed and "the farmers have generally been making good use of their time." Cotton picking and politics were both seasonal, and the newspaper chided local Negroes for their priorities. "The blacks have been indulging a little too much in politics but are getting right again." Iverson Reynolds and Washington Green, always among the community's Republican leadership during the 1870's, served as local election managers again for the 1872 fall elections. The men from Promised Land voted without incident that year.

Civic participation among the Promised Land residents extended beyond partisan politics when the county implemented the new jury law in 1872. There had been no Negro jurors for the trial of the Williams brothers and Colbert Jordan the previous year. Although the inclusion of Negroes in the jury pools was a reform mandated in 1868, four years passed before Abbeville authorities drew up new jury lists from the revised voter registration rolls. The jury law was as repugnant to the whites as Negro suffrage, termed "a wretched attempt at legislation, which surpasses anything which has yet been achieved by the Salons in Columbia." When the new lists were finally completed in 1872 the *Press,* ever the reflection of local white public opinion, predicted that "many of [the freedmen] probably have moved away; and the chances are that not many of them will be forthcoming" in the call to jury duty. Neither the initial condemnation of the law nor the optimistic undertones of the *Press* prediction stopped Pope Moragne and Iverson Reynolds from responding to their notices from the Abbeville Courthouse. Both landowners rode their mules up Five Notch Road from Promised Land to Abbeville and served on the county's first integrated jury in the fall of 1872. Moragne and Reynolds were soon followed by others from the community—Allen Goode, Robert Wideman, William Moragne, James Richie, and Luther (Shack) Moragne. By 1874, less than five years after settlement of Dr. Marshall's farm by the new Negro landowners began, the residents of Promised Land remained actively involved in Abbeville County politics. They were undaunted by the *Press* warning that "just so soon as the colored people lose the confidence and support of the North their doom is fixed. The fate of the red man will be theirs." They were voters, jurors, taxpayers, and trustees of the school their children attended. Their collective identity as an exclusively Negro community was well established. . . .

The representatives to the 1868 South Carolina Constitutional Convention who formulated the state's land redistribution hoped to establish an economically independent Negro yeomanry in South Carolina. The Land Commission intended the purchase and resale of Dr. Marshall's farm to solidify the interests of radical Republicanism in Abbeville County, at least for a time. Both of these designs were realized. A third and unintended consequence also resulted. The land fostered a socially autonomous, identifiable community. Drawing on resources and social structures well established within an extant Negro culture, the men and women who settled Promised Land established churches and schools and a viable economic system based on landownership. They maintained that economic autonomy by subsistence farming and supported many of their routine needs by patronizing the locally owned and operated grist mills and general store. The men were actively involved in Reconstruction politics as well as other aspects of civil life, serving regularly on county juries and paying their taxes. Attracted by the security and prestige Promised Land afforded and the possible hope of eventual landownership, fifty additional landless households moved into the community during the 1870's, expanding the 1880 population to almost twice its original size. Together the eighty-nine households laid claim to slightly more than four square miles of land, and within that small territory they "carved out their own little piece of the world."

Sources

The Meaning of Freedom

What did it mean to be free? As Bethel's account of the settlers of Promised Land indicates, there were many obstacles in the path of every freedman and only a few succeeded in becoming independent small farmers. Some twentieth-century writers have argued that the gains for most blacks were minuscule, that being a poor tenant farmer or share-cropper was often even worse than being a slave. But these writers, of course, never experienced the change from slavery to freedom. Here is a man who did.

Dayton, Ohio, August 7, 1865

To My Old Master, Colonel P. H. Anderson,
Big Spring, Tennessee

Sir: I got your letter and was glad to find you had not forgotten Jourdon, and that you wanted me to come back and live with you again, promising to do better for me than anybody else can. I have often felt uneasy about you. I thought the Yankees would have hung you long before this for harboring Rebs they found at your house. I suppose they never heard about your going to Col. Martin's to kill the Union soldier that was left by his company

From Lydia Maria Child, ed., *The Freedmen's Book* (Boston, 1865), pp. 265–267.

in their stable. Although you shot at me twice before I left you, I did not want to hear of your being hurt, and am glad you are still living. It would do me good to go back to the dear old home again and see Miss Mary and Miss Martha and Allen, Esther, Green, and Lee. Give my love to them all, and tell them I hope we will meet in the better world, if not in this. I would have gone back to see you all when I was working in the Nashville hospital, but one of the neighbors told me Henry intended to shoot me if he ever got a chance.

I want to know particularly what the good chance is you propose to give me. I am doing tolerably well here; I get $25 a month, with victuals and clothing; have a comfortable home for Mandy (the folks here call her Mrs. Anderson), and the children, Milly, Jane and Grundy, go to school and are learning well; the teacher says Grundy has a head for a preacher. They go to Sunday-School, and Mandy and me attend church regularly. We are kindly treated; sometimes we overhear others saying, "Them colored people were slaves" down in Tennessee. The children feel hurt when they hear such remarks, but I tell them it was no disgrace in Tennessee to belong to Col. Anderson. Many darkies would have been proud, as I used to was, to call you master. Now, if you will write and say what wages you will give me, I will be better able to decide whether it would be to my advantage to move back again.

As to my freedom, which you say I can have, there is nothing to be gained on that score, as I got my free-papers in 1864 from the Provost-Marshal-General of the Department at Nashville. Mandy says she would be afraid to go back without some proof that you are sincerely disposed to treat us justly and kindly—and we have concluded to test your sincerity by asking you to send us our wages for the time we served you. This will make us forget and forgive old scores, and rely on your justice and friendship in the future. I served you faithfully for thirty-two years and Mandy twenty years. At $25 a month for me, and $2 a week for Mandy, our earnings would amount to $11,680. Add to this the interest for the time our wages has been kept back and deduct what you paid for our clothing and three doctor's visits to me, and pulling a tooth for Mandy, and the balance will show what we are in justice entitled to. Please send the money by Adams Express, in care of V. Winters, esq, Dayton, Ohio. If you fail to pay us for faithful labors in the past we can have little faith in your promises in the future. We trust the good Maker has opened your eyes to the wrongs which you and your fathers have done to me and my fathers, in making us toil for you for generations without recompense. Here I draw my wages every Saturday night, but in Tennessee there was never any pay day for the negroes any more than for the horses and cows. Surely there will be a day of reckoning for those who defraud the laborer of his hire.

In answering this letter please state if there would be any safety for my Milly and Jane, who are now grown up and both good-looking girls. You know how it was with poor Matilda and Catherine. I would rather stay here and starve and die if it comes to that than have my girls brought to shame by the violence and wickedness of their young masters. You will also please state if there has been any schools opened for the colored children in your neighborhood, the great desire of my life now is to give my children an education, and have them form virtuous habits.

P.S.—Say howdy to George Carter, and thank him for taking the pistol from you when you were shooting at me.

From your old servant,

Jourdon Anderson

The Cartoonist's View of Reconstruction

Thomas Nast was America's foremost political cartoonist. He also was a Radical Republican who had no love for the white South or the Democratic party. The touchstone cause of Radical Republicans was black civil rights—particularly the right to vote—and conflict with the Democrats and the white South often focused on this issue. Nast's drawings in *Harper's Weekly,* as you will notice, illustrated vividly this ongoing battle. The high point for Nast came when Hiram Revels, a black, occupied the Senate seat from Mississippi once held by Jefferson Davis. The low point came shortly afterwards. What effect do you think each cartoon had on the electorate? Were any more compelling than the others?

PARDON.

Columbia.–"Shall I Trust These Men,

FRANCHISE.

And Not This Man?''
Thomas Nast, Harper's Weekly, August 5, 1865. Courtesy of The Research Libraries, The New York Public Library, Astor, Lenox and Tilden Foundations.

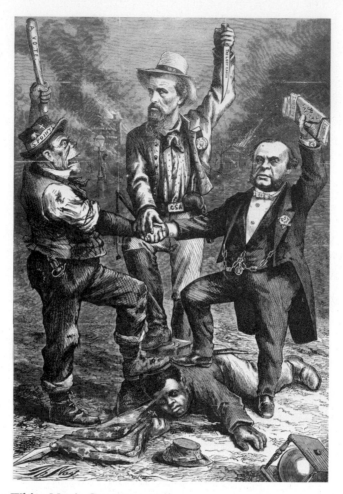

"This Is a White Man's Government."
"We regard the Reconstruction Acts (so called) of Congress as usurpations, and unconstitutional, revolutionary, and void."–*Democratic Platform. Thomas Nast,* Harper's Weekly, *September 5, 1868, Courtesy of The Research Libraries, The New York Public Library, Astor, Lenox and Tilden Foundations.*

"TIME WORKS WONDERS."

IAGO.(JEFF DAVIS.) "FOR THAT I DO SUSPECT THE LUSTY MOOR
HATH LEAP'D INTO MY SEAT: THE THOUGHT WHEREOF
DOTH LIKE A POISONOUS MINERAL GNAW MY INWARDS." — OTHELLO.

Thomas Nast, Harper's Weekly, *April 9, 1870. Courtesy of The Research Libraries, The New York Public Library, Astor, Lenox and Tilden Foundations.*

The Commandments in South Carolina.
"We've pretty well smashed that; but I suppose, Massa Moses, you can get another one." *Thomas Nast,* Harper's Weekly, *September 26, 1874. Courtesy of The Research Libraries, The New York Public Library, Astor, Lenox and Tilden Foundations.*

Thomas Nast, Harper's Weekly, October 24, 1874. Courtesy of The Research Libraries, The New York Public Library, Astor, Lenox and Tilden Foundations.

The Target

". . . They (Messrs. PHELPS & POTTER) seem to regard the White League as *innocent as a Target Company.*"–*Special Dispatch to the "N.Y. Times," from Washington, Jan. 17, 1875. Thomas Nast, Harper's Weekly, February 6, 1875. Courtesy of The Research Libraries, The New York Public Library, Astor, Lenox and Tilden Foundations.*

"To Thine Own Self Be True."
Thomas Nast, Harper's Weekly, April 24, 1875. Courtesy of The Research Libraries, The New York Public Library, Astor, Lenox and Tilden Foundations.

"These Few Precepts in Thy Memory."

Beware of entrance to a quarrel: but, being in,
Bear it that the opposer may beware of thee.
Give every man thine ear, but few thy voice:
Take each man's censure, but reserve thy judgment.
Costly thy habit as thy purse can buy,
But not express'd in fancy; rich, not gaudy:
For the apparel oft proclaims the man.
This above all,—To thine own self be true;
And it must follow, as the night the day,
Thou canst not then be false to any man.

SHAKESPEARE.

The "Civil Rights" Scare Is Nearly Over.
The game of (Colored) fox and (White) goose. *Thomas Nast, Harper's Weekly, May 22, 1875. Courtesy of The Research Libraries, The New York Public Library, Astor, Lenox and Tilden Foundations.*

"Is *This* a Republican Form of Government? Is *This* Protecting Life, Liberty, or Property? Is *This* the Equal Protection of the Laws?"
Mr. Lamar (*Democrat, Mississippi*). "In the words of the inspired poet, 'Thy gentleness has made thee great.'" [Did Mr. LAMAR mean the colored race?] *Thomas Nast,* Harper's Weekly, *September 2, 1876. Courtesy of The Research Libraries, The New York Public Library, Astor, Lenox and Tilden Foundations.*

The South Redeemed

As Nast's cartoons indicate, the crusade for black voting rights and other civil rights ran into stiff opposition and eventually failed. By 1877, white supremacy was firmly re-established throughout the South, and black political voices were almost completely stilled. The South, according to many white Southerners, had been "redeemed" by its white leaders. But the white South did not get back everything it wanted. Black men had refused to work as gang laborers, and black families had refused to let women and children work long hours in the field. Grudgingly, white land owners had let blacks work the land in family plots, usually as either tenant farmers or share-croppers. Thus, despite "redemption," the Southern landscape would look startlingly different after Reconstruction. Here are maps of the same Georgia plantation in 1860 and in 1880. What, in your judgment, were the important features in the new and the old landscape? Do the changes match up with the kinds of attitudes discussed in Bethel's essay? How many of the 1880 families, would you guess, once lived in the old slave quarters?

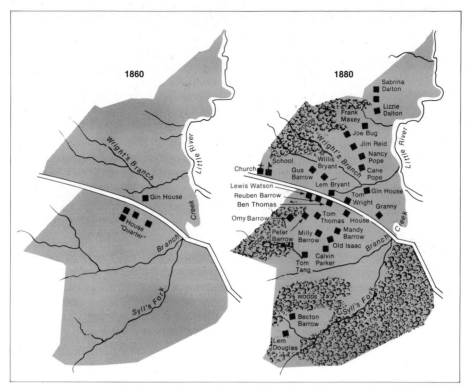

The Barrow Plantation in 1860 and in 1880 *Adapted from* Scribner's Monthly *21 (April 1881): 832–833.*

2

The Gilded Age

Nineteenth-century Americans were obsessed with change, progress, development, and growth. And this obsession reached a new kind of peak during the decades after the Civil War. An American who had matured in the 1850s or 1860s could look backward from 1890 or 1900 and remember a lifetime filled with what seemed to be the most astonishing kinds of transformations.

The facts were there to support such memories of change. The population more than doubled between 1870 and 1900. The telegraph, the telephone, the electric light, and the Linotype were only four of the dozens of inventions that made life—and work—remarkably different. In 1850, most workers were artisans, plying their crafts in small shops under employers working beside them on similar tasks. By 1900, larger industrial enterprises were employing thousands of workers; employers seldom had any personal knowledge of their employees; and much of the skill had been removed from the work process. There were new cities, too—6 in 1900 with populations of more than 500,000. The United States leapfrogged over England, France, and Germany to become the leading industrial nation of the world. Steel production increased 2,000 percent between the Civil War and the end of the century. Many firms for the first time supplied national and urban markets rather than local and rural ones. This meant new opportunities, more intense competition, and, finally, the emergence of the big corporations that have become the hallmark of the American economy. Change was a whirling, accelerating affair that altered the horizons of experience in every decade.

Above the whirl, a kind of official opinion developed, an orthodox opinion that change was "progress." Presidents and senators, newspaper editors and magazine writers, preachers and book publishers—all the molders of what was coming to be thought of as "public opinion"—voiced a belief that industrialization was creating a better life for the republic. Within this view, industrial growth meant opportunity. Competition meant success. All the inventions created leisure and material comfort. The great new factories meant a sort of democracy of well-being for the workers in them. And, in national terms, industrial growth meant the potential triumph in the world of American principles of freedom and equality.

But the awareness of change also generated problems and anxieties. For the wealthy and the sophisticated, there was the possibility that industrialization might lead to a world of materialism, greed, and speculation, a world with only a thin and false veneer of culture and moral values. This fear was a theme of the book that gave a name to the period, Mark Twain and Charles Dudley Warner's *Gilded Age,* published in 1873.

What became known as the "labor question" or the "labor problem" was really a collection of doubts and anxieties. Could the United States absorb the huge pool of immigrants who were attracted to the industrializing cities and towns? Would the new industrial work force tolerate long hours, factory conditions, and gross disparities of wealth, or would they form labor unions and even take to the streets to protest and redress their grievances? Would ordinary Americans continue to believe in the possibilities of success and self-improvement, and so resign themselves to a place in the new order of things? Or would radical ideologies—socialism, communism, anarchism—thrive in the new industrial environment and bring American capitalism crashing down?

Interpretive Essay

Jeremy Brecher

The 1877 Railroad Strike

In the midst of the great economic changes of the latter half of the nineteenth century, most Americans believed that their country could somehow avoid the deep social conflicts and sharp ideological struggles associated with industrialization in Europe. There were, to be sure, disquieting signs. American workers had come together in unions as early as the 1790s, formed workingmen's political parties in the 1820s and 1830s, and, like Philadelphia textile workers in 1844, gone out on strike against their employers. In the decade after the Civil War, national unions, bringing together workers in similar oc-

cupations, had grown dramatically in number and influence, led by
the iron molders and the railroad "brotherhoods." Yet even as
Americans suffered through the depression of the 1870s, it was easy
to believe that race and sectionalism, not class and economics, were
the nation's most critical problems.

With the fourth year of the depression came the rude awakening
known as the 1877 railroad strike. Although less familiar to most students of American history than the Pullman strike and the Homestead strike of the 1890s, the railroad conflict, recounted here by
Jeremy Brecher, was arguably more significant.

While reading Brecher's account, consider the following questions. How did the strike begin, and why did it spread? What did the
railroad workers—and others who became involved—seek to express
through the strike? Did the strikers represent a serious threat to the
social stability of the nation, or even to particular communities? Was
the government's response to the strike justified? In general, was the
strike as significant an event as Brecher seems to think?

In the centers of many American cities are positioned huge armories,
grim nineteenth-century edifices of brick or stone. They are fortresses, complete with massive walls and loopholes for guns. You may have wondered
why they are there, but it has probably never occurred to you that they
were built to protect America, not against invasion from abroad, but against
popular revolt at home. Their erection was a monument to the Great Upheaval
of 1877.

July, 1877, does not appear in many history books as a memorable date,
yet it marks the first great American mass strike, a movement which was
viewed at the time as a violent rebellion. Strikers stopped and seized the
nation's most important industry, the railroads, and crowds defeated or won
over first the police, then the state militias, and in some cases even the Federal
troops. General strikes stopped all activity in a dozen major cities, and strikers
took over social authority in communities across the nation.

It all began on Monday, July 16th, 1877, in the little railroad town of
Martinsburg, West Virginia. On that day, the Baltimore and Ohio Railroad
cut wages ten percent, the second cut in eight months. In Martinsburg, men
gathered around the railroad yards, talking, waiting through the day. Toward
evening the crew of a cattle train, fed up, abandoned the train, and other
trainmen refused to replace them.

As a crowd gathered, the strikers uncoupled the engines, ran them into
the roundhouse, and announced to B&O officials that no trains would leave
Martinsburg till the pay cut was rescinded. The Mayor arrived and conferred
with railroad officials. He tried to soothe the crowd and was booed; when
he ordered the arrest of the strike leaders they just laughed at him, backed

From Jeremy Brecher, *Strike!* (Boston: South End Press, 1972), pp. 1–22. Reprinted by permission
of the publisher.

up in their resistance by the angry crowd. The Mayor's police were helpless against the population of the town. No railroad workers could be found willing to take out a train, so the police withdrew and by midnight the yard was occupied only by a guard of strikers left to enforce the blockade.

That night, B&O officials in Wheeling went to see Governor Matthews, took him to their company telegraph office, and waited while he wired Col. Charles Faulkner, Jr., at Martinsburg, to have his Berkeley Light Guards preserve the peace "if necessary, . . . prevent any interference by rioters with the men at work, and also prevent the obstruction of the trains."

Next morning, when the Martinsburg Master of Transportation ordered the cattle train out again, the strikers' guard swooped down on it and ordered the engineer to stop or be killed. He stopped. By now, hundreds of strikers and townspeople had gathered, and the next train out hardly moved before it was boarded, uncoupled, and run into the roundhouse.

About 9:00 A.M., the Berkeley Light Guards arrived to the sound of a fife and drum; the crowd cheered them. Most of the militiamen were themselves railroaders. Now the cattle train came out once more, this time covered with militiamen, their rifles loaded with ball cartridges. As the train pulled through the yelling crowd, a striker named William Vandergriff turned a switch to derail the train and guarded it with a pistol. A soldier jumped off the train to reset the switch; Vandergriff shot him and in turn was fatally shot himself.

At this, the attempt to break the blockade at Martinsburg was abandoned. The strikebreaking engineer and fireman climbed down from the engine and departed. Col. Faulkner called in vain for volunteers to run the train, announced that the Governor's orders had been fulfilled, dismissed his men, and telegraphed the governor that he was helpless to control the situation.

With this confrontation began the Great Upheaval of 1877, a spontaneous, nationwide, virtually general strike. The pattern of Martinsburg—a railroad strike in response to a pay cut, an attempt by the companies to run trains with the support of military forces, the defeat or dissolution of those forces by amassed crowds representing general popular support—became that same week the pattern for the nation.

With news of success at Martinsburg, the strike spread to all divisions of the B&O, with engineers, brakemen, and conductors joining with the firemen who gave the initial impetus. Freight traffic was stopped all along the line, while the men continued to run passenger and mail cars without interference. Seventy engines and six hundred freight cars were soon piled up in the Martinsburg yards.

The Governor, resolved to break the strike, promised to send a company "in which there are no men unwilling to suppress the riots and execute the law." He sent his only available military force, sixty Light Guards from Wheeling. But the Guards were hardly reliable, for sentiment in Wheeling supported the strike strongly. They marched out of town surrounded by an excited crowd, who, a reporter noted, "all expressed sympathy with the strikers;" box and can makers in Wheeling were already on strike and soon people would be discussing a general strike of all labor. When the Guards' train arrived in Martinsburg, it was met by a large, orderly crowd. The militia's commander conferred with railroad and town officials, but dared not use the troops, lest they "further exasperate the strikers." Instead, he marched them away to the courthouse.

At this point the strike was virtually won. But hardly had the strike broken out when the president of B&O began pressing for the use of the U.S. Army against the strikers in West Virginia. "The loss of an hour would most seriously affect us and imperil vast interests," he wrote. With Federal troops, "the rioters could be dispersed and there would be no difficulty in the movement of trains." The road's vice-president wired his Washington agent, saying that the Governor might soon call for Federal troops, and telling him "to see the Secretary of War and inform him of the serious situation of affairs, that he may be ready to send the necessary force to the scene of action at once." Although a newspaperman on the scene of action at Martinsburg reported "perfect order," and other correspondents were unable to find violence to report, the Colonel of the Guards wired the Governor:

> The feeling here is most intense, and the rioters are largely cooperated with by civilians. . . . The disaffection has become so general that no employee could now be found to run an engine even under certain protection. I am satisfied that Faulkner's experiment of yesterday was thorough and that any repetition of it today would precipitate a bloody conflict, with the odds largely against our small force. . . .

On the basis of this report, the Governor in turn wired the President:

To His Excellency, R. B. Hayes,
President of the U.S.
Washington, D.C.:

Owing to unlawful combinations and domestic violence now existing at Martinsburg and at other points along the line of the Baltimore and Ohio Railroad, it is impossible with any force at my command to execute the laws of the State. I therefore call upon your Excellency for the assistance of the United States military to protect the law abiding people of the State against domestic violence, and to maintain supremacy of the law.

The president of the B&O added his appeal, wiring the President that West Virginia had done all it could "to suppress this insurrection" and warning that "this great national highway [the B&O] can only be restored for public use by the interposition of U.S. forces." In response, President Hayes sent 300 Federal troops to suppress what his Secretary of War was already referring to publicly as "an insurrection."

This "insurrection" was spontaneous and unplanned, but it grew out of the social conditions of the time and the recent experience of the workers. The tactics of the railroad strikers had been developed in a series of local strikes, mostly without trade union support, that occurred in 1873 and 1874. In December, 1873, for example, engineers and firemen on the Pennsylvania Railroad system struck in Chicago, Pittsburgh, Cincinnati, Louisville, Columbus, Indianapolis, and various smaller towns, in what the *Portsmouth* [Ohio] *Tribune* called "the greatest railroad strike" in the nation's history. Huge crowds gathered in depot yards and supported the strikers against attempts to run the trains. State troops were sent into Dennison, Ohio, and Logansport, Indiana, to break strike strongholds. At Susquehanna Depot, Pennsylvania, three months later, shop and repair workers struck. After electing a "Workingmen's Committee," they seized control of the repair shops; within twenty minutes the entire works was reported "under complete control of the men." The strike was finally broken when 1,800 Philadelphia soldiers with thirty pieces of cannon established martial law in this town of 8,000.

The strikes were generally unsuccessful; but, as Herbert Gutman wrote, they "revealed the power of the railroad workers to disrupt traffic on many roads." The employers learned that "they had a rather tenuous hold on the loyalties of their men. Something was radically wrong if workers could successfully stop trains for from two or three days to as much as a week, destroy property, and even 'manage' it as if it were their own." And, Gutman continued, ". . . the same essential patterns of behavior that were widespread in 1877 were found in the 1873–1874 strikes. Three and a half years of severe depression ignited a series of local brush fires into a national conflagration . . ."

The more immediate background of the 1877 railroad strike also helps explain why it took the form of virtual insurrection, for this struggle grew out of the failure of other, less violent forms of action.

The wage cut on the B&O was part of a general pattern which had started June 1st on the Pennsylvania Railroad. When the leaders of the Brotherhoods of Engineers, Conductors, and Firemen made no effort to combat the cut, the railroad workers on the Pennsylvania system took action themselves. A week before the cut went into effect, the Newark, New Jersey division of the Engineers held an angry protest meeting against the cut. The Jersey City lodge met the next day, voted for a strike, and put out feelers to other workers; by the day the cut took effect, engineers' and firemen's locals throughout the Pennsylvania system had chosen delegates to a joint grievance committee, ignoring the leadership of their national union. Nor was the wage cut their only grievance; the committee proposed what amounted to a complete reorganization of work. They opposed the system of assigning trains, in which the first crew into town was the first crew out, leaving them no time to rest or see their families; they wanted regular runs to stabilize pay and working days; they wanted passes home in case of long layovers; they wanted the system of "classification" of workers by length of service and efficiency— used to keep wages down—abolished.

But the grievance committee delegates were easily intimidated and cajoled by Tom Scott, the masterful ruler of the Pennsylvania Railroad, who talked them into accepting the cut without consulting those who elected them. A majority of brakemen, many conductors, and some engineers wanted to repudiate the committee's action; but, their unity broken, the locals decided not to strike.

Since the railroad brotherhoods had clearly failed, the workers' next step was to create a new, secret organization, the Trainmen's Union. It was started by workers on the Pittsburgh, Fort Wayne and Chicago. Within three weeks, lodges had sprung up from Baltimore to Chicago, with thousands of members on many different lines. The Trainmen's Union recognized that the privileged engineers "generally patched things up for themselves," so it included conductors, firemen, brakemen, switchmen, and others besides engineers. The union also realized that the various railroad managements were cooperating against the workers, one railroad after another imitating the Pennsylvania with a ten percent wage cut. The union's strategy was to organize at least three-quarters of the trainmen on each trunk line, then strike against the cuts and other grievances. When a strike came, firemen would not take engineers' jobs, and men on non-striking roads would not handle struck equipment.

But the union was full of spies. On one railroad the firing of members began only four days after the union was formed, and others followed suit: "Determined to stamp it out," as one railroad official put it, the company has issued orders to discharge all men belonging to "the Brotherhood or Union." Nonetheless, on June 24th, forty men fanned out over the railroads to call a general railroad strike for the following week. The railroads learned about the strike through their spies, fired the strike committee in a body, and thus panicked part of the leadership into spreading false word that the strike was off. Local lodges, unprepared to act on their own, flooded the union headquarters with telegrams asking what to do. Union officials were denied use of railroad telegraphs to reply, the companies ran their trains, and the strike failed utterly.

Thus, the Martinsburg strike broke out because the B&O workers had discovered that they had no alternative but to act completely on their own. Not only were their wages being cut, but, as one newspaper reported, the men felt they were "treated just as the rolling stock or locomotives"—squeezed for every drop of profit. Reduced crews were forced to handle extra cars, with lowered pay classifications, and extra pay for overtime eliminated.

A similar spontaneous strike developed that same day in Baltimore in response to the B&O wage cut, but the railroad had simply put strikebreakers on the trains and used local police to disperse the crowds of strikers. What made Martinsburg different? The key to the strike, according to historian Robert Bruce, was that "a conventional strike would last only until strikebreakers could be summoned." To succeed, the strikers had to "beat off strikebreakers by force, seize trains, yards, roundhouses . . ." This was possible in Martinsburg because the people of the town so passionately supported the railroad workers that they amassed and resisted the state militia. It was now the support of others elsewhere which allowed the strikers to resist the Federal troops as well.

On Thursday, 300 Federal troops arrived in Martinsburg to quell the "insurrection" and bivouacked in the roundhouse. With militiamen and U.S. soldiers guarding the yards, the company was able to get a few trains loaded with regulars through the town. When 100 armed strikers tried to stop a train, the Sheriff and the militia marched to the scene and arrested the leader. No one in Martinsburg would take out another train, but with the military in control, strikebreakers from Baltimore were able to run freights through unimpeded. The strike seemed broken.

But the population of the surrounding area also now rallied behind the railroad workers. Hundreds of unemployed and striking boatmen on the Chesapeake and Ohio Canal lay in ambush at Sir John's Run, where they stoned the freight that had broken the Martinsburg blockade, forced it to stop, and then hid when the U.S. regulars attacked. The movement soon spread into Maryland, where at Cumberland a crowd of boatmen, railroaders, and others swarmed around the train and uncoupled the cars. When the train finally got away, a mob at Keyser, West Virginia, ran it onto a side track and took the crew off by force—while the U.S. troops stood helplessly by. Just before midnight, the miners of the area met at Piedmont, four miles from Keyser, and resolved to go to Keyser in the morning and help stop trains. Coal miners and others—"a motley crowd, white and black"—halted a train guarded by fifty U.S. regulars after it pulled out of Martinsburg. At Piedmont a handbill was printed warning the B&O that 15,000 miners, the united citizenry of local communities, and "the working classes of every state in the Union" would support the strikers. "Therefore let the clashing of arms be heard . . . in view of the rights and in the defense of our families we shall conquer, or we shall die."

The result was that most of the trains sent west from Martinsburg never even reached Keyser. All but one, which was under heavy military escort, were stopped by a crowd of unemployed rolling-mill men, migrant workers, boatmen, and young boys at Cumberland, Maryland, and even on the one that went through a trainman was wounded by a gunshot. When two leaders of the crowd were arrested, a great throng went to the Mayor's house, demanded the release of the prisoners, and carried them off on their shoulders.

Faced with the spread of the strike through Maryland, the president of the B&O now persuaded Governor Carrol of Maryland to call up the National Guard in Baltimore and send it to Cumberland. They did not reckon, however, on the reaction of Baltimore to the strike. "The working people everywhere are with us," said a leader of the railroad strikers in Baltimore. "They know what it is to bring up a family on ninety cents a day, to live on beans and corn meal week in and week out, to run in debt at the stores until you cannot get trusted any longer, to see the wife breaking down under privation and distress, and the children growing up sharp and fierce like wolves day after day because they don't get enough to eat."

The bells rang in Baltimore for the militia to assemble just as the factories were letting out for the evening, and a vast crowd assembled as well. At first they cheered the troops, but severely stoned them as they started to march. The crowd was described as "a rough element eager for disturbance; a proportion of mechanics [workers] either out of work or upon inadequate pay, whose sullen hearts rankled; and muttering and murmuring gangs of boys, almost outlaws, and ripe for any sort of disturbance." As the 250 men of the first regiment marched out, 25 of them were injured by the stoning of the crowd, but this was only a love-tap. The second regiment was unable even to leave its own armory for a time. Then, when the order was given to march anyway, the crowd stoned them so severely that the troops panicked and opened fire. In the bloody march that followed, the militia killed ten and seriously wounded more than twenty of the crowd, but the crowd continued to resist, and one by one the troops dropped out and went home, and changed into civilian clothing. By the time they reached the station, only 59 of the original 120 men remained in line. Even after they reached the depot, the remaining troops were unable to leave for Cumberland, for a crowd of about 200 drove away the engineer and firemen of the waiting troop train and beat back a squad of policemen who tried to restore control. The militia charged the growing crowd, but were driven back by brickbats and pistol fire. It was at that stage that Governor Carrol, himself bottled up in the depot by the crowd of 15,000, in desperation wired President Hayes to send the U.S. Army.

Like the railroad workers, others joined the "insurrection" out of frustration with other means of struggle. Over the previous years they had experimented with one means of resistance after another, each more radical than the last. First to prove their failure had been the trade unions. In 1870, there were about thirty-three national unions enrolling perhaps five percent of non-farm workers; by 1877, only about nine were left. Total membership plummeted from 300,000 in 1870 to 50,000 in 1876. Under depression conditions, they were simply unable to withstand the organized attack levied by lockouts and blacklisting. Unemployment demonstrations in New York had been ruthlessly broken up by police. Then the first major industrial union in the United States, the Workingmen's Benevolent Association of the anthracite miners, led a strike which was finally broken by the companies, one of which claimed the conflict had cost it $4 million. Next the Molly Maguires—a secret terrorist organization the Irish miners developed to fight the coal operators—were infiltrated and destroyed by agents from the Pinkerton Detective Agency, which specialized in providing spies, agents provocateurs, and private armed forces for employers combatting labor organizations. Thus, by the summer of 1877 it had become clear that no single group of workers—whether through peaceful demonstration, tightly-knit trade unions, armed terrorism, or surprise strikes—could stand against the power of the companies, their armed guards, the Pinkertons, and the armed forces of the Government.

Indeed, the Great Upheaval had been preceded by a seeming quiescence on the part of workers. The general manager of one railroad wrote, June 21st: "The experiment of reducing the salaries has been successfully carried out by all the Roads that have tried it of late, and I have no fear of any trouble with our employees if it is done with a proper show of firmness on our part and they see that they must accept it cheerfully or leave." The very day the strike was breaking out at Martinsburg, Governor Hartranft of Pennsylvania was agreeing with his Adjutant General that the state was enjoying such a calm as it had not known for several years. In less than a week, it would be the center of the insurrection.

Three days after Governor Hartranft's assessment, the Pennsylvania Railroad ordered that all freights eastward from Pittsburgh be run as "double-headers"—with two engines and twice as many cars. This meant in effect a speed-up—more work and increased danger of accidents and layoffs. The trains were likely to break and the sections collide, sending fifty or sixty men out of work. Then Pennsylvania trainmen were sitting in the Pittsburgh roundhouse listening to a fireman read them news of the strike elsewhere when the order came to take out a "double-header." At the last minute a flagman named Augustus Harris, acting on his own initiative, refused to obey the order. The conductor appealed to the rest of the crew, but they too refused to move the train. When the company sent for replacements, twenty-five brakemen and conductors refused to take out the train and were fined on the spot. When the dispatcher finally found three yard brakemen to take out the train, a crowd of twenty angry strikers refused to let the train go through. One of them threw a link at a scab, whereupon the volunteer yardmen gave up and went away. Said flagman Andrew Hice, "It's a question of bread or blood, and we're going to resist."

Freight crews joined the strike as their trains came in and were stopped, and a crowd of mill workers, tramps, and boys began to gather at the crossings, preventing freight trains from running while letting passenger trains go through. The company asked the Mayor for police, but since the city was nearly bankrupt the force had been cut in half, and only eight men were available. Further, the Mayor was elected by the strong working-class vote of the city, and shared the city's upper crust's hatred for the Pennsylvania Railroad and its rate discrimination against Pittsburgh. At most the railroad got seventeen police, whom it had to pay itself.

As elsewhere, the Trainmen's Union had nothing to do with the start of the strike. Its top leader, Robert Ammon, had left Pittsburgh to take a job elsewhere, and the president of the Pittsburgh Division didn't even know that trouble was at hand; he slept late that morning, didn't hear about the strike until nearly noon—his first comment was "Impossible!"—and he busied himself primarily at trying to persuade his colleagues to go home and keep out of trouble.

The Trainmen's Union did, however, provide a nucleus for a meeting of the strikers and representatives of such groups as the rolling-mill workers. "We're with you," said one rolling-mill man, pledging the railroaders support from the rest of Pittsburgh labor. "We're in the same boat. I heard a reduction of ten percent hinted at in our mill this morning. I won't call employers despots, I won't call them tyrants, but the term capitalists is sort of synonymous and will do as well." The meeting called on "all workingmen to make common cause with their brethren on the railroad."

In Pittsburgh, railroad officials picked up the ailing Sheriff, waited while he gave the crowd a *pro forma* order to disperse, and then persuaded him to appeal for state troops. That night state officials ordered the militia called up in Pittsburgh but only part of the troops called arrived. Some were held up by the strikers, others simply failed to show up. Two-thirds of one regiment made it; in another regiment not one man appeared. Nor were the troops reliable. As one officer reported to his superior, "You can place little dependence on the troops of your division; some have thrown down their arms, and others have left, and I fear the situation very much." Another officer explained why the troops were unreliable. "Meeting an enemy on the field of battle, you go there to kill. The more you kill, and the quicker you do it, the better. But here you had men with fathers and brothers and relatives mingled in the crowd of rioters. The sympathy of the people, the sympathy of the troops, my own sympathy, was with the strikers proper. We all felt that those men were not receiving enough wages." Indeed, by Saturday morning the militiamen had stacked their arms and were chatting with the crowd, eating hardtack with them, and walking up and down the streets with them, behaving, as a regular army lieutenant put it, "as though they were going to have a party." "You may be called upon to clear the tracks down there," said a lawyer to a soldier. "They may call on me," the soldier replied, "and they may call pretty damn loud before they will clear the tracks."

The *Pittsburgh Leader* came out with an editorial warning of "The Talk of the Desperate" and purporting to quote a "representative workingman": " 'This may be the beginning of a great civil war in this country, between labor and capital. It only needs that the strikers . . . should boldly attack and rout the troops sent to quell them—and they could easily do it if they tried. . . . The workingmen everywhere would all join and help . . . The laboring people, who mostly constitute the militia, will not take up arms to put down their brethren. Will capital, then, rely on the United States Army? Pshaw! These ten or fifteen thousand available men would be swept from our path like leaves in the whirlwind. The workingmen of this country can capture and hold it if they will only stick together. . . . Even if so-called law and order should beat them down in blood . . . we would, at least, have our revenge on the men who have coined our sweat and muscles into millions for themselves, while they think dip is good enough butter for us.' "

All day Friday, the crowds controlled the switches and the officer commanding the Pittsburgh militia refused to clear the crossing with artillery because of the slaughter that would result. People swarmed aboard passenger trains and rode through the city free of charge. The Sheriff warned the women and children to leave lest they be hurt when the army came, but the women replied that they were there to urge the men on. "Why are you acting this way, and why is this crowd here?" the Sheriff asked one young man who had come to Pittsburgh from Eastern Pennsylvania for the strike. "The Pennsylvania has two ends," he replied, "one in Philadelphia and one in Pittsburgh. In Philadelphia they have a strong police force, and they're with the railroad. But in Pittsburgh they have a weak force, and it's a mining and manufacturing district, and we can get all the help we want from the laboring elements, and we've determined to make the strike here." "Are you a railroader?" the Sheriff asked. "No, I'm a laboring man," came the reply.

Railroad and National Guard officials, realizing that the local Pittsburgh militia units were completely unreliable, sent for 600 fresh troops from its commercial rival, Philadelphia. A Pittsburgh steel manufacturer came to warn railroad officials not to send the troops out until workingmen were back in their factories. "I think I know the temper of our men pretty well, and you would be wise not to do anything until Monday. . . . If there's going to be firing, you ought to have at least ten thousand men, and I doubt if even that many could quell the mob that would be brought down on us." These words were prophetic. But, remembering the 2,000 freight cars and locomotives lying idle in the yards, and the still-effective blockade, the railroad official replied, "We must have our property." He looked at his watch and said, "We have now lost an hour and a half's time." He had confidently predicted that "the Philadelphia regiment won't fire over the heads of the mob." Now the massacre he counted on—and the city's retaliation—was at hand.

As the imported troops marched toward the 28th Street railroad crossing, a crowd of 6,000 gathered, mostly spectators. The troops began clearing the tracks with fixed bayonets and the crowd replied with a furious barrage of stones, bricks, coal, and possibly revolver fire. Without orders, the Philadelphia militia began firing as fast as they could, killing twenty people in five minutes as the crowd scattered. Meanwhile, the local Pittsburgh militia stood on the hillside at carry arms and broke for cover when they saw the Philadelphians' Gatling gun come forward. Soon they went home or joined the mob.

With the crossing cleared, the railroad fired up a dozen doubleheaders, but even trainmen who had previously declined to join the strike now refused to run them, and the strike remained unbroken. Their efforts in vain, the Philadelphia militia retired to the roundhouse.

Meanwhile, the entire city mobilized in a fury against the troops who had conducted the massacre and against the Pennsylvania Railroad. Workers rushed home from their factories for pistols, muskets and butcher knives. A delegation of 600 workingmen from nearby Temperanceville marched in with a full band and colors. In some cases the crowd organized itself into crude armed military units, marching together with drums. Civil authority collapsed in the face of the crowd; the Mayor refused to send police or even to try to quiet the crowd himself.

The crowd peppered the troops in the roundhouse with pistol and musket fire, but finally decided, as one member put it, "We'll have them out if we have to roast them out." Oil, coke, and whiskey cars were set alight and pushed downhill toward the roundhouse. A few men began systematically to burn the yards, despite rifle fire from the soldiers, while the crowd held off fire trucks at gunpoint. Sunday morning, the roundhouse caught fire and the Philadelphia militia were forced to evacuate. As they marched along the street they were peppered with fire by the crowd and, according to the troops' own testimony, by Pittsburgh policemen as well. Most of the troops were marched out of town and found refuge a dozen miles away. The few left to guard ammunition found civilian clothes, sneaked away, and hid until the crisis was over. By Saturday night, the last remaining regiment of Pittsburgh militia was disbanded. The crowd had completely routed the army.

Sunday morning, hundreds of people broke into the freight cars in the yards and distributed the goods to the crowds below—on occasion with assistance from police. Burning of cars continued. (According to Carroll D. Wright, first U.S. Commissioner of Labor, "A great many old freight cars which must soon have been replaced by new, were pushed into the fire by agents of the railroad company," to be added to the claims against the country.) The crowd prevented firemen from saving a grain elevator, though it was not owned by the railroad, saying "it's a monopoly, and we're tired of it," but workers pitched in to prevent the spread of the fire to nearby tenements. By Monday, 104 locomotives, more than 2,000 cars, and all of the railroad buildings had been destroyed.

Across the river from Pittsburgh, in the railroad town of Allegheny, a remarkable transfer of authority took place. Using the pretext that the Governor was out of the state, the strikers maintained that the state militia was without legal authority, and therefore proposed to treat them as no more than a mob. The strikers armed themselves—by breaking into the local armory, according to the Mayor—dug rifle pits and trenches outside the Allegheny depot, set up patrols, and warned civilians away from the probable line of fire. The strikers took possession of the telegraph and sent messages up and down the road. They took over management of the railroad, running passenger trains smoothly, moving the freight cars out of the yards, and posting regular armed guards over them. Economic management and political power had in effect been taken over by the strikers. Of course, this kind of transfer of power was not universally understood or approved of, even by those who supported the strike. For example, a meeting of rolling-mill men in Columbus, Ohio, endorsed the railroad strikers, urged labor to combine politically and legislate justice, but rejected "mobbism" as apt to destroy "the best form of republican government."

The strike spread almost as fast as word of it, and with it the conflict with the military. In Columbia, Meadville, and Chenago, Pennsylvania, strikers seized the railroads, occupied the roundhouses, and stopped troop trains. In Buffalo, New York, the militia was stoned on Sunday but scattered the crowd by threatening to shoot. Next morning a crowd armed with knives and cudgels stormed into the railroad shops, brushed aside militia guards and forced shopmen to quit work. They seized the Erie roundhouse and barricaded it. When a militia company marched out to recapture the property, a thousand people blocked and drove them back. By Monday evening, all the major U.S. roads had given up trying to move anything but local passenger trains out of Buffalo. Court testimony later gave a good picture of how the strike spread to Reading, Pennsylvania. At a meeting of workers on the Reading Railroad, the chairman suggested that it would not be a bad idea to do what had been done on the B&O. "While it is hot we can keep the ball rolling," someone chimed in. After some discussion, men volunteered to head off incoming trains. Next day a crowd of 2,000 assembled while twenty-five or fifty men, their faces blackened with coal dust, tore up track, fired trains, and burned a railroad bridge. That evening seven companies of the National Guard arrived. As they marched through a tenement district to clear the tracks, the people of the neighborhood severely stoned them, wounding twenty with missiles and pistol shots. The soldiers opened fire without orders and killed eleven. As in Pittsburgh, the population grew furious over the killings. They plundered freight cars, tore up tracks, and broke into an arsenal, taking sixty rifles. Next day the companies which had conducted the massacre marched down the track together with newly arrived troops; the crowd stoned the former and fraternized with the latter. When the hated Grays turned menacingly toward the crowd, the new troops announced that they would not fire on the people, turned some of their ammunition over to the crowd, and told the Grays, "If you fire at the mob, we'll fire at you."

Such fraternization between troops and the crowd was common. When the Governor sent 170 troops to Newark, Ohio, they were so unpopular that the county commissioners refused to provide their rations. Thereupon the strikers themselves volunteered to feed them. By the end of the day strikers and soldiers were fraternizing in high good humor. Similarly, when the Governor of New York sent 600 troops to the railroad center of Hornellsville, in response to the strike on the Erie, the troops and strikers fraternized, making commanders doubtful of their power to act. When the entire Pennsylvania National Guard was called up in response to the Pittsburgh uprising, a company in Lebanon, Pennsylvania, mutinied and marched through town amidst great excitement. In Altoona, a crowd captured a westbound train carrying 500 militiamen. The troops gave up their arms with the best of will and fraternized with the crowd. The crowd refused to let them proceed, but was glad to let them go home—which one full company and parts of the others proceeded to do. A Philadelphia militia unit straggling home decided to march to Harrisburg and surrender. They entered jovially, shook hands all around, and gave up their guns to the crowd.

Persuasion worked likewise against would-be strikebreakers. When a volunteer started to take a freight train out of Newark, Ohio, a striking fireman held up his hand, three fingers of which had been cut off by a railroad accident. "This is the man whose place you are taking," shouted another striker. "This is the man who works with a hand and a half to earn a dollar and a half a day, three days in the week, for his wife and children. Are you going to take the bread out of his mouth and theirs?" The strikebreaker jumped down amidst cheers.

By now, the movement was no longer simply a railroad strike. With the battles between soldiers and crowds drawn from all parts of the working population, it was increasingly perceived as a struggle between workers as a whole and employers as a whole. This was now reflected in the rapid development of general strikes. After the burning of the railroad yards in Pittsburgh, a general strike movement swept through the area. At nearby McKeesport, workers of the National Tube Works gathered early Monday morning and marched all over town to martial music, calling fellow workers from their houses. From the tube workers the strike spread first to a rolling mill, then a car works, then a planing mill. In mid-morning, 1,000 McKeesport strikers marched with a brass band to Andrew Carnegie's great steel works, calling out planing-mill and tin-mill workers as they went. By mid-afternoon the Carnegie workers and the Braddocks car workers joined the strike. At Castle Shannon, 500 miners struck. On the South Side, laborers struck at Jones and Laughlin and at the Evans, Dalzell & Co. pipe works.

In Buffalo, New York, crowds roamed the city trying to bring about a general strike. They effectively stopped operations at planing mills, tanneries, car works, a bolt and nut factory, hog yards, coal yards, and canal works. In Harrisburg, Pennsylvania, factories and shops throughout the city were closed by strikes and crowd action. In Zanesville, Ohio, 300 unemployed men halted construction on a hotel, then moved through town shutting down nearly every factory and foundry and sending horse-cars to the barns. Next morning a meeting of workingmen drew up a schedule of acceptable wages. In Columbus, a crowd growing from 300 to 2,000 went through town spreading a general strike, successfully calling out workers at a rolling mill, pipe works, fire clay works, pot works, and planing mill. "Shut up or burn up" was the mob's slogan. An offshoot of a rally to support the railroad workers in Toledo, Ohio, resolved to call a general strike for a minimum wage of $1.50 a day. Next morning a large crowd of laborers, grain trimmers, stevedores, and others assembled and created a committee of safety composed of one member from every trade represented in the movement. Three hundred men formed a procession four abreast while a committee called on the management of each factory; workers of those not meeting the demands joined in the strike.

In Chicago, the movement began with a series of mass rallies called by the Workingman's Party, the main radical party of the day, and a strike by forty switchmen on the Michigan Central Railroad. The switchmen roamed through the railroad property with a crowd of 500 others, including strikers from the East who had ridden in to spread the strike, calling out other workers and closing down those railroads that were still running. Next the crowd called out the workers at the stockyards and several packinghouses. Smaller crowds spread out to broaden the strike; one group, for example, called out 500 planing-mill workers, and with them marched down Canal Street and Blue Island Avenue closing down factories. Crews on several lake vessels struck. With transportation dead, the North Chicago rolling mill and many other industries closed for lack of coke and other supplies. Next day the strike spread still further: streetcars, wagons and buggies were stopped; tanneries, stoneworks, clothing factories, lumber yards, brickyards, furniture factories, and a large distillery were closed in response to roving crowds. One day more and the crowds forced officials at the stockyards and gasworks to sign promises to raise wages to $2.00 a day, while more dock and lumber yard workers struck. In the midst of this, the Workingman's Party proclaimed: "Fellow Workers . . . Under any circumstances keep quiet until we have given the present crisis a due consideration."

The general strikes spread even into the South, often starting with black workers and spreading to whites. Texas and Pacific Railroad workers at Marshall, Texas, struck against the pay cut. In response, black longshoremen in nearby Galveston struck for and won pay equal to that of their white fellow workers. Fifty black workers marched down the Strand in Galveston, persuading construction men, track layers and others to strike for $2.00 a day. The next day committees circulated supporting the strike. White workers joined in. The movement was victorious, and $2.00 a day became the going wage for Galveston. In Louisville, Kentucky, black workers made the round of sewers under construction, urging a strike for $1.50 a day. At noon, sewer workers had quit everywhere in town. On Tuesday night a march of 500 stoned the depot of the Louisville and Nashville Railroad, which was refusing a wage increase for laborers. By Wednesday, most of Louisville's factories were shut down by roving crowds, and Thursday brought further strikes by coopers, textile and plow factory workers, brickmakers, and cabinetworkers.

The day the railroad strike reached East St. Louis, the St. Louis Workingman's Party marched 500 strong across the river to join a meeting of 1,000 railroad workers and residents. Said one of the speakers, "All you have to do, gentlemen, for you have the numbers, is to unite on one idea—that the workingmen shall rule the country. What man makes, belongs to him, and the workingmen made this country." The St. Louis General Strike, the peak of the Great Upheaval, for a time nearly realized that goal.

The railroad workers at that meeting voted for a strike, set up a committee of one man from each railroad, and occupied the Relay Depot as their headquarters. The committee promptly posted General Order No. 1, forbidding freight trains from leaving any yard.

That night, across the river in St. Louis, the Workingman's Party called a mass meeting, with crowds so large that three separate speakers' stands were set up simultaneously. "The workingmen," said one speaker, "intend now to assert their rights, even if the result is shedding of blood. . . . They are ready to take up arms at any moment."

Next morning, workers from different shops and plants began to appear at the party headquarters, requesting that committees be sent around to "notify them to stop work and join the other workingmen, that they might have a reason for doing so." The party began to send such committees around, with unexpected results. The coopers struck, marching from shop to shop with a fife and drum shouting, "Come out, come out! No barrels less than nine cents." Newsboys, gasworkers, boatmen, and engineers struck as well. Railroadmen arrived from East St. Louis on engines and flatcars they had commandeered, moving through the yards enforcing General Order No. 1 and closing a wire works.

That day, an "Executive Committee" formed, based at the Workingman's Party headquarters, to coordinate the strike. As one historian wrote, "Nobody ever knew who that executive committee really was; it seems to have been a rather loose body composed of whomsoever chanced to come in and take part in its deliberations."

In the evening, 1,500 men, mostly molders and mechanics, armed themselves with lathes and clubs and marched to the evening's rally. To a crowd of 10,000 the first speaker, a cooper, began, "There was a time in the history of France when the poor found themselves oppressed to such an extent that forbearance ceased to be a virtue, and hundreds of heads tumbled into the basket. That time may have arrived with us." Another speaker called upon the workingmen to organize into companies of ten, twenty, and a hundred, to establish patrols to protect property, and to "organize force to meet force." Someone suggested that "the colored men should have a chance." A black steamboatman spoke for the roustabouts and levee workers. He asked the crowd would they stand behind the levee strikers, regardless of color? "We will!" the crowd shouted back.

The general strike got under way in earnest the next morning. The employees of a beef cannery struck and paraded. The coopers met and discussed their objectives. A force of strikers marched to the levee, where a crowd of steamboatmen and roustabouts "of all colors" forced the captains of boat after boat to sign written promises of fifty percent higher pay. Finally everyone assembled for the day's great march. Six hundred factory workers marched up behind a brass band; a company of railroad strikers came with coupling pins, brake rods, red signal flags and other "irons and implements emblematic of their calling." Strikers' committees went out ahead to call out those still working, and as the march came by, a loaf of bread on a flag-staff for its emblem, workers in foundries, bagging companies, flour mills, bakeries, chemical, zinc and white lead works poured out of their shops and into the crowd. In Carondolet, far on the south side of the city, a similar march developed autonomously, as a crowd of iron workers closed down two zinc works, the Bessemer Steel Works, and other plants. In East St. Louis, there was a parade of women in support of the strike. By sundown, nearly all the manufacturing establishments in the city had been closed. "Business is fairly paralyzed here," said the *Daily Market Reporter*.

But economic activities did not cease completely; some continued under control or by permission of the strikers. The British Consul in St. Louis noted how the railroad strikers had "taken the road into their own hands, running the trains and collecting fares"; "it is to be deplored that a large portion of the general public appear to regard such conduct as a legitimate mode of warfare." It was now the railroad managements which wanted to stop all traffic. One official stated frankly that by stopping all passenger trains, the companies would cut the strikers off from mail facilities and prevent them from sending committees from one point to another along the lines.

Railroad officials, according to the *St. Louis Times,* saw advantage in stopping passenger trains and thus "incommoding the public so as to produce a revolution in the sentiment which now seems to be in favor of the strikers." From the strikers' point of view, running non-freights allowed them to coordinate the strike and show their social responsibility.

The strikers had apparently decided to allow the manufacture of bread, for they permitted a flour mill to remain open. When the owner of the Belcher Sugar Refinery applied to the Executive Committee for permission to operate his plant for forty-eight hours, lest a large quantity of sugar spoil, the Executive Committee persuaded the refinery workers to go back to work and sent a guard of 200 men to protect the refinery. Concludes one historian of the strike, "the Belcher episode revealed . . . the spectacle of the owner of one of the city's largest industrial enterprises recognizing the *de facto* authority of the Executive Committee."

But the strikers here and elsewhere failed to hold what they had conquered. Having shattered the authority of the status quo for a few short days, they faltered and fell back, unsure of what to do. Meanwhile, the forces of law and order—no longer cowering in the face of overwhelming mass force—began to organize. Chicago was typical: President Hayes authorized the use of Federal regulars; citizens' patrols were organized ward by ward, using Civil War veterans; 5,000 special police were sworn in, freeing the regular police for action; big employers organized their reliable employees into armed companies—many of which were sworn in as special police. At first the crowd successfully out-maneuvered the police in the street fighting that ensued, but after killing at least eighteen people the police finally gained control of the crowd and thus broke the back of the movement.

Behind them stood the Federal government. "This insurrection," said General Hancock, the commander in charge of all Federal troops used in the strike, must be stifled "by all possible means." Not that the Federal troops were strong and reliable. The Army was largely tied down by the rebellion of Nez Perces Indians, led by Chief Joseph. In the words of Lieutenant Philip Sheridan, "The troubles on the Rio Grande border, the Indian outbreak on the western frontier of New Mexico, and the Indian war in the Departments of the Platte and Dakota, have kept the small and inadequate forces in this division in a constant state of activity, almost without rest, night and day." Most of the enlisted men had not been paid for months—for the Congress had refused to pass the Army Appropriations Bill so as to force the withdrawal of Reconstruction troops from the South. Finally, the Army included many workers driven into military service by unemployment. As one union iron molder in the Army wrote, "It does not follow that a change of dress involves a change of principle." No mutinies occurred, however, as the 3,000 available Federal troops were rushed under direction of the War Department from city to city, wherever the movement seemed to grow out of control. "The strikers," President Hayes noted emphatically in his diary, "have been put down by *force.*" More than 100 of them were killed in the process.

The Great Upheaval was an expression of the new economic and social system in America, just as surely as the cities, railroads and factories from which it had sprung. The enormous expansion of industry after the Civil War had transformed millions of people who had grown up as farmers and self-employed artisans and entrepreneurs into employees, growing thousands of whom were concentrated within each of the new corporate empires. They were no longer part of village and town communities with their extended families and stable, unchallenged values, but concentrated in cities, with all their anonymity and freedom; their work was no longer individual and competitive, but group and cooperative; they no longer directed their own work, but worked under control of a boss; they no longer controlled the property on which they worked or its fruits, and therefore could not find fruitful employment unless someone with property agreed to hire them. The Great Upheaval grew out of their intuitive sense that they needed each other, had the support of each other, and together were powerful.

This sense of unity was not embodied in any centralized plan or leadership, but in the feelings and action of each participant. "There was no concert of action at the start," the editor of the *Labor Standard* pointed out. "It spread because the workmen of Pittsburgh felt the same oppression that was felt by the workmen of West Virginia and so with the workmen of Chicago and St. Louis." In Pittsburgh, concludes historian Robert Bruce, "Men like Andrew Hice or Gus Harris or David Davis assumed the lead briefly at one point or another, but only because they happened to be foremost in nerve or vehemence." In Newark, Ohio, "no single individual seemed to command the . . . strikers. They followed the sense of the meeting, as Quakers might say, on such proposals as one or another of them . . . put forward. Yet they proceeded with notable coherence, as though fused by their common adversity."

The Great Upheaval was in the end thoroughly defeated, but the struggle was by no means a total loss. Insofar as it aimed at preventing the continued decline of workers' living standards, it won wage concessions in a number of cases and undoubtedly gave pause to would-be wage-cutters to come, for whom the explosive force of the social dynamite with which they tampered had now been revealed. Insofar as it aimed at a workers' seizure of power, its goal was chimerical, for the workers as yet still formed only a minority in a predominantly farm and middle-class society. But the power of workers to virtually stop society, to counter the forces of repression, and to organize cooperative action on a vast scale was revealed in the most dramatic form.

It was not only upon the workers that the Great Upheaval left its mark. Their opponents began building up their power as well, symbolized by the National Guard Armories whose construction began the following year, to contain upheavals yet to come.

Certain periods, wrote Irving Bernstein, bear a special quality in American labor history. "There occurred at these times strikes and social upheavals of extraordinary importance, drama, and violence which ripped the cloak of civilized decorum from society, leaving exposed naked class conflict." Such periods were analyzed before World War I by Rosa Luxemburg and others under the concept of mass strikes. The mass strike, she wrote, signifies not just a single act but a whole period of class struggle.

> Its use, its effects, its reasons for coming about are in a constant state of flux . . . political and economic strikes, united and partial strikes, defensive strikes and combat strikes, general strikes of individual sections of industry and general strikes of entire cities, peaceful wage strikes and street battles, uprisings with barricades—all run together and run alongside each other, get in each other's way, overlap each other; a perpetually moving and changing sea of phenomena.

The Great Upheaval was the first—but by no means the last—mass strike in American history.

Sources

Helen Campbell

Prisoners of Poverty: Domestic Service

We tend to think of labor history as the history of *organized* labor and to mark the progress of working-class Americans by their success in organizing national trade unions and umbrella organizations, such as Samuel Gompers's American Federation of Labor (AFL), established in 1886. Yet throughout the nation's history, only a minority of workers—less than 25 percent—have been organized at any particular time. Women, blacks, workers lacking technical skills— these groups remained almost entirely unorganized until the 1930s.

By the 1880s, when Helen Campbell published her book about women wageworkers, more women were employed in domestic service—as maids, laundresses, and cooks in the households of others— than in any other occupation. None of them belonged to unions.

This passage consists of interviews with women who had left domestic service to take up work in a factory or an office. Consider the interviews as a kind of "window" through which we can see some of the tensions generated by social stratification in Gilded Age America. What is it that these women disliked most about domestic service? If we assume that the concerns of these women were similar to those of other workers, what conclusions might we draw about the "mind" of the working class?

From Helen Campbell, *Prisoners of Poverty: Women Wage-Workers, Their Trades and Their Lives* (1887; reprint, New York: Garrett Press, 1970), pp. 222–231.

Our interest lies in discovering what is at the bottom of the objection to domestic service; how far these objections are rational and to be treated with respect, and how they may be obviated. The mistress's point of view we all know. We know, too, her presentation of objections as she fancies she has discovered them. What we do not know is the ground taken by sensible, self-respecting girls, who have chosen trades in preference, and from whom full detail has been obtained as to the reasons for such choice. In listening to the countless stories of experiment in earning a living, the passage from one industry to another, and the uncertainties and despairs before the right thing had shown itself, the question has always been asked, "How did it happen that you did not try to get a place in some good family?". . .

In the present case it seems well to take the individual testimony, each girl whose verdict is chosen representing a class, and being really its mouth-piece.

First on the list stands Margaret M———, an American, twenty-three years old, and for five years in a paper-box factory. Seven others nodded their assent, or added a word here and there as she gave her view, two of them Irish-Americans who had had some years in the public schools.

"It's freedom that we want when the day's work is done. I know some nice girls, Bridget's cousins, that make more money and dress better and everything for being in service. They're waitresses, and have Thursday afternoon out and part of every other Sunday. But they're never sure of one minute that's their own when they're in the house. Our day is ten hours long, but when it's done it's done, and we can do what we like with the evenings. That's what I've heard from every nice girl that ever tried service. You're never sure that your soul's your own except when you are out of the house, and I couldn't stand that a day. Women care just as much for freedom as men do. Of course they don't get so much, but I know I'd fight for mine."

"Women are always harder on women than men are," said a fur-sewer, an intelligent American about thirty. "I got tired of always sitting, and took a place as chambermaid. The work was all right and the wages good, but I'll tell you what I couldn't stand. The cook and the waitress were just common, uneducated Irish, and I had to room with one and stand the personal habits of both, and the way they did at table took all my appetite. I couldn't eat, and began to run down; and at last I gave notice, and told the truth when I was asked why. The lady just looked at me astonished: 'If you take a servant's place, you can't expect to be one of the family,' she said. 'I never asked it,' I said; 'all I ask is a chance at common decency.' 'It will be difficult to find an easier place than this,' she said, and I knew it; but ease one way was hardness another, and she couldn't see that I had any right to complain. That's one trouble in the way. It's the mixing up of things, and mistresses don't think how they would feel in the same place."

Third came an Irish-American whose mother had been cook for years in one family, but who had, after a few months of service, gone into a jute-mill, followed gradually by five sisters.

"I hate the very words 'service' and 'servant,' " she said. "We came to this country to better ourselves, and it's not bettering to have anybody ordering you round."

"But you are ordered in the mill."

"That's different. A man knows what he wants, and doesn't go beyond it; but a woman never knows what she wants, and sort of bosses you everlastingly. If there was such a thing as fixed hours it might be different, but I tell every girl I know, 'Whatever you do, don't go into service. You'll always be prisoners and always looked down on.' You can do things at home for them as belongs to you that somehow it seems different to do for strangers. Anyway, I hate it, and there's plenty like me."

"What I minded," said a gentle, quiet girl, who worked at a stationer's, and who had tried household service for a year,—"what I minded was the awful lonesomeness. I went for general housework, because I knew all about it, and there were only three in the family. I never minded being alone evenings in my own room, for I'm always reading or something, and I don't go out hardly at all, but then I always know I can, and that there is somebody to talk to if I like. But there, except to give orders, they had nothing to do with me. It got to feel sort of crushing at last. I cried myself sick, and at last I gave it up, though I don't mind the work at all. I know there are good places, but the two I tried happened to be about alike, and I sha'n't try again. There are a good many would feel just the same."

"Oh, nobody need to tell me about poor servants," said an energetic woman of forty, Irish-American, and for years in a shirt factory. "Don't I know the way the hussies'll do, comin' out of a bog maybe, an' not knowing the names even, let alone the use, of half the things in the kitchen, and asking their twelve and fourteen dollars a month? Don't I know it well, an' the shame it is to 'em! but I know plenty o' decent, hard-workin' girls too, that give good satisfaction, an' this is what they say. They say the main trouble is, the mistresses don't know, no more than babies, what a day's work really is. A smart girl keeps on her feet all the time to prove she isn't lazy, for if the mistress finds her sitting down, she thinks there can't be much to do and that she doesn't earn her wages. Then if a girl tries to save herself or is deliberate, they call her slow. They want girls on tap from six in the morning till ten and eleven at night. 'T isn't fair. And then, if there's a let-up in the work, maybe they give you the baby to see to. I like a nice baby, but I don't like having one turned over to me when I'm fit to drop scrabbling to get through and sit down a bit. I've naught to say for the girls that's breaking things and half doing the work. They're a shameful set, and ought to be put down somehow; but it's a fact that the most I've known in service have been another sort that stayed long in places and hated change. There's many a good place too, but the bad ones outnumber 'em. Women make hard mistresses, and I say again, I'd rather be under a man, that knows what he wants. That's the way with most."

"I don't see why people are surprised that we don't rush into places," said a shop-girl. "Our world may be a very narrow world, and I know it is; but for all that, it's the only one we've got, and right or wrong, we're out of it if we go into service. A teacher or cashier or anybody in a store, no matter if they have got common-sense, doesn't want to associate with servants. Somehow you get a sort of smooch. Young men think and say, for I have heard lots of them, 'Oh, she can't amount to much if she hasn't brains enough to make a living outside of a kitchen!' You're just down once for all if you go into one."

"I don't agree with you at all," said a young teacher who had come with her. "The people that hire you go into kitchens and are not disgraced. What I felt was, for you see I tried it, that they oughtn't to make me go into livery.* I was worn out with teaching, and so I concluded to try being a nurse for a while. I found two hard things: one, that I was never free for an hour from the children, for I took meals and all with them, and any mother knows what a rest it is to go quite away from them, even for an hour; and the other was that she wanted me to wear the nurse's cap and apron. She was real good and kind; but when I said, 'Would you like your sister, Miss Louise, to put on cap and apron when she goes out with them?' she got very red, and straightened up. 'It's a very different matter,' she said; 'you must not forget that in accepting a servant's place you accept a servant's limitations.' That finished me. I loved the children, but I said, 'If you have no other thought of what I am to the children than that, I had better go.' I went, and she put a common, uneducated Irish girl in my place. I know a good many who would take nurse's places, and who are sensible enough not to want to push into the family life. But the trouble is that almost every one wants to make a show, and it is more stylish to have the nurse in a cap and apron, and so she is ordered into them.". . .

"My trouble was," said another, who had been in a cotton-mill and gone into the home of one of the mill-owners as chambermaid, "I hadn't any place that I could be alone a minute. We were poor at home, and four of us worked in the mill, but I had a little room all my own, even if it didn't hold much. In that splendid big house the servants' room was over the kitchen,—hot and close in summer, and cold in winter, and four beds in it. We five had to live there together, with only two bureaus and a bit of a closet, and one washstand for all. There was no chance to keep clean or your things in nice order, or anything by yourself, and I gave up. Then I went into a little family and tried general housework, and the mistress taught me a great deal, and was good and kind, only there the kitchen was a dark little place and my room like it, and I hadn't an hour in anything that was pleasant and warm. A mistress might see, you'd think, when a girl was quiet and fond of her home, and treat her different from the kind that destroy everything; but I suppose the truth is, they're worn out with that kind and don't make any difference. It's hard to give up your whole life to somebody else's orders, and always feel as if you was looked at over a wall like; but so it is, and you won't get girls to try it, till somehow or other things are different."

* Livery is the black-and-white uniform worn by servants.—*Ed.*

Home and Family

"Lizzie Borden, with an Ax . . ."

In the summer of 1892, Lizzie Borden apparently killed her father, Andrew Jackson Borden, and her stepmother. (She was never convicted; but after she died, the murder weapon, an ax, was found on the family property in Fall River, Massachusetts.) According to one theory, she committed the crime after her father had threatened to rewrite his will and leave all his property to his wife. Guilty or not, Lizzie Borden was ostracized by the Fall River community for the rest of her life.

We might begin by examining how Andrew Jackson Borden and his family fit into Gilded Age society. Borden was a self-made man in an age that worshiped self-made men. Born into poverty in 1822, he made his first money as an undertaker. The Dun and Bradstreet reports illuminate Borden's success in his middle years. But the late nineteenth century was also an age of conspicuous display, and Borden may have been less adept at this facet of Gilded Age behavior. Do the credit ratings, the floor plan of the Borden house, and the description of the neighborhood form a coherent package? To what extent could Lizzie Borden's crime—if she committed it—have been a result of stresses produced within her family by the expectations of the middle class in the Gilded Age?

Dun and Bradstreet Credit Reports on Andrew Jackson Borden and His Partner

Dec. 8, 1852: "We are well acquainted with both these men and consider them good. They have been in business together some eight years and have always maintained a good reputation. Both have families and appear good for wants."

Oct. 13, 1853: "Good for wants."

March 13, 1854: "Young and good businessmen, attentive and industrious, think means sufficient for the business, in good grade and standing here and considered good for their engagements: making money."

Sept. 1, 1854 through July 1, 1855: "Same."

Jan. 1, 1856: "Good for all wants."

July 17, 1856: "Both are rising young men."

Jan. 28, 1863: "Safe and sound."

Aug. 14, 1863: "Doing well and should pay promptly."

Materials from Stephen Nissenbaum, "Lizzie Borden and Her World," in Stephen Botein et al., eds., *Experiments in Teaching History* (Cambridge, Mass.: Harvard-Danforth Center for Teaching and Learning, 1977), pp. 62–63. Reprinted by permission of the author.

Sept. 8, 1866: "Have just bought real estate for $4,000 in good location. Firm among the best."

Feb. 26, 1867: "Getting rich, own $10,000 worth of real estate in the best parts of the city. Sound as a dollar. Doing good business worth $40,000–50,000, good for wants."

Aug. 3, 1867: "Worth at least $60,000."

April 23, 1868: "Good enough they buy for cash."

Oct. 22, 1868: "Doing good business and gaining."

March 6, 1869: "Good enough, worth $75,000 sure and in good credit."

Sept. 10, 1869: "Same."

March 3, 1870: "Good, honest and reliable men doing sound business, worth nearly $60,000–70,000, own real estate worth about $50,000, are good and sound."

Sept. 14, 1870: "Doing good business and are good for all wants."

March 8, 1871: "Are safe and reliable, doing a large business, worth $75,000–100,000, and gaining all the time. Perfectly sound."

March 18, 1872: "Worth $100,000–125,000, sound and substantial."

Sept. 7, 1872: "Means large, doing well, and in excellent standing."

Floor Plan of the Borden House

# Indicates where bodies were found—Mr. Borden in sitting room and Mrs. Borden upstairs.

Where the Bordens Lived

Ward 4,B   Second Street

No.	Name	Age	Occupt'n
89	Doughlas, Oscar F.	48	Photographer
89	Paltz, Harold	25	Clerk
89	Young, Frank M.	42	Paver
89	Burton, Austin L.	25	"
89	Robinson, Frank M.	21	"
89	" Alfred	25	"
89	Dowd, Andrew	41	Foreman
89	Welch, Thomas	51	Paver
89	Simmons, Charles	23	Clerk
89	Austin, Anson G.	25	
89	Deloiry, James	21	Laborer
89	Finney, John	50	Peddler
89	Condon, John	36	Machinist
90	Hamilton, Charles	54	Decorator
90	" Elmer	20	"
90	Gormley, John H.	32	Butcher
91	Bowen, Seabury W.	42	Physician
92	Borden, Andrew J.	67	Retired Mer.
93	Miller, Southard H.	80	Carpenter
93	" Franklin H.	43	Artist
96	Kelley, Michael	35	Physician
98	Chace, Nathan	64	Driver
98	" David	29	Clerk
98	" Mark	54	Hostler
100	Lee, Chew	36	Laundryman
100	Sing, Yenk	39	"
104	Hughes, Christopher	52	Clergyman
104	O'Keefe, John D.	30	"
104	Sheedy, David F.	27	"
106	Brennan, George H.	27	Editor
110	Kelly, George H.	48	Restaurateur
110	Whitehead, Edward	61	Clerk
110	Barry, Patrick	31	Tailor
110	Creeden, Edward	31	"
110	Rouke, William	30	Clerk
110	Pike, Nathan	55	Stonemason
116	Robinson, John	54	Confectioner
120	Lee, Hop	53	Laundryman
120	Airlie, Gardner	31	Clerk

Victorian Photographs

The following photographs portray the experience of well-to-do
Victorian families—families in many respects not unlike that headed
by Andrew Jackson Borden. "Bedroom in the Finch House" requires
that we ask the meaning of possessions for these late-nineteenth-century elites and that we try to come up with some reason why the
feeling, or tone, of this room is so different from what we would expect to find in its late-twentieth-century equivalent.

"Family Gathering Around a Portrait of Its Patriarch" also tells
us something about Victorian family life and especially, of course,
about patriarchy (a form of community in which the father is the supreme authority in the family). Was the notion of patriarchy still rel-
evant to the society of the Gilded Age? Might there be some connection between the family relationships suggested in this photograph
and Lizzie Borden's alleged murder of her father?

Bedroom in the Finch House, 1884. *Minnesota Historical Society, St. Paul; photo by
T. W. Ingersoll, St. Paul.*

Family Gathering Around a Portrait of Its Patriarch, c. 1890.
Photograph by Charles Currier. *Library of Congress.*

3

Cities and Immigrants

In 1860 there were only 16 cities in the United States with populations over 50,000, and only 3 cities of more than 250,000. By 1900 the corresponding figures were 78 and 15. In the half-century after 1850, the population of Chicago grew from less than 30,000 to more than 1 million. For older, eastern cities, growth meant change in function and structure. Boston, in 1850 a concentrated merchant city of some 200,000 persons, dependent on ocean-going commerce, was by 1900 a sprawling industrial city with a population of more than 1 million.

Entirely new cities arose to meet particular demands of time and place. For George Pullman, of sleeping-car fame, big cities were sordid and disorderly places that spawned crime and violence. He planned and built an entirely new community isolated from disruptive influences where (so he believed) his workers would always be happy (he was mistaken). Western cities also expanded rapidly, usually by virtue of some nearby exploitable resource. Wichita was one of several Kansas towns founded on the cattle trade. Seattle was a timber city. Denver had its origins in the 1857 gold rush, but it remained to service the Great Plains much as Chicago did the Midwest.

The new urban residents were often either immigrants from abroad or migrants from the nation's small towns and rural areas. In 1910 perhaps one-third of the total urban population were native Americans of rural origin; another one-quarter were foreign-born. Although the non-urban population increased absolutely in each decade before 1950, it diminished relatively. During and after the Civil War, the widespread adoption of a variety of labor-saving devices, including cultivators, reapers, mowers, threshers, and corn planters, allowed fewer and fewer farmers to feed the urban populace. Certain areas, such as rural New England, showed marked reductions in population. "We cannot all live in cities," wrote Horace Greeley in the 1860s, "yet nearly all seem determined to do so."

The migration into the United States from abroad was, simply put, a major folk migration. There were 4.1 million foreign-born in the United States in 1860, 13.5 million foreign-born in 1910. And to these numbers must be added the children of the foreign-born—15.6 million in 1900, 18.9 million (more than one out of every five Americans) by 1910.

Some cities attracted a disproportionate share of the foreign-born. By 1910, New York City and two older Massachusetts cities, Fall River and Lowell, had more than 40 percent foreign-born. Twelve major cities, including Boston, Chicago, Milwaukee, Detroit, and San Francisco, had between 30 and 40 percent foreign-born. Seventeen other cities, including Seattle, Portland, Omaha, and Oakland, had over 20 percent foreign-born. (Most Southern cities had less than 10 percent.)

After 1880, another change of importance occurred. The national origin of the nation's foreign-born population shifted from the Northern and Western European mix characteristic of previous decades to the Southern and Eastern European, Jewish and Catholic, mix dominant in 1900. In contrast to the earlier immigrants, a larger proportion of the later immigrants concentrated in the ghettos of northeastern industrial cities. On New York City's Lower East Side, more than 30,000 people were squeezed into half a dozen city blocks.

Ethnic clustering was nothing new, but the unfamiliar languages, customs, and religious practices of the Italians, Russians, Poles, and Slavs seemed to many observers to be associated with slums, unemployment, delinquency, and disease. The later immigrants were also held responsible for the growth of "alien" ideologies—anarchism and socialism—in large American cities in the last quarter of the century. And there was enough truth in this charge to give it some credence. "Red" Emma Goldman, one of the nation's most active anarchists, was Russian-born. Her friend Alexander Berkman, who was born in Poland, made an unsuccessful attempt to kill steel magnate Henry Clay Frick during the 1892 Homestead strike. In Chicago, a center of working-class politics, radical political ideas were especially well represented, and radical leaders were more often than not German-born. Germany, after all, had produced Karl Marx, and Russia, the anarchist Mikhail Bakunin. Europe simply had a more well-developed radical tradition than the United States.

Many new immigrants had with them some portion of this tradition when they set foot on American shores.

This chapter explores several aspects of late-nineteenth-century urban history. How did urban political structures respond to increased population and to the new immigrants? How and why did urban residential patterns change? Were the cities of 1900 simply larger versions of their ancestors of the 1860s, or did they function in different ways? Most important, we shall be concerned with how the urban experience affected ordinary Americans. Were immigration and ghetto life uprooting and seriously disruptive experiences, or did immigrants easily become attached to new values, customs, and institutions as the old ones were stripped away? How did urban residents perceive their lives in the new cities, and how did they change their behavior based on those perceptions?

Interpretive Essay

Irving Howe

World of Our Fathers

We are, in a sense, all immigrants. We leave the "world of our fathers" and locate ourselves in new lives. We leave our homes in Chicago for the opportunities of Phoenix. We leave the protections of childhood for the terrors of adulthood. We leave the truths of our parents to find what is true for us.

The men and women who came to the United States in the late nineteenth century experienced all these dislocations, but with an intensity alien to our own, more stable, round of life. Historians, impressed by this intensity, for years characterized the immigrant experience as one of profound alienation. "The life of the immigrant," wrote Oscar Handlin in his book *The Uprooted,* "was that of a man diverted by unexpected pressures away from the established channels of his existence. Separated, he was never capable of acting with the assurance of habit; always in motion, he could never rely upon roots to hold him up. Instead he had ever to toil painfully from crisis to crisis, as an individual alone, make his way past the discontinuous obstacles of a strange world."

Irving Howe's study of Jewish life on New York City's Lower East Side in the last decades of the nineteenth century offers another perspective. What elements of Handlin's view would Howe accept, and with what would he disagree? Were these Jewish immigrants

**passive victims of forces beyond their control? Or did they find a
way to exert a meaningful influence over the quality and content of
their lives?**

For about thirty or forty years, a mere moment in history, the immigrant
Jews were able to sustain a coherent and self-sufficient culture. It was different
from the one they had left behind, despite major links of continuity, and it
struggled fiercely to keep itself different from the one they found in America,
despite the pressures for assimilation. Between what they had brought and
half preserved from the old world and what they were taking from the new,
the immigrant Jews established a tense balance, an interval of equilibrium.

Traditional faith still formed the foundation of this culture, if only by
providing norms from which deviation had to be measured. The influence
of Russian intellectual styles, in their moral gravity and self-conscious idealism,
remained strong, especially among younger men and women aspiring to the
life of the spirit. Secular Jewishness became a major source of ideas, blending
with elements of religion to create a culture that served as surrogate for
nationhood: a structure of values neither strictly religious nor rigidly skeptical.
And then of course all things American kept pouring into the Jewish streets:
ideas, styles, manners, language, more or less transformed by their absorption
into the culture of *Yiddishkeit*.

Released from the constraints of Europe but not yet tamed by the demands
of America, Jewish immigrant life took on a febrile hurry of motion and
drive. After centuries of excessive discipline, life overflowed—its very shape-
lessness gave proof of vitality. Moral norms, while no longer beyond challenge, continued for a time to be those implanted by Orthodox Judaism,
but manners changed radically, opening into a chaos of improvisation. The
fixed rituals that had bound the east European Jews broke down under the
weight of American freedom. The patterns of social existence had to be remade
each day. The comedy of social dislocation gave edge and abundance to life.

Richer in morals than manners, stronger in ideals than amenities, the
world of the immigrant Jews could not, in any ordinary sense, be called a
"high" culture. It lacked an aristocracy to emulate or attack, it lacked a leisure
class that could validate the pursuit of pleasure, it lacked an aesthetic celebrating the idea of pure art. It had no symphonies or operas, no ballets or museums;
its approach to the treasures of the West was decidedly tentative. There were
many persons of native courtesy and refined bearing in the immigrant world,
but the aesthetics of behavior, a matter of deep moral consequence in traditional Judaism, could hardly be a prime concern on the East Side. The nuances
flourishing in a society secure with its economic surplus and political strength
had yet to appear; visions of life exalting the supremacy of play seemed
distant; the European cult of the gentlemen was barely recognized. It was a

society in which the energies of moral aspiration had not yet become settled, or dissipated, into a system of manners.

There had been rigorous, even rigid systems of manners governing every moment of life in the old world, but these had broken down with migration to America. Gradually, as they rebuilt the foundations of their life, the immigrant Jews re-formed its surface. David Blaustein lectured them on the need to "knock at the door" before going into someone else's room—a courtesy that would have more point once "someone else" had a room of his or her own. Abraham Cahan wrote in the *Forward* that table manners should not simply be dismissed as bourgeois adornments: "Not all rules are silly. You would not like my sleeve to dip into your soup as I reach over your plate to get the salt; it is more reasonable for me to ask you to 'pass the salt, please.'" And Marie Ganz remembered a striking incident when her landlord, Mr. Zalkin, barged into the apartment of Mr. Lipsky, demanding "de rent." "Never mind de rent," answered Mr. Lipsky, "What right you got to come in without being told 'come in'? . . . Take off your hat, go outside, knock on the door, and when I say, 'come in,' and not before, you can come in."

What the East Side lacked in sophistication, it made up in sincerity. It responded to primal experiences with candor and directness. It cut through to the essentials of life: the imperative to do right and the comfort of social bonds. Torn apart, as it soon would be, by insoluble conflicts of value, it lived out its inner struggles and confusions to the very brim of its energy.

At the Heart of the Family

An old man remembering his East Side childhood would say that on coming home from school he had a recurrent fear that his cot in the dining room would again be occupied by a relative just off the boat from Europe and given shelter by his parents. How many other Americans could share, even grasp, this order of experience? Space was the stuff of desire; a room to oneself, a luxury beyond reach. "Privacy in the home was practically unknown. The average apartment consisted of three rooms: a kitchen, a parlor, and a doorless and windowless bedroom between. The parlor became a sleeping-room at night. So did the kitchen when families were unusually large. . . . Made comparatively presentable after a long day of cooking, eating and washing of dishes and laundry, the kitchen was the scene of formal calls at our house and of the visits of friends and prospective suitors." Cramming everything into the kitchen during the evenings had a practical purpose: it saved money on gas and electricity. During the 1890's desperate families had put "three boarders in the front room and two *borderkes* [female boarders] in the kitchen, but today the rooms are too small," noted the *Forward* in 1904. Once boarders could be assigned separate rooms and neither kitchen nor dining room needed to be let, a major advance had been registered in domestic economy.

Only in the kitchen could the family come together in an approximation of community. On most days everyone ate helter-skelter, whenever he could, but on Friday nights, in the mild glow of the Sabbath, the whole family would eat together. Decorum reigned again, the pleasure of doing things as everyone knew they should be done. When a son failed to show up for Friday-night dinners, that was a signal of serious estrangement—not the least use of rules being that they lend clear meaning to violations.

Sitting around the wooden kitchen table that was covered with a white or checkered oilcloth, fathers read newspapers, mothers prepared food, children did homework, boarders gobbled meals. The father's eyes "often fell on the youth at the table who is studying 'Virgil' or on the girl seated in the rocking chair with the big geography on her lap serving as a desk. The atmosphere of the room was not altogether pleasant . . . due to the pail of refuse under the burning stove, which must remain in the house over night by an edict of the janitor." When families took in work, perhaps "finishing" dresses, it was done in the kitchen. Night after night *landslayt* from the old country, recalls Sophie Ruskay, would come to sit in the kitchen, "waiting uncomplainingly until Mama was at leisure. . . . In Yiddish and with eloquent gestures they told the stories of their hardships." For the kitchen was the one place where immigrants might recall to themselves that they were not mere creatures of toil and circumstances, but also human beings defined by their sociability. The kitchen testified to the utterly plebeian character of immigrant Jewish life; the kitchen was warm, close, and bound all to the matrix of family; sometimes of course it could also be maddeningly noisy and crowded—"my own private Coney Island," Zero Mostel has remembered—and then the sole escape was behind the locked door of a toilet or down the steps and into the streets.

In the kitchen the Jewish mother was sovereign. "My mother," recalls Alfred Kazin in his lyrical memoir,

> worked [in the kitchen] all day long, we ate in it almost all meals except the Passover *seder*. . . . The kitchen gave a special character to our lives; my mother's character. All my memories of that kitchen are dominated by the nearness of my mother sitting all day long at her sewing machine, by the clacking of the treadle against the linoleum floor, by the patient twist of her right shoulder as she automatically pushed at the wheel with one hand or lifted her foot to free the needle. . . . The kitchen was her life. Year by year, as I began to take in her fantastic capacity for labor and her anxious zeal, I realized it was ourselves she kept stitching together.

Every recollection of Jewish immigrant life that is concerned with more than the trivia of "local color" notices that as soon as the Jews moved from eastern Europe to America there followed a serious dislocation of the family. Patterns of the family had been firmly set, indeed, had been allowed to become rigid in the old country: the moral authority of the father, the formal submission of the wife together with her frequent dominance in practical affairs, the obedience of children softened by parental indulgences.

An old-world mother—prototype of thousands who would come to America—is sketched by one immigrant:

> She was nervous, clever, restless, obstinate, quick-tempered and very active. She was capable of working from early morning until late at night for her husband and children. . . . Like most Jewish women of those days, she had not been educated. . . . She knew and observed, however, in every particular, all the rules and laws pertaining to the Jewish religion. . . .
>
> The name of God was always on her lips. Always when she was about to start gossiping with other women, she would begin, "May God not punish me for what I am about to say. . . ."
>
> To her children she was a loving despot. For the slightest offense she would curse, threaten, and quite often emphasize her indignation with slaps in the face . . . but soon after she would quietly ask God to forgive her. . . .
>
> "Poor innocent lambs," she would whisper, "it is my fault, not theirs, that we are so poor and they do not get enough to eat. . . ." And so it would go on and on.

In a culture where men were supposed to be—and sometimes were—concerned mainly with the rigors of learning, the mother often became the emotional center of the family, the one figure to whom all turned for comfort and with whom constraints might safely be discarded. Whenever social arrangements demand a harsh discipline, there is likely to be a sanctioned outlet for the overflow of feeling. Among the east European Jews it was the mother. Her mixture of practical sense and emotional abundance was classically celebrated in Jacob Gordin's *Mirele Efros,* a Yiddish play enormously popular in both eastern Europe and America—half culture-myth and half tear-jerker in which errant, ambitious sons come finally to recognize the wisdom of the triumphant matriarch.

Not all or even most Jewish fathers in eastern Europe were learned, nor were all wives prepared to take on the burdens of breadwinning. Still, such families did exist and, more important, they set a standard honored even by those who could not live up to it. Some immigrants tried for a time to continue the old ways. "In our home," remembered Elizabeth Stern, the daughter of a rabbi, "the father was the head, revered and honored. One did not speak to him, nor of him, lightly. He represented an ancient civilization." So he did; yet in the new civilization of America it was to her mother, not her father, that the young Elizabeth turned for practical guidance.

In the turmoil of the American city, traditional family patterns could not long survive. The dispossession and shame of many immigrant fathers has been a major subject for fiction about immigrant Jews, both in English and Yiddish. For the Jewish wife the transition seems to have been a little easier. Having sold herrings in the market place of her *shtetl,* she could sell herrings on Orchard Street—and then, if a little more ambitious, open a grocery or drygoods store. Never having regarded herself as part of a spiritual elite, she did not suffer so wrenching a drop in status and self-regard as her husband. She was a practical person, she had mouths to feed, and, by and large, she saw to it that they were fed.

It was by no means typical of immigrant life that wives should continue to be or become the breadwinners. On the East Side only a tiny fraction of wives worked full time—though most girls did or tried to. If the husband was a responsible man and children began to arrive, the wife usually stayed home, sometimes earning an extra dollar with piecework taken from a garment subcontractor. Not only tradition but practical sense enforced this choice: it was so hard to maintain any sort of decent life in the tenements, it took so much energy just to cook and clean and shop and bring up children, that the immigrant wives, who in any case seldom possessed marketable skills, had to stay home. For both husband and wife, even if there were no children, to spend sixty hours a week in a shop would have made family life all but impossible. Nor did staying home mean leisure or indulgence for the wives. It meant carving out an area of protection for their families, it meant toil and anxiety, which all too often left them worn with fatigue, heavy and shapeless, prematurely aged, their sexuality drained out.

It was from her place in the kitchen that the Jewish housewife became the looming figure who would inspire, haunt, and devastate generations of sons. She realized intuitively that insofar as the outer world tyrannized and wore down her men, reducing them to postures of docility, she alone could create an oasis of order. It was she who would cling to received values and resist the pressures of dispersion; she who would sustain the morale of all around her, mediating quarrels, soothing hurts, drawing a circle of safety in which her children could breathe, and sometimes, as time went on, crushing her loved ones under the weight of her affection. The successful entry of the immigrant Jews into the American business world would require a reassertion of the "male principle," a regathering of authority and aggression—at least outside the home. But in the early years of a family's life in America, it was often the mother who held things together and coped best with the strange new world:

> They were able [reads one account] to maintain the traditional, patriarchal structure. Pauline [the mother], a sensitive woman, declared that the children should not give their household contributions to her, even though she did the shopping and spent most of the cash. She understood the humiliation of Isaac [the unemployed father] and worked to preserve his old role and status, declaring that "Papa should be the manager, he being the head of the household." Thus the forms, if not the entire substance, of family relationships were maintained at the Jacobson home.

To preserve a portion of customary deference to her husband while acquiring the scrappiness demanded by the streets; to gratify her idea of what was morally right while yielding an inch or two to her children; to sustain her personal modesty while beginning to recognize that she was also a woman with desires of her own—it took strength, sometimes an excess of strength, to deal with these conflicting demands.

Quantities of time had to be consumed in finding out where a piece of fresh fish might be gotten for a penny less, or which butcher threw in a few extra bones with a pound of meat. The diet the immigrant mother provided her family was, at the outset, mostly an adaptation of what they had eaten in the old country; poor families were known to subsist for days on herring, bread, and tea, with potatoes and cheap meats like lung among the other staples. Except for horse-radish, carrots, cabbage, and beets, the early immigrants had little fondness for vegetables, though fruit was greatly liked. With time, lettuce and tomatoes came to be "good for the children"—the cult of the vegetable being transmitted to the immigrant kitchen by both the Yiddish newspaper and the American school. (The one provision that was usually delivered to immigrant homes was the plebeian bubbly known as seltzer, in white or blue bottles with a spray on top.)

For both the immigrant mother and her family, food remained at the center of existence. It would be a long time, certainly more than a generation, before one could take for granted having as much food as one might want. Fat meat, the bane of later Americans, seemed a privilege. "The sight of the roast sputtering with hot grease stirred me to ecstasy. In the old home [Europe] I had never had enough meat. . . . Now fat meat was mine for the asking, and what was more I learned that it was cheaper than lean meat, a strange subversion of good taste." To the immigrant mother these words of a young man from the East Side were a matter of course, barely requiring articulation. . . .

Time brought changes. Learning to relish the privileges of suffering, the Jewish mother could become absurdly, outrageously protective. From that condition, especially if linked, as it well might be, with contempt for her husband, she could decline into a brassy scourge, with her grating bark or soul-destroying whine, silver-blue hair, and unfocused aggression. Nor was it unusual for her to employ ingenuity in order to keep her brood in a state of prolonged dependence, as she grew expert at groaning, cajoling, intimidating. Daughters paled, sons fled.

Yet even behind the most insufferable ways of the Jewish mother there was almost always a hard-earned perception of reality. Did she overfeed? Her mind was haunted by memories of a hungry childhood. Did she fuss about health? Infant mortality had been a plague in the old country and the horror of diphtheria overwhelming in this country. Did she dominate everyone within reach? A disarranged family structure endowed her with powers she had never known before, and burdens too; it was to be expected that she should abuse the powers and find advantage in the burdens. The weight of centuries bore down. In her bones, the Jewish mother knew that she and hers, simply by being Jewish, had always to live with a sense of precariousness. When she worried about her little boy going down to play, it was not merely the dangers of Rivington or Cherry Street that she saw—though there *were* dangers on such streets; it was the streets of Kishinev and Bialystok and other towns in which the blood of Jewish children had been spilled. Later, such memories would fade among those she had meant to shield and it would become customary to regard her as a grotesque figure of excess.

Venerated to absurdity, assaulted with a venom that testifies obliquely to her continuing moral and emotional power, the immigrant mother cut her path through the perils and entanglements of American life. Everyone spoke about her, against her, to her, but she herself has left no word to posterity, certainly none in her own voice, perhaps because all the talk about her "role" seemed to her finally trivial, the indulgence of those who had escaped life's primal tasks. Talk was a luxury that her labor would enable her sons to taste.

Boarders, Desertion, Generational Conflict

Composites, by their very nature, omit a wide range of eccentricity and variation. If the Jewish family was a major force making for stability in the immigrant world, it was also peculiarly open to the seepage of alien values. So many demands were made on it that sooner or later it had to show signs of strain and coming apart. No social arrangement as inherently delicate as the family could withstand the assaults that came from all sides—from the school, the street, the theatre, the gangs, the shops, the gentile world, all seemingly united in trying to rip apart the fabric of Jewish life. . . .

The Yiddish press of the early 1900's is filled with articles, some serious and others mere persiflage, concerning the damage wrought by boarders in immigrant homes. The sheer piling in of bodies into small spaces was itself enough to create psychic problems. Samuel Cohen has remembered how his brother Joseph rented a "large two-room flat" for ten dollars a month in order to be able to sublet the bedroom to four boarders, all of them drygoods peddlers, who kept their stock in the same room.

> Each boarder paid seventy-five cents a week, which was to include coffee in the morning and laundering. . . . Each would contribute six cents for a half pound of meat, thus making it two pounds in all, and two cents additional for vegetables in which the meat was cooked. . . . Every morning one of the boarders went down to the grocery store and bought four five-cent rye loaves. They would all breakfast on that with coffee. The remainder of each loaf was laid away for the evening meal. But my sister-in-law could not cut in on the loaves, for they all bore their owners' private marks!

The most severe sign of disturbance was the persistent desertion of families by immigrant husbands. Records of the United Hebrew Charities in New York for the fiscal years 1903 and 1904 show that 1,052, or about 10 percent, of the applications for relief came from deserted women. In Chicago it was 15 percent. The Committee on Desertions of the Conference of Jewish Charities reported that in the period between October 15, 1905, and May 1,

1906, it handled 591 cases of desertion. Fifty-four of these were taken to court, with 33 agreeing to support their families, 18 serving a prison term, 2 released at the wife's request, and one simply destitute; 63 cases were settled out of court, with the husbands either returning to their families or agreeing to support them; 48 cases were pending; and the remainder, somewhat more than half, were "awaiting further information"—that is, the husbands could not be found. In 1911 this work was consolidated on a national scale through the establishment of the National Desertion Bureau. In 1912 it reported 561 cases among Jewish immigrants in New York alone. The reasons given for desertion were: 120, another woman; 47, bad habits; 134, insufficient dowry; 4, wife immoral; 3, another man, and so on. Because many deserted wives, out of shame or fear, failed to report their husbands, many of the men never were in fact discovered. The figures can therefore be taken as, at best, an approximation of how serious the problem was. . . .

An extreme symptom, the desertion of husbands aroused abhorrence among all segments of the immigrant world; but it did not really threaten life at its center, certainly not as much as the friction between parents and children. If conflicts between generations are central to the experience of all immigrant groups, among the Jews these became especially severe because of the persuasion that, at almost any cost, it was necessary to propel sons and daughters into the outer world—or, more precisely, to propel them into the outer world as social beings while trying to keep them spiritually within the Jewish orbit. Morris Raphael Cohen, who grew up on the East Side, saw the conflict between generations mostly as a struggle of ideas: "We called upon the old religion to justify itself on the basis of modern science and culture. But the old generation was not in a position to say how this could be done. . . . What ensued was a struggle between old and new ideals. Homes ceased to be places of peace and in the ensuing discord much of the proverbial strength of the Jewish family was lost." Cohen was surely right in the long run, but it is arguable that during the years when the immigrant culture was at its strongest the clash between generations lent it a kind of vitality, an inner tension generating new energy.

Neither side could have known, nor gained much consolation if it had, that in the cramped precincts of the ghetto they were re-enacting tests of conscience that had shaken European intellectual life throughout the nineteenth century. Denounced as "a daughter of Babylon" when she first brought home earnings from her literary work, and excoriated by a father who cried out that "in America money takes the place of God," Anzia Yezierska was trapped in a heart struggle much like that of George Eliot with her father. The classic war to the death between father and son in Samuel Butler's *The Way of All Flesh* would find a small-scale replica in the fictional memories of Budd Schulberg's *What Makes Sammy Run?*:

> "I hadda chance to make a dollar," Sammy said.
> "Sammy!" his father bellowed. "Touching money on the Sabbath! God should strike you dead!"

The old man snatched the money and flung it down the stairs. . . .

"You big dope!" Sammy screamed at him, his voice shrill with rage. "You lazy son-of-a-bitch."

The old man did not respond. His eyes were closed and his lips were moving. He looked as if he had had a **stroke**. He was praying.

This conflict between generations *had* to be unbearably fierce. Lincoln Steffens, for some years closely involved with the immigrant community, saw

an abyss of many generations. . . . We would pass a synagogue where a score or more of boys were sitting hatless in their old clothes, smoking cigarettes on the steps outside, and their fathers, all dressed in black, with their high hats, uncut beards, and temple curls, were going into the synagogues, tearing their hair and rending their garments. The reporters stopped to laugh; and it was comic; the old men, in their thrift, tore the lapels of their coats very carefully, a very little, but they wept tears, real tears.

It was a struggle beyond conciliation, and the more it raked up old affections the more bitter it grew. Responses that few could allow themselves to recognize or name, responses of embarrassment, guilt, and shame, were brought into the open. One's parents were to be cherished yet kept in the background; to be loved yet brushed aside. Among one's friends, especially if they had some pretensions to culture, it was understood that parents were a cause for uneasiness—a reason, by the way, that so much of the younger generations' social life moved toward the streets. Arthur Goldhaft, son of an immigrant, has expressed with a rare honesty feelings of shame about parents he also loved:

The [immigrant Jews] themselves seemed ready to accept the idea that they were nobodies. They were so scared that they even dropped the pride of a family name. Or maybe they had something deep in them that was a greater pride, that made all this name business a trifle . . . which we, their American children, didn't catch on to. This perhaps is the first key to what disturbed so many of us as we grew up—the feeling that our folks were just nobodies.

How could the younger people understand why their fathers felt that identity rested not in a name—Weisenberg or Weiss or Wiss or even White— but in unbreakable membership in a sanctified people? And even if sons and daughters could understand this, as Goldhaft struggled to, of what earthly use would it be when they began to push their way into American society?

The immigrant leaders and intellectuals tried to cope with the problem, but they were helpless. In 1903 Abraham Cahan printed a *Forward* editorial on baseball, a subject that until then had eluded his public scrutiny. A father had written in bemoaning his son's fondness for baseball: "What is the point of this crazy game? It makes sense to teach a child to play dominoes or chess." But baseball? "The children can get crippled. . . . I want my boy to grow up to be a *mensh,* not a wild American runner." Poor Cahan, trying to cope with problems beyond the wisdom of a Solomon, replied cautiously that Jewish boys should be allowed to play baseball—as if anyone could stop them!—"as long as it does not interfere with their education." Chess was good, "but the body needs to develop also. Baseball is played in the fresh air. The really wild game is football, the aristocratic game in the colleges. Accidents and fights occur in football, but baseball is not dangerous." Even for Cahan there had to be a limit, his Jewish fright and socialist rectitude drawing the line at "aristocratic" football. He ended, however, with his usual good sense: "It is a mistake to keep children locked up in the house. . . . Bring them up to be educated, ethical, and decent, but also to be physically strong so they should not feel inferior.". . .

By 1910, according to [Yiddish poet Abraham] Liessen, one could see an important social change in the East Side. A decade or more earlier, the usual kind of generational clash had occurred between Orthodox parents and radical children, while now it took place between radical parents and worldly, ambitious children. A cruel kind of justice—perhaps the sole answer to Liessen's question "Why don't their intelligent children feel a debt?"

While the generational struggle continued for decades, it would be some years before it seriously threatened the coherence of the immigrant community. Until the First World War large numbers of new immigrants kept arriving, with each new wave forced in part to re-enact the experience of the preceding ones. The institutional structure of the Jewish community kept growing in strength, a barrier against disintegration. And the struggle between old and young continued to be acted out mainly on immigrant territory, even the most rebellious sons still forced by circumstance and feeling to remain within the cultural orbit of their fathers. What would finally doom the immigrant Jewish culture was not any internal development at all, but the ending of immigration in the twenties—for that would signify a decisive tipping of strength in the struggle between old and new.

Sources

The Dumbbell Tenement

Many Lower East Side Jews lived in "dumbbell" tenements, so called because of their shape. Because it was designed as an improvement on existing structures, the dumbbell was, ironically, labeled a "reform." Perhaps it was, but it also had serious deficiencies. Placed side by side, as was the intention, two dumbbells created an airshaft less than 5 feet wide between the buildings.

From the floor plan reproduced below, and from Irving Howe's discussion of Jewish life on the Lower East Side, imagine what it would have been like to live in a dumbbell tenement in the 1880s.

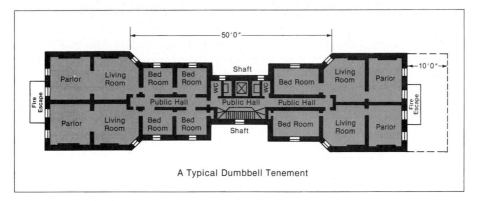

A Typical Dumbbell Tenement

A Typical Dumbbell Tenement. *From Moses Rischin,* The Promised City: New York's Jews, 1870–1914 *(Cambridge, Mass.: Harvard University Press, 1962), p. 83. Reprinted by permission.*

What kinds of experiences would life in such a building promote? And what activities would it inhibit? Speculate on why the building was designed so that the bedrooms in the apartments on the left could be entered from both the living room and the public hallway.

Leonard Covello

What's in a Name?

Leonard Covello came to East Harlem in New York City from Avigliano, Italy, in 1896. In this selection from his autobiography, Covello recalls a quarrel over the family name. What was at stake in the argument? Was there a real difference between how southern Italians and Americans thought about their names? Had Leonard Covello made his name into little more than a commodity, as his mother claimed?

One day I came home from the Soup School with a report card for my father to sign. It was during one of these particularly bleak periods. I remember that my friend Vito Salvatore happened to be there, and Mary Accurso had stopped in for a moment to see my mother. With a weary expression my father glanced over the marks on the report card and was about to sign it. However, he paused with the pen in his hand.

"What is this?" he said. "Leonard Covello! What happened to the *i* in Coviello?"

From Leonard Covello with Guido D'Agostino, *The Heart Is the Teacher* (New York: McGraw-Hill, 1958), pp. 29–31.

My mother paused in her mending. Vito and I just looked at each other.

"Well?" my father insisted.

"Maybe the teacher just forgot to put it in," Mary suggested. "It can happen." She was going to high school now and spoke with an air of authority, and people always listened to her. This time, however, my father didn't even hear her.

"From Leonardo to Leonard I can follow," he said, "a perfectly natural process. In America anything can happen and does happen. But you don't change a family name. A name is a name. What happened to the *i?*"

"Mrs. Cutter took it out," I explained. "Every time she pronounced Coviello it came out Covello. So she took out the *i*. That way it's easier for everybody."

My father thumped Columbus on the head with his fist. "And what has this Mrs. Cutter got to do with my name?"

"What difference does it make?" I said. "It's more American. The *i* doesn't help anything." It was one of the very few times that I dared oppose my father. But even at that age I was beginning to feel that anything that made a name less foreign was an improvement.

Vito came to my rescue. "My name is Victor—Vic. That's what everybody calls me now."

"Vica. Sticka. Nicka. You crazy in the head!" my father yelled at him.

For a moment my father sat there, bitter rebellion building in him. Then with a shrug of resignation, he signed the report card and shoved it over to me. My mother now suddenly entered the argument. "How is it possible to do this to a name? Why did you sign the card? Narduccio, you will have to tell your teacher that a name cannot be changed just like that. . . ."

"Mamma, you don't understand."

"What is there to understand? A person's life and his honor is in his name. He never changes it. A name is not a shirt or a piece of underwear."

My father got up from the table, lighted the twisted stump of a Toscano cigar and moved out of the argument. "Honor!" he muttered to himself.

"You must explain this to your teacher," my mother insisted. "It was a mistake. She will know. She will not let it happen again. You will see."

"It was no mistake. On purpose. The *i* is out and Mrs. Cutter made it Covello. You just don't understand!"

"Will you stop saying that!" my mother insisted. "I don't understand. I don't understand. What is there to understand? Now that you have become Americanized you understand everything and I understand nothing."

With her in this mood I dared make no answer. Mary went over and put her hand on my mother's shoulder. I beckoned to Vito and together we walked out of the flat and downstairs into the street.

"She just doesn't understand," I kept saying.

"I'm gonna take the *e* off the end of my name and make it just Salvator," Vito said. "After all, we're not in Italy now."

Vito and I were standing dejectedly under the gas light on the corner, watching the lamplighter moving from post to post along the cobblestone street and then disappearing around the corner on First Avenue. Somehow or other the joy of childhood had seeped out of our lives. We were only boys, but a sadness that we could not explain pressed down upon us. Mary came and joined us. She had a book under her arm. She stood there for a moment, while her dark eyes surveyed us questioningly.

"But they don't understand!" I insisted.

Mary smiled. "Maybe some day, you will realize that *you* are the one who does not understand."

Urban Barricades: A Photo Essay

By virtue of their size and the new relationships they imposed on their inhabitants, American cities of the late nineteenth century required their residents to live and to communicate in ways unknown just a few decades before. Many of the adjustments that people made—and the institutions they created to facilitate those adjustments—involved either attempts to establish contact where none had existed before or attempts to reduce contact where it was felt to be excessive or inappropriate. Which of the following photographs illustrates each of these efforts? What, for example, is the function of the trademark? Why did it become an important way to market goods in the late nineteenth century? Delmonico's was one of New York City's most elite restaurants and social clubs. What was its purpose? The racial stereotype in the Excelsior ginger ale advertisement suggests the possibility that stereotypes serve a necessary function in an anonymous urban setting. What is that function? Given what you know about Lower East Side Jews from Irving Howe's essay, how do you interpret the gates and fences in the Hebrew Cemetery?

The last photograph is of the Robie house, a so-called prairie house designed by Frank Lloyd Wright. Introduced in 1901, the prairie house was perhaps Wright's most important turn-of-the-century contribution to American architecture and design. More than sixty prairie houses were built in the next decade, many of them in Chicago and surrounding suburbs. What might these houses have offered the families that occupied them? Does the house seem likely to have integrated these families more closely into city life or to have separated them from it?

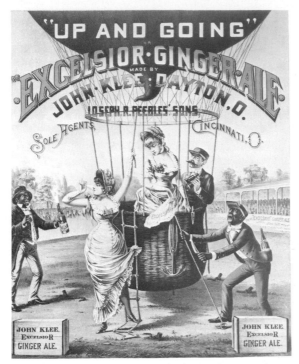

Excelsior Ginger Ale. *Library of Congress.*

Hebrew Cemetery, New York City. *Library of Congress.*

Delmonico's, New York City, 1903. *Library of Congress.*

Frederick C. Robie House, Chicago. *Library of Congress, Historic American Buildings Survey, ILL, 16-Chig., 33–2, No. ILL-1005.*

The Photographer as Reformer: Jacob Riis

Nothing is more embedded in our value structure than the notion that the photograph is objective, a precise rendering of reality ("pictures don't lie"). The photographs taken by Jacob Riis offer an opportunity to assess this belief, for Riis was reformer as well as photographer. A police reporter for two New York City newspapers, Riis wrote an important book about lower-class urban life, *How the Other Half Lives* (1890), founded a settlement house (1901), and was active in the public-park and playground movements. What kind of world view did Riis bring to his work? What did he think of the people clustered at "Bandit's Roost"? Would Riis have argued that the subjects in this photograph were capable of changing their own lives? that their culture was a vital one?

Bandit's Roost, 39½ Mulberry Street, New York City, c. 1888.
Photograph by Jacob A. Riis. *The Jacob A. Riis Collection; Museum of the City of New York.*

4

The
Farming Frontier

The terms "America" and "the West" had seemed synonymous, from the time of the earliest penetration of the Atlantic coastline down into the nineteenth century. But during the years after the Civil War, a new kind of frontier waited to be conquered by white settlers and surrendered in bitter defeat by the Indians. Beyond the Mississippi lay a vast expanse of plains, known officially as "the Great American Desert." Farther west were the seemingly impenetrable mountains and the real deserts of the Southwest. To most Americans, even as late as the 1850s, this half of the continent appeared to be good for little but a permanent reservation for Indian tribes.

Amazingly, in little over a generation, the trans-Mississippi West was settled. The first transcontinental railroad was opened shortly after the Civil War. It was followed by others and by a network of rail lines spreading out into Iowa, Missouri, Texas, and the Dakotas. California became a state on the eve of the Civil War, and by the end of the century the process of state making had filled in almost all the continental map. The last effective Indian resistance was broken in the 1870s and 1880s, when the old policy of war and extermination was replaced with a new form of aggression, called "assimilation." Mining towns sprang from nothing in Nevada, Colorado, and Montana. Texas and Oklahoma became primary cotton-producing states. Cowboys drove Texas longhorns into the new cow towns of Kansas and Nebraska, where the animals could be loaded onto trains headed for eastern slaughterhouses. New techniques of dry farming created one of the world's most productive wheat belts in the western half of the Great Plains. In 1890, just twenty-five years after Grant had accepted Lee's surrender, the

United States Bureau of the Census officially declared that the frontier had ended forever.

The story was not a simple one of geographical expansion. The
settlers of the new West were armed with a new technology that
helped explain the remarkable rapidity of their success. The repeating
rifle and the Gatling gun subdued the Indians. The railroad took the
wheat and cattle east at heretofore incredible speeds. Miners used
steam power and dynamite to pry gold and silver from the mountains. Farmers—the big ones, at least—had the new mechanical
reaper to bring in wheat at a rate that manual labor could not have
approached. Californians were tied to the rest of the Union by the
railroad and the new telegraph.

On the surface, then, the experience was one of triumph—at
least for the white society. But there was a dark side to things, too.
Even dry farming could not overcome periodic droughts, and the
droughts came. There was competition from Russian and Australian
wheat, so prices were very unstable. Some railroads gouged the
farmers. Worst of all, the new technology proved not to be a bless-
ing at all. The new agriculture was just *too* efficient. By 1890, one
farmer could produce and get to market what it had taken eight
farmers to produce fifty years before. Together, they produced more
food than could be sold. So prices fell and stayed down, and farmers
often could not recoup the cost of their seed, much less earn the
money to pay interest on their mortgages and on the loans they had
made to buy their reapers and plows. Agricultural depression was so
severe and frequent that the whole second half of the nineteenth century—except for the war years—was really one long and chronic
economic crisis for farmers, not only in the new West, but everywhere.

Agriculture in the South labored under a different set of burdens. The Civil War created a long-term capital shortage and, of
course, severed the bond that had held slave labor to the plantation.
Southerners responded with two systems. The first, designed to establish a link between free black farm workers and the plantation,
was sharecropping. Under this system, blacks (and poor whites)
agreed to farm the land in return for a share of the crop—usually
one-third. Under the second system, the crop-lien, sharecroppers
and tenant farmers borrowed money and received credit for supplies
and food from merchants and landowners, while pledging in return a
percentage of their crop. Together, sharecropping and the crop-lien
fostered throughout the South a system of peonage, in which poor

whites and blacks were legally bound by debt to work the lands of others.

Farmers sought to redress their grievances through a variety of protest movements, each linked to a particular organization. In the 1860s, Midwestern farmers established the Patrons of Husbandry, better known as the Grange. Its purposes were partly social and partly economic—to lower the costs of shipment and storage of grain. By the 1890s, farmers in the South, the Great Plains, and the Far West had turned to state and national politics. Through the People's party, or Populists, they sought the aid of the national government in inflating a depressed currency and in regulating the railroads and other trusts. Populist influence peaked in 1896, when William Jennings Bryan was the presidential nominee of both the Democrats and the Populists, but declined after Bryan was defeated for the presidency by Republican William McKinley.

There were other, less political, ways of coming to grips with the market revolution, the heritage of slavery, and the dislocation caused by being transplanted, body and soul, onto a remote prairie. Plains farmers brought with them a weapon that helped them overcome the initial reluctance to move onto the hard, unyielding sod of Nebraska and the Dakotas. The weapon was *myth:* the myth that the West was the source of unprecedented opportunity; the myth that climate would respond to the migration of people; the myth that the yeoman farmer—half frontiersman, half man-of-the-soil—could handle anything; the myth that all whites were superior to all Indians.

If the West was all this to the people who lived there, to the majority of Americans, who lived in cities or just "back East," it was a mirror of what Americans were and wanted to be. Frederick Jackson Turner triggered an ongoing debate on the meaning of the West in 1893, when he read an essay, "The Significance of the Frontier in American History," to an audience of fellow historians assembled in Chicago. Turner read American history as the story of the frontier, a continually receding area of free land that had placed generations of Americans on the cutting edge between civilization and savagery. This experience had shaped the national character. It had made Americans intensely individualistic, nationalistic, and democratic. When he linked his frontier thesis to the announcement in the 1890 federal census that the frontier had ceased to exist, Turner implied that these values were in danger—his way, perhaps, of sharing his sadness that an era had come to an end.

Interpretive Essay

Angel Kwolek-Folland

The Elegant Dugout

Almost every American history textbook contains a photograph that purports to describe life on the late-nineteenth-century plains. It usually features a family, sitting stiffly on uncomfortable wooden chairs, their sod house in the background, baking under the prairie sun.

There is a powerful truth in those sod-house photos. But it is a partial truth—an exterior truth, if you will—as the following essay reveals. Using photographs of the interiors of frontier and western homes, Angel Kwolek-Folland describes the remarkable efforts of pioneer women to bring comfort, dignity, and even "civilization" to the Kansas prairies. With its emphasis on the role of women, on space, and on physical culture, the essay is also representative of recent trends in historical writing.

We might begin to examine the essay by comparing and contrasting Kwolek-Folland's description of frontier home life with its urban counterpart, sketched by Irving Howe in Chapter 3. More important, however, is just what conclusions should be drawn from the bewildering array of objects that women imported to the prairies. Were the women who did so necessarily satisfied with their lives? Was it really possible to bring Boston to a Kansas sod house?

Most middle-class American women of the late nineteenth century lived out their lives within the domestic realm, performing tasks that had come to be identified as intrinsically female: caring for small children, tending the ill or aged and managing the daily operations of the household. These things have been so closely identified with Victorian American womanhood that it has been possible to overlook the existence of the physical home as an autonomous cultural creation. Historians frequently have focused on the emotional or political content of the set of beliefs and activities called "domesticity" without analyzing the personal or cultural significance of domestic physical space. Yet for the average late Victorian woman who accepted the conventional wisdom of her time—who was neither a reformer nor a reactionary— the home was a constant physical presence, the arena wherein the behavior of day-to-day life helped to define domesticity. In addition to these personal meanings, the material home was a vital symbol within the context of late Victorian culture, and its continuance as a significant part of American life

Angel Kwolek-Folland, "The Elegant Dugout: Domesticity and Moveable Culture in the United States, 1870–1900," *American Studies* 25 (Fall 1984): 21–37. Reprinted, with author's revisions, from *American Studies,* 25:2. © 1984 Mid-America American Studies Association. Used by permission.

seemed to hinge on whether or not it would adapt to the rapidly-changing society of the late nineteenth century.

Late Victorian definitions of what it meant to be an American derived from an awareness of cultural and physical change and the perceived need to standardize American social institutions. Although mobility always had been a factor in the reality of American political and social institutions, after the Civil War it became a part of the cultural awareness of Americans. The United States Census Bureau, in its documentation of the 1880 census, concentrated almost exclusively on the fact that Americans frequently changed their residence. The attention given by the Bureau to this one aspect of American life at the expense of others illustrates that, perhaps for the first time in American experience, the fact of mobility became a conscious part of national self-definition.

Historians writing about the period 1870 to 1900 have discussed this awareness of change as manifested in areas such as the family, business, religion and politics. Of all these, however, the least-explored is the family and, especially, that construct of feminine experience called "domesticity." The primary purpose of this article is to explore several insistent questions raised by this gap in our knowledge about the late Victorian family. How was domesticity, an essentially conservative construct, reconciled with a mobile society? What was the relationship between women and the mobile physical home? Was personal as well as cultural womanhood bound up with the objects and spaces of the domestic environment? In order to illuminate these questions, I will discuss the behavior of individual women as they created living spaces in both settled and frontier areas of Kansas between 1870 and 1900. Since settlement on the frontier confronted the experience of mobility head on, it magnified phenomena characteristic of the settled life of those who did not choose to become pioneers. Thus, while the pioneer experience was in a certain way unique, in another sense it serves to shed light upon common cultural circumstances.

In addition, this essay will focus on the experience of women settlers, and specifically women's *cultural* role on the frontier in relation to the *physical domestic space* which they occupied and the objects with which they surrounded themselves. The belief in the power of the physical home to transform individual character was an underlying aspect of woman's ideal role in the late nineteenth century. In addition, her ability to create a satisfying domestic environment through the manipulation and placement of domestic objects was an essential part of the late Victorian woman's sense of herself, as well as her awareness of what it meant to be "civilized." The secondary purpose of this article, then, is to explore the cultural role of women in the frontier in relation to the physical arena of domesticity.

i

The settlers of the Kansas frontier of the 1870s and 1880s strove to accommodate rough, make-do living arrangements with ideals of comfort and coziness.

Figure 1. **Interior of Dugout in Ford County, Kansas.** *Kansas State Historical Society.*

The Kansas frontier was not so much conquered as it was domesticated, and women played a leading role in this transformation. The promoters of Kansas settlement expressed their awareness of woman's cultural role when they urged male settlers to cultivate the minds and hearts of the inhabitants by establishing tasteful homes in the new land. "The neat calico dresses and sunshade hats of the ladies, and the cheap but durable raiment of the gentlemen," remarked Evan Jenkins in 1880, "were in harmony with the times, and with the plain domestic spirit that prevailed in the homestead region."

Kansas women, whether in rural, frontier or urban areas, attempted to reproduce the visible symbols of home that were an important part of the late Victorian notion of civilization. Frontierswomen brought with them the furniture and books, the pianos and pans, that would recreate the stable family home wherever they went. Some women compared frontier accommodations favorably to their Eastern background. When Carrie Robbins moved with her husband to Kansas from Quincy, Illinois, soon after their marriage in 1887, they lived in a sod house in the sagebrush and cactus flats west of Dodge City. At a dinner with some neighbors, she commented on the delicious meal which was "well cooked and well served. [The] table was really elegant with nice linen and silverware." Despite the fact that Carrie Robbins found herself on the open spaces of western Kansas, with their nearest neighbor a prairie dog colony, she applied her Illinois standards to Kansas homemaking and did not find it wanting.

To understand the significance of the domestic environment for these women, we must first turn to the physical artifacts of the frontier home. Figure 1 shows the interior of a dugout in Ford County, Kansas. Despite the crowding, the homemaker has found a place for everything. Since the photograph was taken as a permanent record of their living arrangements, she probably set out her best items for the benefit of the family history, or to show relatives or friends "back East" the cultured style of dugout life.

The illustration [shows] the similarity between her present environment and that she had left behind. She propped the family Bible on the hutch, and on the cloth-covered table in the foreground set an impressive fancy tea service. Pictures and a calendar hang on the walls near the stove, and a birdcage and books are prominently displayed. A doll even sits in the infant's chair, in place of a child who would not have remained still for the length of time it took to expose the photograph, but whose presence would help to define a family's rather than an individual's dwelling.

In *The Northern Tier* (1880), Evan J. Jenkins described a Kansas scene that could have taken place in any parlor in the nation: "In one of those dug-outs which I visited on a certain rainy day, an organ stood near the window and the settler's wife was playing 'Home! Sweet Home!' " Jenkins, a surveyor for the Federal Land Office, noted the ability of Kansas women on the western frontier to transmit culture through the objects and arrangement of domestic interiors. He praised the urbane quality of even the most modest Kansas homes and acknowledged that credit for this condition went to women:

> Many of those 'dug-outs' . . . . gave evidence of the refinement and culture of the inmates. . . . . The wife had been reared in the older states, as shown by the neat and tastefully-arranged fixtures around the otherwise gloomy earth walls.

Jenkins' reference to the presence of culture focused on the woman's ability to turn sod walls and a dirt floor into the equivalent of an Eastern parlor. The woman who displayed objects which had cultural significance—birdcages, Bibles, tea sets—was able to give her relatives and neighbors visual proof of her lack of privation, and of the identity of her living arrangements to those she had left behind.

The apparent "sloppiness" of the clothing and other objects hanging on the walls of the Ford County dugout is less aberrant when compared with the calculated casualness of other contemporary interior scenes, suggesting that the crowded interior was not caused solely by a lack of space. Studied casualness was intended to communicate comfort, and an expression of comfort was closely tied to the visual impact of material objects. In an 1871 article for *The Ladies' Repository,* Mrs. Willing explained to her readers that one homemaker "had wrought miracles of comfort—a ten cent paper on the wall, fresh and cheery, a bright rag carpet, a white bed spread, groups of engravings from the Repository and some pencil sketches . . . ," when she decorated the family home. In other words, actual comfort in the form of soft chairs, warm blankets or heated rooms was not as necessary in home decoration as the appearance of comfort communicated through physical objects. Some objects themselves expressed relaxation such as the shawls draped over pictures or the mantle, and the "throw" pillows on chairs or divans. Comfort also could be expressed via a carefully-planned jumble, as though the rooms were "lived-in." In the dugout, where space was at a premium and the items were "arranged" for the picture, there is the same sense of

Figure 2. **View of Kitchen in Unidentified Residence.** *Kansas State Historical Society.*

studied casualness as in the other rooms. The owner of the dugout expressed the ideal of comfortable, inexpensive, pleasant home surroundings by carefully positioning her visual clues to achieve order in a tight space.

Many photographs of architectural interiors focus on the same imagery as the illustrations in popular magazines and books; others represent a type of iconography that is related to traditional domestic genre scenes. They illustrate the transference of at least some portions of the ideal home to the trans-Mississippi West. For example, we can make a further comparison of the intent and content of the Ford County dugout photograph by looking at Figure 2. A table has been set for a meal, in what probably is a lower-middle-class dining room since the chairs do not match one another and the table service is inexpensive ceramic or glass. This type of record occurs often in the family collections of all economic classes. The intent of this type of photograph was to exhibit the abundance of the family and to illustrate the skills of the homemaker who provided this example of the transitory domestic art of table arranging. The preparation of a table for holidays or parties was a "high art" form within the aesthetics of the household; correct positioning in the placement of dishes, silver and glassware expressed a refined, educated sensibility. While acting as housekeeper of her father's sod house in Rice County, Kansas, Emily Combes prepared an elaborate meal with four kinds of meat, three vegetables, jelly and relishes, dessert and coffee. She "added to the table that 'charm of civilization' napkins and a white table cloth using for decoration a bowl of wildflowers and green leaves. . . . I was quite proud of myself," she admitted. Even in the upper-class or upper-middle-class household, where the work of setting a holiday or party table might go to a servant, the homemaker received the credit since this function expressed the homemaker's skill in beautifying the home. By executing this function in small town or frontier areas, homemakers linked themselves to other women across the nation.

In addition to their practical uses, certain objects possessed symbolic meanings. Their presence in a home testified that a cultured sensibility pervaded the household. A typical middle–class genre piece of the late nineteenth century [was] a piano, carefully draped by a shawl, with one or more people in attendance. Women appeared most often in such photographs, but occasionally males were present as spectators or vocalists. Mrs. Sweet, who lived on a farm near Baldwin, Kansas, took piano lessons from a Miss Doyle, who came out once a week to give music lessons and usually stayed for dinner. Small, collapsible pump organs were available in the late nineteenth century, and it probably was this type of instrument which Mr. Jenkins heard in the dugout he visited. A piano or organ was one of the signals which communicated culture and refinement, whether one lived in a dugout, a frame house, or . . . rented rooms. . . .

Books were another signal intended to communicate the degree of a family's culture. Domestic decoration manuals and magazines pictured shelves laden with reading material, as well as vases, plates and pictures. This juxtaposition of items partially transformed the status of the book to that of a decorative object. Figure 3, an interior view of the living room of the Rob Roy ranch house in western Kansas at the turn of the century, has a typical decorative arrangement, with a plate hung over the mantle and statuary and feathers or shells resting nearby. Photographs and diaries indicate that the emblems of cultivated life transferred to the frontier, although the substance of currently fashionable taste was not perfectly reproduced. Emily Combes had to settle for wildflowers instead of cultivated blooms, and the dugout dweller could fit a collapsible organ but not a full-sized piano into the small space.

This necessity for a certain amount of make-shift in the accommodations of Kansas rural and town dwellings was seen by Kansans as both a virtue and a liability. An almost schizophrenic mingling of attitudes appeared in most public and some private statements about the quality of Kansas life. Kansas boosters somewhat defensively claimed that the rough prairie state was healthier than other areas, as they simultaneously averred that all the advantages of civilization were present in Kansas. This seems to have been a general rural phenomenon rather than a regional one. Sociologist Harry Braverman points out that in the late nineteenth century there were far fewer differences among the lives of people in rural areas around the country than between those in urban and those in rural areas. Despite their distance from the more populous East, the women of late nineteenth century Kansas or Nebraska, for example, lived much the same sort of life they would have lived in rural or small town areas of Ohio, New York or Pennsylvania. Braverman notes the persistence of semi-rural and rural areas only a few miles from New York City even as late as 1890.

Newspapers such as *The Rural New Yorker* (which had a large circulation in all farming areas of the country) carried articles or letters to the editor protesting against an image of rural isolation or small-town cultural backwardness. In "A Country Housekeeper's Ideal," Annie L. Jack claimed that it was as easy to lead a "refined" life in the country as in the city. "There

Figure 3. **Living Room of the Rob Roy Ranch, Kansas, c. 1890s.** *Kansas State Historical Society.*

need not be any roughness in our amusements; there is every facility for a beautiful and cultivated life, if one can have flowers and books, even if the other surroundings are simple and inexpensive." Emily Combes wrote to her fiancé in April 1871 from Manhattan, Kansas, that "The houses are neat and pretty, many being built of stone and furnished nicely—plenty of books, carpets, pictures, piano. . . . One meets some very cultured people." Other people claimed that being rough around the edges was a positive quality. An article in the Manhattan (Kansas) *Nationalist* on 13 January 1871, claimed that Kansas women were not ignorant of fashion in house furnishings, but that the family and its needs took precedence over the whims of outsiders.

Kansas women generally evidenced great concern for their role as women responsible for maintaining a congenial and civilized home environment, within the constraints of economy. Contrary to the dictates of magazines, however, their attention to home spaces frequently was as much for themselves as for their families. Mrs. Bingham regretted her move from Junction City to a small farm outside town [about 1870]. Her first experience of the tiny farm dwelling, and her realization of its distance from the tree-lined streets of Junction City, shocked and frightened her. "When I went into the little one-room place, with a loft reached by ladder, the tears came to my eyes, thinking of the contrast with the neat new home we had left." Nevertheless, Mrs. Bingham reconciled herself to her new home once her furniture and fixtures were in place. "We finally got things in shape to live. A bed in one corner, the cupboard in another, the stove in another, with chairs and tables between and around." For Mrs. Bingham, the division and distribution of the interior spaces and objects of the home was an important part of creating a livable situation. Her first thought was for the interior of her home, and she carefully arranged her furniture to create a sense of orderliness even in the small space. Mrs. Sweet, who moved to a farm near Ottawa, Kansas, in

1890, spent her first days in her new home freshening and arranging the fixtures and furniture. Her diary carefully notes each object, and possessively refers to all of them: "I worked at arranging things and unpacking my white dishes . . . I fixed my safe and unpacked my glass dishes." She put down carpet, hung pictures, put up curtains, papered the walls and painted some of her furniture. With these tasks accomplished, she felt she had transformed a house into her home. Home, in this sense, could be anywhere as long as one had the things which made anywhere into one's special place. Home was transportable, in other words, by transporting objects. The essential ideal of home as a domestic ambiance created by women could be physically moved in the form of household articles or interior arrangements. Thus, the homemaker provided stability for the family not by her person but by her ability to obtain and arrange objects.

The western frontier of the 1870s challenged women's capacity to maintain the quality of the home environment. Carrie Robbins noted in her journal that she was not pleased with her first impressions of frontier dwellings, but she remained undiscouraged. ". . . I had my first look at a sod house, rather low, dark and gloomy looking on the outside, yet with floors, windows, and the walls plastered. They are pleasant and comfortable upon the inside. I think I can make ours seem homelike. . . ." The situation frequently was not much better in the towns, where housing was short and women often had to make do with what was available. "I cant [*sic*] bear the idea of living in the Preston house it is so banged up and there are no conveniences either," lamented Emma Denison in 1873. "It is nothing but a dreary house, pretty enough on the outside but ugly enough inside." Carrie Robbins and Emma Denison mentioned the exteriors of their dwellings, but focused sharply on the interiors. For many women, the inside of their homes mattered more to them than the exterior.

The arrangement of the objects in the domestic interior occurred within a time frame that set women's domestic life apart from a clock-regimented society. In the first place, it was tied to the seasonal changes for the household and marked the transitional points of the year in the spring and fall. These changes were the same whether the woman kept house in the city or on a farm, and would not have varied much from New York to Kansas to Oregon. Taking down heavy winter drapes to replace them with lighter summer shades or removing wool carpets in favor of mats or light rag-rugs were seasonal chores that varied little from year to year, but which were always special events in the usual household routine. Susan B. Dimond moved to a farm near Cawker City, Kansas, in 1872. Entry after entry in her diary, beginning when she was in eastern Pennsylvania and continuing while she was in Kansas, simply stated, "Done my usual work," or "Done my housework." Then, in the seasons of change her entries became more detailed, with such comments as "varnished a bedstead" or "commenced to cover our lounge in the evening," "worked on my counterpain, & papered some up stairs and fixed up the chamber."

As further evidence of the importance of this domestic ritual, even women who had regular servants usually reserved the largest part of this seasonal activity for themselves. Mrs. James Horton of Lawrence, Kansas, whose diary almost never mentions her attention to the details of housework unless her servant was ill, noted in April 1874 that she "took up North-chamber carpet & cleaned room." During the course of the month she installed wallpaper in the hall, put down carpets in the bedrooms and on the stairs, removed the blinds so they could be painted, and "arranged Books." Such entries received the same weight as her trips to Leavenworth, her social and literary meetings and her reading habits, which dominate her diary during other months.

For newly-married women, the formation of a home was important as the symbol of conjugal happiness. Martha Farnsworth, whose alcoholic and tubercular husband once threatened her life with a shotgun, lived what she described as a "dreary, lonely life in tears." Nevertheless, her home symbolized the happiness they were unable to achieve in their personal relations. When her husband died, she gave away or "burned up" the silverware, blankets, bedstead and other household items in order not to be reminded of how unhappy she had been. Ridding herself of the physical artifacts of her marriage seemed a way to rid herself of its unpleasant memories. Her second marriage, to Fred Farnsworth, gave her all of the happiness she had missed in the first. While living with his parents, she remarked excitedly that she and Fred purchased a "new Gasoline Stove," their "*first purchase . . .* in household furnishing." They later purchased a small home of their own in Topeka.

With virtually no funds, Mrs. Farnsworth set about to create a pleasant ambiance by decorating the rooms.

> I have one pretty Wolf rug, which I placed in front of a Bench, I made myself and covered, then I have a box, covered and two chairs. I got at [the] grocery, common, manila wrapping paper and made window shades, and we have our Piano, and we have music in our home and are happy. . . .

In late summer she put the final touches on the interior of their home by selecting and installing wallpaper. "Got a lovely Terra Cotta Ingrain, with 18 inch border, for the Parlor; a beautiful pink flowered, gilt for the dining-room and Leavender [sic] flowers for the bed-room and we will have a dear 'little nest' when once we get settled."[20] By combining found objects such as grocery wrapping paper, hoarded treasures such as the Wolf rug and the piano, various purchased wallpapers, a rocker and a home-made bench, Martha Farnsworth created a personal family space to give physical manifestation of her happy marriage. Similarly, in the damp cellar under the Dimond home, where they lived during a particularly cold winter, Susan Dimond assured her family's material and spiritual comfort as well as her own. "We moved our stove and bed down into the basement this afternoon," she noted in her diary on 28 November 1872. "We were over to Dyton['s] to dinner . . .

brought some pictures home to hang in our basement." Lacking funds for commercial wallpaper, she used newspapers to cover the earth walls.

In their diaries and letters, homemakers frequently made allusion to themselves as aristocrats or "queens." This may have indicated an awareness on their part that the home could symbolize economic status. Ella Whitney wrote to her cousin Hattie Parkerson in 1872, "How do you like keeping house on your own responsibility. I expect you feel as grand as a queen and step about." Mrs. Bingham felt the crowning touch in her cottonwood shack was two carpets which she had brought with her from New York. When these were down on the floor, she felt "quite aristocratic." It is also possible that the use of words such as these referred to the contemporary cultural metaphor of the home as a castle. Either way, the central position of the physical home is evident. For Mrs. Bingham, her New York carpets provided links with other homes she had lived in as well as a sense of personal completeness and pride. The objects within the home were inextricably tied to women's concept of self as well as to their cultural role.

ii

The vital soul of an ideal Victorian home was the wife and homemaker who transformed an architectural shell into a "Home" by the selection and arrangement of domestic spaces and objects. Most women were committed to the reality of this ideal to the extent that they seemed unable to separate their self-image from the physical domestic environment. When Eva Moll wanted to bring her absent friend Hattie Parkerson to mind in 1898, she conjured up an image of Hattie in her home in Kansas, where "everything impressed itself so deeply upon my memory that if you have made any changes in furnishings or the arrangement of the furniture, I believe I could put everything where it was when I was there." Eva used the image of an unchanged domestic environment to tell Hattie that their friendship endured in spite of distance. Belle Litchfield, in 1899, sent Hattie a photograph of the exterior of her new home in Southbridge, Massachusetts, and then took careful pains to describe the interior: "The room where the corner Bay Window is, is our library. . . . [she then put herself into the picture] where I now sit writing. The chamber above it is my chamber, and the bay window over that is my studio." Her description would not have satisfied an architect, but that was not Belle's intent. She hoped to recreate for her friend a sense of a home— not of a building—where people lived and moved within the various rooms, where the dramas and comedies of the domestic world played on their own timeless stage.

By locating a part of the home's significance in the presence of particular types of objects, Americans attested to the essentially mobile nature of the physical and spiritual home. In addition, the pianos, pictures and tables set with napkins in the "wilderness," told the world that a cultivated woman was present, one who understood and could communicate her cultural womanhood. Whatever else their ultimate role may have been in providing the institutional marks of culture such as schools and churches, women first "domesticated" the frontier, and linked it to other areas of the nation, by their awareness and use in the home of commonly-accepted cultural symbols. Rather than consider a dugout, a rented room or a damp cellar as temporary living arrangements, and thus not worth improving, they created a stable home by their attention to the domestic interior and the objects which filled it regardless of the size or condition of the dwelling. Like Julia Hand, who began moving her household goods into her sod house before it was finished, the arrangement of domestic space was one of a woman's first considerations in the frontier environment. No doubt a portion of this concern stemmed from the fact that home was a woman's place of work, and organized quarters simplified household tasks. Then too, the objects a woman brought to her new home provided a sense of continuity whether she moved across the nation or across town. Neither of these assumptions, however, explains why Dimond troubled to get pictures to hang in a temporary shelter, or Farnsworth's proud, detailed description of her new wallpaper, or why the anonymous decorator of the Ford County dugout wanted her fancy tea service at center-front for a photograph. In addition to the personal meanings associated with objects, the homemaker also was aware of the cultural significance of domesticity. The [physical] domestic environment, in other words, provided an essential link between personal and cultural womanhood.

Sources

Settling the Great Plains: One Couple's Experience

Charles Wooster left his Michigan home in March 1872 to build a new life in the West. He found his way to Nebraska, where his wife joined him nine months later. Their letters to each other reveal a great deal about how one couple of middling means made a beginning on the Great Plains. How did Wooster choose a place to settle? What kinds of possessions did he consider most essential? Do you think that Helen (Nellie) Wooster was about to be pleasantly surprised or disappointed with what her husband had prepared for her? What do the letters tell us about marital relationships in the nineteenth century? Does the experience of this couple support Angel Kwolek-Folland's interpretation of the settlement experience?

From William F. Schmidt, ed., "The Letters of Charles and Helen Wooster: The Problems of Settlement," *Nebraska History* 46 (1965): 121–137. Reprinted with permission.

Chicago, March 12, 1872
9 P.M.

My Little Wife

    I have been here about 24 hours, as you see by the date of this. I found that I could gain no time by starting towards Minnesota before 5 this afternoon. I have been running about town most of the (day) and have learned nothing worth mentioning. I went to the Office of the Prairie Farmer this forenoon. Saw a man there from Minnesota who had been there twenty years and after talking with him and some others and thinking the matter all over again concluded that I would not go to Minnesota at all. This evening I accidentally met a young man who has just returned from southwestern Kansas. He says everything is awful high there and gives a discouraging account generally. Having concluded not to go to Minnesota I have made up my mind to go to Nebraska and shall look for a place with a house and some improvements. I have half a mind to say I will not write again until I find a permanent stopping place, but still I may. I shall leave here within an hour and shall reach Omaha about 10 tomorrow P.M. . . .

Bye Bye

I think of you all the time and hope to see you soon

Charley

Silver Creek, Nebraska
14   6 P.M.

    This is a station city or village consisting of the depot, a grocery hotel, and one dwelling house . . .

    It [the country] is as much different from anything that you ever saw in Michigan as can possibly be imagined. What I shall do here I can not possibly say. I do not intend to be in a hurry. I shall probably remain here . . . some time and then perhaps [go] to Grand Island . . . You must make up your mind not to get homesick when you come, find what you may. If we find any peace or happiness on this earth, I suppose at least 99 per cent of it will be within our own home . . .

(Unsigned)

Silver Glen, Merrick Co., Nebr.
March 27, 1872

My Little Wife

. . . Although there are Indians to be seen here, almost every day, they are very peaceable and are much more afraid of the whites than the whites are of them. In fact the white people do not fear them at all and I have yet to learn of a woman or child who stands in the slightest dread of them. . . .

When they wish to enter a house they will come and look in at the windows until someone notices them and then if the door is opened they will step right in without further invitation. They most always ask for something to eat, but if one doesn't wish to be troubled with them it is only necessary to refuse and send them on their way.

There is no danger here of raids from wild Indians for the country is settled many miles beyond and the wild Indians are far away . . . So don't give yourself any concern about Indians. You will stand in no more danger of them than in Michigan and when you have been here a little while you will not be a bit afraid of them . . .

Charley

Silver Glen, Neb.
July 28, 1872

My dear little Wife

I do not know what to say to you. You inform me that you are coming this fall. I certainly hope you will do so for it is very unpleasant for me to live alone and do my own house work, no less so perhaps than for you to be without any fixed place in Michigan. But these are only a part of the reasons why we wish to be together. It seems to me however that it would not be very wise for us to undertake to go to keeping house when we have no money even to pay your fare here saying nothing about freight, the cost of enough furniture to enable us to live at all which would be 50$ at least, the incidental expense of living and things which it would be necessary to have to supply our table which the farm will not afford. Fuel would necessarily cost something. How could we live without a cow? A good one would cost 50$—a second rate one might be had for 40$. In the spring if I did not have a team and some farming utensils a little money would be almost a necessity. How should we get the seeds that I had intended to, for hedge plants, fruits and forest trees? True my corn crop ought to be worth 200$, but whether I could realize anything on it would be a very doubtful question. . . . You can estimate our resources and the necessary expenses of settling up here as well as I can.

If I said I could live cheap here alone, it has been proved that I was correct for since the 26 day of April, living, fuel, cooking utensils and all probably has not cost me 10$. I have had no butter for two months and I do not use more than a pound of pork in a week. . . . The more I see of some other places the more I think of my own. I can prove up on it next spring and then I could raise money on it if I wish to, though I do not wish to if possible to avoid it. As heretofore I shall *try* to get along as well as possible but, if in so doing my feet should slip from under me and I should slide into hell, I should endeavor to endure the fry with all fortitude. . . .

Bye bye
Charley

Silver Glen, Neb.
August 28, 1872

My dear little Wife

. . . I think I shall get a yoke of oxen and a second-hand wagon. I think of going down about Columbus to look for them. I can not go till I do four or five days more in haying. I do not want to pay over 150$ for them both. It will be better for me to get them at first if I get them at all as I shall need several days team work preparatory to building. The material for the house will cost altogether 150$, and I am in hopes that I shall be able to do so much of the work myself that it will not be necessary to pay out much for work.

I have bought the heifer I spoke of in my last [letter] and shall pay for her—40$—in a day or two . . . I would not have bought the heifer now, but I was afraid some one else would get her. She is the only one I have seen that pleased me and is, I think, the best one I have seen or heard of.

Charley

Silver Glen, Neb.
Nov. 24, 1872

Little Wife,

Thursday I went to the station partly in hopes of meeting you. I did not know but you would come notwithstanding my letter. Friday night I went again and instead of yourself I found a letter from you. I am sorry you were feeling out of gear. I am sure I have tried to do the best I could. I wanted you here, but what could I do? My means were insufficient, and whenever I did get money it was not enough to meet demands. My expenses have been greater than I anticipated and now I find myself with a house but not a dollar to furnish it. A few days ago I had 60$ with which I intended to get furniture, but unexpectedly I was obliged to get about 20$ worth of stuff for the house when I supposed I had enough. The charges on the goods were upwards of 18$ and yesterday I went to Columbus . . . and spent 27$ or thereabouts for a pump, inside doors, door hangings, etc.

. . . You see then that we have no money and no prospect of getting any for an indefinite length of time unless it can be borrowed. It seems as though some of your brothers or all of them might have money the[y] should be glad to lend . . . and wait till we could pay. If not we must work in some other direction. As I told you . . . I can prove up on my place and give that as security if it's considered necessary, and that would be worth many times all we shall need to borrow.

. . . It is perhaps useless for me to say more. I am sorry for you, sorry for myself and sorry for the devil . . .

. . . Come now if you can. Let us enjoy again each other's love. The future must provide for itself.

Charley

Silver Glen, Neb.
Dec. 3, 1872

Little Wife

. . . The floor is nearly laid now and two or three days work ought to be sufficient, especially if the pantry is not finished before you come, and it probably will not be as I wish you to have it done after your own heart. If I had money, I could be ready for you in three days and so I can in two or three days at any time after getting money. . . .

I have not opened the melodeon, barrel, chest or box of clothes. In the large box I found one of the large jars of quinces was broken probably from the hilt of the sabre pressing upon the top of it . . .

Your little chickens are no more for this world, some skunks dug in while I was away and eat them all, their mother, two or three other hens and two or three other chickens. I caught one of the skunks in a trap and am trying to catch another . . .

What fine times we shall have when you come.

Bye bye
Charley

Hillsdale, Mich.
Dec. 9, 1872

My dear Boy

I'm now soon coming to you and am not going to be fooled out of it much longer, for although I have had a pretty hard time to find money, I have succeeded *at last* just as I gave up all hope and had gone to bed with a nervous sick headache. You must be pleased and not frown at me for taking the money in the way I have for it is all the way I can get any at present.

[My father] signed a note with me to get the money from Lawt Thompson. I should not have known that Lawt had any but Cousin Mart unbeknown to me asked him if he had some and would let you have it with pa for a signer and he said he would. So this morning pa came up to Lawts with me, and Lawt drew the note and I signed Chas. Wooster to it and pa signed H. P. Hitchcock . . . He had only 70$ to let so I took that for six months at 10 per ct. and now you will be pleased than other wise won't you? and don't for Gods sake send it back. . . .

I am going to start a week from tomorrow (Tuesday) so prepare for my coming and don't you write and say that the floor is not quite laid yet, for if it isn't I can soon hammer it down . . .

Write to me as soon as you get this for I want one more letter from you before I go so I can carry it in the cars for company . . .

Bye bye, for now I'm surely coming even if you write me the house is burned to ashes. Bye.

Nellie

Westward Bound: Images

The journey westward was an experience that real people had. But it was also a popular vehicle for artists and photographers, who tried to capture the reality of that journey while adding to it their own notions about the meaning of the American West. Compare these two versions of the westward movement. Why do you suppose they are so different? Would the artist of *Emigrants Crossing the Plains* have agreed with Frederick Jackson Turner that the frontier was the source of individualism and self-reliance? Or would he have claimed some other quality as the West's peculiar contribution to the national character? Also compare these images with the letters of Charles and Nellie Wooster. Which image best expresses the Woosters' particular reality?

Emigrants Crossing the Plains. Photocopy of engraving by H. B. Hall, Jr., after drawing by F. O. C. Darley. *Library of Congress.*

Westward Bound. *Library of Congress.*

Populism

The Election of 1892

By the 1890s, the individualism of a Charles Wooster had yielded to the cooperative enthusiasm of the Farmers' Alliance and, finally, to the formation of a political party. In November 1892, the People's (or populist) party elected governors in Kansas, North Dakota, and Colorado as well as an estimated 1,500 county officials and state legislators. James Weaver, the party's presidential candidate, received more than 1 million votes. In contrast to their success in the Midwest, the Populists did very poorly in the South, where the new organization threatened to upset a regional system of racial control embedded in the Democratic party.

Examine the following map, which shows the voting pattern in the presidential election of 1892. Does it appear that the People's party was successful in reaching debt-ridden sharecroppers in the cotton belt? industrial workers in the urban North? From what you know of Charles Wooster and where his farm was located, how might he have voted in the 1892 election?

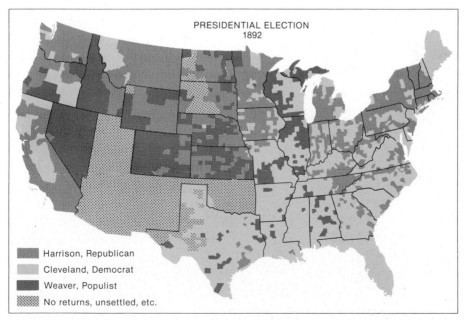

Presidential Election, 1892. *From* Atlas of the Historical Geography of the United States, *ed. Charles O. Paullin (New York: Carnegie Institution of Washington and the American Geographical Society of New York, 1932), copyright Carnegie Institution of Washington.*

Victims of Empire

Quanah Parker

**It was no easy task to remain a simple yeoman farmer while compet-
ing in an international market or struggling with eastern bankers.
And similar pressures fell heavily on the American Indian. This photograph captured Comanche leader Quanah Parker living in two cultures—one Indian and tribal, the other white and commercial.**

Comanche leader Quanah Parker with portrait of his mother in the background.
Photograph Archives, Division of Library Resources, Oklahoma Historical Society.

5

Empire, Crisis, and Reform

In the final years of the nineteenth century, Americans suddenly awoke from their preoccupations with domestic life to find themselves with an empire on their hands. In 1895, while very few Americans paid any attention, inhabitants of Cuba, which was still a Spanish colony, staged an unsuccessful revolution—one more in a series of New World revolutions against European rule that had begun in 1776. But this one failed. The Spanish began a ruthless repression of guerrilla resistance, even herding men, women, and children into concentration camps. The American press took up the Cuban cause in shrill editorials and exaggerated reporting. Before anyone, even those in President McKinley's administration, quite knew what was happening, the American battleship *Maine,* calling at Havana, had been mysteriously sunk, perhaps sabotaged. McKinley asked Congress for a resolution permitting "forcible intervention" in Cuba. An American fleet that Secretary of the Navy Theodore Roosevelt had waiting in the Pacific steamed for Manila Bay in the Philippines to attack Spanish warships there. War was on.

The war lasted for only a few weeks, and when it was over, the United States "possessed" the Philippines and Puerto Rico, and was faced with the task of governing Cuba for a time under military occupation. The British boasted that the sun never set on their empire. Americans could not yet make the same boast, but they could see from a quick look at the map that the sun never set for *long* on American possessions.

This simple story—of being drawn innocently into "a splendid little war," as John Hay called it, and waking up blinkingly to an unanticipated empire—probably is a fairly accurate summary of the way most Americans experienced the events of 1898 and 1899. But the story misses a lot.

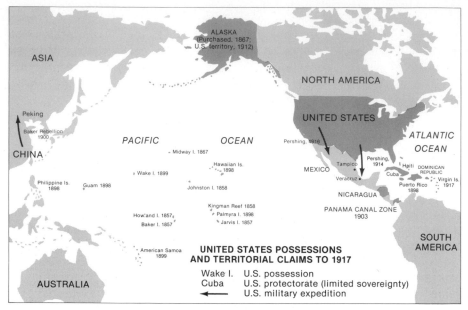

UNITED STATES POSSESSIONS
AND TERRITORIAL CLAIMS TO 1917

Wake I.   U.S. possession
Cuba   U.S. protectorate (limited sovereignty)
⟵   U.S. military expedition

From R. Jackson Wilson et al., *The Pursuit of Liberty: A History of the American People* (New York: Knopf, 1984), vol. 2, p. 703. Copyright © 1984 by Alfred A. Knopf, Inc. Reprinted by permission of the publisher.

It overlooks, to begin with, the fact that the history of the United States could be written as a history of expansion and conquest. Through exploration, purchase, treaty, and war, the United States had become, in the course of the nineteenth century, a vast nation. And all along there had been plans and dreams to expand even further, down into Mexico and the Caribbean. In this way, the Spanish–American War was a logical outcome to a long history.

The Cuban occupation should also be seen as one of the first of many similar interventions over the next two decades that together helped define the distinctly American version of empire. Carried out with the support of presidents known as reformers and progressives, these ventures added up to a major extension of American influence around the globe. Roosevelt's aid to Panamanian rebels in 1903 made possible American domination of the Canal Zone. Under William Taft, the United States asserted its right to intervene and to supervise the collection of customs receipts in Nicaragua, another nation with a potential canal route. Woodrow Wilson sent American forces into Haiti and the Dominican Republic, and in 1914, seeking to topple the Mexican government, he landed American troops and occupied the coastal city of Veracruz.

But this new expansion occurred in a new atmosphere. The

1890s was a decade of deep economic and social crisis. The depression of 1893 to 1897 was the worst in the nation's history and gave rise to the specter of collapse, as bands of tramps wandered the countryside in numbers large enough to be called "armies." Two of the most violent strikes in American history—one at Homestead, Pennsylvania, in 1892; the second at Pullman, Illinois, in 1894—intensified the sense that the country was at a desperate crossroads. For many, particularly for people like Theodore Roosevelt, the war and the chance to be an imperial power were a welcome relief from the brooding sense of decline and collapse that the decade had engendered.

In addition, whatever its origins, the new empire appeared to many Americans to be an opportunity, both for commercial and military development and for reform. The connection may seem odd in retrospect, but many Americans looked on the chance to govern Cuba or the Philippines as a chance to recover a sense of mission, to bring to "backward" nations government that was honest, efficient, enlightened, and democratic. In the process, such people hoped, the nation might begin to set its own house in order. Indeed, the experience of empire may have contributed as much as Populism did to the emergence of the atmosphere of reform that was to give the first decades of the new century their characteristic flavor.

Interpretive Essay

Howard Gillette, Jr.

The Military Occupation of Cuba: Workshop for American Progressivism

In this essay on the military occupation of Cuba, Howard Gillette, Jr., tries to get at the significance of the creation of an American empire in a new way. Instead of asking why Americans got involved in the war with Spain, he asks what they expected of their new empire once they found it on their hands. If Gillette is correct, and if Cuba was typical, what would you say defined the peculiar American *uses* of empire? Was American imperialism in Cuba any different from

the kind of empire the United States had exercised over the Plains Indians in the 1880s? or that progressive-era reformers would extend to children (see "A Play Census of Cleveland Pupils" in Chapter 6)?

The Spanish-American War marked an important turning point in American domestic as well as foreign policy. The intervention on behalf of Cuban independence generated a national sense of mission, not only to uplift the oppressed people of other countries, but also to improve domestic conditions at home. The war and the resulting policy of extraterritorial expansion, according to such a major contributor to progressivism as Herbert Croly "far from hindering the process of domestic amelioration, availed, from the sheer force of the national aspirations it aroused, to give a tremendous impulse to the work of national reform."

The agents of the occupation in Cuba* brought the prospects of American civilization—good government, education and business efficiency. In this sense the occupation was profoundly conservative, a reflection of already well-established American values and programs. On the other hand Leonard Wood, the second military governor of the island, established an overall pattern of political action which contrasted sharply with previous reform movements of both populists and Mugwumps.† Rejecting both the populist appeal to the masses and the negative Mugwump commitment to laissez-faire and puritan moralism, the Wood administration provided a model of new government powers in the hands of "responsible" leadership. It combined the Mugwump bias for elitism with the belief of populists in government activism. As such it serves as an important, previously neglected, link between old and new reform movements in America. In a real sense the occupation of Cuba served as a workshop for progressivism.

The issues surrounding the early occupation emerged out of the long-term conflict between Mugwump reformers and their opponents. Indeed, John R. Proctor, president of the U.S. Civil Service Commission, could not resist moralizing on Cuba's fate on the occasion of its transfer to American control:

> We do not feel personally responsible for misgovernment in New York or Philadelphia, but every American citizen will feel a personal responsibility for mis-

---

*I have chosen to concentrate here on Cuba rather than the other Spanish possessions, because of its central role as the source for the Spanish-American War and Theodore Roosevelt's close connection with the island. The secondary literature on the administration of the Philippines and Puerto Rico suggests that the Cuban reform effort was not atypical for the possessions generally. Cuba should then serve as a proper focus for depicting the ties between the war and emerging progressivism.

†[As the author uses this term, "Mugwump" refers to the genteel reformers who reached the peak of their influence in the Gilded Age—men like E. L. Godkin of *The Nation* and landscape architect Frederick Law Olmsted. Mugwumps were committed to laissez-faire economics, distrusted the masses, believed in the natural hegemony of an elite, and were expansionists in foreign policy.—*Ed.*]

government in Havana, Santiago, and Manila, and will hold any party to a strict accountability, and any party daring to apply the partisan spoils system to the government of our colonies or dependencies will be hurled from power by the aroused conscience of the American people.

Following as it did the excesses of the Gilded Age, the war inevitably inspired charges from anti-imperialists that it was only the product of greedy business interests wishing to exploit Cuba's natural resources. Such charges made Congress sensitive enough to declare its own good intention through the Teller amendment to the Paris peace treaty: "That the United States hereby disclaims any disposition or intention to exercise sovereignty, jurisdiction, or control over [Cuba] except for the pacification therein and asserts its determination, when that is accomplished, to leave the government of the Island to its people." To insure that the new territory would not be subject to economic exploitation, Congress passed the Foraker Amendment to the Army Appropriations bill in February 1899, prohibiting the granting of franchises or concessions in Cuba to American companies during the period of military occupation. President McKinley himself stressed America's good intentions in an effort to distinguish his foreign policy from the prevailing drive among European nations for colonial possessions. The Spanish territories, McKinley claimed in a recurrent theme of his administration, "have come to us in the providence of God, and we must carry the burden, whatever it may be, in the interest of civilization, humanity and liberty."

Cuba's first military governor, John Brooke, a career soldier who made his reputation in the Spanish War by leading invading columns through the virtually bloodless conquest of Puerto Rico, did his best to effect the outlines of good government promised in Washington. He initiated programs to build new schools and to provide basic sanitation facilities for the island. Among his appointees he counted as military governor of Havana William Ludlow, a man who had already established a credible record in the United States as a good government reformer. During his tenure as director of the Water Department in Philadelphia, according to a New York *Times* report, "political heelers who had won sinecures by carrying their wards were discharged and their places filled by efficient men. Political bosses stood aghast at such independence and after trying all kinds of 'influence' and 'pulls' were compelled to leave the Water Department alone as long as Colonel Ludlow remained at its head." Ludlow expressed his confidence in the effectiveness of transporting America's campaign against corruption to the island, claiming in his first annual report in 1900 that, "For the first time, probably in its history, Havana had an honest and efficient government, clean of bribery and speculation, with revenues honestly collected and faithfully and intelligently expended."

But the problems facing Brooke required more than basic services and clean government. The devastation and near anarchy of the island suggested immediately the need for extensive social, economic and political reconstruction. Yet lacking both administrative experience and any philosophical commitment to government activism, Brooke dampened every effort to provide government services whose need he did not find absolutely compelling. At one point he rejected a plan for long-term low-interest loans to destitute farmers, calling the program a kind of paternalism which would destroy the self-respect of the people.

The prospect for more comprehensive reform was discouraged by the lack of direction from Washington. Despite his repeated promise to carry out an American mission in Cuba, President McKinley outlined no general policy for the island. Henry Adams complained in January 1899, that "the government lets everything drift. It professes earnestly its intention to give Cuba its independence, but refuses to take a step toward it, and allows everyone to act for annexation." Fully a year after the military occupation began, McKinley admitted, "Up to this time we have had no policy in regard to Cuba or our relations therewith, for the simple reason that we have had no time to formulate a policy." Under the circumstances Brooke was forced, as he said, to conduct the government by induction.

Without clear direction from Washington, Brooke lapsed into a narrow strain of reform directed at purifying Cuba's social system. Among his first circulars were orders to abolish gambling, to close business houses on Sunday and to prohibit public games and entertainments on Sunday. In perhaps his most misguided effort at reform he ordered in the interest of public safety the confiscation of all machetes on the island, not realizing that the law, if executed faithfully, would ruin the island's sugar business. Brooke's announced restrictions on theaters and dance halls led the Washington *Post* to editorialize: "Our first duty in Cuba is not morals or customs, but the establishment of institutions of law and order . . . if we begin by interference in their private lives, with puritanical compulsion and missionary irritation, the problem of Cuban rehabilitation will be set back twenty years."

The Brooke administration provoked its first serious internal criticism from Leonard Wood, past commander of the Rough Rider brigade Teddy Roosevelt made famous and military governor of the province of Santiago. As a young activist who felt well-tested by the war, Wood bridled at Brooke's timidity. "The condition of the Island is disheartening," he wrote his friend Roosevelt in August 1899. "I tell you absolutely that no single reform has been initiated which amounts to anything to date." Publicly he made no effort to conceal his discontent, telling a New York *Times* reporter, "The Cuban problem can easily be solved. With the right sort of administration everything could be straightened out in six months. Just now there is too much 'tommy-rot.' What is needed is a firm and stable military government in the hands of men who would not hesitate to use severe measures should the occasion arise."

Roosevelt took Wood's complaints seriously and launched a campaign to promote him to Brooke's position. Five days after Wood penned his scathing report on Brooke Roosevelt replied: "Your letter makes me both worried and indignant . . . I am going to show it privately and confidentially to [Secretary of War Elihu] Root. I do not know what to say. Root is a thoroughly good fellow and I believe is going to steadily come around to your way of looking at things." As early as July 1 Roosevelt had touted Wood for Military Governor, writing Secretary of State John Hay that he doubted whether "any nation in the world has now or has had within recent time, anyone so nearly approaching the ideal of military administrator of the kind now required in Cuba." Wood, Roosevelt argued, "has a peculiar facility for getting on with the Spaniards and Cubans. They like him, trust him, and down in their hearts are afraid of him." Roosevelt's campaign had its effect, for in December 1899, Wood succeeded to Brooke's position.

Wood accepted his appointment as no ordinary assignment. "He is further impressed with the idea he has a mission—is charged with a great reformation," Brooke's retiring chief of staff noted. Such a mission demanded not just the establishment of civil order as sought by Brooke but reconstruction of the island as a thriving nation state. Though he showed some sensitivity to differences between Latin and Anglo-Saxon cultures, Wood could not resist promoting Americanization of the island—in the administration of justice, the training of police and general administrative practice—where proven methods could speed up goals of efficiency and uplift. As he wrote President McKinley explaining his ultimate objective, "We are going ahead as fast as we can, but we are dealing with a race that has steadily been going down for a hundred years and into which we have got to infuse new life, new principles and new methods of doing things."

Unlike Brooke, Wood established the administrative credibility to effect the changes he sought. He assiduously avoided imposition of puritanical social reforms on the Cuban people. "The main thing," he wrote, "is to avoid the appearance of correcting abuses which do not exist." Instead he emphasized adoption of "a business-like way of doing things," which he had complained was missing from the Brooke administration. His interest in corporate administrative efficiency drew sustenance and support from McKinley's new Secretary of War Elihu Root who had left his job as a New York corporate lawyer to take responsibility both for administering the Spanish possessions and modernizing the Army along efficient corporate lines. Together they shared the goals of an emerging social type in America which stressed organization and efficiency as touchstones of the progress of civilization.

As a start new lines of organization were drawn for the entire administrative system of the island. Wood revamped Brooke's education program, for example, because it lacked precision. Though Brooke's minister of education succeeded in building new schools and increasing enrollment, he developed no institutional controls over the system. With the application of a new approach fashioned after Ohio law, school administration was divided according to function. A commissioner of education handled all executive matters, including purchasing supplies and making appointments, while a superintendent of schools developed educational policy. Together with six provincial commissioners he formed a board of education authorized to determine and introduce proper methods of teaching in the public schools. Each school district was granted local autonomy, though individual teachers were held responsible to central authority through a system of reports. The school board required teachers to complete reports monthly and yearly. Salaries were withheld for failure to comply. All teachers were also required to spend the first two summers of the American occupation in school and pass a certification exam at the end of their second year. The rigorous system was completely new to Cuba, where no public school system had previously existed and where teaching standards had never been defined.

Next to education, Cuban law was the most important object of Wood's administrative reorganization. In his annual report for 1900, Wood said that no department was "more in need of thorough and radical reform, rigid inspection, and constant supervision," than the department of justice which "was lacking in efficiency, energy and attention to duty." He complained that the Cuban judiciary and legal body had "surrounded itself with a cobweb of tradition and conservatism and adopted a procedure so cumbersome and slow of execution as to render impossible a prompt administration of justice." But he believed progress had been made under his administration. "Incompetent and neglectful individuals have been dismissed, the number of correctional courts has been very greatly increased, the audiencias supplied with necessary material, and very much done to improve the court houses."

Wood also launched a massive program of public works to reconstruct the island's cities. This municipal reform effort started under the crudest conditions. Wood's sanitary engineer in Santiago wrote that when he took office "not a shovel or a broom [was available], and for several days, pieces of oil cans and brushes of trees, and palm branches, were the only implements available." By the close of 1900 chief engineer William Black could report that the streets of the island's major cities were sprinkled and swept nightly. In 1901 Black reported a wide range of services planned for the island, including new sewer systems; modern street pavements; construction of water mains to new buildings; water pollution controls; public parks; construction of new schools and public buildings; a modern slaughterhouse designed after the best Chicago examples and a system of subways for wires for transmission of electricity for light power, telegraph and telephone service.

The Department of Public Works not only provided a wide range of public services, but under Black it reorganized its internal operation to promote efficient conduct of city business. Cuban street cleaners could no longer be haphazard in their work or their dress. Each man was assigned a particular district responsibility and was uniformed smartly in white cotton-duck suits with brown cord trimmings, white metal badges and brown hats. In addition, the department prepared codes for municipal operations, including a list of plumbing specifications that set standard requirements for every class of pipe and fitting.

In order to institutionalize the improved efficiency of municipal departments in particular, Wood urged adoption of a new city charter in Havana. Soon after his promotion, Wood appointed a commission of American and Cuban experts to draw up a model city charter. The commission was given copies of recent American charters, in which the fundamental principles en-

couraged were "simplicity, effectiveness, responsibility, and the largest measure of autonomy that could with safety be authorized." Following the argument for home rule in the United States, the new charter prevented the
central and provincial governments from intervening in municipal affairs,
granting the city control of "all matters within its boundary." Specifically
city government was held responsible for "the comfort and health of the
inhabitants, and the security of their persons and property." Significantly
the charter provided for regulation of all public utilities at a time when municipal reformers in America were attempting to write the same provision into
law. The charter also incorporated an order previously adopted on the island
which simplified the tax system by eliminating the ill-defined system of shared
responsibility between city and province and making a direct connection between the tax rate and benefits received from city government.

The new city charter pointed the way to the best of American municipal
reform. It established the dictum, which would be stated most precisely by
Herbert Croly, that government must be efficient and to be efficient its powers
must equal its responsibilities. Not only was the city authorized to use broad
powers in the public interest, it was held responsible to promote that interest.
As such, the charter reflected the general enthusiasm for positive government
intervention in public affairs shared by Wood, Root, Roosevelt and Croly.
Wood worked to define similar powers of public responsibility at a national
level in Cuba through the creation of a railroad commission. He was offended,
as he said, that the railroads "have always been able to buy the government
and run things about as they saw fit." But much more he felt the state had
a responsibility to protect public welfare. "I'm going to insist on state intervention in regulating rates," he wrote President Roosevelt in 1902, "when it is
evident that such rates are prejudicial to the public interest."

When the railroads balked at possible state regulation Wood received
encouragement from E. H. Moseley, Secretary of the U.S. Interstate Commerce Commission. "The demand of the railroads of Cuba that they should
be allowed to control at pleasure, consulting their own interest only, the
arteries of the internal commerce of the country is preposterous," he wrote
Wood in January 1902. "I'm convinced that the railroad commission, composed of men of high character, is determined to follow the reasonable and
correct course, dealing fairly with all, and while having the interest of the
State and welfare of the people fully in view, do no act of injustice to the
railroads."

The Cuban railroad law enacted a month later incorporated all the major
features of the Interstate Commerce Act adopted in the United States in
1887. It forbade railroads to engage in discriminatory practices, required them
to publish their rate schedules, prohibited them from entering pooling arrangements to keep rates high and declared that rates should be "reasonable and
just." The Cuban law attempted to avoid the major pitfall of its predecessor
by holding a ruling valid until revoked by the Supreme Court. Under the
American law, where the I.C.C. relied on the Supreme Court for enforcement,

fifteen of the first sixteen cases appealed had been decided in favor of the railroads against the commission.

Recent scholarship has revealed how legislation for the I.C.C., though stimulated by agrarian discontent, ultimately reflected the concerns of commercial interests, which wished to rationalize the system for their own profits. Taken out of the American context the Cuban reform represented an ideal in itself divorced from the factions which originally shaped the bill. Significantly, Wood gave it new purpose in protecting middle-class producers and planters for whom, he wrote Root, lower rates would be "a very substantial gain."

Indeed Wood built his program around the establishment of a conservative middle-class ruling elite. He distrusted the Cuban politicians who had gained office in the first elections and who, he said, appeared to be "in a certain sense doctors without patients, lawyers without practice and demagogues living in the subscription of the people and their friends." Planters and producers, on the other hand, appealed to him as "an honest, warm-hearted class of people," who were most appreciative of good order and protection of life and property. Wood often called the planter class conservative in a positive sense, consciously identifying them with the better class of citizens in America who unfortunately, he thought, had bypassed public service. He continued to believe, however, that their success, both political and commercial, was essential to the future of Cuba, for ultimately they would have to provide both the tax revenues to pay for needed services on the island and the leadership to effect those services. Wood underscored his belief in working hard for reciprocal trade agreements:

> The resources on which Cuba must depend for the income necessary to establish a stable government, requiring, as any government does, good schools, good courts, a system of public works, means of communication, hospitals, charities, etc., are those which will be derived from the sale of her two most stable products, and, if we continue to legislate against these, we cannot, with any degree of sincerity, expect the new government to be able to maintain such conditions as constitute stable government.

Ultimately Wood revealed the kind of commitment to conservative political capitalism which Gabriel Kolko has described as characteristic of progressivism. His hope for Cuba lay in a working relationship of responsible businessmen in both countries. He assigned highest priority to sanitation measures, for instance, largely because he believed adequate safeguards against disease were a prerequisite for American investment in the island. Part of his desire to standardize Cuban law derived from reports from American businessmen that the principal reason for the lack of confidence in Cuban investments was the threat of costly time-consuming litigation in native courts. Wood risked criticism from Cuban patriots for limiting popular suffrage because, as he wrote Root, "if it were known to be a fact that we were going to give universal suffrage, it would stop investments and advancement in this island to an extent which would be disastrous in its results."[*]

Wood clearly opposed outright business exploitation, but he could not avoid a bias for conservative middle-class business ideology. In the final year of his administration he worked actively for a stipulation gained in the controversial Platt Amendment to the Army Appropriations bill which guaranteed the preservation of American commercial interests through the right of intervention. All orders of the military government were granted permanence in Article IV which declared that "all acts of the United States in Cuba during its military occupancy thereof are ratified and validated, and all lawful rights acquired thereunder shall be maintained and protected." Americanization of the island was thus completed, with legal assurance that it would not be quickly or easily overturned.

By every American standard the occupation had been a tremendous success. In guiding Cuba to its independence without succumbing to colonialism, business exploitation or government corruption, Wood rested the worst fears of the Mugwump reformers. Jacob Riis, the New York social reformer, granted the occupation that degree of success, in terms widely adopted by the press at the time:

> Cuba is free, and she thanks President Roosevelt for her freedom. But for his insistence that the nation's honor was bound up in the completion of the work his Rough-Riders began at Las Guasimas and on San Juan hill, a cold conspiracy of business greed would have left her in the lurch, to fall by and by reluctantly into our arms, bankrupt and helpless, while the sneer of the cynics that we were plucking that plum for ourselves would have been justified.

Beyond these essentially negative results, however, the administration provided a positive achievement through government activism which separated Wood and his contemporaries from the Mugwumps. Wood himself stressed this activism, in contrast to Brooke's timid administration, in summarizing his record. He had, as he wrote in 1903, completed work "which called for practically a rewriting of the administrative law of the land, including the law of charities, hospitals and public works, sanitary law, school law, and railway law; meeting and controlling the worst possible sanitary conditions; putting the people to school; writing an electoral law and training the people in the use of it, establishing an entirely new system of accounting and auditing." Not without pride he concluded that the work called for and accomplished "the establishment, in a little over three years, in a Latin military colony, in one of the most unhealthy countries of the world, a republic modeled closely upon the lines of our own great Anglo-Saxon republic."

[*] Wood to Root, Feb. 23, 1900, Wood Papers. On another occasion he wrote Root, "The people ask me what we mean by a stable government in Cuba. I tell them that when money can be borrowed at a reasonable rate of interest and when capital is willing to invest in the island, a condition of stability will have been reached."

Our understanding of the special nature of the Wood reform ethic is heightened through a brief analysis of its reception in Cuba. For a country whose economic and social identity lay largely in the countryside, Wood could well have concentrated government expenditures in a program of agricultural reconstruction modeled after methods being instituted in the American South and suggested by Governor James Wilson of Matanzas Province. "I do not consider the future of Cuba depends chiefly upon schools, road-making, improved sanitation or judiciary reform," Wilson said. "The best the United States can do for Cuba and the Cubans is to give every opportunity for improving the value of the land by putting it to the best uses. In this way capital could do an immense amount of good here as well as get returns." Wood rejected Wilson's plea, resting his hopes for Cuba's future not in small farms but in the cities. He stressed this urban orientation when he wrote Roosevelt in August 1899, "All we want here are good courts, good schools and all the public work we can pay for. Reform of municipal government and a business way of doing things."

Wood's emphasis on urban development ran counter to established Cuban tradition. While his work in Havana drew praise in America, it received a less welcome reception among Cubans. The Havana ayuntamiento (city council) overwhelmingly rejected the charter commission report, although the proposal purportedly incorporated the best features of American law. According to one councilman, the new plan was but one more of the great many fancies which had been thrust on the Cubans by force.

Beyond Wood's urban orientation lay a bias for government authority which again rankled the Cubans. As governor of Santiago, Wood had gained tremendous popularity by criticizing the centralization of authority in Havana. When Brooke decreed that all customs revenues would be distributed from Havana, Wood took the case for decentralized distribution to Washington and became a hero among Cubans. Wood's act struck a responsive chord with a people who hoped for a substitution of American decentralized administration for the highly centralized Spanish system. The Spanish law of 1878 governing local administration outwardly allowed local autonomy. But a provision making the alcalde (mayor) removable at will placed the executive authority and the towns generally at the mercy of the central government. The Cubans moved toward greater local independence with the Autonomist Constitution of 1897 which stipulated that the ayuntamientos and not the central government made the final selection of alcaldes.

Wood's reputation as champion of Santiago's independence encouraged the Cubans to believe that he would complete the decentralization begun by the Autonomist Constitution. Wood did encourage municipal autonomy. He eliminated many municipalities which had been created during the war solely to act as agents of the Spanish government, making the remaining cities real functioning units with their own taxing and spending power. But with a lack of administrative experience at the local level, cities repeatedly exceeded their budgets, depending on national revenues to remain solvent. Wood's own personal vigor and the fact that he was so insistent on his directives helped sustain all final authority in Havana. As one sensitive observer of America's overseas policy, Leo S. Rowe, said, "The leaders in the work of civic reorganization were determined to put an end to the highly centralized administration of Spanish times, but in actual development of the system the force of tradition has proved stronger than conscious purpose. Although the municipalities enjoy more extensive powers in law, in fact they remain subservient to the central government."

Wood's authoritarian bent must have reflected a military man's desire to get a job done. He recognized, for instance, no restraints in effecting sanitation measures in Santiago. According to President McKinley's special commissioner to the island, Robert Porter, "The doors of houses had to be smashed in; people making sewers of the thoroughfares were publicly horsewhipped in the streets of Santiago; eminently respectable citizens were forcibly brought before the commanding general and sentenced to aid in cleaning the streets they were in the habit of defiling." As A. Hunter Dupree has pointed out, Wood managed to institute his sanitation program in Cuba because island administrators held powers which "would have been entirely unavailable to the President of the United States had the infected city been New Orleans instead of Havana." Wood himself credited his success in Cuba to the wide scope of his power, indicating that if he were to take a role in administering the Philippines "I should like to have a go at the situation with the same authority I have had here. Without such full authority I believe the Islands will be the burial ground of the reputation of those who go there."

Had Wood shared the philosophical restraints of Brooke or other Mugwump leaders of his generation on the limited use of government power he might not have aroused the kind of opposition in Cuba he did. The important factor for the historian of American reform, however, lies in the example Wood held up to his countrymen back home and its reception there, whatever his own motivations for seeking government authority in Cuba. By carefully selecting among existing precedents in the United States those models which allowed the greatest government activism, Wood presented fellow reformers in America with a new spirit of administrative technique and law. His reforms emphasizing administrative efficiency served as a bridge between Root's reorganization of the Army and Gifford Pinchot's program for a professionally managed forest system and later administrative reforms instituted by Theodore Roosevelt as president.

In a general sense Wood's administration, undertaken as it was in the full glare of national publicity, provided a visibility for reform which had been badly lacking in earlier good government movements. The emergence of Roosevelt, Root and Wood from virtual obscurity to national heroes helped dramatize a new spirit of reform and suggested to the public at large the dawn of a new moral leadership for America. "The war with Spain," Secretary of the Navy William H. Moody claimed in a speech in 1902, "disclosed the enormous resources of this country, its wealth, its power, its strength, but it disclosed more. It disclosed the character of our people, and we know that where the Tafts, and the Roots, and the Days, and the Woods, and the

Roosevelts came from, there are many more like them to come to the service of the country when their country calls." Wood's heralded decision to turn down a $25,000-a-year street railway presidency offered during his term as military governor set him apart from public figures of the Gilded Age and gave substance to a new leadership ideal, articulated by Roosevelt as early as 1897 when he was still Assistant Secretary of the Navy that: "The fight well fought, the life honorably lived, the death bravely met—those count far more in building a fine type of temper in a nation than any possible success in the stock-market, than any possible prosperity in commerce or manufactures."

In a more direct sense the philosophical connection between the occupation and emerging progressivism was tied through personal links, the most important of which was Wood's close relationship with Theodore Roosevelt. Among more specialized progressive leaders, Leo Rowe of the University of Pennsylvania recognized immediately the importance of administrative innovation in the Spanish possessions. Though recognized as an expert on municipal reform in America, Rowe found the study of the Spanish possessions irresistible. He wrote not only extensive articles on the administration of Cuba and the Philippines but also a book on the occupation of Puerto Rico, where he served as chairman of the island's code commission. He predicted in March 1899, that the workshop provided by the Spanish possessions would turn America's political philosophy away from limited protection of individual liberties to one of activist intervention for national development. "The readjustment of the country's international relations, which must follow the recent struggle with Spain, will supply the connecting link between economic and political development," he wrote in *The Forum*. "Its influence, however, will extend far beyond these limits. It will modify our political ideas, develop a broader view of the country's relation to the larger affairs of the world, and react upon domestic politics, with the result of raising the level of public life."

In his urban work Rowe reached theoretical conclusions which Wood coincidentally put into pragmatic effect. In 1897 Rowe argued that even though American cities had reached a nadir in the American experience they would have to serve nonetheless as the chief agent of civilization. The reformer's role, then, lay clearly in upgrading the urban environment, precisely the approach Wood took in Cuba. Indeed, Wood's administration both reflected Rowe's philosophy and gave it sustenance through the apparent triumph of urban-oriented programs to give the island the services sought in America through the city beautiful movement, particularly good schools, grand public buildings and clean streets.

On another level the experiments in the Caribbean served to inspire activists among two other major elements of the emerging reform movement, the journalists who would soon become known as muckrakers and the social welfare activists. Robert Bannister cites the tremendous impact the activism of Wood and Roosevelt had on Ray Stannard Baker in converting him from a Mugwump to a progressive. Indeed Baker seems to have absorbed himself the chief principles of Roosevelt's strenuous life, writing in his journal, "A warrior is not made by the battles he avoids but by the battles he fights." Another entry suggests a parallel drive with Roosevelt, Wood and Rowe to take up the challenge of remaking society: "What we must be thankful for is not perfection, not the solution of all our problems; this condition we can never hope to attain—but let us praise God for the struggle! Completeness we can not attain, but where there is restless activity, there is also health and hope. Not beautification, perfection: that is heaven, but turmoil and struggle, progress; that is human life." For the social reformer Jacob Riis, the example of the American occupation was no less inspiring. "How jolly it is to think of you and Roosevelt being both where you are," he wrote Wood in February 1900. "This is a good world anyway, and the pessimists lie like the Dickens."

Despite our recognition today that Wood's specific programs as well as his desire to civilize Cuba generally reflected already established American values, we should not underestimate the impact of the overall reform effort on the United States. For a country in which administrative reform had not yet emerged as a national goal and in which urban reconstruction remained rather a hope than a reality, Wood's achievement must have provided, as Croly said, a tremendous stimulus for domestic reform. The Cuban occupation provided progressives not only with a programmatic cohesion which had been lacking in earlier reform movements but also the kind of favorable national publicity which could give new efforts momentum at home. The success of the occupation, by American standards, underscored the belief that the United States had fulfilled its mandate to lift the Cuban people into the forward stream of Western civilization, and in so doing, it provided for a new generation of progressives faith in man's ability to remake and reform the world around him.

Sources

Theodore Roosevelt

Behind the "Big Stick"

Theodore Roosevelt is the physical embodiment of American imperialism. Generations of students have become familiar with an image of Roosevelt, sleeves rolled up, shoveling dirt out of what would become the Panama Canal. The image is important, not simply because of Roosevelt's undeniable role in shaping our Caribbean empire, but also because it says so much about *why* Roosevelt thought the nation should be there. In "The Strenuous Life," a famous

speech delivered in 1899 and reprinted in part below, Roosevelt ex-
pounds on the virtues of striving, which was so strongly identified
with his character.

It is worth noting that this emphasis on the strenuous life was
new. An earlier generation had been more attuned to the lessons of
George M. Beard's *American Nervousness: Its Causes and Consequences*
(1881). Beard found modern civilization, which he broke down into
five elements—the press, the telegraph, the sciences, steam power,
and the "mental activity of women"—at the root of the matter. Because the nervous system had not grown sufficiently to compensate
for the additional strains imposed by an overspecialized, urban society, nervous disorders had multiplied. Beard counseled Americans to
conserve their limited supply of nervous energy.

Here are two theories of physical energy, each distinctive and
each, apparently, representative of its own time. Why was Roosevelt
so fond of the strenuous life, whereas Beard thought it so dangerous?
What changes in the late nineteenth century might account for the
change?

In speaking to you, men of the greatest city of the West, men of the
State which gave to the country Lincoln and Grant, men who preëminently
and distinctly embody all that is most American in the American character,
I wish to preach, not the doctrine of ignoble ease, but the doctrine of the
strenuous life, the life of toil and effort, of labor and strife; to preach that
highest form of success which comes, not to the man who desires mere
easy peace, but to the man who does not shrink from danger, from hardship,
or from bitter toil, and who out of these wins the splendid ultimate triumph.

A life of slothful ease, a life of that peace which springs merely from
lack either of desire or of power to strive after great things, is as little worthy
of a nation as of an individual. . . . If you are rich and are worth your salt,
you will teach your sons that though they may have leisure, it is not to be
spent in idleness; for wisely used leisure merely means that those who possess
it, being free from the necessity of working for their livelihood, are all the
more bound to carry on some kind of non-remunerative work in science, in
letters, in art, in exploration, in historical research—work of the type we
most need in this country, the successful carrying out of which reflects most
honor upon the nation. We do not admire the man of timid peace. We admire
the man who embodies victorious effort; the man who never wrongs his
neighbor, who is prompt to help a friend, but who has those virile qualities
necessary to win in the stern strife of actual life. It is hard to fail, but it is
worse never to have tried to succeed. . . . When men fear work or fear
righteous war, when women fear motherhood, they tremble on the brink
of doom; and well it is that they should vanish from the earth, where they

From Theodore Roosevelt, *The Strenuous Life: Essays and Addresses* (1899; reprint, New York:
Century, 1901), pp. 1–2, 4–13, 17–18, 20–21.

are fit subjects for the scorn of all men and women who are themselves strong and brave and high-minded. . . .

We of this generation do not have to face a task such as that our fathers faced, but we have our tasks, and woe to us if we fail to perform them! We cannot, if we would, play the part of China, and be content to rot by inches in ignoble ease within our borders, taking no interest in what goes on beyond them, sunk in a scrambling commercialism; heedless of the higher life, the life of aspiration, of toil and risk, busying ourselves only with the wants of our bodies for the day, until suddenly we should find, beyond a shadow of question, what China has already found, that in this world the nation that has trained itself to a career of unwarlike and isolated ease is bound, in the end, to go down before other nations which have not lost the manly and adventurous qualities. If we are to be a really great people, we must strive in good faith to play a great part in the world. We cannot avoid meeting great issues. All that we can determine for ourselves is whether we shall meet them well or ill. In 1898 we could not help being brought face to face with the problem of war with Spain. All we could decide was whether we should shrink like cowards from the contest, or enter into it as beseemed a brave and high-spirited people; and, once in, whether failure or success should crown our banners. So it is now. We cannot avoid the responsibilities that confront us in Hawaii, Cuba, Porto Rico, and the Philippines. All we can decide is whether we shall meet them in a way that will redound to the national credit, or whether we shall make of our dealings with these new problems a dark and shameful page in our history. To refuse to deal with them at all merely amounts to dealing with them badly. We have a given problem to solve. If we undertake the solution, there is, of course, always danger that we may not solve it aright; but to refuse to undertake the solution simply renders it certain that we cannot possibly solve it aright. The timid man, the lazy man, the man who distrusts his country, the over-civilized man, who has lost the great fighting, masterful virtues, the ignorant man, and the man of dull mind, whose soul is incapable of feeling the mighty lift that thrills "stern men with empires in their brains"—all these, of course, shrink from seeing the nation undertake its new duties; shrink from seeing us build a navy and an army adequate to our needs; shrink from seeing us do our share of the world's work, by bringing order out of chaos in the great, fair tropic islands from which the valor of our soldiers and sailors has driven the Spanish flag. . . .

No country can long endure if its foundations are not laid deep in the material prosperity which comes from thrift, from business energy and enterprise, from hard, unsparing effort in the fields of industrial activity; but neither was any nation ever yet truly great if it relied upon material prosperity alone. All honor must be paid to the architects of our material prosperity, to the great captains of industry who have built our factories and our railroads, to the strong men who toil for wealth with brain or hand; for great is the debt of the nation to these and their kind. But our debt is yet greater to the men whose highest type is to be found in a statesman like Lincoln, a soldier like

Grant. They showed by their lives that they recognized the law of work, the law of strife; they toiled to win a competence for themselves and those dependent upon them; but they recognized that there were yet other and even loftier duties—duties to the nation and duties to the race.

So much for the commercial side. From the standpoint of international honor the argument is even stronger. The guns that thundered off Manila and Santiago left us echoes of glory, but they also left us a legacy of duty. If we drove out a medieval tyranny only to make room for savage anarchy, we had better not have begun the task at all. It is worse than idle to say that we have no duty to perform, and can leave to their fates the islands we have conquered. Such a course would be the course of infamy. It would be followed at once by utter chaos in the wretched islands themselves. Some stronger, manlier power would have to step in and do the work, and we would have shown ourselves weaklings, unable to carry to successful completion the labors that great and high-spirited nations are eager to undertake. . . .

But in the early eighties the attention of the nation became directed to our naval needs. Congress most wisely made a series of appropriations to build up a new navy, and under a succession of able and patriotic secretaries, of both political parties, the navy was gradually built up, until its material became equal to its splendid personnel, with the result that in the summer of 1898 it leaped to its proper place as one of the most brilliant and formidable fighting navies in the entire world. We rightly pay all honor to the men controlling the navy at the time it won these great deeds, honor to Secretary Long and Admiral Dewey, to the captains who handled the ships in action, to the daring lieutenants who braved death in the smaller craft, and to the heads of bureaus at Washington who saw that the ships were so commanded, so armed, so equipped, so well engined, as to insure the best results. But let us also keep ever in mind that all of this would not have availed if it had not been for the wisdom of the men who during the preceding fifteen years had built up the navy. . . .

And, gentlemen, remember the converse, too. Remember that justice has two sides. Be just to those who built up the navy, and, for the sake of the future of the country, keep in mind those who opposed its building up. Read the "Congressional Record." Find out the senators and congressmen who opposed the grants for building the new ships; who opposed the purchase of armor, without which the ships were worthless; who opposed any adequate maintenance for the Navy Department, and strove to cut down the number of men necessary to man our fleets. The men who did these things were one and all working to bring disaster on the country. They have no share in the glory of Manila, in the honor of Santiago. They have no cause to feel proud of the valor of our sea-captains, of the renown of our flag. Their motives may or may not have been good, but their acts were heavily fraught with evil. They did ill for the national honor, and we won in spite of their sinister opposition. . . .

The problems are different for the different islands. Porto Rico is not large enough to stand alone. We must govern it wisely and well, primarily in the interest of its own people. Cuba is, in my judgment, entitled ultimately to settle for itself whether it shall be an independent state or an integral portion of the mightiest of republics. But until order and stable liberty are secured, we must remain in the island to insure them, and infinite tact, judgment, moderation, and courage must be shown by our keeping the island pacified, in relentlessly stamping out brigandage, in protecting all alike, and yet in showing proper recognition to the men who have fought for Cuban liberty. The Philippines offer a yet graver problem. Their population includes half-caste and native Christians, warlike Moslems, and wild pagans. Many of their people are utterly unfit for self-government, and show no signs of becoming fit. Others may in time become fit but at least can only take part in self-government under a wise supervision, at once firm and beneficent. We have driven Spanish tyranny from the island. If we now let it be replaced by savage anarchy, our work has been for harm and not for good. I have scant patience with those who fear to undertake the task of governing the Philippines, and who openly avow that they do fear to undertake it, or that they shrink from it because of the expense and trouble; but I have even scanter patience with those who make a pretense of humanitarianism to hide and cover their timidity, and who cant about "liberty" and the "consent of the governed," in order to excuse themselves for their unwillingness to play the part of men. Their doctrines, if carried out, would make it incumbent upon us to leave the Apaches of Arizona to work out their own salvation, and to decline to interfere in a single Indian reservation. Their doctrines condemn your forefathers and mine for ever having settled in these United States. . . .

I preach to you, then, my countrymen, that our country calls not for the life of ease but for the life of strenuous endeavor. The twentieth century looms before us big with the fate of many nations. If we stand idly by, if we seek merely swollen, slothful ease and ignoble peace, if we shrink from the hard contests where men must win at hazard of their lives and at the risk of all they hold dear, then the bolder and stronger peoples will pass us by, and will win for themselves the domination of the world. Let us therefore boldly face the life of strife, resolute to do our duty well and manfully; resolute to uphold righteousness by deed and by word; resolute to be both honest and brave, to serve high ideals, yet to use practical methods. Above all, let us shrink from no strife, moral or physical, within or without the nation, provided we are certain that the strife is justified, for it is only through strife, through hard and dangerous endeavor, that we shall ultimately win the goal of true national greatness.

Edgar Rice Burroughs

The Search for the Primitive: Tarzan of the Apes

Early-twentieth-century advocates of American empire often defended the nation's involvement abroad as part of a larger "civilizing" mission. "The Republic," proclaimed progressive Senator Albert J. Beveridge, "never retreats. Why should it retreat? The Republic is the highest form of civilization, and civilization must advance."

Theodore Roosevelt's allusions to "wild pagans" and "half-caste . . . Christians" in the preceding speech barely conceal a similar enthusiasm. But for Roosevelt, civilization was a two-edged sword; one must be civilized, but not "overcivilized."

The following selection, from Edgar Rice Burroughs's epic adventure tale, *Tarzan of the Apes* (1912), raises the possibility that America's outward thrust was somehow related to the concept of "civilization." The story concerns an Englishman, Lord Greystoke (Tarzan), raised from infancy entirely by apes and mothered by the ape Kala, whose death—at the hands of a black man—Tarzan revenges.

Burroughs was an ordinary American, and his book was extraordinarily popular with his compatriots. What message did it have for Americans about civilization? about the consequences of empire? Would readers of *Tarzan* have felt more comfortable or less comfortable in their pursuit of overseas territories?

Tarzan of the Apes lived on in his wild, jungle existence with little change for several years, only that he grew stronger and wiser, and learned from his books more and more of the strange worlds which lay somewhere outside his primeval forest.

To him life was never monotonous or stale. There was always Pisah, the fish, to be caught in the many streams and the little lakes, and Sabor, with her ferocious cousins to keep one ever on the alert and give zest to every instant that one spent upon the ground.

Often they hunted him, and more often he hunted them, but though they never quite reached him with those cruel, sharp claws of theirs, yet there were times when one could scarce have passed a thick leaf between their talons and his smooth hide.

Quick was Sabor, the lioness, and quick were Numa and Sheeta, but Tarzan of the Apes was lightning.

With Tantor, the elephant, he made friends. How? Ask not. But this is known to the denizens of the jungle, that on many moonlit nights Tarzan of the Apes and Tantor, the elephant, walked together, and where the way was clear Tarzan rode, perched high upon Tantor's mighty back.

Many days during these years he spent in the cabin of his father, where still lay, untouched, the bones of his parents and the skeleton of Kala's baby. At eighteen he read fluently and understood nearly all he read in the many and varied volumes on the shelves.

Also could he write, with printed letters, rapidly and plainly, but script he had not mastered, for though there were several copy books among his treasure, there was so little written English in the cabin that he saw no use for bothering with this other form of writing, though he could read it, laboriously.

Thus, at eighteen, we find him, an English lordling, who could speak no English, and yet who could read and write his native language. Never had he seen a human being other than himself, for the little area traversed by his tribe was watered by no greater river to bring down the savage natives of the interior.

High hills shut it off on three sides, the ocean on the fourth. It was alive with lions and leopards and poisonous snakes. Its untouched mazes of matted jungle had as yet invited no hardy pioneer from the human beasts beyond its frontier.

But as Tarzan of the Apes sat one day in the cabin of his father delving into the mysteries of a new book, the ancient security of his jungle was broken forever.

At the far eastern confine a strange cavalcade strung, in single file, over the brow of a low hill.

In advance were fifty black warriors armed with slender wooden spears with ends hard baked over slow fires, and long bows and poisoned arrows. On their backs were oval shields, in their noses huge rings, while from the kinky wool of their heads protruded tufts of gay feathers.

Across their foreheads were tattooed three parallel lines of color, and on each breast three concentric circles. Their yellow teeth were filed to sharp points, and their great protruding lips added still further to the low and bestial brutishness of their appearance.

Following them were several hundred women and children, the former bearing upon their heads great burdens of cooking pots, household utensils and ivory. In the rear were a hundred warriors, similar in all respects to the advance guard.

That they more greatly feared an attack from the rear than whatever unknown enemies lurked in their advance was evidenced by the formation of the column; and such was the fact, for they were fleeing from the white man's soldiers who had so harassed them for rubber and ivory that they had turned upon their conquerors one day and massacred a white officer and a small detachment of his black troops.

For many days they had gorged themselves on meat, but eventually a stronger body of troops had come and fallen upon their village by night to revenge the death of their comrades.

That night the black soldiers of the white man had had meat a-plenty, and this little remnant of a once powerful tribe had slunk off into the gloomy jungle toward the unknown, and freedom.

But that which meant freedom and the pursuit of happiness to these savage blacks meant consternation and death to many of the wild denizens of their new home.

For three days the little cavalcade marched slowly through the heart of this unknown and untracked forest, until finally, early in the fourth day, they came upon a little spot near the banks of a small river, which seemed less thickly overgrown than any ground they had yet encountered.

Here they set to work to build a new village, and in a month a great clearing had been made, huts and palisades erected, plantains, yams and maize planted, and they had taken up their old life in their new home. Here there were no white men, no soldiers, nor any rubber or ivory to be gathered for cruel and thankless taskmasters.

Several moons passed by ere the blacks ventured far into the territory surrounding their new village. Several had already fallen prey to old Sabor, and because the jungle was so infested with these fierce and bloodthirsty cats, and with lions and leopards, the ebony warriors hesitated to trust themselves far from the safety of their palisades.

But one day, Kulonga, a son of the old king, Mbonga, wandered far into the dense mazes to the west. Warily he stepped, his slender lance ever ready, his long oval shield firmly grasped in his left hand close to his sleek ebony body.

At his back his bow, and in the quiver upon his shield many slim, straight arrows, well smeared with the thick, dark, tarry substance that rendered deadly their tiniest needle prick.

Night found Kulonga far from the palisades of his father's village, but still headed westward, and climbing into the fork of a great tree he fashioned a rude platform and curled himself for sleep.

Three miles to the west slept the tribe of Kerchak.

Early the next morning the apes were astir, moving through the jungle in search of food. Tarzan, as was his custom, prosecuted his search in the direction of the cabin so that by leisurely hunting on the way his stomach was filled by the time he reached the beach.

The apes scattered by ones, and twos, and threes in all directions, but ever within sound of a signal of alarm.

Kala had moved slowly along an elephant track toward the east, and was busily engaged in turning over rotted limbs and logs in search of succulent bugs and fungi, when the faintest shadow of a strange noise brought her to startled attention.

For fifty yards before her the trail was straight, and down this leafy tunnel she saw the stealthy advancing figure of a strange and fearful creature.

It was Kulonga.

Kala did not wait to see more, but, turning, moved rapidly back along the trail. She did not run; but, after the manner of her kind when not aroused, sought rather to avoid than to escape.

Close after her came Kulonga. Here was meat. He could make a killing and feast well this day. On he hurried, his spear poised for the throw.

At a turning of the trail he came in sight of her again upon another straight stretch. His spear hand went far back the muscles rolled, lightning-like, beneath the sleek hide. Out shot the arm, and the spear sped toward Kala.

A poor cast. It but grazed her side.

With a cry of rage and pain the she-ape turned upon her tormentor. In an instant the trees were crashing beneath the weight of her hurrying fellows, swinging rapidly toward the scene of trouble in answer to Kala's scream.

As she charged, Kulonga unslung his bow and fitted an arrow with almost unthinkable quickness. Drawing the shaft far back he drove the poisoned missile straight into the heart of the great anthropoid.

With a horrid scream Kala plunged forward upon her face before the astonished members of her tribe.

Roaring and shrieking the apes dashed toward Kulonga, but that wary savage was fleeing down the trail like a frightened antelope.

He knew something of the ferocity of these wild, hairy men, and his one desire was to put as many miles between himself and them as he possibly could.

They followed him, racing through the trees, for a long distance, but finally one by one they abandoned the chase and returned to the scene of the tragedy.

None of them had ever seen a man before, other than Tarzan, and so they wondered vaguely what strange manner of creature it might be that had invaded their jungle.

On the far beach by the little cabin Tarzan heard the faint echoes of the conflict and knowing that something was seriously amiss among the tribe he hastened rapidly toward the direction of the sound.

When he arrived he found the entire tribe gathered jabbering about the dead body of his slain mother.

Tarzan's grief and anger were unbounded. He roared out his hideous challenge time and again. He beat upon his great chest with his clenched fists, and then he fell upon the body of Kala and sobbed out the pitiful sorrowing of his lonely heart.

To lose the only creature in all his world who ever had manifested love and affection for him was the greatest tragedy he had ever known.

What though Kala was a fierce and hideous ape! To Tarzan she had been kind, she had been beautiful.

Upon her he had lavished, unknown to himself, all the reverence and respect and love that a normal English boy feels for his own mother. He had never known another, and so to Kala was given, though mutely, all that would have belonged to the fair and lovely Lady Alice had she lived.

After the first outburst of grief Tarzan controlled himself, and questioning the members of the tribe who had witnessed the killing of Kala he learned all that their meager vocabulary could convey.

It was enough, however, for his needs. It told him of a strange, hairless, black ape with feathers growing upon its head, who launched death from a slender branch, and then ran, with the fleetness of Bara, the deer, toward the rising sun.

Tarzan waited no longer, but leaping into the branches of the trees sped rapidly through the forest. He knew the windings of the elephant trail along which Kala's murderer had flown, and so he cut straight through the jungle to intercept the black warrior who was evidently following the tortuous detours of the trail.

At his side was the hunting knife of his unknown sire, and across his shoulders the coils of his own long rope. In an hour he struck the trail again, and coming to earth examined the soil minutely.

In the soft mud on the bank of a tiny rivulet he found footprints such as he alone in all the jungle had ever made, but much larger than his. His heart beat fast. Could it be that he was trailing a MAN—one of his own race?

There were two sets of imprints pointing in opposite directions. So his quarry had already passed on his return along the trail. As he examined the newer spoor a tiny particle of earth toppled from the outer edge of one of the footprints to the bottom of its shallow depression—ah, the trail was very fresh, his prey must have but scarcely passed.

Tarzan swung himself to the trees once more, and with swift noiselessness sped along high above the trail.

He had covered barely a mile when he came upon the black warrior standing in a little open space. In his hand was his slender bow to which he had fitted one of his death dealing arrows.

Opposite him across the little clearing stood Horta, the boar, with lowered head and foam flecked tusks, ready to charge.

Tarzan looked with wonder upon the strange creature beneath him—so like him in form and yet so different in face and color. His books had portrayed the *Negro,* but how different had been the dull, dead print to this sleek thing of ebony, pulsing with life.

As the man stood there with taut drawn bow Tarzan recognized him not so much the *Negro* as the *Archer* of his picture book——

A stands for Archer

How wonderful! Tarzan almost betrayed his presence in the deep excitement of his discovery.

But things were commencing to happen below him. The sinewy black arm had drawn the shaft far back; Horta, the boar, was charging, and then the black released the little poisoned arrow, and Tarzan saw it fly with the quickness of thought and lodge in the bristling neck of the boar.

Scarcely had the shaft left his bow ere Kulonga had fitted another to it, but Horta, the boar, was upon him so quickly that he had no time to discharge it. With a bound the black leaped entirely over the rushing beast and turning with incredible swiftness planted a second arrow in Horta's back.

Then Kulonga sprang into a near-by tree.

Horta wheeled to charge his enemy once more; a dozen steps he took, then he staggered and fell upon his side. For a moment his muscles stiffened and relaxed convulsively, then he lay still.

Kulonga came down from his tree.

With a knife that hung at his side he cut several large pieces from the boar's body, and in the center of the trail he built a fire, cooking and eating as much as he wanted. The rest he left where it had fallen.

Tarzan was an interested spectator. His desire to kill burned fiercely in his wild breast, but his desire to learn was even greater. He would follow this savage creature for a while and know from whence he came. He could kill him at his leisure later, when the bow and deadly arrows were laid aside.

When Kulonga had finished his repast and disappeared beyond a near turning of the path, Tarzan dropped quietly to the ground. With his knife he severed many strips of meat from Horta's carcass, but he did not cook them.

He had seen fire, but only when Ara, the lightning, had destroyed some great tree. That any creature of the jungle could produce the red-and-yellow fangs which devoured wood and left nothing but fine dust surprised Tarzan greatly, and why the black warrior had ruined his delicious repast by plunging it into the blighting heat was quite beyond him. Possibly Ara was a friend with whom the Archer was sharing his food.

But, be that as it may, Tarzan would not ruin good meat in any such foolish manner, so he gobbled down a great quantity of the raw flesh, burying the balance of the carcass beside the trail where he could find it upon his return.

And then Lord Greystoke wiped his greasy fingers upon his naked thighs and took up the trail of Kulonga, the son of Mbonga, the king; while in far-off London another Lord Greystoke, the younger brother of the real Lord Greystoke's father, sent back his chops to the club's *chef* because they were underdone, and when he had finished his repast he dipped his finger-ends into a silver bowl of scented water and dried them upon a piece of snowy damask.

All day Tarzan followed Kulonga, hovering above him in the trees like some malign spirit. Twice more he saw him hurl his arrows of destruction— once at Dango, the hyena, and again at Manu, the monkey. In each instance the animal died almost instantly, for Kulonga's poison was very fresh and very deadly.

Tarzan thought much on this wondrous method of slaying as he swung slowly along at a safe distance behind his quarry. He knew that alone the tiny prick of the arrow could not so quickly dispatch these wild things of the jungle, who were often torn and scratched and gored in a frightful manner as they fought with their jungle neighbors, yet as often recovered as not.

No, there was something mysterious connected with these tiny slivers of wood which could bring death by a mere scratch. He must look into the matter.

That night Kulonga slept in the crotch of a mighty tree and far above him crouched Tarzan of the Apes.

When Kulonga awoke he found that his bow and arrows had disappeared. The black warrior was furious and frightened, but more frightened than furious. He searched the ground below the tree, and he searched the tree above the ground; but there was no sign of either bow or arrows or of the nocturnal marauder.

Kulonga was panic-stricken. His spear he had hurled at Kala and had not recovered; and, now that his bow and arrows were gone, he was defenseless except for a single knife. His only hope lay in reaching the village of Mbonga as quickly as his legs would carry him.

That he was not far from home he was certain, so he took the trail at a rapid trot.

From a great mass of impenetrable foliage a few yards away emerged Tarzan of the Apes to swing quietly in his wake.

Kulonga's bow and arrows were securely tied high in the top of a giant tree from which a patch of bark had been removed by a sharp knife near to the ground, and a branch half cut through and left hanging about fifty feet higher up. Thus Tarzan blazed the forest trails and marked his caches.

As Kulonga continued his journey Tarzan closed on him until he traveled almost over the black's head. His rope he now held coiled in his right hand; he was almost ready for the kill.

The moment was delayed only because Tarzan was anxious to ascertain the black warrior's destination, and presently he was rewarded, for they came suddenly in view of a great clearing, at one end of which lay many strange lairs.

Tarzan was directly over Kulonga, as he made the discovery. The forest ended abruptly and beyond lay two hundred yards of planted fields between the jungle and the village.

Tarzan must act quickly or his prey would be gone; but Tarzan's life training left so little space between decision and action when an emergency confronted him that there was not even room for the shadow of a thought between.

So it was that as Kulonga emerged from the shadow of the jungle a slender coil of rope sped sinuously above him from the lowest branch of a mighty tree directly upon the edge of the fields of Mbonga, and ere the king's son had taken a half dozen steps into the clearing a quick noose tightened about his neck.

So quickly did Tarzan of the Apes drag back his prey that Kulonga's cry of alarm was throttled in his windpipe. Hand over hand Tarzan drew the struggling black until he had him hanging by his neck in mid-air; then Tarzan climbed to a larger branch drawing the still threshing victim well up into the sheltering verdure of the tree.

Here he fastened the rope securely to a stout branch, and then, descending, plunged his hunting knife into Kulonga's heart. Kala was avenged.

Tarzan examined the black minutely, for he had never seen any other human being. The knife with its sheath and belt caught his eye; he appropriated them. A copper anklet also took his fancy, and this he transferred to his own leg.

He examined and admired the tattooing on the forehead and breast. He marveled at the sharp filed teeth. He investigated and appropriated the feathered headdress, and then he prepared to get down to business, for Tarzan of the Apes was hungry, and here was meat; meat of the kill, which jungle ethics permitted him to eat.

How may we judge him, by what standards, this ape-man with the heart and head and body of an English gentleman, and the training of a wild beast?

Tublat, whom he had hated and who had hated him, he had killed in a fair fight, and yet never had the thought of eating Tublat's flesh entered his head. It could have been as revolting to him as is cannibalism to us.

But who was Kulonga that he might not be eaten as fairly as Horta, the boar, or Bara, the deer? Was he not simply another of the countless wild things of the jungle who preyed upon one another to satisfy the cravings of hunger?

Suddenly, a strange doubt stayed his hand. Had not his books taught him that he was a man? And was not The Archer a man, also?

Did men eat men? Alas, he did not know. Why, then, this hesitancy! Once more he essayed the effort, but a qualm of nausea overwhelmed him. He did not understand.

All he knew was that he could not eat the flesh of this black man, and thus hereditary instinct, ages old, usurped the functions of his untaught mind and saved him from transgressing a worldwide law of whose very existence he was ignorant.

Quickly he lowered Kulonga's body to the ground, removed the noose, and took to the trees again.

The cover of the
September 10, 1912,
issue of *The All-
Story* magazine, in
which *Tarzan of the
Apes* was first
published. *Copyright
© 1912 by Frank A.
Munsey Co.
Trademark
TARZAN ® owned
by Edgar Rice
Burroughs, Inc. and
Used by Permission.*

6

Progressivism:
The Age of Reform

Historian Richard Hofstadter gave us the theme for this chapter in 1955 when he published his conclusions about Populism and progressivism in a book titled *The Age of Reform*. Thirty years later, it is not at all clear what this phenomenon called "progressivism" was, or whether its agents, the "progressives," were really very progressive. Hofstadter in fact argued that at the heart of progressivism was a vision of the past, an attempt to restore economic individualism and political democracy, values that had been buried under giant corporations, burgeoning unions, and corrupt political bosses. With the exception of Theodore Roosevelt, who believed that most big business could not and should not be eliminated, progressives, according to Hofstadter, generally tried to disassemble existing institutions. The progressive movement, he wrote, was "the complaint of the unorganized against the consequences of organization."

Others have argued that progressivism was not nostalgic but aggressively future-oriented. According to this view, progressivism cannot be separated from the "organizational revolution" taking place at the turn of the century. Products of that revolution include trade associations, new government agencies, the organized professions, and an increased willingness to use federal rather than state and local agencies to achieve economic and social goals. But there are real problems even in placing specific movements within this organizational context. Did new government regulations represent the past or the future? Were they designed to bring change or to preserve the status quo?

The title of Hofstadter's study implies the ability to recognize a reform when we see one, and much of the history of the progressive period has been written from this assumption. But here, too, there are difficulties. When Theodore Roosevelt broke with the Republican party in 1912 and campaigned for the presidency under the banner of the Progressive party (not to be confused with the more general term "progressivism"), his Bull Moose platform was a classic summary of social reforms long identified with progressivism—minimum wages for women, prohibition of child labor, the eight-hour workday, and workmen's compensation. For years, however, Roosevelt had been involved with birth-control advocate Margaret Sanger and with Stanford University president David Starr Jordan and other luminaries in another "reform" effort, the eugenics movement, which many progressives found unappealing. In a letter written in 1914, Roosevelt described and explained his interest in eugenics:

> I wish very much that the wrong people could be prevented entirely from breeding; and when the evil nature of these people is sufficiently flagrant, this should be done. Criminals should be sterilized and feeble-minded persons forbidden to leave offspring behind them. But as yet there is no way possible to devise a system which could prevent all undesirable persons from breeding.

For Roosevelt, eugenics deserved the label "reform" every bit as much as the movement to abolish child labor. Others, including historians, have disagreed, and therein lies a central problem with the word "reform."

Nor is the difficulty resolved simply by focusing on what seem to be clearly benign reforms. One of the most popular progressive-period programs was state workmen's compensation legislation, under which injured workers were compensated according to predetermined schedules, rather than by virtue of what they could recover through legal action. By what standards is workmen's compensation "reform"? Is it an example of progressivism? Feminists of the 1970s and 1980s would raise similar, and worthwhile, questions about the many progressive-era laws that regulated hours and conditions for working women. In 1910 those laws seemed to be important measures of protection; today they seem to be obstacles to equality of the sexes. Were those laws, even in 1910, a clear example of social progress?

Still, certain features of progressivism stand out. One need only mention the major regulatory measures of the period to grasp the importance of regulation (a word, it should be emphasized, with no more real content than "reform"). Out of a financial panic in 1907 came the Federal Reserve System, created in 1913 to provide a more flexible currency. Several pieces of railroad legislation, including the Elkins Act (1903) and the Hepburn Act (1906), were designed to limit rebates (unfair price cutting by the carriers) and to give the Interstate Commerce Commission, then two decades old, the authority to fix maximum rates. Congress also provided for federal inspection of meat packers that shipped in interstate commerce and created the Federal Trade Commission (1914) to supervise the competitive relations of interstate businesses. State and local governments were also active in the regulatory movement and were the major agencies of change in such social-justice areas as hours of labor, child labor, and tenement-house reform. The progressive period is also well known for a series of measures designed to change the terms of access to the political system: the direct election of United States senators, direct primaries for the nomination of elective officials, initiative, referendum, and recall.

Aside from the dramatic rise in the use of government as a social tool, the qualities that gave unity to progressivism were attitudinal and ideological. Progressives believed in data. They believed in the possibilities of "scientific" social welfare, supported by research; of market research in selling; and of measuring the abilities of employees through psychological testing. This faith in science was often accompanied by a fear of national moral collapse. It was this kind of thinking that led to the founding of the Boy Scouts of America in 1910 and to Roosevelt's enchantment with eugenics.

Finally, progressivism was not, at least on the surface, a matter of class interests, of one group seeking hegemony over another. For progressives, the political system was not a device by which conflicting interests compromised (or failed to compromise) their essential differences; it was a means through which the essential harmony of all interests might be expressed. Perhaps because of this emphasis on harmony, the declaration of war in April 1917 ushered in a brief period in which the progressive spirit of reform was reincarnated as a struggle against German autocracy. Led by Woodrow Wilson, Americans came to understand the war as a holy crusade, a great struggle, as Wilson put it, to "make the world safe for democracy."

Interpretive Essay

David J. Rothman

The State as Parent

David Rothman, the author of the following essay, shares the skepticism about progressivism described in the introduction to this chapter. While he acknowledges that the progressives confronted real and

serious social problems—poverty, widowhood, industrial accidents,
child labor, juvenile delinquency, and the like—he questions the
progressives' reliance on the state to solve those problems and the
progressives' *attitude* toward the poor, women, children, immigrants,
and workers—all of whom were the objects of progressive reform
campaigns. According to Rothman, progressives resembled parents
in their relationship to their children; they assumed that they knew
what was good and right for the widow with dependent children,
the child who labored in the mine or factory, or the adolescent criminal. Rothman's argument is especially important today, when the
welfare state—the descendant of progressive reform—struggles to
survive against the assaults of the political right and left.

In this selection, Rothman examines a quintessential progressive
institution—the juvenile court. Why is Rothman critical of the court?
Is it the solution itself, or just the attitude with which it was imposed, that troubles him? What kinds of alternatives does Rothman
suggest or imply? What alternatives can you think of? Finally, imagine that you were a youthful "offender." Would you have wanted
your case to be handled in a juvenile court?

In the field of juvenile justice, the character of Progressive innovations emerges
in clear and stark fashion. Between 1900 and 1920, reformers revolutionized
social policy toward the delinquent and created a new mechanism, the juvenile
court, that would dominate both the administration of justice and all right-
minded thinking on the subject for at least the first half of this century.
Even by Progressive standards, the champions of the juvenile court acted
with exceptional audacity; and of all the reform measures, this one remains
the most controversial. It was the first Progressive program in criminal justice
to be successfully challenged by a new wave of activists in the post-1960's
as arbitrary and counterproductive in its exercise of discretionary authority
(witness their victory in the Supreme Court Gault decision). Yet even today
the program continues to attract dedicated support and remains surprisingly
invulnerable to fundamental change. All of which, of course, constitutes an
open invitation to historical inquiry. To understand the origins and consequences of the juvenile court movement is to examine Progressivism at its
most aggressive and influential.

It is not surprising that such aggressiveness should have involved procedures for juveniles, for Progressive programs were to a remarkable degree
child-oriented. From child labor legislation to compulsory schooling laws,
from kindergartens to playgrounds, from widows' pension provisions to municipal bureaus of child health and hygiene, Progressives sought to insure
the proper physical, mental, and moral development of the child. Inevitably,

From *Conscience and Convenience: The Asylum and Its Alternatives in Progressive America* by David
J. Rothman. Copyright © 1980 by David J. Rothman. By permission of Little, Brown and
Company.

this orientation encouraged Progressives to reexamine the fundamentals of juvenile justice, to see how this system too could be made more responsive to the best interests of the child.

In part, the child-centeredness of Progressives reflected their response to the hordes of immigrants who were crowding into American cities. However unsettling it was for native-born Americans to confront strange ghettos where oddly dressed newcomers spoke in a babble of tongues, it was still more disturbing, or at least challenging, to watch their countless children (and they seemed countless to those limiting their family size to two or three children) continue to follow Old World ways. Admittedly, reformers' ability to affect the life style or life chances of the first-generation immigrant was circumscribed—but surely they could influence the second generation. There was both ample opportunity and ample reason to make the child of the immigrant understand and then fulfill the promise of American life, to win his allegiance to the American way by letting him reap its rewards.

Each of the Progressive child welfare measures looked to this goal. The kindergartens and settlement clubs would inculcate the right attitudes in children, thereby promoting their chances for success and, perforce, their love of country. They would teach the newcomers such mottoes as "The clock helps us to be good," and "patriotic songs and stories of the great men who have made America what she is." The municipal clinics had their important contribution: to impart the rules of preventive medicine so that sickly and puny children would become sturdy youth and thus take full advantage of American opportunities. Since this aim seemed so realizable and significant, Progressives were not afraid to introduce the coercive force of law. Immigrant parents did not understand that removing their children from the classroom and putting them to work as common laborers doomed them to a permanent place in the factory and subjected them to grave risks of injury. Therefore, reformers moved to ban children from the labor force and to compel them to attend schools—which would increase the likelihood of their becoming healthy, vigorous, and upwardly mobile adults.

However important these considerations, the Progressives' orientation toward the child had a second source of inspiration. Not only their view of American society but their concept of the intrinsic nature of childhood inspired their programs. Probably the best starting point is with the work of G. Stanley Hall, the psychologist at Clark University who made the first systematic studies of child development in the United States. Hall's influence was large, not only within the academy (where he trained a host of students in child study) but among the general public. Hall introduced and popularized an idea of childhood as composed of a series of distinct stages: the child moved from level to level in his growth, and each level demanded a particular kind of response. In the early years, a child should be trained to habits: "Never again will there be such susceptibility to drill and discipline." Then, in adolescence (a stage to which Hall ascribed particular significance), "individuality must have a longer tether." To treat the adolescent as a ten-year-old was to invite disaster. Hall went on to instruct mothers (not fathers; we are still in

1900) to learn about childhood and, more, to observe their children closely—
for in no other way would they be able to react appropriately to each stage.
Childhood, in other words, was a vastly more complicated phenomenon
than had heretofore been imagined. Maternal instinct was not enough—now
one needed insight.

Hall's contribution helped to change the way a generation of women
thought about motherhood and the way a generation of Americans thought
about child care. Mothers were to be trained to their responsibilities, to learn
the intricate lessons necessary for guiding proper child development. . . .

G. Stanley Hall himself extended his perspective to delinquency. No
one, he explained, could understand the juvenile offender without appreciating
individual differences. "Criminaloid youth is more sharply individualized than
the common good child. . . . Virtue is more uniform and monotonous than
sin. There is one right but there are many wrong ways, hence they need to
be individually studied." Traditional procedures, Hall insisted, violated these
precepts. "Those smitten with the institution craze or with any extreme correc-
tionalist views will never solve the problem of criminal youths." If Hall and
his followers complained that the public schools had "too much uniformity,
mechanism, and routine," imagine how acute their distress with the reformatory.

Hall next identified several causes of delinquency. That they were mostly
environmental points to his close fit with the new social sciences—in part
he reflected and in part he promoted this kind of outlook. The causes ranged
from "heredity, bad antenatal conditions, bad homes, unhealthful infancy
and childhood," to "overcrowded slums with their promiscuity and squalor,
which are always near the border of lawlessness, and perhaps are the chief
cause of crime." In fact, Hall returned frequently to environmental considerations. "There is much reason to suspect," he declared, "that the extremes
of wealth and poverty are more productive of crime than ignorance, or even
intemperance." Hall's roster of causes was practically a checklist for Progressive action: the health bureaus were to combat maternal and child diseases,
and innumerable other measures were to alleviate poverty.

From these premises, Hall strongly advocated a juvenile court system.
Obviously the program "must have marked reformatory elements." That
end was as old as the house of refuge and no one debated it. Rather, the
novelty lay in Hall's means. First, juveniles had to be treated completely
apart from adults. "The problems of criminology for youth cannot be based
on the principles now recognized for adults"; and here Hall was referring to
the Jacksonian asylum's traditional principles of fixity, uniformity, and the
like. "The greatest need of the penologist and criminologist," Hall contended,
"is the further study, by expert methods, of individual cases and their relations
to the social environment. We must fathom and explore the deeper strata of
the soul, personal and collective, to make our knowledge really preventive,
and recognize the function of the psychologist, pedagogue, and the physician."
Once again, an individual (and expert) approach presupposed wide discretion;
and since the object of treatment was a youth, Hall was ready to expand

this discretion well past recognizable adult standards: "We must pass beyond the clumsy apparatus of a term sentence or the devices of a jury, clumsier yet, for this purpose." With this statement, we are at the heart of the juvenile court ideal. . . .

The design for the juvenile court set out to realize these precepts. The court was to represent a wholly new and Progressive way of responding to the delinquent. Heretofore, reformers contended, the state had to adopt one of two equally objectionable tactics, to choose, as it were, between evils. It could move against the young offender with the full rigor of the adult criminal law: detain him in a jail, prosecute and try him with all the strictness appropriate to criminal procedure, and sentence him to a prison-like institution. In short, it could adopt a tactic that almost certainly would transform a juvenile delinquent into an adult criminal. Or, shying away from so disastrous an intervention, the state could refrain from acting, turn the delinquent loose again, and in so doing know that it had encouraged him to resume his life in crime. The brilliance of the juvenile court solution lay in its ability to follow a middle course that would substitute rehabilitation for punishment or neglect.

This course was to alter every aspect of the state's actions. A special children's court, oriented to the individual case and administered under the most flexible procedures, would, as one reformer announced, "banish entirely all thought of crime and punishment," moving beyond the "mere attempt at punishment." The delinquent, upon being apprehended, would go to a juvenile detention center, not to a jail. The court hearing would be an informal investigation that looked to the needs of the child, not to his guilt or innocence. The disposition of the case would aim for rehabilitation, not punishment, in most (though not all) instances through probationary work. Here was a program that promised to be both helpful and effective, that would satisfy the needs of the child and the welfare of the society. As one of its most active supporters, Bernard Flexner, phrased it, the great discovery of the juvenile court was that "individual welfare coincided with the well-being of the state. Humanitarian and social considerations thus recommended one and the same procedure. . . . Sympathy, justice and even the self-interest of society were all factors in bringing about the changed attitude."

The innovation seemed so capable of solving the problem of delinquency without sacrificing anyone's interests that reformers did not anticipate objections. "Only ignorance of what it really is could make anyone oppose the juvenile court," one proponent declared—and, in fact, opposition was scarce. As we shall see, the court plan made friends for the best of reasons and the worst of reasons: in juvenile justice, as in adult justice, reforms satisfied the most humanitarian of impulses and, at the same time, some very narrow and self-interested considerations. But here again, the proper starting point for understanding both the structure and the popularity of the court is with its doing-good quality. The groups that campaigned most enthusiastically and effectively on its behalf carried outstanding credentials as philanthropists.

The most active among them, as might be expected, were the club women, particularly the members of the National Congress of Mothers. It was not a maudlin sentimentality for childhood (as some historians have charged) that motivated them, but quite the reverse, their sense that the delinquent required very sophisticated and particular attention, in effect, the prescriptions that G. Stanley Hall was offering. Chicago's first juvenile court judge, Richard Tuthill, understood their aims and political contribution well: "The women's clubs are the parents of all children. They have taught the state how to be a parent. . . . The women got the juvenile law passed." And women carried the court idea to other states as well. In Ohio, for example, the National Congress of Mothers was so active that one court supporter pleaded "that the men not leave all the work of securing passage to the women."

Other prestigious organizations and leaders testified to the benevolence and wisdom of the court idea. The first founders of schools of social work, like Henry Thurston, and their counterparts in the settlement house movement, like Jane Addams and Julia Lathrop, heartily approved the measure. Those who first administered the new system were also among its most articulate advocates. It is difficult to exaggerate the significance of the founding of the juvenile court in Chicago to the movement as a whole precisely because its judge, Richard Tuthill, and its chief administrator, Timothy Hurley, were indefatigable in popularizing the program. Hurley, in fact, from 1900 to 1910 published a monthly, the *Juvenile Court Record,* which not only reported every step in the progress of the movement but issued countless editorials and columns promoting it as well. And Tuthill and Hurley were not the exceptions. Denver's juvenile court judge, Ben Lindsey, was a one-man traveling road show; and if most of his speeches were variations on the theme of the insights of Lindsey, still he did find time to praise the concept of the court too. Further, by 1910, psychologists and psychiatrists, with William Healy the most active among them, not only endorsed the program but were eager to assume a major role in it. With such exemplary and diverse supporters, the court seemed to represent a significant victory for humanity and progress.

The speed with which states rushed to enact the appropriate legislation confirms the power of the rhetoric and the alliance. The first formally constituted juvenile court opened in Chicago in 1899. Within five years, ten states had implemented similar procedures, and by 1920 every state except three provided for a juvenile court. As one New York official aptly concluded: "Considering the slowness with which changes in judicial procedure are brought about, the rapid extension of the children's court is extraordinary and bears witness to its social need and constructive worth."

The juvenile court was to concern itself first not with the specific charge facing the delinquent, but with his character and life style, his psychological strengths and weaknesses, the advantages and disadvantages of his home environment. It was not his act but, in Hall's term, his soul, that was at issue. As Chicago's juvenile court judge, Julian Mack, promised: the court intended to discover "what he is, physically, mentally, morally, and then, if he is treading the path that leads to criminality," to take charge, "not so much to punish as to reform, not to degrade but to uplift, not to crush but to develop, to make him not a criminal but a worthy citizen." So, too, it was obvious to Boston's juvenile judge Harvey Baker that "of course the court does not confine its attention to just the particular offense which brought the child to its notice." If a boy came to the court "for some trifle," like failing to wear the badge entitling him to sell newspapers, but he turned out to be a chronic truant, then the court would respond to the more serious problem. The boy arrested for playing ball in the street who turned out to be a loafer, a gambler, and a petty thief would be treated not for the stated offense but for his vicious habits.

Since a court that was determined to explore the soul of the delinquent could not be bound by formal and technical rules, proponents everywhere moved to relax the style of its proceedings, to make them non-adversarial. Although judges could not banish a lawyer from the courtroom altogether, they did not consider his presence either appropriate or necessary. Minnesota juvenile court judge Grier Orr boasted that in his courtroom "the lawyers do not do very much . . . and I do not believe I can recall an instance where the same attorney came back a second time; he found that it was useless for him to appear . . . for an attorney has not very much standing when it comes to the disposition of children in the juvenile court."

In a similar spirit, juvenile courts were not to follow the rules of testimony appropriate to adult trials. Not that the codes establishing juvenile courts invariably and explicitly gave judges the authority to disregard such stipulations. Rather, as Judge Orr accurately noted: "The laws of evidence are sometimes forgotten or overlooked, because the juvenile court was a court of inquiry and not of prosecution; it is to find out the good that is within the boy or the child and to point out the way to reform, not to punish." The docket entry was not "the State versus Johnny Smith," and therefore "the laws of evidence could not be referred to in a law school as being exemplary." In almost every anecdote that judges or other proponents recounted about the workings of the court, a gentle and clever judge persuaded a stubborn or recalcitrant offender to "fess up," to tell the truth. Obviously this represented not a violation of the individual's right against self-incrimination but the first step of the delinquent toward rehabilitation.

Trial by jury seemed equally out of place in a juvenile court. The judge who was competent to act as lawyer and district attorney was equipped to find the facts as well. Juries were useful when a court wanted to know precisely what an offender had done. But here the act was irrelevant and the "facts" were not traditional facts; they involved the social background, the psychological make-up, and the level of maturity of the child. And judges, better than juries, could master and respond to such data. . . .

The single most important component of the juvenile court program was probation. Indeed, it assumed a significance to these proceedings that was still greater than in adult criminal justice. Probation represented, in the words of Timothy Hurley, "the keystone which supports the arch of this law." In the more elaborate phrases of Judge Tuthill, it was "the cord upon which all the pearls of the juvenile court are strung. . . . Without it, the juvenile court could not exist."

The first task of the probation officer was to provide the juvenile court judge with all the appropriate information for understanding the personality and condition of the child. The Illinois legislature charged probation officers "to make a personal inquiry into the facts of the case with the view to assist the court in what ought to be done. To this end, it will be necessary to record the history and the circumstances of the child as fully as possible. . . . The court will desire to ascertain the character, disposition and tendencies and school record of the child; also the character of the parents and their capability for governing and supporting the child, together with the character of the home, as to comforts, surroundings." To satisfy so far-reaching a mandate, the law gave the probation officer full latitude in making an investigation. "This information will be obtained in your own way, from the child, from the parents, neighbors, teachers, clergymen, police officials, and from the records of the poor department, the police department, and the various charitable agencies." In addition, the probation officer (or the judge himself) was to enlist the services of experts in child psychology and psychiatry to understand the peculiarities of each case. Indeed, this commitment was so much stronger for the delinquent than for the adult criminal that reformers recommended that the court itself hire a staff of psychologists or psychiatrists or have a very close working relationship with a clinic. The search for knowledge about the child had to lead everywhere.

The second task of the probation officer was to supervise the young offender released into the community. Given the strong sense that juvenile institutions were too rigid or, conversely, that only a mother would respond to the complex and changing nature of the child, proponents anticipated that most court dispositions would be probation. "No two of the boys coming to a juvenile court are alike," observed child welfare advocate Homer Folks, and accordingly, "The probation system offers many and varied things for many and varied kinds of boys." Reformers did not doubt the difficulty of this assignment; since the child was in trouble, his family and social circumstances were bound to be inadequate. The probation officer would have to assume the duties of an educated mother and at the same time train other family members and even neighbors to fulfill their responsibilities. But at least no legal restrictions were to interfere with the job. "With the great right arm and force of the law," declared Judge Tuthill, "the probation officer can go into the home and demand to know the cause of the dependency or the delinquency of a child. . . . He becomes practically a member of the family and teaches them lessons of cleanliness and decency, of truth and integrity." Admittedly, Tuthill continued, "Threats may be necessary in some instances to enforce the learning of the lessons he teaches, but whether by threats or cajolery, by appealing to their fear of the law or by rousing the ambition that lies latent in each human soul, he teaches the lesson and transforms the entire family into individuals which the state need never again hesitate to own as citizens." So once again proponents confidently enlarged the scope of state action. The same latitude and discretion that characterized juvenile courtroom procedure and pre-sentence investigations belonged to probation supervision as well.

Reformers were fully prepared to empower the courts to exercise still another option: to incarcerate the juvenile offender. In some cases of delinquency (and estimates of the frequency of these cases varied widely), institutionalization was a fully legitimate response, an integral part of a rehabilitative program. Yes, probation was a proper first resort. To incarcerate children, such a champion of probation as Homer Folks explained, "is to administer opiates to the community. It is to turn its mind away from its own serious problems." Nevertheless, Folks and his fellow reformers acknowledged that "juvenile probation is not proposed nor advisable for all cases of delinquency." Some boys simply would not take probation seriously and so institutionalization was an appropriate back-up sanction. Also, as Richmond, Virginia, juvenile court judge James Ricks noted, if "the child's parents are hopelessly weak or morally bad, or if he has no home, he should then be given a chance in a good institution or foster home." Moreover, the confirmed delinquent certainly belonged in an institution. Far better for him to be incarcerated in a setting, in Judge Tuthill's terms, "where he can be taught even against his own will the primary duty of obedience to authority," than to be left alone with his "vicious habits and demoralizing associates." Commitment to an institution could well be in the child's best interest and the court, therefore, could order it without tightening procedures.

In fact, many juvenile court proponents were also determined to expand the types of institutional programs for the delinquent. "The information which we are slowly accumulating as a result of more scientific investigation," declared Louis Robinson, the chief probation officer in Philadelphia, "does not show us that there will be no need for institutions in the future but rather that there is great need for institutions of a new and better type." Or, as his counterpart in Milwaukee insisted: "The new law was not a protest against institutionalism, for that was not the weak point. It was a protest against a criminal system which provided nothing better than suspended sentence or jail to cut delinquency at its first stages." . . .

Reformers' willingness to incarcerate at least some among the delinquent was but one example of their general readiness to elevate the power of the juvenile court over the family. Indeed, to many proponents, the most notable feature of the new court law was its clear expression of this principle. "The juvenile court laws," concluded one survey, "are usually so broad that the State, in its capacity of *parens patriae* . . . will take jurisdiction over practically every significant situation where it appears it should do so in the interests of the child." In part, this posture reflected Progressives' determination to rescue the immigrant child; his welfare was too important to allow the family the final say, whether the issue was the parents' right to put the child to work or to keep him out of school—or their right to discipline or fail to discipline him in their own fashion. In part too, it revealed reformers' confidence in their own program. Given the complex character of the child, the better part of wisdom was to trust to the court and its expert allies.

Whatever the motive, supporters eagerly justified the state's entitlement. The first case histories that Timothy Hurley reprinted in the *Juvenile Court Record* were frankly designed to give legitimacy to the extended reach of the state. Hurley recounted how he once "stood outside the door of a shanty and watched 'Mother Shevlin' teach a beautiful young boy to steal a handkerchief out of a coat pocket without being detected." (Hurley was a master salesman—the story was about "shanty" Irish, and the victim was a "beautiful boy," as though good looks ought to have precluded delinquency.) To be sure, Hurley continued, existing statutes would have permitted court intervention in this instance, but under the older system the boy could have been sent to an institution for only a brief time and "the rest of the family of degenerate children was, perforce, left to pursue its infamously criminal way, because there was no law on the statute books of the state of Illinois whereby they could be brought into court and cared for as they should have been." It was such cases as the Shevlin family, concluded Hurley, that led his organization (the Chicago Visitation and Aid Society) and others as well, such as the city's women's clubs and the Bar Association, to advocate a new law that would "provide a more comprehensive way . . . to bring about desired results than any that had been so far devised."

Hurley's perspective was widely shared. Mrs. Martha Falconer, a Chicago probation officer, was quick to tell the 1901 meeting of the National Congress of Mothers that "the women who cannot control their boys of eight or nine years of age should not have the care of them." Fully aware that she was addressing middle-class women on the problems of lower-class children, that it was other mothers, less capable and prepared than they, who had to be censured, Falconer promoted the juvenile court's discretionary authority because "I want those boys in a reform school; I feel there is no love there in the home, and that his home is no place for that boy." And she urged her audience not to be fooled for a moment by the public protests of the parents. "Those who neglect their children most are the ones who weep and wail loudest about them in court. To those women I say, 'You will keep your children off the streets or the city of Chicago will do it for you.'" In no less unequivocal terms the police matron of St. Louis made the same point to her state legislature. She had recently asked a little girl who was sitting around the jail where her mother was, to be told that she was "down in the Holdover drunk." The police matron had been able to get this child away from her mother and thus rescue her from a disastrous upbringing, but she had accomplished it "with difficulty." "Had we a juvenile court, these many cases could be easily settled and save the lives, and also the souls, of hundreds of just such unfortunate little ones." . . .

Reformers had fashioned a rationale and a program whose goals seemed to offer something to everyone, and it is small wonder that their synthesis lasted for most of this century. The juvenile court rhetoric and procedures were at once benevolent and tough-minded, helpful and rigorous, protective of the child and altogether mindful of the safety of the community. One might debate endlessly, and futilely, whether reformers used benign language to cloak a repressive innovation, whether "social control" motivations were more significant than humanitarian concerns. The critical point is that reformers saw no conflict here; they did not believe they were in an either/or position. There was nothing hypocritical in their approach, no covert message that had to be sorted out, no code language that had to be cracked. Openly and optimistically they presented a program that seemed so very right and necessary precisely because it did not require trade-offs. The welfare of the child was synonymous with the welfare of society. The juvenile court, the whole program for understanding and combating delinquency, was in the best interests of everyone.

Thus the rhetoric of helpfulness that would open a speech or pamphlet on behalf of the juvenile court would effortlessly give way to a rhetoric of repression and public safety. The most important organ of the movement, the *Juvenile Court Record,* demonstrated this capacity well. Its columns asked its readers to be "patient and forgiving: Whereas, it is often necessary to bring the little ones to court in order that they may be taught to discriminate between right and wrong, in truth we must hold them guiltless. . . . Would we have done better in their places?" But its motto, prominently displayed in every issue, declared: "Every homeless child is a menace to society and the State." In just this way Judge Franklin Hoyt, of the New York juvenile court, opened his anecdotal account of his service with gentle phrases addressed by the "spirit of justice" to the "spirit of youth." "You are bruised and bewildered . . . but you need not fear. . . . Trust in me, for I am here to help you. . . . In me you will find no fair-weather friend, but a guide and protector who will stand by you through storm and stress." Hoyt then proceeded to fill his pages with stories of how he combated the various "isms" of the young, and to tell how he won "recruits for law and order." To Hoyt, the wisdom of the juvenile court arrangements were never better demonstrated than in a certain case when a boy came before him on a petty charge, but upon discussion revealed himself to be a Socialist. Then the judge had the chance to teach someone who thought "that our established institutions are but forms of slavery" the Progressive credo: "Kindliness, common sense, and humane justice can exist side by side with the enforcement of law and order."

In juvenile justice particularly, the ease with which proponents moved from one message to another, from the promise to uplift to the threat to coerce, testified to their ultimate confidence in the moral and social superiority of the American system. There was no conflict between the helping power and the policing power because both sought to adjust the youthful deviant to an environment that provided optimal conditions for promoting his own well-being. Since the delinquent was by definition young and oftentimes immigrant, in two senses a newcomer to the scene, he was doubly blind to the American promise. Hence the rights and wrongs of the situation were easily drawn up: intemperance, vulgarity, antiquated customs, loose street life, ignorance, were on one side of the ledger; the careful nurture of the child, education, training to lawfulness, obedience, close supervision, on the other. The juvenile court was the bridge between the two.

Sources

The State as Parent: Mothering Through Public Health

This undated photograph captures the progressive spirit in action. On what grounds might Rothman object to what is taking place here?

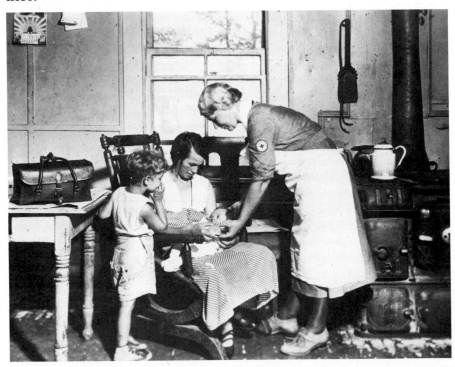

The public health nurse teaches the mothers of limited means the proper feeding of babies and children. *National Archives, RG 90, Public Health Service, No. 90-G-2926.*

Mother's Day

Women shaped the content of reform in important ways. Alice Hamilton, for example, tramped from one mine or factory to another, crusading for occupational health and safety; Florence Kelley headed the factory-inspection staff of the state of Illinois; Jane Addams and Lillian Wald spearheaded the settlement-house movement. Others lobbied for woman suffrage, which was granted just as the progressive era closed.

In the midst of this remarkable activity, another progressive, Woodrow Wilson, chose to honor a certain category of women— mothers. How does the Mothers' Day Proclamation fit with the aggressive politics of the era's women reformers? And how can one square the proclamation's celebration of motherhood with the critical view of American mothers suggested in the photograph on page 138?

Congress and the President

Legalize and Immortalize

Mothers' Day

Second Sunday in May

A PROCLAMATION

"Whereas, by a joint resolution, approved May 8, 1914, designating the second Sunday in May as Mothers' Day, and for other purposes, the President is authorized and requested to issue a proclamation calling upon the government officials to display the United States flag on all government buildings, and the people of the United States to display the flag at their homes, or other suitable places on the second Sunday in May, as a public expression of our love and reverence for the mothers of our country;

"And, Whereas, by the said joint resolution it is made the duty of the President to request the observance of the second Sunday in May as provided for in the said joint resolution;

"Now, therefore, I, Woodrow Wilson, President of the United States of America, by virtue of the authority vested in me by the said joint resolution, do hereby direct the government officials to display the United States flag on all government buildings, and do invite the people of the United States to display the flag at their homes, or other suitable places, on the second Sunday of May, as a public expression of our love and reverence for the mothers of our country. In witness whereof I have set my hand and caused the seal of the United States to be hereunto affixed.

"Done at the city of Washington this 9th day of May, in the year of our Lord, one thousand nine hundred and fourteen and of the Independence of the United States one hundred and thirty-eight.

"WOODROW WILSON.
"By the President.
"WILLIAM JENNINGS BRYAN.
"Secretary of State."

"Mothers' Day Proclamation" from America's Families: A Documentary History, *edited by Donald M. Scott and Bernard Wishy. Copyright © 1982 by Donald M. Scott and Bernard Wishy. Reprinted by permission of Harper & Row, Publishers, Inc.*

Woodrow Wilson Proclaims Mother's Day, 1914.

Education and Childhood

Progressive-period reformers were anxious to set education on a new and "scientific" footing. And they were just as concerned with the problem of "wayward" youth. All across the nation, there were studies of how children spent their time. And in institutions for "delinquent" children there was a similar determination to classify in scientific terms the kinds of vices that young people were prey to. Behind the science—and not far behind it, either—was an obvious moralism. The officials who made the studies that follow were sure that they knew what a good life was, and just as certain that *knowledge* was the key to solving the problem. The two photographs from the George Junior Republic speak more clearly than words about the kinds of ideological purposes that lay behind the statistics. What does the Cleveland play census reveal about the people who compiled it? What do you suppose the census takers meant when they recorded the children "doing nothing"? What kind of play did Cleveland reformers wish to see? What typically progressive traits are mirrored in the statistics on "delinquent" boys? For example, where were boys sent when discharged from the Maine State School for Boys? What characteristics of youth were found most offensive at the Indiana Boys' School, and why? Finally, how might David J. Rothman use these materials to support his critique of progressivism?

Recreation

A Play Census of Cleveland Pupils

A play census, taken June 23, 1913, under the direction of the Chief Medical Inspector and Assistant Superintendent in charge of Physical Education in Cleveland, seemed to show this same lack of relationship between the school and the out-of-school activities of children. The results of this study are shown in Table 7.

Conclusions Drawn From This Census
1. That just at the age (under 15) when play and activity are the fundamental requirements for proper growth and development 41 per cent of the children seen were doing nothing. The boy without play is father to the man without a job.
2. Fifty-one per cent of all the children seen were in the streets, in the midst of all the traffic, dirt, and heat, and in an environment conducive to just the wrong kind of play.
3. That only six per cent of the children seen were on vacant lots despite the fact that in most of the districts vacant lots were available as play spaces. A place to play does not solve the problem: there must be a play leader.

Table 7. What 14,683 Cleveland Children Were Doing on June 23, 1913

		Boys	*Girls*	*Total*
Where they were seen	On streets	5,241	2,558	7,799
	In yards	1,583	1,998	3,581
	In vacant lots	686	197	883
	In playgrounds	997	872	1,869
	In alleys	413	138	551
What they were doing	Doing nothing	3,737	2,234	5,961
	Playing	4,601	2,757	7,358
	Working	719	635	1,354
What games they were playing	Baseball	1,448	190	1,638
	Kites	482	49	531
	Sand piles	241	230	471
	Tag	100	53	153
	Jackstones	68	257	325
	Dolls	89	193	282
	Sewing	14	130	144
	Housekeeping	53	191	244
	Horse and wagon	89	24	113
	Bicycle riding	79	13	92
	Minding baby	19	41	60
	Reading	17	35	52
	Roller-skating	18	29	47
	Gardening	13	14	27
	Caddy	6	0	6
	Marbles	2	0	2
	Playing in other ways mostly just fooling	1,863	1,308	3,171

From George E. Johnson, *Education Through Recreation* (Cleveland: The Survey Committee of the Cleveland Foundation, 1916), pp. 48–51. Reprinted with permission.

4. That even though 36 playgrounds were open and 16 of them with apparatus up, only 1869, or 11 per cent, of the children seen within four blocks of a playground were playing on playgrounds. Last Friday 6488 children played on playgrounds.
5. That of the 7358 children reported to have been playing, 3171 were reported to have been playing by doing some of the following things: fighting, teasing, pitching pennies, shooting craps, stealing apples, "roughing a peddler," chasing chickens, tying can to dog, etc., but most of them were reported to have been "just fooling"—not playing anything in particular.
6. We need more and better playgrounds and a better trained leadership.

The Recreational Interests of Cleveland Pupils

That the play interests of children and youth answer to deep-seated needs and are essential for fullest development and education is now so universally admitted that only the mere statement is here necessary. It is also evident that these play interests are the prototypes of the great lines of human interest, endeavor, and achievement represented in adult life and in education work today.

Crime and Reformation

Causes for which Boys Were Committed to Louisville, Kentucky, Industrial School, 1906

	White	*Colored*	*Total*
Incorrigibility	72	27	99
Delinquency	43	13	56
Larceny	4	3	7
Petit larceny	13	9	22
Grand larceny	8	1	9
Burglary	4	3	7
Burglary and larceny	19	3	22
Vagrancy and larceny	1	0	1
Vagrancy	8	2	10
Vagrancy and incorrigibility	3	0	3
Incorrigibility and immorality	1	0	1
Assault	2	1	3
Manslaughter in fourth degree	1	0	1
Felony	1	0	1
Attempted rape	0	1	1
Destruction of property	2	0	2
Obstructing railroad	1	0	1
Disturbing the peace	2	0	2

State School for Boys, South Portland, Maine, 1906. Students Were Heavily Concentrated in the 10–15 Age Group.

Facts Connected with the Moral Condition of the Boys When Received	
Whole number received	2,615
Have intemperate parents	881
Lost father	816
Lost mother	654
Relatives in prison	335
Step parents	491
Idle	1,658
Much neglected	907
Truants	1,140
Sabbath breakers	992
Untruthful	2,053
Profane	1,908

Disposition of Those Discharged Since Opening of the School

Discharged on expiration of sentence	223
Discharged by trustees	731
Indentured to—	
Barber	1
Blacksmith	1
Boarding mistress	1
Boilermaker	1
Cabinetmaker	6
Carpenters	13
Cooper	1
Farmers	287
Harness makers	3
Laborers	9
Lumbermen	3
Machinists	5
Manufacturers	2
Mason	1
Miller	1
Sea captains	5
Shoemakers	14
Tailors	3
Tallow chandler	1
Allowed to leave on trial	1,026
Allowed to enlist	19
Illegally committed	19
Remanded	64
Pardoned	15
Finally escaped	81
Violated trust	49
Died	49
Delivered to courts	24
Returned to masters	4

Nativity of All Committed

Foreigners	278
Born in United States	2,295
Nativity not known	41

Demerit Offenses, Indiana Boys' School, Plainfield, 1906

Talk	10
Disobedience	10
Disorder	10
Laziness	10
Vandalism	10
Willful waste	20
Quarreling	50
Dormitory	50
Shielding	50
Profanity	50
Fighting	100
Tobacco or money	100
Falsehood	100
Theft	100
Obscenity	100
Disrespect and impudence	100
Vulgarity	200
Insubordination	200
Planning escape	500
Escape	1,000
Secret vice	1,000
Planning immoral association	1,000
Immoral association	2,000

From U.S. Congress, House Committee on the Judiciary, *Juvenile Crime and Reformation, Including Stigmata of Degeneration,* Being a Hearing on the Bill (H. R. 16733) to Establish a Laboratory for the Study of the Criminal, Pauper, and Defective Classes, by Arthur MacDonald, 60th Cong. (Washington, D.C., 1908), pp. 115, 107.

The George Junior Republic

The George Junior Republic was a progressive-era camp for destitute and delinquent youth. It had strong appeal for Theodore Roosevelt, economist John R. Commons, and General Robert Baden-Powell (British founder of the Boy Scouts, another progressive-era institution). According to these photos, what was the cause of delinquency among youth? What did the George Junior Republic choose to do about it?

The Court, c. 1905. A citizen judge presides. *Department of Manuscripts and University Archives, Cornell University, Ithaca, N.Y.*

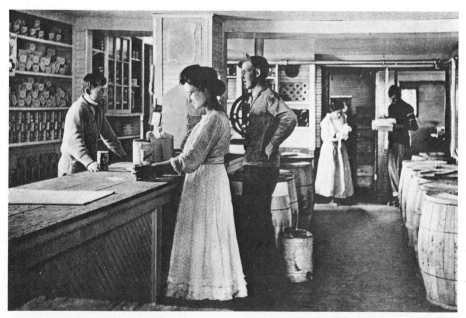

The Republic Store, c. 1910. Citizens exchange Republic currency for groceries. *Department of Manuscripts and University Archives, Cornell University, Ithaca, N.Y.*

Progressivism Goes to War: The Jailing of Eugene Debs

The Wilsonian vision of the European conflict as a great democratic crusade against autocracy no doubt helped Americans summon the courage and dedication to fight World War I. At the same time, however, it contributed to an atmosphere of mindless intolerance.

Among the many victims of this intolerance was socialist leader Eugene Debs. Imprisoned in the 1890s for his role in the Pullman strike, he emerged to found what became the Socialist Party of America. In 1912, he received almost 1 million votes in a run for the presidency, indicative of the appeal and strength of socialism during the Progressive era.

During World War I, Debs came up against the Sedition Act (1918), which made it illegal for people to make false statements that interfered with the prosecution of the war and to use "disloyal, profane, scurrilous, or abusive language" to describe the American form of government. The act was enforced mainly against pacifists and socialists such as Debs.

The speech that landed Debs in jail (he would serve three years of a ten-year term) was delivered in Canton, Ohio, on June 16, 1918, before 1,200 socialists gathered for a party convention. A jury found Debs guilty of having willfully and knowingly tried to obstruct the operation of the Selective Service Act (1917) and, thus, of having interfered with the war effort. In your opinion, was there any legal—or ethical—justification for imprisoning Debs?

Comrades, friends and fellow workers, for this very cordial greeting, this very hearty reception, I thank you all with the fullest appreciation of your interest in and your devotion to the cause for which I am to speak to you this afternoon. [*Applause.*]

To speak for labor; to plead the cause of the men and women and children who toil; to serve the working class, has always been to me a high privilege [*applause*]; a duty of love.

I have just returned from a visit over yonder [*pointing to the workhouse*] [*laughter*], where three of our most loyal comrades [*applause*] are paying the penalty for their devotion to the cause of the working class. [*Applause.*] They have come to realize, as many of us have, that it is extremely dangerous to exercise the constitutional right of free speech in a country fighting to make democracy safe in the world. [*Applause.*] . . .

If it had not been for the men and women who, in the past, have had the moral courage to go to jail, we would still be in the jungles. [*Applause.*]

From Jean Y. Tussey, ed., *Eugene V. Debs Speaks* (New York: Pathfinder Press, 1970), pp. 244, 254–255, 260–261, 267, 271–272, 278–279. Reprinted by permission of Pathfinder Press. Copyright © 1970 by Pathfinder Press, Inc.

This assemblage is exceedingly good to look upon. I wish it were possible for me to give you what you are giving me this afternoon. [*Laughter.*] What I say here amounts to but little; what I see here is exceedingly important. [*Applause.*] You workers in Ohio, enlisted in the greatest cause ever organized in the interest of your class, are making history today in the face of threatening opposition of all kinds—history that is going to be read with profound interest by coming generations. [*Applause.*]

There is but one thing you have to be concerned about, and that is that you keep foursquare with the principles of the international Socialist movement. [*Applause.*] It is only when you begin to compromise that trouble begins. [*Applause.*] So far as I am concerned, it does not matter what others may say, or think, or do, as long as I am sure that I am right with myself and the cause. [*Applause.*] There are so many who seek refuge in the popular side of a great question. As a Socialist, I have long since learned how to stand alone. [*Applause.*] . . .

Who appoints our federal judges? The people? In all the history of the country, the working class have never named a federal judge. There are 121 of these judges and every solitary one holds his position, his tenure, through the influence and power of corporate capital. The corporations and trusts dictate their appointment. And when they go to the bench, they go, not to serve the people, but to serve the interests that place them and keep them where they are.

Why, the other day, by a vote of five to four—a kind of craps game— come seven, come 'leven [*laughter*]—they declared the child labor law unconstitutional—a law secured after twenty years of education and agitation on the part of all kinds of people. And yet, by a majority of one, the Supreme Court, a body of corporation lawyers, with just one exception, wiped that law from the statute books, and this in our so-called democracy, so that we may continue to grind the flesh and blood and bones of puny little children into profits for the junkers of Wall Street. [*Applause.*] And this in a country that boasts of fighting to make the world safe for democracy! [*Laughter.*] The history of this country is being written in the blood of the childhood the industrial lords have murdered . . .

Wars throughout history have been waged for conquest and plunder. In the Middle Ages when the feudal lords who inhabited the castles whose towers may still be seen along the Rhine concluded to enlarge their domains, to increase their power, their prestige and their wealth they declared war upon one another. But they themselves did not go to war any more than the modern feudal lords, the barons of Wall Street go to war. [*Applause.*] The feudal barons of the Middle Ages, the economic predecessors of the capitalists of our day, declared all wars. And their miserable serfs fought all the battles. The poor, ignorant serfs had been taught to revere their masters; to believe that when their masters declared war upon one another, it was their patriotic duty to fall upon one another and to cut one another's throats for the profit and glory of the lords and barons who held them in contempt. And that is war in a nutshell. The master class has always declared the wars;

the subject class has always fought the battles. The master class has had all to gain and nothing to lose, while the subject class has had nothing to gain and all to lose—especially their lives. [*Applause.*]

They have always taught and trained you to believe it to be your patriotic duty to go to war and to have yourselves slaughtered at their command. But in all the history of the world you, the people, have never had a voice in declaring war, and strange as it certainly appears, no war by any nation in any age has ever been declared by the people.

And here let me emphasize the fact—and it cannot be repeated too often—that the working class who fight all the battles, the working class who make the supreme sacrifices, the working class who freely shed their blood and furnish the corpses, have never yet had a voice in either declaring war or making peace. It is the ruling class that invariably does both. They alone declare war and they alone make peace.

> Yours not to reason why;
> Yours but to do and die.

That is their motto and we object on the part of the awakening workers of this nation.

If war is right let it be declared by the people. You who have your lives to lose, you certainly above all others have the right to decide the momentous issue of war or peace. [*Applause.*] . . .

You need at this time especially to know that you are fit for something better than slavery and cannon fodder. [*Applause.*] You need to know that you were not created to work and produce and impoverish yourself to enrich an idle exploiter. You need to know that you have a mind to improve, a soul to develop, and a manhood to sustain. . . .

They are continually talking about your patriotic duty. It is not *their* but *your* patriotic duty that they are concerned about. There is a decided difference. Their patriotic duty never takes them to the firing line or chucks them into the trenches.

And now among other things they are urging you to "cultivate" war gardens, while at the same time a government war report just issued shows that practically 52 percent of the arable, tillable soil is held out of use by the landlords, speculators and profiteers. They themselves do not cultivate the soil. They could not if they would. Nor do they allow others to cultivate it. They keep it idle to enrich themselves, to pocket the millions of dollars of unearned increment. . . .

And now for all of us to do our duty! The clarion call is ringing in our ears and we cannot falter without being convicted of treason to ourselves and to our great cause.

Do not worry over the charge of treason to your masters, but be concerned about the treason that involves yourselves. [*Applause.*] Be true to yourself and you cannot be a traitor to any good cause on earth. . . .

7

From War to Normalcy

The generation that came of age in the 1920s did so in the shadow of World War I. A nation led to expect that the struggle would be morally satisfying—that had boldly announced in song that "the Yanks are coming"—would be reduced to seeking meaning in an unidentifiable soldier, buried in Arlington, Virginia. That a war of such short duration—direct American involvement lasted little more than eighteen months—could have had such an impact may seem surprising. But part of an explanation may be found by examining how Americans experienced the conflict and what they were led to believe it would achieve.

Several groups experienced the war years as a time of increased opportunity. Blacks—migrating from the South into Chicago, Detroit, New York, and other industrial cities—and women—heretofore denied most jobs open to men—found themselves suddenly employable. The same circumstances allowed organized labor to double its membership in the four years after 1914. Farmers prospered because of rising European demand and, after 1917, because of government price guarantees. Soldiers, however, experienced the typical wartime "tax" on income, and many lost their positions on promotional ladders.

Continued deficit spending fueled the economy during demobilization. In 1919, activity in automobile production and building construction, two industries held back by the war, helped the nation avoid a prolonged postwar tailspin. But economic crisis could be postponed for only so long. By mid-1921, the economy was mired in a serious depression that cut industrial output by some 20 percent. It seems likely that a downturn in the postwar economy, deeply affecting a people who had no history of planning for such events, helped to dissolve the aura of economic progress and personal suc-

cess that had been part of the war and to inaugurate a decade of conflict between young and old, employer and employee, country and
city, religion and science, nation and locality. In the minds of many
Americans, depression was inseparably linked to demobilization and
the peace settlement.

Unlike World War II, World War I was not an especially popular conflict with Americans. Few German-Americans wanted to see
the United States declare war on Germany. Irish-Americans feared
that United States entry into the war would mean assistance to Britain in its struggle against Irish revolutionaries. Socialists—an influential faction in the 1910s—strongly opposed the American declaration
of war, branding it "a crime against the people of the United
States." This antiwar stance brought Socialist candidates in the 1917
municipal elections 34 percent of the vote in Chicago and 44 percent
in Dayton, Ohio. Hundreds of thousands refused to register or to be
inducted into the military.

The war had to be sold, systematically and unabashedly, like
any other product. The government's advertising agency was the
Committee on Public Information, headed by journalist George
Creel. The Creel Committee employed an elaborate publicity apparatus to educate Americans to proper wartime values. In one advertisement, a smiling American soldier clenched a White Owl cigar between his teeth and said:

> Did I bayonet my first Hun?
> Sure! How did it feel? It *doesn't*
> feel! There *he* is. There *you*
> are. One of you has got to go.
> I preferred to stay.
>
> So when sergeant says,
> "Smash 'em, boys"—we do.
> And we go them one better
> like good old Yankee Doodle
> Yanks. For bullets and bayo-
> nets are the only kind of lingo
> that a Hun can *understand!*
>
> (*Saturday Evening Post,* August
>   31, 1918; reprinted by per-
>   mission of General Cigar and
>   Tobacco Co.)

Efforts to eliminate criticism of the war effort took many forms.
At Columbia University, a professor who opposed United States entry into the war was summarily dismissed. More than 1,500 persons

were arrested under the Espionage Act of 1917 and the Sedition Act of 1918. One was Eugene Debs—in 1912 a candidate for the presidency—who served time in Atlanta Penitentiary for criticizing the war. The Industrial Workers of the World (IWW), popularly known as Wobblies, a radical labor group that was strongest on the West Coast, was viciously harassed. Although the organization took no official position on American involvement and although the IWW was involved in only 3 of more than 500 wartime strikes, over 100 Wobblies were tried in 1918 on charges of sabotage and conspiracy to obstruct the war. On the flimsiest of evidence, a jury found all defendants guilty. Fifteen received prison sentences of twenty years; thirty-three were given ten years; and another thirty-five received five years.

Perhaps fighting a war—especially a war with which large numbers of the population disagreed—required a kind of artificially imposed unity. This would explain the Wobbly trials and the Creel Committee propaganda. But when the fighting stopped—when the great crusade was over—a new crusade, called the Red Scare, took the place of wartime coercion of dissidents. When this latest hysteria subsided in the spring of 1920, hundreds of radicals of every persuasion—socialists, Wobblies, syndicalists, communists, even ordinary union members—had been arrested, beaten, lynched, tried, or deported.

Just as wartime coercion had yielded to the Red Scare, so was the Red Scare reincarnated in the politics of Warren Harding. In May 1920, emphasizing that "too much has been said about Bolshevism in America," Harding coined the word that would capture his appeal and win him the presidency, urging a return to "not heroism, but healing, not nostrums, but normalcy." With "normalcy," Harding and the American people seemed to be rejecting the world that Woodrow Wilson had sought to create—the world in which words replaced concrete realities, in which dreams of world government (the League of Nations) transcended political facts. The Creel Committee had described the war as "a Crusade not merely to re-win the tomb of Christ, but to bring back to earth the rule of right, the peace, goodwill to men and gentleness he taught." When it proved much less than this, Americans beat an emotional retreat to the comfort of Harding's slogans.

The 1920s had powerful currents of individualism, of course. In fact, the decade has been rightly famed for its affection for jazz, for its compulsion for mah-jongg and flagpole sitting, for the flapper, and for the iconoclast H. L. Mencken (for whom every group, even the New England town meeting, was a mob run by demagogues). Harding's "normalcy," however, seemed to center on a program of cultural conformity, and it was to infect the entire decade. The Ku Klux Klan, revived at a Georgia meeting in 1915, grew rapidly in the early 1920s through campaigns against blacks, Catholics, Jews, and immigrants. National prohibition, which required millions to give up deeply ingrained drinking habits or evade the law, was in effect throughout the decade. The first law establishing immigration quotas was passed in 1921; a second measure passed three years later was designed to reduce immigration from Eastern and Southern Europe—the later immigrants discussed in Chapter 3. If "normalcy" is broad enough to encompass these aspects of the 1920s, then perhaps wartime coercion, the Red Scare, and "normalcy" were all variations on a theme—a theme perhaps placed in bold relief by the war, demobilization, and postwar economic crisis, but ultimately one set more deeply in the nation's character and its institutions than any of these events.

Interpretive Essay

Stanley Coben

The American Red Scare, 1919–1920

In the following essay, historian Stanley Coben describes and analyzes the causes of the Red Scare of 1919 and 1920. Like the introduction to this chapter, Coben stresses how important it is to place the Red Scare in the context of larger factors such as American nativism and the cultural shock of the Great War. He also suggests that history might have taken a different turn, and the Red Scare might have been much less intense, had Americans not been rendered vulnerable by high rates of unemployment and inflation. But why, if the real problems were economic conditions such as inflation and unemployment, did so many Americans respond so irrationally, picking out enemies that were far removed from those real concerns? One might imagine a returning veteran having some difficulty identifying his enemies; but what of A. Mitchell Palmer, Woodrow Wilson's attorney general? Why did Palmer join the hunt? Was he irresponsible? politically motivated perhaps? Or is it possible that he regarded the

**Red Scare as a curious capstone for progressivism and Wilsonian re-
form? Finally, consider another portion of Coben's explanation: the
idea that Americans behaved so aggressively because they needed an
"island of . . . security." Nothing sounds more reasonable. But why
did they choose to define the *nation* as that island? Why not the family, the church, their state or region, or the community?**

At a victory loan pageant in the District of Columbia on May 6, 1919,
a man refused to rise for the playing of "The Star-Spangled Banner." As
soon as the national anthem was completed an enraged sailor fired three
shots into the unpatriotic spectator's back. When the man fell, the *Washington
Post* reported, "the crowd burst into cheering and handclapping." In February
of the same year, a jury in Hammond, Indiana, took two minutes to acquit
the assassin of an alien who yelled, "To Hell with the United States." Early
in 1920, a clothing store salesman in Waterbury, Connecticut, was sentenced
to six months in jail for having remarked to a customer that Lenin was "the
brainiest," or "one of the brainiest" of the world's political leaders. Dramatic
episodes like these, or the better known Centralia Massacre, Palmer Raids,
or May Day riots, were not everyday occurrences, even at the height of the
Red Scare. But the fanatical one hundred per cent Americanism reflected by
the Washington crowd, the Hammond jury, and the Waterbury judge pervaded a large part of our society between early 1919 and mid-1920.

Recently, social scientists have produced illuminating evidence about the
causes of eruptions like that of 1919–1920. They have attempted to identify
experimentally the individuals most responsive to nativistic appeals, to explain
their susceptibility, and to propose general theories of nativistic and related
movements. These studies suggest a fuller, more coherent picture of nativistic
upheavals and their causes than we now possess, and they provide the framework for this attempt to reinterpret the Red Scare.

Psychological experiments indicate that a great many Americans—at least
several million—are always ready to participate in a "red scare." These people
permanently hold attitudes which characterized the nativists of 1919–1920:
hostility toward certain minority groups, especially radicals and recent immigrants, fanatical patriotism, and a belief that internal enemies seriously threaten
national security.

In one of the most comprehensive of these experiments, psychologists
Nancy C. Morse and Floyd H. Allport tested seven hypotheses about the
causes of prejudice and found that one, national involvement or patriotism,
proved to be "by far the most important factor" associated with prejudice.
Other widely held theories about prejudice—status rivalry, frustration-aggres-
sion, and scapegoat hypotheses, for example—were found to be of only secondary importance. Summarizing the results of this and a number of other

From Stanley Coben, "A Study in Nativism: The American Red Scare of 1919–1920," *Political
Science Quarterly* 79, no. 1 (March 1964): 52–75. Reprinted with permission.

psychological experiments, Gordon W. Allport, a pioneer in the scientific study of prejudice, concluded that in a large proportion of cases the prejudiced person is attempting to defend himself against severe inner turmoil by enforcing order in his external life. Any disturbance in the social *status quo* threatens the precarious psychic equilibrium of this type of individual, who, according to Allport, seeks "an island of institutional safety and security. The nation is the island he selects . . . It has the definiteness he needs."

Allport pointed out that many apprehensive and frustrated people are not especially prejudiced. What is important, he found,

> is the way fear and frustration are handled. The institutionalistic way—especially the nationalistic—seems to be the nub of the matter. What happens is that the prejudiced person defines "nation" to fit his needs. The nation is first of all a protection (the chief protection) of him as an individual. It is his in-group. He sees no contradiction in ruling out of its beneficent orbit those whom he regards as threatening intruders and enemies (namely, American minorities). What is more, the nation stands for the status quo. It is a conservative agent; within it are all the devices for safe living that he approves. His nationalism is a form of conservatism.

Substantial evidence, then, suggests that millions of Americans are both extraordinarily fearful of social change and prejudiced against those minority groups which they perceive as "threatening intruders." Societal disruption, especially if it can easily be connected with the "intruders," not only will intensify the hostility of highly prejudiced individuals, but also will provoke many others, whose antagonism in more stable times had been mild or incipient, into the extreme group. . . .

According to Anthony F. C. Wallace, who has gone farthest toward constructing a general theory of cult formation, when the disruption has proceeded so far that many members of a society find it difficult or impossible to fulfill their physical and psychological needs, or to relieve severe anxiety through the ordinary culturally approved methods, the society will be susceptible to what Wallace has termed a "revitalization movement." This is a convulsive attempt to change or revivify important cultural beliefs and values, and frequently to eliminate alien influences. Such movements promise and often provide participants with better means of dealing with their changed circumstances, thus reducing their very high level of internal stress. . . .

Dominant as well as conquered peoples, Ralph Linton has pointed out, undergo nativistic movements. Dominant groups, he observed, are sometimes threatened "not only by foreign invasion or domestic revolt but also by the invidious process of assimilation which might, in the long run, destroy their distinctive powers and privileges." Under such circumstances, Linton concluded, "the frustrations which motivate nativistic movements in inferior or dominated groups" are "replaced by anxieties which produce very much the same [nativistic] result" in dominant groups. . . .

The ferocious outbreak of nativism in the United States after World

War I was not consciously planned or provoked by any individual or group, although some Americans took advantage of the movement once it started. Rather, the Red Scare, . . . was brought on largely by a number of severe social and economic dislocations which threatened the national equilibrium. The full extent and the shocking effects of these disturbances of 1919 have not yet been adequately described. Runaway prices, a brief but sharp stock market crash and business depression, revolutions throughout Europe, widespread fear of domestic revolt, bomb explosions, and an outpouring of radical literature were distressing enough. These sudden difficulties, moreover, served to exaggerate the disruptive effects already produced by the social and intellectual ravages of the World War and the preceding reform era, and by the arrival, before the war, of millions of new immigrants. This added stress intensified the hostility of Americans strongly antagonistic to minority groups, and brought new converts to blatant nativism from among those who ordinarily were not overtly hostile toward radicals or recent immigrants.

Citizens who joined the crusade for one hundred per cent Americanism sought, primarily, a unifying force which would halt the apparent disintegration of their culture. The movement, they felt, would eliminate those foreign influences which the one hundred per centers believed were the major cause of their anxiety.

Many of the postwar sources of stress were also present during World War I, and the Red Scare, as John Higham has observed, was partly an exaggeration of wartime passions. In 1917–1918 German-Americans served as the object of almost all our nativistic fervor; they were the threatening intruders who refused to become good citizens. "They used America," a patriotic author declared in 1918 of two million German-Americans, "they never loved her. They clung to their old language, their old customs, and cared nothing for ours. . . . As a class they were clannish beyond all other races coming here." Fear of subversion by German agents was almost as extravagant in 1917–1918 as anxiety about "reds" in the postwar period. Attorney General Thomas Watt Gregory reported to a friend in May 1918 that "we not infrequently receive as many as fifteen hundred letters in a single day suggesting disloyalty and the making of investigations."

Opposition to the war by radical groups helped smooth the transition among American nativists from hatred of everything German to fear of radical revolution. The two groups of enemies were associated also for other reasons. High government officials declared after the war that German leaders planned and subsidized the Bolshevik Revolution. When bombs blasted homes and public buildings in nine cities in June 1919, the director of the Justice Department's Bureau of Investigation asserted that the bombers were "connected with Russian bolshevism, aided by Hun money." In November 1919, a year after the armistice, a popular magazine warned of "the Russo-German movement that is now trying to dominate America. . . ."

Even the wartime hostility toward German-Americans, however, is more understandable when seen in the light of recent anthropological and psychological studies. World War I disturbed Americans not only because of the real threat posed by enemy armies and a foreign ideology. For many citizens it had the further effect of shattering an already weakened intellectual tradition. When the European governments decided to fight, they provided shocking evidence that man was not, as most educated members of Western society had believed, a rational creature progressing steadily, if slowly, toward control of his environment. When the great powers declared war in 1914, many Americans as well as many Europeans were stunned. The *New York Times* proclaimed a common theme—European civilization had collapsed: The supposedly advanced nations, declared the *Times,* "have reverted to the condition of savage tribes roaming the forests and falling upon each other in a fury of blood and carnage to achieve the ambitious designs of chieftains clad in skins and drunk with mead." Franz Alexander, director for twenty-five years of the Chicago Institute of Psychoanalysis, recently recalled his response to the outbreak of the World War:

> The first impact of this news is [*sic*] unforgettable. It was the sudden intuitive realization that a chapter of history had ended. . . . Since then, I have discussed this matter with some of my contemporaries and heard about it a great deal in my early postwar psychoanalytic treatments of patients. To my amazement, the others who went through the same events had quite a similar reaction. . . . It was an immediate vivid and prophetic realization that something irrevocable of immense importance had happened in history.

Americans were jolted by new blows to their equilibrium after entering the war. Four million men were drafted away from familiar surroundings and some of them experienced the terrible carnage of trench warfare. Great numbers of women left home to work in war industries or to replace men in other jobs. Negroes flocked to Northern industrial areas by the hundreds of thousands, and their first mass migration from the South created violent racial antagonism in Northern cities.

During the war, also, Americans sanctioned a degree of government control over the economy which deviated sharply from traditional economic individualism. Again, fears aroused before the war were aggravated, for the reform legislation of the Progressive era had tended to increase government intervention, and many citizens were further perturbed by demands that the federal government enforce even higher standards of economic and social morality. By 1919, therefore, some prewar progressives as well as conservatives feared the gradual disappearance of highly valued individual opportunity and responsibility. Their fears were fed by strong postwar calls for continued large-scale government controls—extension of federal operation of railroads and of the Food Administration, for example.

The prime threat to these long-held individualistic values, however, and the most powerful immediate stimulus to the revitalistic response, came from Russia. There the Bolshevik conquerors proclaimed their intention of exporting Marxist ideology. If millions of Americans were disturbed in 1919 by the specter of communism, the underlying reason was not fear of foreign invasion—Russia, after all, was still a backward nation recently badly defeated by German armies. The real threat was the potential spread of communist ideas. These, the one hundred per centers realized with horror, possessed a genuine appeal for reformers and for the economically underprivileged, and if accepted they would complete the transformation of America.

A clear picture of the Bolshevik tyranny was not yet available; therefore, as after the French Revolution, those who feared the newly successful ideology turned to fight the revolutionary ideals. So the *Saturday Evening Post* declared editorially in November 1919 that "History will see our present state of mind as one with that preceding the burning of witches, the children's crusade, the great tulip craze and other examples of softening of the world brain." The *Post* referred not to the Red Scare or the impending Palmer Raids, but to the spread of communist ideology. Its editorial concluded: "The need of the country is not more idealism, but more pragmatism; not communism, but common sense." One of the most powerful patriotic groups, the National Security League, called upon members early in 1919 to "teach 'Americanism.' This means the fighting of Bolshevism . . . by the creation of well defined National Ideals." Members "must preach Americanism and instil the idealism of America's Wars, and that American spirit of service which believes in giving as well as getting." New York attorney, author, and educator Henry Waters Taft warned a Carnegie Hall audience late in 1919 that Americans must battle "a propaganda which is tending to undermine our most cherished social and political institutions and is having the effect of producing widespread unrest among the poor and the ignorant, especially those of foreign birth."

When the war ended Americans also confronted the disturbing possibility, pointed up in 1919 by the struggle over the League of Nations, that Europe's struggles would continue to be their own. These factors combined to make the First World War a traumatic experience for millions of citizens. As Senator James Reed of Missouri observed in August 1919, "This country is still suffering from shell shock. Hardly anyone is in a normal state of mind . . . A great storm has swept over the intellectual world and its ravages and disturbances still exist."

The wartime "shell shock" left many Americans extraordinarily susceptible to psychological stress caused by postwar social and economic turbulence. Most important for the course of the Red Scare, many of these disturbances had their greatest effect on individuals already antagonistic toward minorities. First of all, there was some real evidence of danger to the nation in 1919, and the nation provided the chief emotional support for many Americans who responded easily to charges of an alien radical menace. Violence flared throughout Europe after the war and revolt lifted radicals to power in several Eastern and Central European nations. Combined with the earlier Bolshevik triumph in Russia these revolutions made Americans look more anxiously at radicals here. Domestic radicals encouraged these fears; they became unduly optimistic about their own chances of success and boasted openly of their coming triumph. Scores of new foreign language anarchist and communist journals, most of them written by and for Southern and Eastern European immigrants, commenced publication, and the established radical press became more exuberant. These periodicals never tired of assuring readers in 1919 that "the United States seems to be on the verge of a revolutionary crisis." American newspapers and magazines reprinted selections from radical speeches, pamphlets, and periodicals so their readers could see what dangerous ideas were abroad in the land. Several mysterious bomb explosions and bombing attempts, reported in bold front page headlines in newspapers across the country, frightened the public in 1919. To many citizens these seemed part of an organized campaign of terror carried on by alien radicals intending to bring down the federal government. The great strikes of 1919 and early 1920 aroused similar fears.

Actually American radical organizations in 1919 were disorganized and poverty-stricken. The Communists were inept, almost without contact with American workers and not yet dominated or subsidized by Moscow. The IWW was shorn of its effective leaders, distrusted by labor, and generally declining in influence and power. Violent anarchists were isolated in a handful of tiny, unconnected local organizations. One or two of these anarchist groups probably carried out the "bomb conspiracy" of 1919; but the extent of the "conspiracy" can be judged from the fact that the bombs killed a total of two men during the year, a night watchman and one of the bomb throwers, and seriously wounded one person, a maid in the home of a Georgia senator.

Nevertheless, prophesies of national disaster abounded in 1919, even among high government officials. Secretary of State Robert Lansing confided to his diary that we were in real peril of social revolution. Attorney General A. Mitchell Palmer advised the House Appropriations Committee that "on a certain day, which we have been advised of," radicals would attempt "to rise up and destroy the Government at one fell swoop." Senator Charles Thomas of Colorado warned that "the country is on the verge of a volcanic upheaval." And Senator Miles Poindexter of Washington declared, "There is real danger that the government will fall." A West Virginia wholesaler, with offices throughout the state, informed the Justice Department in October 1919 that "there is hardly a respectable citizen of my acquaintance who does not believe that we are on the verge of armed conflict in this country." William G. McAdoo was told by a trusted friend that "Chicago, which has always been a very liberal minded place, seems to me to have gone mad on the question of the 'Reds.' " Delegates to the Farmers National Congress in November 1919 pledged that farmers would assist the government in meeting the threat of revolution.

The slight evidence of danger from radical organizations aroused such wild fear only because Americans had already encountered other threats to cultural stability. However, the dislocations caused by the war and the menace of communism alone would not have produced such a vehement nativistic response. Other postwar challenges to the social and economic order made the crucial difference.

Of considerable importance was the skyrocketing cost of living. Retail prices more than doubled between 1915 and 1920, and the price rise began gathering momentum in the spring of 1919. During the summer of 1919 the dominant political issue in America was not the League of Nations; not even the "red menace" or the threat of a series of major strikes disturbed the public as much as did the climbing cost of living. The *Washington Post* early in August 1919 called rising prices, "the burning domestic issue. . . ." Democratic National Chairman Homer Cummings, after a trip around the country, told President Woodrow Wilson that more Americans were worried about prices than about any other public issue and that they demanded government action. When Wilson decided to address Congress on the question the Philadelphia *Public Ledger* observed that the administration had "come rather tardily to a realization of what is uppermost in the minds of the American people."

Then the wave of postwar strikes—there were 3,600 of them in 1919 involving over 4,000,000 workers—reached a climax in the fall of 1919. A national steel strike began in September and nationwide coal and rail walkouts were scheduled for November 1. Unions gained in membership and power during the war, and in 1919 labor leaders were under strong pressure to help workers catch up to or go ahead of mounting living costs. Nevertheless, influential government officials attributed the walkouts to radical activities. Early in 1919, Secretary of Labor William B. Wilson declared in a public speech that recent major strikes in Seattle, Butte, Montana, and Lawrence, Massachusetts, had been instituted by the Bolsheviks and the IWW for the sole purpose of bringing about a nationwide revolution in the United States. During the steel strike of early fall, 1919, a Senate investigating committee reported that "behind this strike there is massed a considerable element of I.W.W.'s, anarchists, revolutionists, and Russian soviets. . . ." In April 1920 the head of the Justice Department's General Intelligence Division, J. Edgar Hoover, declared in a public hearing that at least fifty per cent of the influence behind the recent series of strikes was traceable directly to communist agents.

Furthermore, the nation suffered a sharp economic depression in late 1918 and early 1919, caused largely by sudden cancellations of war orders. Returning servicemen found it difficult to obtain jobs during this period, which coincided with the beginning of the Red Scare. The former soldiers had been uprooted from their homes and told that they were engaged in a patriotic crusade. Now they came back to find "reds" criticizing their country and threatening the government with violence, Negroes holding good jobs in the big cities, prices terribly high, and workers who had not served in the armed forces striking for higher wages. A delegate won prolonged applause from the 1919 American Legion Convention when he denounced radical aliens, exclaiming, "Now that the war is over and they are in lucrative positions while our boys haven't a job, we've got to send those scamps to hell." The major part of the mobs which invaded meeting halls of immigrant organizations and broke up radical parades, especially during the first half of 1919, was comprised of men in uniform.

A variety of other circumstances combined to add even more force to the postwar nativistic movement. Long before the new immigrants were seen as potential revolutionists they became the objects of widespread hostility. The peak of immigration from Southern and Eastern Europe occurred in the fifteen years before the war; during that period almost ten million immigrants from those areas entered the country. Before the anxious eyes of members of all classes of Americans, the newcomers crowded the cities and began to disturb the economic and social order. Even without other postwar disturbances a nativistic movement of some strength could have been predicted when the wartime solidarity against the German enemy began to wear off in 1919.

In addition, not only were the European revolutions most successful in Eastern and to a lesser extent in Southern Europe, but aliens from these areas predominated in American radical organizations. At least ninety per cent of the members of the two American Communist parties formed in 1919 were born in Eastern Europe. The anarchist groups whose literature and bombs captured the imagination of the American public in 1919 were composed almost entirely of Italian, Spanish, and Slavic aliens. Justice Department announcements and statements by politicians and the press stressed the predominance of recent immigrants in radical organizations. Smoldering prejudice against new immigrants and identification of these immigrants with European as well as American radical movements, combined with other sources of postwar stress to create one of the most frenzied and one of the most widespread nativistic movements in the nation's history.

The result . . . was called Americanism or one hundred per cent Americanism. Its objective was to end the apparent erosion of American values and the disintegration of American culture. By reaffirming those beliefs, customs, symbols, and traditions felt to be the foundation of our way of life, by enforcing conformity among the population, and by purging the nation of dangerous foreigners, the one hundred per centers expected to heal societal divisions and to tighten defenses against cultural change.

Panegyrics celebrating our history and institutions were delivered regularly in almost every American school, church, and public hall in 1919 and 1920. Many of these fervent addresses went far beyond the usual patriotic declarations. Audiences were usually urged to join a crusade to protect our hallowed institutions. Typical of the more moderate statements was Columbia University President Nicholas Murray Butler's insistence in April 1919 that "America will be saved, not by those who have only contempt and spite for her founders and her history, but by those who look with respect and reverence upon the great series of happenings extending from the voyage of the Mayflower. . . ."

What one historian has called "a riot of biographies of American heroes—statesmen, cowboys, and pioneers" appeared in this brief period. Immigrants as well as citizens produced many autobiographical testimonials to the superiority of American institutions. These patriotic tendencies in our literature were as short-lived as the Red Scare, and have been concealed by "debunking" biographies of folk heroes and skeptical autobiographies so common later in the nineteen-twenties. An unusual number of motion pictures about our early history were turned out immediately after the war and the reconstruction of colonial Williamsburg and of Longfellow's Wayside Inn was begun. With great fanfare, Secretary of State Lansing placed the original documents of the Constitution and the Declaration of Independence on display in January 1920, and the State Department distributed movies of this ceremony to almost every town and city in the United States. Organizations like the National Security League, the Association for Constitutional Government, the Sons and Daughters of the American Revolution, the Colonial Dames of America, with the cooperation of the American Bar Association and many state Bar Associations, organized Constitution Day celebrations and distributed huge numbers of pamphlets on the subject throughout the country.

The American flag became a sacred symbol. Legionaires demanded that citizens "Run the Reds out from the land whose flag they sully." Men suspected of radical leanings were forced to kiss the stars and stripes. A Brooklyn truck driver decided in June 1919 that it was unpatriotic to obey a New York City law obliging him to fly a red cloth on lumber which projected from his vehicle. Instead he used as a danger signal a small American flag. A policeman, infuriated at the sight of the stars and stripes flying from a lumber pile, arrested the driver on a charge of disorderly conduct. Despite the Brooklyn patriot's insistence that he meant no offense to the flag, he was reprimanded and fined by the court.

Recent immigrants, especially, were called upon to show evidence of real conversion. Great pressure was brought to bear upon the foreign-born to learn English and to forget their native tongues. As Senator William S. Kenyon of Iowa declared in October 1919, "The time has come to make this a one-language nation." An editorial in the *American Legion Weekly* took a further step and insisted that the one language must be called "American. Why even in Mexico they do not stand for calling the language the Spanish language."

Immigrants were also expected to adopt our customs and to snuff out remnants of Old World cultures. Genteel prewar and wartime movements to speed up assimilation took on a "frightened and feverish aspect." Welcoming members of an Americanization conference called by his department, Secretary of the Interior Franklin K. Lane exclaimed in May 1919, "You have been gathered together as crusaders in a great cause. . . . There is no other question of such importance before the American people as the solidifying and strengthening of true American sentiment." A Harvard University official told the conference that "The Americanization movement . . . gives men a new and holy religion. . . . It challenges each one of us to a renewed consecration and devotion to the welfare of the nation." The National Security League boasted, in 1919, of establishing one thousand study groups to teach teachers how to inculcate "Americanism" in their foreign-born students. A critic of the prevailing mood protested against "one of our best advertised American mottoes, 'One country, one language, one flag,'" which, he complained, had become the basis for a fervent nationwide program.

As the postwar movement for one hundred per cent Americanism gathered momentum, the deportation of alien nonconformists became increasingly its most compelling objective. Asked to suggest a remedy for the nationwide upsurge in radical activity, the Mayor of Gary, Indiana, replied, "Deportation is the answer, deportation of these leaders who talk treason in America and deportation of those who agree with them and work with them." "We must remake America," a popular author averred. "We must purify the source of America's population and keep it pure. . . . We must insist that there shall be an American loyalty, brooking no amendment or qualification." As Higham noted, "In 1919, the clamor of 100 per centers for applying deportation as a purgative arose to an hysterical howl. . . . Through repression and deportation on the one hand and speedy total assimilation on the other, 100 per centers hoped to eradicate discontent and purify the nation."

Politicians quickly sensed the possibilities of the popular frenzy for Americanism. Mayor Ole Hanson of Seattle, Governor Calvin Coolidge of Massachusetts, and General Leonard Wood became the early heroes of the movement. The man in the best political position to take advantage of the popular feeling, however, was Attorney General A. Mitchell Palmer. In 1919, especially after the President's physical collapse, only Palmer had the authority, staff, and money necessary to arrest and deport huge numbers of radical aliens. The most virulent phase of the movement for one hundred per cent Americanism came early in 1920, when Palmer's agents rounded up for deportation over six thousand aliens and prepared to arrest thousands more suspected of membership in radical organizations. Most of these aliens were taken without warrants, many were detained for unjustifiably long periods of time, and some suffered incredible hardships. Almost all, however, were eventually released.

After Palmer decided that he could ride the postwar fears into the presidency, he set out calculatingly to become the symbol of one hundred per cent Americanism. The Palmer raids, his anti-labor activities, and his frequent pious professions of patriotism during the campaign were all part of this effort. Palmer was introduced by a political associate to the Democratic party's annual Jackson Day dinner in January 1920 as "an American whose Americanism cannot be misunderstood." In a speech delivered in Georgia shortly before the primary election (in which Palmer won control of the state's delegation to the Democratic National Convention), the Attorney General asserted: "I am myself an American and I love to preach my doctrine before undiluted one hundred per cent Americans, because my platform is, in a word, undiluted Americanism and undying loyalty to the republic." The same theme dominated the address made by Palmer's old friend, John H. Bigelow of Hazleton, Pennsylvania, when he placed Palmer's name in nomination at the 1920 National Convention. Proclaimed Bigelow: "No party could survive today that did not write into its platform the magic word 'Americanism.'. . . The Attorney-General of the United States has not merely professed, but he has proved his true Americanism . . . Behind him I see a solid phalanx of true Americanism that knows no divided allegiance."

Unfortunately for political candidates like Palmer and Wood, most of the social and economic disturbances which had activated the movement they sought to lead gradually disappeared during the first half of 1920. The European revolutions were put down; by 1920 communism seemed to have been isolated in Russia. Bombings ceased abruptly after June 1919, and fear of new outrages gradually abated. Prices of food and clothing began to recede during the spring. Labor strife almost vanished from our major industries after a brief railroad walkout in April. Prosperity returned after mid-1919 and by early 1920 business activity and employment levels exceeded their wartime peaks. At the same time, it became clear that the Senate would not pass Wilson's peace treaty and that America was free to turn its back on the responsibilities of world leadership. The problems associated with the new immigrants remained; so did the disillusionment with Europe and with many old intellectual ideals. Nativism did not disappear from the American scene; but the frenzied attempt to revitalize the culture did peter out in 1920. The handful of unintimidated men, especially Assistant Secretary of Labor Louis F. Post, who had used the safeguards provided by American law to protect many victims of the Red Scare, found increasing public support. On the other hand, politicians like Palmer, Wood, and Hanson were left high and dry, proclaiming the need for one hundred per cent Americanism to an audience which no longer urgently cared.

It is ironic that in 1920 the Russian leaders of the Comintern finally took charge of the American Communist movement, provided funds and leadership, and ordered the Communist factions to unite and participate actively in labor organizations and strikes. These facts were reported in the American press. Thus a potentially serious foreign threat to national security appeared just as the Red Scare evaporated, providing a final illustration of the fact that the frenzied one hundred per centers of 1919–1920 were affected less by the "red menace" than by a series of social and economic dislocations.

Although the Red Scare died out in 1920, its effects lingered. Hostility toward immigrants, mobilized in 1919–1920, remained strong enough to force congressional passage of restrictive immigration laws. Some of the die-hard one hundred per centers found a temporary home in the Ku Klux Klan until that organization withered away during the mid-twenties. As its most lasting accomplishments, the movement for one hundred per cent Americanism fostered a spirit of conformity in the country, a satisfaction with the *status quo,* and the equation of reform ideologies with foreign enemies. Revitalization movements have helped many societies adapt successfully to new conditions. The movement associated with the American Red Scare, however, had no such effect. True, it unified the culture against the threats faced in 1919–1920; but the basic problems—a damaged value system, an unrestrained business cycle, a hostile Russia, and communism—were left for future generations of Americans to deal with in their own fashion.

Sources

Vigilante Patriot

The following newspaper account was the basis for the first three sentences of Stanley Coben's essay on the Red Scare. While Coben's use of it is surely reasonable, there is more to this curious piece than his summary reveals. Why was George Goddard shot? What was the attitude of the reporter who wrote the story? What tensions came together in 1919 to produce the event described?

Disrespect for the American flag and a show of resentment toward the thousands who participated in a victory loan pageant here [Chicago] tonight may cost George Goddard his life. He was shot down by a sailor of the United States navy when he did not stand and remove his hat while the band was playing the "Star-Spangled Banner."

Goddard had a seat of vantage in the open amphitheater. When he failed to stand he was the most conspicuous figure among the throng. When he fell at the report of the "sailor's" gun the crowd burst into cheers and handclapping. When Goddard failed to respond to the first strains of the national anthem Samuel Hagerman, sailor in the guard of honor, asked him to get up.

"What for?" demanded Goddard.

Hagerman touched him with his bayonet.

"Get up. Off with your hat."

Goddard muttered, and drew a pistol.

With military precision Hagerman stepped back a pace and slipped a shell into his gun.

Goddard started away. As the last notes of the anthem sounded the sailor commanded him to halt. Then he fired into the air.

"Halt!"

Goddard paid no attention.

The sailor aimed and fired three times. Goddard fell wounded. Each shot found its mark.

When he was searched, an automatic pistol, in addition to the one he had drawn, was found. Another pistol and fifty cartridges were found in a bag he carried. He said he was a tinsmith, out of work. Papers showed he had been at Vancouver and Seattle and it was believed by the authorities he had come here for the I.W.W.* convention.

*Industrial Workers of the World. See the introduction to this chapter.—*Ed.*
"Chicagoans Cheer Tar Who Shot Man," *Washington Post*, May 7, 1919, p. 2.

Ernest Hemingway

"Soldier's Home"

"Soldier's Home" was among Ernest Hemingway's favorite short stories. First published in 1925, it describes one young man's attempt to put the war, his family, his community, and his own growing up into one coherent framework. The issue was a real one for Hemingway, who at eighteen had left his job as a reporter for the *Kansas City Star* and volunteered for ambulance duty in Europe with the American Red Cross.

The central figure in the story is Harold Krebs, who returns home from a war that has affected him profoundly and personally. He soon discovers, however, that no one wants to hear what he has to say about the war; the prevailing orthodoxy has no room for a perception of army life and Germany very different from that of the Creel Committee.

What is Krebs's reaction to the war? Why does he have such difficulty describing his feelings about the conflict to others? What are the historical roots of that difficulty? In addition, read the story as a document in family history. What has happened to the family described here that renders it incapable of serving as an "island" for Krebs? Throughout, pay special attention to Hemingway's style. Does the style mesh easily with the assembly line, the speak-easy, the flapper, and other characteristic images of the 1920s?

Krebs went to the war from a Methodist college in Kansas. There is a picture which shows him among his fraternity brothers, all of them wearing exactly the same height and style collar. He enlisted in the Marines in 1917 and did not return to the United States until the second division returned from the Rhine in the summer of 1919.

There is a picture which shows him on the Rhine with two German girls and another corporal. Krebs and the corporal look too big for their uniforms. The German girls are not beautiful. The Rhine does not show in the picture.

By the time Krebs returned to his home town in Oklahoma the greeting of heroes was over. He came back much too late. The men from the town who had been drafted had all been welcomed elaborately on their return. There had been a great deal of hysteria. Now the reaction had set in. People seemed to think it was rather ridiculous for Krebs to be getting back so late, years after the war was over.

At first Krebs, who had been at Belleau Wood, Soissons, the Champagne, St. Mihiel and in the Argonne did not want to talk about the war at all. Later he felt the need to talk but no one wanted to hear about it. His town had heard too many atrocity stories to be thrilled by actualities. Krebs found that to be listened to at all he had to lie, and after he had done this twice he, too, had a reaction against the war and against talking about it. A distaste for everything that had happened to him in the war set in because of the lies he had told. All of the times that had been able to make him feel cool and clear inside himself when he thought of them; the times so long back when he had done the one thing, the only thing for a man to do, easily and naturally, when he might have done something else, now lost their cool, valuable quality and then were lost themselves.

His lies were quite unimportant lies and consisted in attributing to himself things other men had seen, done or heard of, and stating as facts certain apocryphal incidents familiar to all soldiers. Even his lies were not sensational at the pool room. His acquaintances, who had heard detailed accounts of German women found chained to machine guns in the Argonne forest and who could not comprehend, or were barred by their patriotism from interest in, any German machine gunners who were not chained, were not thrilled by his stories.

Krebs acquired the nausea in regard to experience that is the result of untruth or exaggeration, and when he occasionally met another man who had really been a soldier and they talked a few minutes in the dressing room at a dance he fell into the easy pose of the old soldier among other soldiers: that he had been badly, sickeningly frightened all the time. In this way he lost everything.

During this time, it was late summer, he was sleeping late in bed, getting up to walk down town to the library to get a book, eating lunch at home, reading on the front porch until he became bored and then walking down through the town to spend the hottest hours of the day in the cool dark of the pool room. He loved to play pool.

In the evening he practised on his clarinet, strolled down town, read and went to bed. He was still a hero to his two young sisters. His mother would have given him breakfast in bed if he had wanted it. She often came in when he was in bed and asked him to tell her about the war, but her attention always wandered. His father was noncommittal.

Before Krebs went away to the war he had never been allowed to drive the family motor car. His father was in the real estate business and always wanted the car to be at his command when he required it to take clients out into the country to show them a piece of farm property. The car always stood outside the First National Bank building where his father had an office on the second floor. Now, after the war, it was still the same car.

Nothing was changed in the town except that the young girls had grown up. But they lived in such a complicated world of already defined alliances and shifting feuds that Krebs did not feel the energy or the courage to break into it. He liked to look at them, though. There were so many good-looking young girls. Most of them had their hair cut short. When he went away only little girls wore their hair like that or girls that were fast. They all wore sweaters and shirt waists with round Dutch collars. It was a pattern. He liked to look at them from the front porch as they walked on the other side of the street. He liked to watch them walking under the shade of the trees. He liked the round Dutch collars above their sweaters. He liked their silk stockings and flat shoes. He liked their bobbed hair and the way they walked.

When he was in town their appeal to him was not very strong. He did not like them when he saw them in the Greek's ice cream parlor. He did not want them themselves really. They were too complicated. There was something else. Vaguely he wanted a girl but he did not want to have to work to get her. He would have liked to have a girl but he did not want to have to spend a long time getting her. He did not want to get into the intrigue and the politics. He did not want to have to do any courting. He did not want to tell any more lies. It wasn't worth it.

He did not want any consequences. He did not want any consequences ever again. He wanted to live along without consequences. Besides he did not really need a girl. The army had taught him that. It was all right to pose as though you had to have a girl. Nearly everybody did that. But it wasn't true. You did not need a girl. That was the funny thing. First a fellow boasted how girls mean nothing to him, that he never thought of them, that they could not touch him. Then a fellow boasted that he could not get along without girls, that he had to have them all the time, that he could not go to sleep without them.

That was all a lie. It was all a lie both ways. You did not need a girl unless you thought about them. He learned that in the army. Then sooner or later you always got one. When you were really ripe for a girl you always got one. You did not have to think about it. Sooner or later it would come. He had learned that in the army.

Now he would have liked a girl if she had come to him and not wanted to talk. But here at home it was all too complicated. He knew he could never get through it all again. It was not worth the trouble. That was the thing about French girls and Germans girls. There was not all this talking. You couldn't talk much and you did not need to talk. It was simple and you were friends. He thought about France and then began to think about Germany. On the whole he had liked Germany better. He did not want to leave Germany. He did not want to come home. Still, he had come home. He sat on the front porch.

He liked the girls that were walking along the other side of the street. He liked the look of them much better than the French girls or the German girls. But the world they were in was not the world he was in. He would like to have one of them. But it was not worth it. They were such a nice pattern. He liked the pattern. It was exciting. But he would not go through all the talking. He did not want one badly enough. He liked to look at them all, though. It was not worth it. Not now when things were getting good again.

He sat there on the porch reading a book on the war. It was a history and he was reading about all the engagements he had been in. It was the most interesting reading he had ever done. He wished there were more maps. He looked forward with a good feeling to reading all the really good histories when they would come out with good detail maps. Now he was really learning about the war. He had been a good soldier. That made a difference.

One morning after he had been home about a month his mother came into his bedroom and sat on the bed. She smoothed her apron.

"I had a talk with your father last night, Harold," she said, "and he is willing for you to take the car out in the evenings."

"Yeah?" said Krebs, who was not fully awake. "Take the car out? Yeah?"

"Yes. Your father has felt for some time that you should be able to take the car out in the evenings whenever you wished but we only talked it over last night."

"I'll bet you made him," Krebs said.

"No. It was your father's suggestion that we talk the matter over."

"Yeah. I'll bet you made him." Krebs sat up in bed.

"Will you come down to breakfast, Harold?" his mother said.

"As soon as I get my clothes on," Krebs said.

His mother went out of the room and he could hear her frying something downstairs while he washed, shaved and dressed to go down into the dining-room for breakfast. While he was eating breakfast his sister brought in the mail.

"Well, Hare," she said. "You old sleepy-head. What do you ever get up for?"

Krebs looked at her. He liked her. She was his best sister.

"Have you got the paper?" he asked.

She handed him *The Kansas City Star* and he shucked off its brown wrapper and opened it to the sporting page. He folded *The Star* open and propped it against the water pitcher with his cereal dish to steady it, so he could read while he ate.

"Harold," his mother stood in the kitchen doorway, "Harold, please don't muss up the paper. Your father can't read his *Star* if it's been mussed."

"I won't muss it," Krebs said.

His sister sat down at the table and watched him while he read.

"We're playing indoor over at school this afternoon," she said. "I'm going to pitch."

"Good," said Krebs. "How's the old wing?"

"I can pitch better than lots of the boys. I tell them all you taught me. The other girls aren't much good."

"Yeah?" said Krebs.

"I tell them all you're my beau. Aren't you my beau, Hare?"

"You bet."

"Couldn't your brother really be your beau just because he's your brother?"

"I don't know."

"Sure you know. Couldn't you be my beau. Hare, if I was old enough and if you wanted to?"

"Sure. You're my girl now."

"Am I really your girl?"

"Sure."

"Do you love me?"

"Uh, huh."

"Will you love me always?"

"Sure."

"Will you come over and watch me play indoor?"

"Maybe."

"Aw, Hare, you don't love me. If you loved me, you'd want to come over and watch me play indoor."

Krebs's mother came into the dining-room from the kitchen. She carried a plate with two fried eggs and some crisp bacon on it and a plate of buckwheat cakes.

"You run along, Helen," she said. "I want to talk to Harold."

She put the eggs and bacon down in front of him and brought in a jug of maple syrup for the buckwheat cakes. Then she sat down across the table from Krebs.

"I wish you'd put down the paper a minute, Harold," she said.

Krebs took down the paper and folded it.

"Have you decided what you are going to do yet, Harold?" his mother said, taking off her glasses.

"No," said Krebs.

"Don't you think it's about time?" His mother did not say this in a mean way. She seemed worried.

"I hadn't thought about it," Krebs said.

"God has some work for every one to do," his mother said. "There can be no idle hands in His Kingdom."

"I'm not in His Kingdom," Krebs said.

"We are all of us in His Kingdom."

Krebs felt embarrassed and resentful as always.

"I've worried about you so much, Harold," his mother went on. "I know the temptations you must have been exposed to. I know how weak men are. I know what your own dear grandfather, my own father, told us about the Civil War and I have prayed for you. I pray for you all day long, Harold."

Krebs looked at the bacon fat hardening on his plate.

"Your father is worried, too," his mother went on. "He thinks you have lost your ambition, that you haven't got a definite aim in life. Charley Simmons, who is just your age, has a good job and is going to be married. The boys are all settling down; they're all determined to get somewhere;

you can see that boys like Charley Simmons are on their way to being really a credit to the community."

Krebs said nothing.

"Don't look that way, Harold," his mother said. "You know we love you and I want to tell you for your own good how matters stand. Your father does not want to hamper your freedom. He thinks you should be allowed to drive the car. If you want to take some of the nice girls out riding with you, we are only too pleased. We want you to enjoy yourself. But you are going to have to settle down to work, Harold. Your father doesn't care what you start in at. All work is honorable as he says. But you've got to make a start at something. He asked me to speak to you this morning and then you can stop in and see him at his office."

"Is that all?" Krebs said.

"Yes. Don't you love your mother, dear boy?"

"No," Krebs said.

His mother looked at him across the table. Her eyes were shiny. She started crying.

"I don't love anybody," Krebs said.

It wasn't any good. He couldn't tell her, he couldn't make her see it. It was silly to have said it. He had only hurt her. He went over and took hold of her arm. She was crying with her head in her hands.

"I didn't mean it," he said. "I was just angry at something. I didn't mean I didn't love you."

His mother went on crying. Krebs put his arm on her shoulder.

"Can't you believe me, mother?"

His mother shook her head.

"Please, please, mother. Please believe me."

"All right," his mother said chokily. She looked up at him. "I believe you, Harold."

Krebs kissed her hair. She put her face up to him.

"I'm your mother," she said. "I held you next to my heart when you were a tiny baby."

Krebs felt sick and vaguely nauseated.

"I know, Mummy," he said. "I'll try and be a good boy for you."

"Would you kneel and pray with me, Harold?" his mother asked.

They knelt down beside the dining-room table and Krebs's mother prayed.

"Now, you pray, Harold," she said.

"I can't," Krebs said.

"Try, Harold."

"I can't."

"Do you want me to pray for you?"

"Yes."

So his mother prayed for him and then stood up and Krebs kissed his mother and went out of the house. He had tried so to keep his life from being complicated. Still, none of it had touched him. He had felt sorry for his mother and she had made him lie. He would go to Kansas City and get a job and she would feel all right about it. There would be one more scene maybe before he got away. He would not go down to his father's office. He would miss that one. He wanted his life to go smoothly. It had just gotten going that way. Well, that was all over now, anyway. He would go over to the schoolyard and watch Helen play indoor baseball.

Edward L. Bernays

"Reach for a Lucky . . ."

"The business of America," remarked President Calvin Coolidge in 1925, "is business." Coolidge was right. Relieved of the burden of the Great War and victorious over the forces of alien radicalism, Americans gave themselves up to the world of business with an abandon not matched until the 1980s. Advertising executive Bruce Barton captured the tone of the age in *The Man Nobody Knows,* a 1925 best seller that described Jesus Christ as a top-notch salesman.

Barton's depiction of Jesus as a salesman (rather than as a crafts-man or producer) marks the book as a typical product of a new gen-eration of businessmen obsessed with marketing goods. A nine-teenth-century businessman assumed that goods would find a buyer. His twentieth-century counterpart, well aware that increases in pro-ductivity might make it difficult to sell all that was produced, as-sumed no such thing. As a result, advertising, marketing, and public relations—all methods of stimulating consumption—flowered in the 1920s.

Edward L. Bernays, the author of the following account, was among those who cut their public-relations teeth in the Creel Com-mittee's wartime propaganda campaigns. In this selection, from his autobiography, Bernays describes his efforts on behalf of George Washington Hill's American Tobacco Company.

If these efforts are an example of public relations, how might we define that profession? What kinds of tools did public relations utilize in the 1920s? On what assumptions—about human nature and behav-ior—was public relations based? Were Bernays's activities socially re-sponsible?

From Edward L. Bernays, *Biography of an Idea: Memoirs of Public Relations Counsel Edward L. Bernays* (New York: Simon & Schuster, 1965), pp. 372–373, 377, 383–387. Reprinted by permis-sion of Harold Ober Associates Incorporated. Copyright © 1965 by Doris F. and Edward L. Bernays.

My assignment as counsel on public relations to the American Tobacco Company, a blue-chip corporation that made cigarettes and cigars, followed close on the heels of our relationship with Procter & Gamble.

The doughboys in World War I had popularized cigarettes. Up to that time manufactured cigarettes, called tailor-mades, had been thought *déclassé*. My father would not permit cigarette smoking at home. In some quarters, smoking cigarettes was considered a mark of effeminacy. But when the boys returned from France, where they had rolled their own, they took up ready-made packaged varieties. Three cigarette companies—Liggett & Myers, R. J. Reynolds and American Tobacco—had the major share of the cigarette market. For many years American had spread its advertising allotment over 50 different tobacco products, making no large dent on the public with any one of them. Lucky Strike had been a late entry in the cigarette sweepstakes; its name had formerly belonged to a chewing tobacco. Albert Lasker, who headed the Lord & Thomas advertising agency of Chicago, persuaded Percival Hill, then president of the company, to throw his entire advertising appropriation into promoting Lucky Strike cigarettes. Within three years sales zoomed from 25 million to 150 million cigarettes a day, and Lucky Strike gained first place among cigarettes, a position it held for two decades.

I worked with American after George Washington Hill had taken over the presidency from his father. . . .

Hill's main interest in life—indeed, his only one—was to see that Luckies retained first place in the race with Chesterfields and Camels. I did not know of any activities he took part in outside of his business—no charities, horse racing, paintings or yachts. If he had a point of view on topics other than Luckies and his business, I never heard it expressed. He gave no public speeches or press interviews. He was a rugged individualist, a residual phenomenon left over from the late nineteenth century.

He spent his waking hours thinking of ideas that might induce more people to buy Luckies. He left the production of cigarettes to subordinates. His field was selling. He seized recklessly, fearlessly any idea he thought would sell Luckies. Some of his selling ideas had far-reaching social effects. In the first year of our direct relationship, 1928–1929, Hill became obsessed by the prospect of winning over the large potential female market for Luckies. "If I can crack that market, I'll get more than my share of it," he said to me one day. "It will be like opening a new gold mine right in our front yard." He had an idea that might do it, he said. He had coined the slogan "Reach for a Lucky instead of a sweet" to meet the problem.

The thesis that excess weight affected health adversely was beginning to impress the public. Hill's campaign brought instantaneous response from women on two grounds: health and fashion, both of which stressed slenderness. An earlier campaign based on people's interest in their health, the "no throat irritation" theme, had advanced Luckies' fortunes. But this new concept was even more telling. Hill made the claim that cigarettes dulled appetites and thereby enhanced health by reducing weight.

My activities now focused on the slogan "Reach for a Lucky instead of a sweet." In November my good friend Nickolas Muray, then a crack young commercial photographer, at my suggestion sent a letter to influential photographers and commercial artists praising slender women who lit cigarettes instead of eating sweets and asking their support for the ideal of slimness. Muray was eager for publicity and recognized that the publicity would help him. When his story was sent to the newspapers, photographers and artists took their cue from Muray, and the public soon became more and more oriented toward slenderness. We also publicized the slim fashions, which Paris then emphasized, flooding fashion editors with photographs of thin Parisian models in *haute couture* dresses.

The sugar interests protested vociferously, counterattacking with statements that Hill's advertising was unjustified and not cricket. But Hill kept up the battle, reveling in the controversy he had started and convinced it would recruit new Lucky smokers from among the stout.

I urged Hill to have a scientific study made of medical literature showing the effects of the excessive use of sugar on the human body. "I'll engage a physician," I said, "to make a research of the literature supporting our contention and we'll publish it." Hill agreed. The published findings strengthened our hand.

I knew the sugar industry was trying to align science on their side. Bruce Bliven said years ago, "The cure for propaganda is more propaganda." The competition of ideas in the American market place is an essential democratic process, for then the public can make its own choice. Even when ideas conflict and confuse, public debate clarifies the issues and makes for a sounder choice, in the long run.

When battles were shaping up or got hot, Hill would call me in. I assume he also called in Ivy Lee and Albert Lasker, but we were never brought face to face in a joint conference to work out strategy and tactics. Hill didn't function that way. He got Machiavellian pleasure in seeing our individual points of view without confrontation.

"What'll we do to get these s.o.b.'s?" he would ask. "How'll we meet this g.d. situation?"

In one conflict, when he was under criticism by commentators in the journals of opinion and advertising trade press who said his advertising was in the worst taste, Hill hired outstanding artists to illustrate the Lucky Strike advertisements. We collected comments by distinguished artists on the importance of using good artists to stimulate taste in advertising. These comments, sent out as news releases, were picked up in newspapers and the trade press.

Hill had a flair for recognizing what was just below the surface of the public mind. He relied principally on intuition, and his intuition was generally right. The disadvantage of this method of procedure, however, is that, although you may often be right, you miss opportunities that reason might uncover. Hill believed, for instance, that only mass circulation publications were suitable advertising media for American, that publications with small and influential circulation, such as *The Nation, New Republic, Harper's, Atlantic Monthly,* etc., were unimportant to his products. Nevertheless, I have worked with few men of action so receptive to unproved ideas and so imaginative in carrying out new concepts. Skywriting was still an unproved advertising medium when someone brought it to Hill's attention. Soon he had thousands of city dwellers throughout the country gaping at spirals of smoke in the sky spelling out to their delighted astonishment, "Smoke Lucky Strikes." He intuitively recognized that the public would get an intensified desire for smoking Luckies from the smoke in the sky.

In December 1928 Hill asked me to devise a plan to strengthen public support for a new advertising campaign stressing moderation, a modification of the "reach for a Lucky" theme. After the excesses of the first eight years of the 1920s, America was receptive to the idea of restraint. Commentators on the contemporary scene in serious newspapers and magazines were pointing out the dangers and impossibilities of a manic state carrying on indefinitely. I proposed the organization of a Moderation League, to be formed and launched, coincidentally, with the advertising. We planned to enlist the co-operation of many organizations—the Automobile Association to urge moderation in driving, the air transport groups to call for moderation in stunt flying, the antiprofanity leagues to work toward moderation in speech, the architects' societies to urge moderation in the size of buildings to relieve traffic congestion, and art dealers' associations to promote moderation in the prices of Old Masters.

I felt, even before the 1929 crash that sobered up America, that as a nation we needed to practice moderation. I am sure Hill didn't actually care a whit about moderation itself. The fact that it would sell Luckies was his concern.

Hill was not at all receptive to my comprehensive plan for a broad, integrated moderation campaign; he was interested only in the next specific action I proposed. This attitude surprised me then, but I have since discovered that most tycoons tend to regard intermediate and long-range planning as impractical, eccentric and a nuisance. They don't want to be bothered with interpretive thinking and weighing intangibles. They want *ad hoc* action. A proposal for a onetime act takes less effort and time to read, understand, okay and carry out. The commitments and risks are fewer.

When I saw that Hill did not want to proceed by plan, I proposed enlisting Ziegfeld beauties in our moderation campaign. He acquiesced immediately. With the help of Ziegfeld's publicity man, six glamorous and beautiful *Follies* girls appeared at the Ritz-Carlton Hotel and pledged themselves to moderation and organized the Ziegfeld Contour, Curve and Charm Club, which had as its motto "Moderation, sense and not sensation." They would demonstrate moderation by their ideal "modern figure with its tantalizing, sinuous curves." When the *Follies* toured the country moderation became part of the publicity theme.

We followed up the Ziegfeld tie-in by asking newsworthy groups and individuals to speak out for moderation. "Moderation has become the mode in women's fashions," intoned Jacques Worth, our famous French couturier. Soon clippings of news stories and editorial comment on the blessings of restraint were coming in from all over the country. Obviously the newspaper statements on moderation helped develop cumulative interest in the idea. By March the campaign was moving ahead effectively on its own momentum despite its *ad hoc* character. What we did had all the effect of a long-range program, for as soon as one action was gaining momentum we proposed another and carried that out. Hill was happy.

Next, Hill thought the time had arrived for a direct, vigorous campaign to induce women to smoke in public places. In 1929 it was acceptable for women to smoke at home, but a woman seen smoking in public was labeled a hussy or worse.

Hill called me in. "How can we get women to smoke on the street? They're smoking indoors. But, damn it, if they spend half the time outdoors and we can get 'em to smoke outdoors, we'll damn near double our female market. Do something. Act!"

"There's a taboo against such smoking," I said. "Let me consult an expert, Dr. A. A. Brill, the psychoanalyst. He might give me the psychological basis for a woman's desire to smoke, and maybe this will help me."

"What will it cost?"

"I suppose just a consultation fee."

"Shoot," said Hill.

Brill explained to me: "Some women regard cigarettes as symbols of freedom," he told me. "Smoking is a sublimation of oral eroticism; holding a cigarette in the mouth excites the oral zone. It is perfectly normal for women to want to smoke cigarettes. Further, the first woman who smoked probably had an excess of masculine components and adopted the habit as a masculine act. But today the emancipation of women has suppressed many of their feminine desires. More women now do the same work as men do. Many women bear no children; those who do bear have fewer children. Feminine traits are masked. Cigarettes, which are equated with men, become torches of freedom."

In this last statement I found a way to help break the taboo against women smoking in public. Why not a parade of women lighting torches of freedom—smoking cigarettes?

The Easter Sunday Parade on Fifth Avenue seemed a natural occasion on which to launch the idea. One of my friends who worked for *Vogue* gave us a list of thirty debutantes. We sent each the following telegram, signed by my secretary, Bertha Hunt, from our office:

IN THE INTERESTS OF EQUALITY OF THE SEXES AND TO FIGHT ANOTHER SEX TABOO I AND OTHER YOUNG WOMEN WILL LIGHT ANOTHER TORCH OF FREEDOM BY SMOKING CIGARETTES WHILE STROLLING ON FIFTH AVENUE EASTER SUNDAY. WE ARE DOING THIS TO COMBAT THE SILLY PREJUDICE THAT THE CIGARETTE IS SUITABLE FOR THE HOME, THE RESTAURANT, THE TAXICAB, THE THEATER LOBBY BUT NEVER NO NEVER FOR THE SIDEWALK. WOMEN SMOKERS AND THEIR ESCORTS WILL STROLL FROM FORTY-EIGHTH STREET TO FIFTY-FOURTH STREET ON FIFTH AVENUE BETWEEN ELEVEN-THIRTY AND ONE O'CLOCK.

We expressed similar sentiments in an advertisement in the New York newspapers that was signed by Ruth Hale, a leading feminist, who was glad to find a platform for her views, which happened to coincide with American's. Ten young debutantes agreed to march.

Our parade of ten young women lighting "torches of freedom" on Fifth Avenue on Easter Sunday as a protest against woman's inequality caused a national stir. Front-page stories in newspapers reported the freedom march in words and pictures. For weeks after the event editorials praised or condemned the young women who had paraded against the smoking taboo.

The demonstration became almost a national issue. E. H. Gauvreau, editor of the New York *Graphic,* wanted us to reassemble the girls for a special photograph; another, the editor of the Ventura, California, *Star,* in a headline—"SWATS ANOTHER TABOO"—acknowledged that the parade had accomplished its purpose. Women's clubs throughout the country expressed grief that women would smoke in public; papers in Boston, Detroit, Wheeling, West Virginia, and San Francisco reported women smoking on the streets as a result of the New York parade. Age-old customs, I learned, could be broken down by a dramatic appeal, disseminated by the network of media. Of course the taboo was not destroyed completely. But a beginning had been made, one I regret today.

The Lindbergh Phenomenon

Charles Lindbergh's 1927 solo flight across the Atlantic brought an adulation unprecedented in intensity and duration. Not since Andrew Jackson defeated the British at New Orleans in 1814 had a single individual taken on such heroic proportions. In some sense, Lindbergh was a commodity—created by the media, consumed by the public. But it is also safe to say that Americans badly needed a hero in 1927 and that Lindbergh suited them perfectly. What do the following photos tell us about what Americans wanted to be or what they feared they had become? Why, for example, did one sculptor put Lindbergh in a greasy mechanic's suit? One possibility is that Lindbergh and his plane, the *Spirit of St. Louis,* appealed to people because of what their journey said, in a symbolic way, about work, technology, and the new consumer mentality.

Original Caption: "San Diego, Cal., May 24, 1932— On this field at San Diego, California, now known as Lindbergh Field, the citizens of the city have erected this statue in honor of Col. Charles A. Lindbergh. It was at this field that the "Lone Eagle" first started to learn to fly and the statue depicts him in his old, rough, greasy clothes that made him a familiar figure around the field." *National Archives.*

Collection of Statuary Received by Lindbergh, Thomas Jefferson Memorial Building, St. Louis, Missouri, 1930. *National Archives.*

Work and Play

The two photographs that follow show Americans at play. Or are they at work? Why is it difficult to tell which is which? How had attitudes of efficiency and productivity infiltrated the recreational activities of these individuals? In the second photograph, why are no men present?

Original Caption: "Leo Reisman, musical director of the Central Park Casino, discovers that the average couple covers ten miles in an evening's dancing. He is shown here watching William E. Cook and Ethel Rosevere, both of whom are wearing a pedometer on their ankles, which indicates the ground covered." 1929. *National Archives.*

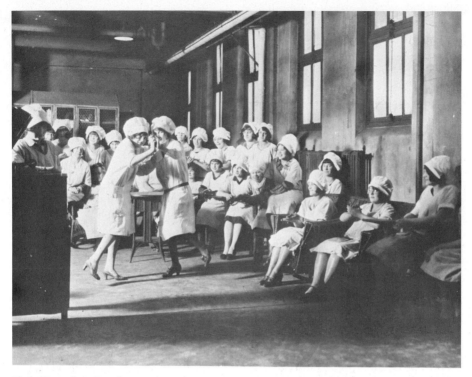

Girls Dancing During Noon Hour at Armour & Company Plant, 1927.
National Archives.

8

The Great
Depression and
the New Deal

The economic decline that followed the stock market crash of October 1929 was unparalleled in the nation's history. Over 4 million people were unemployed in 1930, 8 million in 1931, and almost 13 million, or close to one-quarter of the total civilian labor force, in 1933. Detroit, a city symbolic of the high-flying consumer economy of the 1920s, suffered in proportion to its earlier prosperity. Of the city's 690,000 gainful workers in October 1930, 223,000 were without jobs in March 1931. Because millions of small farmers reacted to falling prices by continuing to produce full crops, agricultural production fell little; farm income, however, was halved in the four years after 1929.

Work for wages was the heart of the economy of the early 1930s, and when it faltered, the effects rippled through every area of American life. In one sixty-day period in Detroit, for example, some 50,000 homeowners lost the equity in their property—the banks foreclosed on their mortgages and took their homes. Black children went to school without food. Throughout that city, people of all races rummaged through garbage cans in the city's alleys, stole dog biscuits from the pound, and even tried to dig homes in the ground.

Herbert Hoover was not a do-nothing president. His attempts to persuade business to maintain wage rates were moderately successful for more than two years. Through the Agricultural Marketing Act, passed four months prior to the crash, the national government sought to maintain agricultural prices. National expenditures on public works increased. The Reconstruction Finance Corporation lent funds to banks, railroads, building and loan associations, and in-

surance companies. It saved a number of institutions from bank-
ruptcy.

Perhaps Hoover's greatest failure was his firm opposition to national expenditures for relief. Private charity and city government,
the primary agencies of relief, soon proved inadequate. Even in
Philadelphia, where philanthropic traditions ran deep, the city's
Community Council described its situation in July 1932 as one of
"slow starvation and progressive deterioration of family life." Detroit, with its highly developed *public* welfare system, in 1931 debated whether to cut its welfare rolls in half or reduce payments by
50 percent—whether to "feed half the people or half-feed the people."

As people gradually became aware just how deep the crisis
went, and as the government under Hoover failed to deal with it, it
became obvious that fundamental change of one kind or another
might be the only solution. One possible direction of change was
dictatorship. The Great Depression was not a domestic crisis only.
European nations were just as severely hit as the United States. And
there, turning to an authoritarian figure—a Hitler in Germany or a
Mussolini in Italy—at least promised to restore order and a sense of
purpose. Europe's dictators frightened many Americans. But they
also led many to think of strong leadership as a necessary phenomenon of the age, a prerequisite to the restoration of international order
and domestic prosperity.

Another possible direction—a threat or a promise, depending on
where one stood politically—was revolution. To many, some sort of
socialist or communist transformation of the economic and political
order seemed the only answer. Early in the decade, the Communist
party did make some gains. The party tried to organize unemployed
urban workers into "councils," built around neighborhoods, blocks,
or even apartment houses. In 1930, these Unemployed Councils
managed a series of demonstrations in major cities, drawing crowds
ranging from 5,000 to 35,000. Later, after they deemphasized their
talk of immediate revolution, the Communists had some substantial
successes within the Congress of Industrial Organizations (CIO), a
new and powerful labor union. Large numbers of intellectuals—writers, scientists, teachers, and bureaucrats—also joined the party. The
Socialist party, too, began a vigorous program of recruitment and
political campaigning, with the very popular Norman Thomas as its
presidential candidate.

Into this atmosphere of uncertainty came Franklin Delano Roosevelt. A master at capturing the national mood in his speeches,

Roosevelt talked of action, of advance, of what he called a New Deal for the American people.

It was not all talk, of course. Within three months of his inauguration in March 1933—the so-called Hundred Days—Roosevelt had signed into law a bewildering variety of legislation, much of it designed either to restructure the economy or to bring recovery. In the Emergency Banking Act, Congress gave the president broad discretionary powers over financial transactions. The Government Economy Act cut government employees' salaries and veterans' pensions in an attempt to balance the federal budget. The Agricultural Adjustment Act granted subsidies to farmers who voluntarily reduced acreage or crops. In an act of boldness not to be repeated, development of the Tennessee River Valley was turned over to a public corporation.

Akin to the policy toward agriculture but more comprehensive, the National Industrial Recovery Act (NIRA) attempted to promote recovery by granting businesses the right to cooperate. Each industry wrote its own code of fair competition—setting minimum wages and maximum workweeks, limiting construction of new capacity, even fixing prices by prohibiting sales below cost. In addition, section 7(a) of the NIRA appeared to give workers the right to bargain collectively with employers. (The NIRA is perhaps the best evidence that the New Deal sought to strengthen capitalism rather than replace it with socialism.)

Relief efforts went well beyond those of the Hoover administration. To absorb the unemployed, Congress created the Civilian Conservation Corps (CCC) and set up the Public Works Administration to promote construction in the public interest. In 1935, the Works Progress Administration (WPA) was established to coordinate public works. The Emergency Relief Act directed Hoover's Reconstruction Finance Corporation to make relief funds available to the states and signaled the shift away from Hoover's opposition to using federal money for relief. The Social Security Act of 1935 brought the national government into old-age assistance and insurance and unemployment compensation.

Historians have long debated whether the New Deal had any significant effect on the depression. But of one thing there can be little doubt. Roosevelt did manage to steal the rhetorical thunder from *both* the advocates of dictatorship and the proponents of revolution. And he did so by adopting some of the language of each side. When he presented his legislative program to Congress, he could sound as though he meant to do everything that any European leader could do, asking for "broad Executive power to wage a war against the emergency, as great as the power that would be given to me if we were in fact invaded by a foreign foe." And he could sound like a bit of a socialist when the need was there, as when he talked bitterly about the way that "economic royalists" controlled the nation's wealth and had led the people blindly into depression.

Historians have also argued about whether Roosevelt's New Deal "saved" American capitalism or fundamentally altered it. What he was probably most anxious to save, however, was not the economic system, or even the political structure, but the faith of his constituents *in* the system. The nation did not respond to calls for revolution. The actual power of the Communist party probably declined after Roosevelt's election. The "deal" he offered the people may not have been as "new" as he made it sound, but he did convince most Americans that he was in charge of the only game in town.

Interpretive Essay

Alan Brinkley

Voices of Protest

Franklin Delano Roosevelt was elected president four times, the first in 1932. In retrospect, he was vulnerable only once, in 1936, and that vulnerability was much reduced when his most serious challenger, Senator Huey Long of Louisiana, was fatally wounded on the steps of the state capitol in Baton Rouge in 1935.

As Alan Brinkley's essay demonstrates, Long was a strange and yet remarkable man. The "Kingfish," as he came to be known, had acquired his political skills as a traveling salesman, small-town lawyer, and state railroad commissioner. Whether as governor or senator, he was the dominant political force in Louisiana, where he taxed the oil interests to build roads and expand the state university.

Long is usually dismissed as a "demagogue." But, as Brinkley reminds us, his politics were not all that unreasonable. Do you think that Long was, in some important sense, a "threat" to the nation? Was Roosevelt's treatment of him clearly justified? Given the special problems of the 1930s, was his Share Our Wealth Plan a viable and legitimate program?

From Alan Brinkley, *Voices of Protest: Huey Long, Father Coughlin, and the Great Depression* (New York: Alfred A. Knopf, 1982), pp. 57–66, 68, 70–74, 79–81, as edited. Copyright © 1982 by Alan Brinkley. Reprinted by permission of Alfred A. Knopf, Inc.

Early in October 1932 a political cartoon appeared in the Republican Washington *Star* deriding the apparent alliance between Huey Long and Franklin Roosevelt. The future President lay propped up in bed beaming proudly at a
row of infants lying docilely beside him. The babies bore familiar faces: Cor-
nelius Vanderbilt Whitney, Vincent Astor, Hiram Johnson, George Norris.
And at the end of the row, gazing contentedly into space, was the pudgy
visage of Huey Long. Roosevelt, admiring them all,. was exclaiming trium-
phantly, "Just look at my little darlings!"

Long and Roosevelt may have looked like the best of friends for a while
in 1932, but they themselves knew otherwise. Their relationship was a troubled one from the beginning; and as both men moved further and further
into the center of national politics, it did nothing but deteriorate. Each viewed
the other with suspicion and some fear. Each knew the other would ultimately
be an obstacle to his own goals. Both spoke hopefully at first of friendship
and cooperation, but soon the lines of battle were openly drawn. . . .

Early in October, Roosevelt invited Long to join him for lunch at his
country home in Hyde Park, New York. It was not an auspicious encounter.
Roosevelt displayed no irritation at Huey's outrageous costume (a loud suit,
clashing shirt, and pink tie) or at his effort to dominate the conversation
during lunch, lecturing the candidate like a schoolboy. Roosevelt's mother,
however, was not so tactful. "Who is that *awful* man?" she said in a loud
whisper. Everyone pretended not to hear, but Long almost certainly took
note. "By God, I feel sorry for him," he later remarked of Roosevelt. "He's
got more sonsofbitches in his family than I got in mine." He was not much
impressed by the candidate himself either. "I like him," he said condescend-
ingly after this first meeting. "He's not a strong man, but he means well."

A visit to Warm Springs, Georgia, a few weeks after the election only
deepened Long's doubts. The conversation was friendly enough, but Huey
left puzzled and disturbed by Roosevelt's congenial evasiveness. "When I
talk to him, he says 'Fine! Fine! Fine!' " he complained. "But Joe Robinson
goes to see him the next day and again he says 'Fine! Fine! Fine!' Maybe he
says 'Fine!' to everybody."

When Roosevelt arrived in Washington late in January for meetings with
party leaders and members of Congress, he managed to pacify Long briefly.
Huey emerged from a meeting in the President-elect's suite at the Mayflower
Hotel smiling and content, promising to do whatever Roosevelt asked and
praising him as "the same old Frank, . . . all wool and a yard wide." Only
days later, however, the cordiality had vanished, as an arrogant and presump-
tuous message Long sent to Roosevelt suggested. Noting press reports of
some disagreement among Roosevelt advisors over a Cabinet appointment,
Long wired: "Glad to see you told Farley, Walker and others you wanted
none of their advice. I figured all the time you wanted men like me to advise
you.". . . .

The antagonisms increased with startling rapidity in the first weeks of
the new Administration. So desperate had the economic crisis become by
the time Roosevelt took office that even the most entrenched conservatives

and the most impatient progressives seemed willing at first to follow the new President almost blindly. But not Huey Long. The special session of Congress Roosevelt had called to consider emergency legislation was only a few moments old when Huey seized the floor to stake out his own position on dealing with the crisis.

Long's first complaint was about the bank holiday Roosevelt had proclaimed four days earlier in an effort to halt the alarming wave of bank failures across the nation. The President should have acted to subsidize the banks, not close them, he argued. Roosevelt's first piece of legislation, moreover, had serious deficiencies. The Emergency Banking Act, drafted so quickly that there had not even been time for copies to be printed before the Senate debate, would save the great national banks, Long claimed, but "the little banks in the counties and in the parishes and in the States are most in need of protection." So he offered an amendment "to give the President the right to save the State banks," an amendment that would entitle Roosevelt to declare local banks members of the Federal Reserve System (and thus eligible for increased government assistance) without meeting the stringent capital requirements imposed on larger, national institutions.

The Banking Act was, as Long claimed, an intensely conservative document, drafted in large part by bankers and by conservative holdovers from the Hoover Administration. In an atmosphere that some believed would have enabled Roosevelt to transform the very nature of the banking system, even to nationalize it, he had chosen instead simply to use government funds to stabilize the existing structure. And, as Long claimed, there was little in the bill to help small, local banks, little to guarantee that the crisis would not become a vehicle for the large financial institutions to drive smaller competitors out of business. But while Long, alone among members of the Senate, spoke at great length and with great passion on this question, his colleagues were in no mood to listen. They defeated his amendment by voice vote (Long could not even muster enough support to demand a roll call) and went on to pass the Banking Act unamended that same afternoon.

Long was even more distressed by the second piece of emergency legislation to arrive from the White House: the Government Economy Act, which proposed slashing more than half a billion dollars from the budget largely by cutting veterans' benefits and reducing the salaries of government employees. The bill was the work of bankers and financiers, Long claimed, of "Mr. Morgan" and "Mr. Rockefeller." And it would have "disastrous consequences." If the President was concerned about balancing the budget, then he should support new taxes on private fortunes to raise additional funds, not cut payments to men and women already in need. Administration forces, however, fended off all opposition and won almost immediate passage of one of the most conservative pieces of legislation to move through the Congress in three years. Long was one of only thirteen Senators to vote against it.

As the Roosevelt juggernaut continued to roll through Congress, erecting the basic framework of the early New Deal during the first "Hundred Days" of the Congressional session, the relationship between Long and the Administration worsened. . . .

The National Industrial Recovery Act, the keystone of the New Deal program, Long denounced more bitterly than anything else. Although he supported its provisions for public-works expenditures, he lashed out at the system of wage and price codes it established. The codes, he predicted (correctly, as it turned out), would be written largely by the leaders of the industries involved and would become an excuse for price-fixing, for cartelization, for large interests driving small ones out of business. "Every fault of socialism is found in this bill, without one of its virtues," he complained. "Every crime of monarchy is in here, without one of the things that would give it credit.". . .

These legislative skirmishes were, however, peripheral to Long's main battle with the Administration—a battle he waged, characteristically, over an issue of his own devising. It was the issue upon which he had long ago decided to build his national career: the limitation of fortunes and the redistribution of wealth.

The Roosevelt Presidency was barely two weeks old when Long introduced legislation placing strict ceilings on personal incomes, private fortunes, and inheritances. It was an open challenge to the Administration to fulfill what Long insisted had been the major promise of the 1932 Democratic campaign. Yet Long apparently never really expected the President to endorse his proposals, for he moved almost immediately to mobilize public support for them in a way the Administration could not but view as threatening. Five days after Franklin Roosevelt delivered his first "Fireside Chat" over the radio to explain the provisions of the Emergency Banking Act, Long took to the air himself. On free network time provided by the National Broadcasting Company (in accordance, NBC officials claimed, with a long-standing but seldom used policy of allowing access to the air to any member of Congress on request), he delivered the first of what was to become a three-year series of folksy radio addresses designed to move himself to the forefront of the popular consciousness.

Long was no stranger to radio. He had used it effectively in building his popularity in Louisiana, in promoting his cotton-holiday plan in 1931, and in the Caraway campaign of the previous summer. His experience was evident in the skillful and deceptively benign speech he delivered March 17. With liberal use of passages from the Bible and quotations from such popular American heroes as Daniel Webster, William Jennings Bryan, and Theodore Roosevelt, Long made his economic proposals sound simple, logical, and moderate. Even more impressive was his caginess in dealing with Roosevelt. There was no hint in this address of disillusionment with the Administration. On the contrary, he insisted, "our great President . . . has not only kept faith before his nomination, but he kept faith after nomination." In campaign speeches, even in his Inaugural Address, Roosevelt had "declared to help decentralize the wealth of this country." But the new President would need assistance. "He has a hard task ahead," and Huey Long was ready to come to his aid.

To his supporters, Long was presenting himself as a champion of the common man, working selflessly to help a popular President fulfill his campaign promises. To the Administration, however, he was beginning to seem a shrewd and dangerous foe. Long was taking the President's vague commitment to the principle of wealth redistribution and using it to create in the public mind an expectation of specific legislative action. He was maneuvering Roosevelt into an awkward and profitless position.

For a few months, the Administration remained willing to put up with all of this—with the attacks on its legislative proposals, the maligning of New Deal officials, the attempts to appeal over the President's head directly to the public. But by the middle of June, Roosevelt had apparently decided that Long could not be appeased, and he summoned him to the White House for what he told aides would be a "showdown."

The meeting did not have the appearance of a showdown. Long bounded into the President's office dressed in a brilliant white suit and began reminding Roosevelt pointedly of his own great work at the Chicago convention. For a while, he failed to remove his straw hat, except occasionally to tap the President's knee or elbow with it when making a point. James Farley and Marvin McIntyre, also present, were incensed at what they considered a deliberate discourtesy, but Roosevelt remained calm and superficially amiable. By the end of the interview, however, he had made his intentions clear: Huey would no longer be consulted on the distribution of federal patronage in Louisiana.

Long may not have realized fully at first how completely the President had written him off. Although he growled to Farley after the meeting about Roosevelt's evasiveness, he assured reporters cheerily as he left the White House that "The President and I are never going to fall out. I'll be satisfied whichever way matters go." But as the summer wore on and Long watched more and more federal appointments going to his enemies in Louisiana, what little loyalty he may still have felt toward the Administration eroded. In October, he all but formalized the break. First, he directed the Louisiana state government to refuse any federal funds that would be spent under the supervision of his political enemies. Then, when Interior Secretary Harold Ickes began to criticize him for his petulance, Long called a press conference, launched a spirited attack on New Deal officials in Louisiana, and concluded angrily: "While you are at it, pay them my further respects up there in Washington. Tell them they can go to hell."

Why had it happened? And why so quickly? By any normal standards, there seemed to be every reason for both Long and Roosevelt to avoid a public falling out. The President, in the first critical days of an Administration that faced an uncertain future, could hardly have been eager to win the enmity of a powerful and increasingly popular member of his own party. And Long, whose national reputation was still in its earliest stages of development, would seem to have had little to gain from a break with the man who had won the overwhelming confidence of the American people.

For the President, the explanation seems relatively simple. Already, Long was making it clear that he was no friend of the Administration, that he would support it only on his own terms, terms that were unacceptable to Roosevelt. It was becoming apparent, moreover, that Long's attempts to pressure the President into supporting his programs were having some effect upon the public. Members of the White House staff worried when they received letters from people like William Dombrow of Chicago, who wrote of his admiration for the President and added that "Here in Illinois the people would rejoice if they had a leader, such as the Hon. Sen. Huey P. Long. His bill that he recently introduced in Congress on Decentralization of Wealth, is one of the greatest pieces of legislation that was ever introduced"; and from groups like an Irish-American political organization, which sent Roosevelt a resolution praising "Senator Long's zeal for honest execution of the 'New Deal.' " The President could not afford to let Long continue creating the impression that his wealth-redistribution proposals were part of the Administration's program. The longer he waited, the costlier the break would be when it inevitably came. It was better to do it quickly and minimize the damage.

For Long's part, the reasons are more obscure. Perhaps he was, as he claimed, genuinely disillusioned with Roosevelt. Perhaps he simply over-estimated the amount of public abuse the President was willing to take. What seems most likely, however, is that Long quickly realized that Franklin Roosevelt was a more formidable adversary than he had anticipated, and that anyone with national aspirations of his own would tie himself to the Administration at his peril. "He's so doggone smart," Long remarked in the affected back-country dialect he sometimes adopted, "that fust thing I know I'll be working fer him—and I ain't goin' to." Later, he explained further. The only difference between Hoover and Roosevelt, he claimed, was that Hoover was a hoot owl while Roosevelt was a scrootch owl. "A hoot owl bangs into the roost and knocks the hen clean off, and catches her while she's falling. But a scrootch owl slips into the roost and talks softly to her. And the hen just falls in love with him, and the first thing you know, *there ain't no hen*."

Franklin Roosevelt was taking a calculated gamble when he cast Long adrift. He was wagering that his own popularity would more than offset Long's; that without public identification with the New Deal, Huey's national strength would languish and ultimately die. For a while, it seemed that the gamble had paid off. During the second half of 1933, it did appear that Long had entered an irreversible decline—not only in the nation but in his hitherto unassailable bastion, Louisiana. . . .

Long's greatest problem in 1933, however, was one of his own making, a result of the loose and flamboyant life-style he had adopted since his arrival in Washington. During a visit to New York in August, Huey accompanied some friends to a party at a country club in Sands Point, Long Island. He spent several hours getting pleasantly drunk, flirting with pretty women (his wife, as usual, was at home in Louisiana), and bouncing from table to table glad-handing and back-slapping, until finally he disappeared into the men's room.

What happened next has never been entirely clear; but what seems most plausible is that Huey, always impatient, tried to use an occupied urinal by relieving himself between the legs of someone in front of him, succeeding only in soaking the man's trousers. He emerged from the washroom with a bleeding and badly swollen eye. Although Long and his party quickly left the club and drove back to the city, several other guests caught a glimpse of the injured Kingfish; within hours, reports of the incident appeared in the press. For days, even weeks, the stories and editorials continued, presenting one version after another of the fight. Long had never been popular among New York journalists, and they seemed now to vie with one another in ridiculing him. Newspapers and magazines around the country picked up the story off the wires and gave it front-page attention, until soon the incident was as widely known as any in Long's career. . . .

As the publicity surrounding the incident grew, Long apparently reasoned that an even fuller response was necessary. At first, he had attributed the attack vaguely to the dark forces that had threatened him throughout his career. Within a few days, he became more specific. The assailants, he claimed, had been "members of the House of Morgan," Wall Street hit men hired to eliminate the most powerful threat to the financial oligarchy. "The only reason he wasn't killed," one Long-inspired circular maintained, "was because he managed to get away too soon for the men to finish the job.". . .

Hodding Carter was more realistic than many others of Long's enemies, and he realized that, for all the setbacks, Huey "isn't down yet." He "can always make himself heard," Carter grudgingly admitted. For "as long as there are prejudices to appeal to, as long as the voting mass can be swayed by a demagogue preaching discontent and hitting below the belt at the easiest targets, Huey P. Long will be up and about." Long himself, while he would not have shared Carter's venomous characterization of his appeal, also realized that he was far from through. "I have more enemies in the United States than any little man I know of," he boasted defiantly to a Louisiana audience in the midst of his troubles. "I am proud of my enemies." And he would, he promised, beat them yet. . . .

Having secured his position in Louisiana, Long began to repair the damage his setbacks of 1933 had done to his national prestige. He gave up drinking and avoided the racy nightspots at which he had become a fixture in Washington. He started a rigorous diet and shed more than thirty pounds. He even took his wife, with whom he had seldom been seen in recent years, on a belated "honeymoon" to Hot Springs, Arkansas. The time for playing the clown had passed. Long now wanted to appear sober, responsible, and statesmanlike.

More important than these cosmetic moves was a series of practical steps to help him communicate his message directly to the people. In October 1933, after working on it intermittently for a year or more, he published an autobiography, *Every Man a King*. A lively and entertaining if less than fully candid book, it portrayed a sincere and selfless Huey Long whose every thought and effort had been directed toward aiding the common people of America. Reviewers scoffed at it. "There is hardly a law of English usage or a rule of English grammar that its author does not break somewhere," sneered the *New York Times Book Review*. The work made clear, wrote Allan Nevins in the *Saturday Review,* that Long "is unbalanced, vulgar, in many ways ignorant, and quite reckless." But *Every Man a King* was not meant for the East Coast literati. Bound in a striking (some would say garish) gold cover, priced at a profit-denying one dollar a copy, it was intended for men and women not in the habit of reading books. When bookstores managed to sell only about 20,000 copies of the 100,000 Long had had printed, he simply gave the rest of them away.

He also resumed publishing his own newspaper. The *Louisiana Progress,* the propaganda organ he had created to counter the hostility of the established press in his home state, had died quietly in 1932. Now, less than a year later, it reappeared in a new guise—renamed the *American Progress* and aimed at a national, not a regional audience. Like its predecessor, the *American Progress* was an unabashed advocate of the career and the programs of Huey P. Long. It did not, however, devote much space to Long's accomplishments in Louisiana. Instead, it focused on the broader issue of redistribution of wealth. Published weekly for about seven months, monthly thereafter, it had only a small formal subscription list. For the most part, Long mailed it free to whomever he chose—to an audience that averaged 300,000 per issue but that occasionally grew to 1.5 million. It was financed, like everything else Long did, by political contributions from his organization in Louisiana.

By the spring of 1934, Long had established the foundations of a genuinely independent communications network. Just as he had once done in Louisiana, so now in the nation he was ensuring that never again would he have to rely solely upon the establishment press for publicity. His autobiography painted for his followers a picture of his life far more flattering than anything an outsider might publish. His newspaper would supply them with regular accounts of his activities, would interpret his legislative activities in a congenial light, and would explain the virtues of his program. A staff of sixty stenographers, the largest in Congress, would supply the men and women on Long's enormous mailing list with a flood of letters, circulars, and pamphlets proclaiming Huey's message and extolling his triumphs. Most important of all, radio speeches would bring his voice to millions of Americans so that, using his considerable broadcasting skill, he could soothe their fears about him and exhort them to ever greater efforts on his behalf. He used the radio only intermittently in 1933 and 1934, but by early 1935 he had become a frequent speaker on NBC and at times, according to the crude audience estimates of the day, one of the network's biggest attractions.

Long used his new tools of publicity to promote a freshly refined set of economic proposals: a plan that took his long-standing commitment to wealth redistribution and translated it into a specific program for reform. Late in 1934, he unveiled what was to be the cornerstone of the rest of his public career: the Share Our Wealth Plan.

The underlying argument for the new proposals was a simple one. The wealth of America, while abundant, was limited, Long said. Each citizen had a basic right to a decent share of what wealth there was. But for too long, a few rich men had been permitted to own so large a proportion of the nation's assets that they had not left enough for all the others. It was, he explained, as if everyone in America had been invited to a great barbecue. "God invited us all to come and eat and drink all we wanted. He smiled on our land and we grew crops of plenty to eat and wear. He showed us in the earth the iron and other things to make everything we wanted. He unfolded to us the secrets of science so that our work might be easy. God called: 'Come to my feast.'" But what had happened? "Rockefeller, Morgan, and their crowd stepped up and took enough for 120,000,000 people and left only enough for 5,000,000 for all the other 125,000,000 to eat. And so many millions must go hungry and without these good things God gave us unless we call on them to put some of it back."

Long did at times explain the problem in more sophisticated terms. He cited figures (usually from such questionable sources as the *Saturday Evening Post* or from obscure government studies made decades before) to show that "2 percent of the people owned 60 percent of the wealth," or that "about 85 percent of the wealth is owned by 5 percent of the people." The specific numbers, however, were never as important as the broader image: of a problem so obvious that only willful ignorance could obscure it.

The solution, the Share Our Wealth Plan (or, as he often called it, the Long Plan), was as simple as the problem. A new set of harshly confiscatory tax codes would place strict limits on the amount of wealth any one man could own and on the amount he could pass on to his heirs. Each person would be permitted to own capital worth $1 million with impunity. But on every million he owned over that amount he would be required to pay a sharply increasing "capital levy tax." On the second million, the rate would be one percent; on the third, two percent; on the fourth, four percent; on the fifth, eight percent; and so on. Once a personal fortune exceeded $8 million, the tax would become 100 percent. At first, this would permit individuals to retain fortunes of close to $7 million; but since the levy would be reimposed each year, before long "No one would have much more than three to four million dollars to the person."

The proposals for income and inheritance taxes were even simpler. His income-tax plan extended the existing laws "to the point that, once a man makes the net sum of one million dollars in one year, that he gives the balance of what he makes that year to the government." Likewise, the government would confiscate all inheritances of more than one million dollars. The plan would, Huey insisted, "injure no one." It would not abolish millionaires;

it might even increase their number ("I'd cut their nails and file their teeth," he admitted with some chagrin, "and let them live"); but his proposals would prevent anyone from accumulating a truly obscene fortune and would make an enormous fund of wealth available to the rest of the people.

That fund would enable the government to enact the second major component of the Share Our Wealth Plan: guaranteed subsistence for everyone in America. Each needy family would receive a basic "household estate" of $5,000, "enough for a home, an automobile, a radio, and the ordinary conveniences." And this would be only a "start." There would be a government guarantee, too, of an adequate annual income for each family, "a minimum of from $2,000 to $2,500 . . . per year," enough, he claimed, to "maintain a family in comfort" once it had acquired the basic necessities that the initial $5,000 allowance would allow it to purchase. There were other proposals: government support for education, old-age pensions, improved benefits to veterans, increased federal assistance to farmers, government-supported public-works projects, limitation of working hours, and more. Some of these provisions survived only briefly as part of the Long program; some of them proved durable. But the limiting of large fortunes and the distribution of the surplus formed its unchanging core.

The Share Our Wealth Plan was politically attractive in many ways. Economically, however, it had serious—indeed, insurmountable—problems. Long failed to provide any clear explanation of the mechanics of redistribution. Not all wealth, of course, was in the form of money. Many, perhaps most of the holdings of the nation's wealthiest men and women were in the form of capital investments—industrial plants, real estate, stocks, bonds, and the like—that could not be easily evaluated, liquidated, or redistributed. Yet Long apparently never gave much thought to such problems. When pressed on the matter, he simply shrugged and admitted that "I am going to have to call in some great minds to help me."

A more fundamental flaw was that the vast surplus wealth Long claimed could finance his program simply did not exist. There were not enough John D. Rockefellers with idle millions lying in bank vaults to satisfy the needs of the nation. One scholarly survey in 1935 suggested that if the government confiscated all wealth owned by those worth $1 million or more (a step even more drastic than Long envisioned) and distributed it among those worth $5,000 or less (precisely what Long proposed), the recipients would receive only a little more than $400 each. According to other estimates (and, given the difficulty in measuring "wealth," such estimates were necessarily crude ones), for every family to receive the minimum $5,000 homestead Long promised would mean that no family could retain more than about $7,000 in wealth. For each family to receive the annual $2,500 income Long promised, no family would be able to keep more than about $3,000 of its earnings a year. Long liked to suggest that effective redistribution was an easy matter, that it involved only skimming the excess from a few large fortunes. "Let no one tell you that it is difficult to redistribute the wealth of this land," he told a national radio audience in 1934. "It is simple." But it was not simple.

To effect the sort of reallocation of resources Long promised would have required a process far more drastic and painful than he admitted or realized.

It was hardly surprising, therefore, that Long's critics denounced his program as cynical demagoguery and accused him of pandering openly to ignorance and prejudice in his pursuit of public support. He was, H. L. Mencken once venomously charged (in a description that echoed the views of many), "simply a backwoods demagogue of the oldest and most familiar model—impudent, blackguardly, and infinitely prehensile." Yet to dismiss the Share Our Wealth Plan as demagoguery is to dismiss it too easily. It was a simplistic program, seriously, perhaps fatally, flawed. It was not, however, an attempt to divert attention away from real problems; it did not focus resentment on irrelevant scapegoats or phony villains. It pointed, instead, to an issue of genuine importance; for the concentration of wealth was, even if not in precisely the form Long described it, a fundamental dilemma of the American economy. Few economists would have disagreed that in referring to the problem Long was, in a crude way, describing one of the basic causes of the Depression: the insufficient distribution of purchasing power among the populace, the inability of the economy to provide markets for the tremendous productivity of American industry and agriculture. For all its faults, the Share Our Wealth Plan was not without elements of economic truth. . . .

It was not through the Senate, however, that Long intended to chart his political future. If he was to become the power he intended, if he was to make his program for redistribution of wealth the overriding concern of the nation, he would need a vehicle entirely his own. In February 1934, he created one.

Speaking over a national radio hookup for the first time in almost a year, Long announced that he was forming a new political organization: the Share Our Wealth Society, to be composed of a nationwide system of local clubs. Anyone committed to the idea of redistribution of wealth could join. It was time, he argued, "to hit the root with the ax. . . . Enroll with us. Let us make known to the people what we are going to do. . . . Share Our Wealth societies are now being organized, and people have it within their power to relieve themselves from this terrible situation."

The idea for the Share Our Wealth Clubs had apparently occurred to Long spontaneously at three o'clock one morning, and he had excitedly roused Earle Christenberry, his secretary, from bed to work out the details with him. But the concept of creating an independent organization for himself was not a new one. It had its roots in his political career in Louisiana. While he could not hope to re-create on a national scale the iron-clad and pervasive organizational hegemony he had achieved in his own state, he could work to establish a widespread network of supporters with whom he could retain constant communication. And upon them, he hoped, he could build a national following of enough size and power to allow him to achieve his dreams.

How extravagant those dreams were was rapidly becoming clear. It took no great prescience to recognize the thin line dividing the establishment of a national political organization from the establishment of a political party. The formation of the Share Our Wealth Society was the decisive signal that Long was not merely attempting to pressure and cajole the Administration and the Democratic Party, but was planning to supplant it. "It is more and more evident in Washington," wrote Arthur Krock early in 1935, "that many Democrats feel he is getting ready to pounce upon their party and absorb all or a large part of it in 1936."

Such Democrats included officials as powerful as the President himself. Roosevelt was no longer content simply to deny Long patronage and to cut off federal funds in Louisiana. Now that Huey was creating a potentially threatening national organization, the Administration considered more drastic measures. In September 1934, the President went so far as to flirt with the idea of sending federal troops into Louisiana to "restore Republican government" in the state. Members of the Justice Department and the FBI drew up elaborate legal and tactical memoranda before Roosevelt finally abandoned the rash and explosive scheme.

By 1935, the Administration had apparently settled on a different approach. No longer would it attempt simply to pressure or threaten Long; it would co-opt him. Franklin Roosevelt's widely heralded "turn to the left" in 1935 (a series of ambitious proposals often described as the "Second New Deal") was the result of many political considerations. There can be little doubt, however, that Long was one of them. As one "prominent" Democratic Senator with close ties to the White House disclosed to a reporter early in the year, "We are obliged to propose and accept many things in the New Deal that otherwise we would not because we must prevent a union of discontent around [Long]. The President is the only hope of the conservatives and liberals; if his program is restricted, the answer may be Huey Long."

One New Deal proposal in particular had the stamp of Long clearly across its face: Roosevelt's tax message of June 1935. After months of uncertainty, the President had accepted a Treasury Department proposal for sharply graduated increases in income- and inheritance-tax rates, and he presented it to Congress as an attempt "to prevent an unjust concentration of wealth and economic power." Long expressed enthusiastic approval at first, but he soon made clear that the Administration plan was not nearly drastic enough to satisfy him. The President's proposal was, he charged (with some accuracy), little more than a cosmetic move. It would make no fundamental difference in the distribution of national wealth.

Whether Roosevelt's tax plan and his other new proposals would ultimately have succeeded in undermining Huey's appeal is impossible to determine, for less than three months later Long was dead. At the moment, however, they had no appreciable effect. Long's national reputation grew at an astounding rate through the spring and summer of 1935, and the size and distribution of his Share Our Wealth Clubs grew with it. In the sixth year of the Depression and the third year of the New Deal, Long seemed to many to be on the verge of creating a genuine new force in American politics, one whose ultimate power nobody could yet predict. And there was little doubt that he intended to use this force to play an instrumental role in the 1936 election. "What is quietly tipped off as being the Huey Long 1936 campaign badge has made its appearance in Washington," the San Francisco *Examiner* noted in March 1935. "It is a small gold kingfish, with a crown on its head and labeled 'Louisiana,' worn in the buttonhole. It is, unlike Huey, exceedingly modest."

Unlike Huey indeed, for, while Long usually insisted that he had as yet made no concrete plans for 1936, every now and then he let evidence of his real ambitions slip out. "I'll tell you here and now," he told reporters one afternoon late in the summer, "that Franklin Roosevelt will not be the next President of the United States. If the Democrats nominate Roosevelt and the Republicans nominate Hoover, Huey Long will be your next President."

Sources

Stella Nowicki

Organizing the Stockyards

During the 1920s, organized labor faced severe political and technological challenges. Employers joined hands with the courts to deprive workers of the right to picket effectively; new or growing automobile, chemical, and service industries created thousands of jobs, but nearly all of them were for unskilled workers. Weak and under attack, the American Federation of Labor (AFL) proved unwilling to abandon its traditional emphasis on the organization of skilled "crafts" (cigarmaking, typography, for example) for a new "industrial" approach that would bring all workers in a given industry under one union. Unskilled workers in steel, rubber, automobiles, and other mass-production industries plunged into the desperate 1930s without a major ally.

Help came from Franklin Roosevelt's New Deal and from John L. Lewis's Congress of Industrial Organizations (CIO), created in response to the AFL's timidity and committed to industrial unionism. But the CIO did not exist until 1935, and, as Stella Nowicki's recollection suggests, New Deal legislation did not instantly make organized workers out of unorganized ones or cause employers to stop resisting unions. Much of the tough, grass-roots organizing of the depression years was done by rank-and-file workers like Nowicki.

What made Nowicki a radical? Was her communism acceptable to her co-workers? How did her objectives differ from those of the American Federation of Labor?

I ran away from home at age 17. I had to because there was not enough money to feed the family in 1933 during the Depression.

I was brought up on a farm. We really roughed it. We had no electricity. We had outdoor privies. We baked our own bread, churned our own butter, raised and butchered our own hogs, made our own sausage, did our own smoking of meat. All the things young people are into today we did because it was a necessity. We worked hard and long hours.

We used to fell our own oak trees, my older sister and I. We would cut eight or nine foot logs with a cross cut saw and we'd lift those logs up on the wagon and drive home, then pick them up and run a buzz saw on them. We did all kinds of other heavy work.

My father was a coal miner at one time and he instilled pro-unionism in us as youngsters. The coal miners, at least the foreign born, were of socialist background. My father bought a few books about Lenin and Gorky from socialists in the coal fields. I learned Polish through these revolutionary books but only years later did I make the connection.

I remember when Sacco and Vanzetti were executed. The foreign-born people were in mourning for a week after that, and they were not all pro-socialist. My mother was and still is a practicing Catholic.

My father used to have this slogan, "No work, no eat." That's a socialist slogan, he said. It was really carried out at home. If we didn't work we really didn't eat.

I would challenge my father many times. Before I left home I had gone to a dance with a group of girls against my father's word. For two or three nights I slept in the barn and my mother would bring me food.

Agnes, a woman from Chicago, was on our farm for her health. She was going to have an experimental operation in which a bone would be transplanted from her leg to her back to help correct a curvature. She asked me to come back to Chicago with her. We hitch-hiked to Benton Harbor and then caught the boat. I then lived with Agnes and her family who were radicals.

One of the family was Herbert March. Herb March was a member of the Young Communist League. He was a young man. When he was just out of college at seventeen or eighteen years old, he felt that here was this country, very rich, yet all these people were out of work. Maybe college didn't mean much and maybe he should go into organizing people for social-ism, maybe capitalism wasn't the answer.

I was not really introduced to socialism until I came to Chicago and the Marches began telling me about it. I lived with them at 59th and Ashland. They lived on the second floor and on the third floor they had bedrooms and an attic room. Anyone who didn't have some place to live could always find room there. It was near the streetcar intersection and when there were meetings blacks could come. (This was a real problem at that time.) The Marches would have meetings of the YCL in the attic and they'd ask me to sit in. The terminology was like a foreign language. I thought that I better join this outfit so that I would know what they were talking about.

They pointed out things to me that, in my very unsophisticated and farm-like way, I saw. There was so much food being dumped—the government bought it up—and people were hungry and didn't have enough to eat. (There were days when I didn't have anything to eat. That's when I picked up smoking. Somebody said, "Here, smoke. It'll kill your appetite." And it did.) I realized that there was this tremendous disparity. The people in our YCL group told me that the government was set up to keep it this way. They thought that instead of just thinking about ourselves we should be thinking about other people and try to get them together in a union and organize and then maybe we would have socialism where there would not be hunger, war, etc. They initiated me into a lot of political ideas and gave me material to read. We had classes and we would discuss industrial unionism, the craft unions and the history of the labor movement in this country. We talked about Debs,* we talked about the eight hour day, many things.

I was doing housework for $4 a week and I hated it. I would cry and cry. I was horribly homesick because I hated the restraint of being in a house all the time. I was used to being out a lot on the farm. So Herb suggested that I get a job in the stockyards.

Herb was working at Armour's at the time. He bought me a steel, with which one sharpens a knife, and I took it with me. He took me down to the stock yards and (he tells this story) I said, "Those beautiful cows! They can't kill those beautiful cows!" At home we just had cows for milking. But here were all these cows and they were going to be killed and they were crying, mooing, as they were going to be killed. But one had to get a job!

One of the ways to get a job was to go down to the employment office. Every morning you got there by six or six-thirty. There were just so many benches and they would all be filled early. They would only need one, maybe two people. This woman, Mrs. McCann, women's hiring director, would look around for the biggest and brawniest person. At seventeen I weighed 157 pounds coming from the farm, rosy-cheeked and strong. "Have you had experience?" I said, "Well not in the stock yards but we used to butcher our own hogs at home." I carried this big steel and that impressed her. Mrs. McCann hired me.

I was in the cook room. At that time the government bought up drought cattle and they were killed, canned, and given to people on relief to eat. The meat would be cut into big hunks and steamed. Then it would come on a rail and be dumped out on the table. The women would be all around the table and we would cut the meat up, remove the gristle and bad parts, and make hash out of it. The government inspector would come around to see that bad meat wasn't being thrown into the hash. But as soon as his back would be turned, the foreman would push this stuff right down the chute to go into the cans—all this stuff we had put aside to be thrown away

---

*Eugene Debs, see pages 146–148.—*Ed.*

he would push right down in, including gloves, cockroaches, anything. The company didn't give a damn.

The meat would be so hot and steamy your fingers almost blistered but you just stayed on. In 1933–34 we worked six hour shifts at 37½ cents an hour. We would have to work at a high rate of speed. It was summer. It would be so hot that women used to pass out. The ladies' room was on the floor below and I would help carry these women down almost vertical stairs into the washroom.

We started talking union. The thing that precipitated it is that on the floor below they used to make hotdogs and one of the women, in putting the meat into the chopper, got her fingers caught. There were no safety guards. Her fingers got into the hotdogs and they were chopped off. It was just horrible.

Three of us "colonizers" had a meeting during our break and decided this was the time to have a stoppage and we did. (Colonizers were people sent by the YCL or CP [Communist party] into points of industrial concentration that the CP had designated. These included mass basic industries: steel, mining, packing, and railroad. The colonizers were like red missionaries. They were expected to do everything possible to keep jobs and organize for many years.) All six floors went on strike. We said, "Sit, stop." And we had a sit-down. We just stopped working right inside the building, protesting the speed and the unsafe conditions. We thought that people's fingers shouldn't go into the machine, that it was an outrage. The women got interested in the union.

We got the company to put in safety devices. Soon after the work stoppage the supervisors were looking for the leaders because people were talking up the action. They found out who was involved and we were all fired. I was blacklisted.

I got a job doing housework again and it was just horrible. Here I was taking care of this family with a little spoiled brat and I had to pick up after them—only Thursday afternoon off and every other Sunday—and all for four dollars a week of which I sent two dollars home. I just couldn't stand it. I would rather go back and work in a factory, any day or night.

A friend of mine who had been laid off told me that she got called to go back to work. Meanwhile she had a job in an office and she didn't want to go back to the stockyards, so she asked me if I wanted to go in her place. She had used the name Helen Ellis. I went down to the stockyards and it was the same department, exactly the same job on the same floor where I had been fired. But it was the afternoon and Mrs. McCann wasn't there. Her assistant was there. Her assistant said, "Can you do this work?" I said, "Oh yes, I can. I've done it." She told me that I would start work the following afternoon.

I came home and talked with Herb and Jane. We decided that I would have to go to the beauty shop. I got my hair cut really short and hennaed (similar to tinting today). I thinned my eyebrows and penciled them, wore a lot of lipstick and painted my nails. Because I hadn't been working, I had a suntan. I wore sandals and I had my toenails painted, which I would never have done before. I came in looking sharp and not like a country girl, so I passed right through and I was hired as Helen Ellis on the same job, the same forelady!

After several days the forelady, Mary, who was also Polish, came around and said, "OK, Helen, I know you're Stella. I won't say anything but just keep quiet" if I wanted to keep the job. I answered her in Polish that I knew that the job wouldn't last long and I thanked her. She knew I was pro-union and I guess she was too, so I kept the job as Helen Ellis until I got laid off. (Later on I was blacklisted under the name Ellis.)

Out of the fifteen dollars, I'd have to try to save half of it almost, to carry me when I was out of work. I remember that at one time I had a three-room furnished apartment on East 47th Street and I was paying fifteen dollars a month rent. Sometimes there would be fourteen people living there besides myself. Those who worked supported those who didn't. Anybody who worked put the money in the one pot and we shared it.

At this time, Herb was in the AFL and was asking for an industrial form of organization. The American Federation of Labor was organized along a craft basis. In the stockyards there might have been some electricians or some steam fitters or mechanics who were organized in their own separate unions. The mass of workers who were working on the assembly lines and on the kills—the sheep kill, the beef kill, the hog kill—and in the canning rooms, the women, they were not organized. The wage scale was way down.

The AFL really wasn't interested in getting masses of people in because large numbers threatened their position. Being as they were in crafts they didn't want to see the expansion because they would lose control. They had nice-paying jobs. They were bought off in a sense.

There were many battles within the AFL. A group of people, including Herb March, would raise questions at union meetings whenever they could get the floor. Many times they couldn't get the floor to speak and were carried out of union meetings bodily because they insisted on speaking on questions that the workers were concerned with—conditions of employment, wages, and other things. Herb nearly lost his life a couple of times because AFL racketeers were tied up with the meat-packers. Then the left-wing group organized a Trade Union Unity League as sort of an answer to the craft organization.

The Trade Union Unity League used to meet on 47th and State. We would walk [a couple of miles] from 47th and Ashland to 47th and State for meetings—we didn't have car fare and were out of work much of the time— to get together and talk about how we were going to organize the stockyards. The meetings were with blacks and whites.

Even at that time we raised the question of more Negroes on skilled jobs. The proportion of Negroes when I started in 1933 was, I suppose, fifteen to twenty per cent at most. By the time I left in 1945 it was maybe sixty per cent. . . .

It was very underground because if you even talked union you were fired. Jobs were at a premium. You didn't have the law which guaranteed people the right to organize.* So we actually had secret meetings. Everybody had to vouch for anyone that they brought to the meeting, that they were people that we could trust, because as soon as the company found out that people were trying to organize, they would try to send in stool pigeons. They paid people to come in and try to get information.

What they didn't know was that the secretary to the vice-president of one of the companies was the wife of one of the people who was interested in organizing. We were able to take advantage of this. We made copies of material and were able to use it to expose many of the anti-union tactics of the company.

I remember one of the first big CP meetings when we had William Foster† come to talk. The hall wasn't big enough. Somebody had gotten hold of a loudspeaker (they were very difficult to get in those days) and we hooked that up so that people could hear down the steps and into the street.

We had a YCL/CP unit. (There weren't enough people in either the YCL or the CP to meet separately and so we met together, younger and older people.) We would have meetings and marches and classes on Marxism and Leninism. . . .

. . . . We had people at Armour's and we had some people in Wilson's but there was nobody at Swift and Company. They employed anywhere from two to five thousand workers and we wanted to get some of them into the CIO.

Swift's was in a different class than Armour's. Everyone who worked in Swift's was thought to be a higher class worker—they got more money. Swift's had a group bonus system called the Bedaux system. After you produced so much then each person in the gang got that much more money. It's diabolical. One worker slits the throat of another. They keep going so that the group production is great enough that they can all get a bonus.

Swift and Company had a strong entrenched company union with a paternalistic system to keep people sort of quiescent and controlled. The company actually selected the representatives from the different departments. They called it an "Independent Employees Organization." Anybody who spoke up about it was a troublemaker and they got rid of him.

I went to Swift's to get a job. The personnel director said they weren't hiring but what were my qualifications, where did I work last. I told her Independent Casing. "Well, why aren't you there now?" I told her that I got a scholarship to go to the University of Wisconsin through the Y that previous summer. And she said, "Well that's my Alma Mater!" So she hired me for the casing department.

Later I got sent to the sliced bacon department which is the elite department. It was the cleanest job and you made the most money. They had this

---

* Actually, the right to organize was guaranteed by law before the New Deal. What was at issue was the right to use organization to achieve another objective, such as collective bargaining.—*Ed.*
† William Foster was head of the Communist party.—*Ed.*

visitors' ramp where people went by and would look down. We were freezing our asses off in this cooler of about forty degrees. I wore two pairs of wool socks and a couple of wool sweaters under my uniform and a cap. We'd have to go every two or three hours into the washroom to thaw out and spill out.

Swift and Company had a slogan that the premium bacon was "not touched by human hands." The sliced bacon came down on this conveyor belt and we women sat three on either side facing forward, sitting with a scale in front of us. One woman would just put the plastic see-through cover on the bacon. Then we would catch the bacon with our tongs, turn it over on the scale to make sure that each package was about eight ounces in weight— a quarter ounce less or more—then we would wrap them up, put them back on the belt and on they would go to the packer at the end of the line.

The women themselves had gotten together and they would turn out a hundred and forty-four packages an hour of bacon. We were making $15 a week at 37½ cents an hour, but if we each produced 144 packages an hour we got $7 more in our pay. We made 50 per cent more than anybody else but we produced 90 per cent more than the set group rate. A new girl would come in and the oldtimers would train her. They would help her out so that gradually by the end of a certain period of time she was doing the 144. But they would never let anyone go beyond that 144 packages. They maintained that limit and they did it without a union. One smart-aleck girl came in there once and she was going to show them and go beyond that number because she wanted to earn more money: all the bacon that she got from the girls further up the line was messed up and scrappy and she'd have to straighten it up to put it in the package. She couldn't make a hundred packages an hour. (We took a loss just to show her.)

The checker would come around with the stop watch. You learned to wrap a package of bacon using a lot of extra motions because it was a time study thing. When he wasn't there we eliminated all those motions and did it simply. This was done everywhere—sausage, wrap and tie, bacon, everywhere. (It's all done by machine now.) There is always a faster way to do something, a simpler way where you save energy and time. The older women, in terms of experience, would show the new women. It was a tremendous relationship of solidarity. But they weren't about to join the union. They weren't about to put out a buck a month in union dues.

At first the women were afraid. It took quite a bit of courage to join. They were concerned about their jobs. Many of them were sole breadwinners. Also the Catholic Church said that the CIO was red: you join the CIO and you are joining a red organization. To talk about the CIO then was like talking about socialism to some people today. Even to talk union, you talked about it in whispers. You had to trust the person and know the person very well because he could be a stool pigeon.

When I was at the University of Wisconsin, John Lewis made his speech that he was breaking away the coal miners union from the AFL and they were going to set up the CIO. We set up an organizing committee for the stockyards. There were seventeen of us that met, three women and fourteen men. One of them was an Irishman by the name of McCarthy who became the acting chairman of the Packinghouse Workers Organizing Committee. We met behind a tavern on Honore Street. The organizing of these seventeen people was on Communist Party initiative and we worked through contacts in the IWO, the International Workers Order.* In this group of seventeen there were some Poles and some Slovaks who were indigenous to the community. . . .

The National Labor Relations Act had been passed, giving workers the right to organize. But this was not easy because people were laid off. I was laid off, for instance, in the gut shanty and they tried to break my seniority. We had departmental seniority and I would be shifted all around. Besides casing and sliced bacon, I got to work in wrap and tie (hams), soap, glue, fresh sausage, pork trim, almost every department. By being shifted around I became acquainted with many more women. I kept the names and addresses of all the women because I knew that some day I would need them. When we started organizing I knew women all over the whole plant. I would call them and get information as to pro-labor union sentiment, problems and issues, and so forth. We would print it up in the CIO news—the *Swift Flashes* we called it.

The same women who had hired me at Swift's approached me and asked me if I'd like to work in personnel—they tried to buy me off. They offered me better-paying jobs. . . .

Women had an awfully tough time in the union because the men brought their prejudices there. The fellows couldn't believe that women in the union were there for the union's sake. They thought that they were there to get a guy or something else. Some thought that we were frivolous. I would be approached by men for dates and they would ask me why I was in the union, so I would tell them that I was for socialism and I thought that this was the only way of bringing it about.

Some of my brothers, who believed in equality and that women should have rights, didn't crank the mimeograph, didn't type. I did the shit work, until all hours, as did the few other women who didn't have family obligations. And then when the union came around giving out jobs with pay, the guys got them. I and the other women didn't. It was the men who got the organizing jobs. Men who worked in plants got paid for their time loss—women didn't. I never did. But we were a dedicated group. We worked in coolers and from there I would go to the union hall and get out leaflets, write material for shop papers, turn in dues, etc., get home and make supper, get back. These guys had wives to do this but there was nobody to do mine. Sometimes I'd be up until eleven, twelve, or one o'clock and then have to get up early and be punched in by quarter to seven and be working on the job by seven. . . .

---

*A fraternal insurance agency dominated by the Communist party.

The women felt the union was a man's thing because once they got through the day's work they had another job. When they got home they had to take care of their one to fifteen children and the meals and the house and all the rest, and the men went to the tavern and to the meetings and to the racetrack and so forth. The fellows were competing for positions and the women didn't feel that that was their role. They were brainwashed into thinking that this union was for men.

The union didn't encourage women to come to meetings. They didn't actually want to take up the problems that the women had. I did what I could to get the women to come to the meetings but very few came—only when there was a strike. I tried to make the meetings more interesting than just a bunch of guys talking all evening. . . .

About socialism, you didn't talk about socialism per se. You talked about issues and saw how people reacted. You talked about how one could attain these things. The only time I ever heard anyone from the union talk about socialism outside of the small meetings was the head of another CIO local, a Scotsman. After negotiations and they didn't get all they wanted, the guys were turning down the contract. He said, "Look, you bunch of bastards, you're not going to get all of this stuff, not until you have socialism." That's the way he put it to them and I thought it was great. "This is a limited contract under capitalism." I think the workers got the message. It all depends what your relationship is to the people you are talking with.

The Civilian Conservation Corps

The legislation creating the Civilian Conservation Corps (CCC) in 1933 authorized the agency to provide work for 250,000 jobless male citizens between the ages of 18 and 25, in soil erosion, reforestation, and similar projects. Enrollees were salaried at $30 per month, a portion of which was sent to dependents.

The CCC became a very popular program, but like other New Deal projects that were unfamiliar, it first had to be sold to the American people. The two photographs that follow, with their original captions, were part of an ongoing public-relations effort carried out by the agency. They are visual evidence of what the CCC was designed to achieve (beyond youth employment). Do they, for example, suggest an effort to fundamentally change the nature of American capitalism? From them, we can also take a guess or two at what ordinary Americans thought about the corps and the kinds of doubts they had about becoming a part of this social experiment.

Original Caption: "Camp Roosevelt, Edinburg, Virginia, July 22, 1940—*Miscellaneous Activities:* Enrollee Robert Daily of Pittsburgh, Pennsylvania, enjoying a pleasant Saturday evening with his girlfriend, Ruth Copp, at her home near Woodstock, Virginia. Looking to the future, they enjoy examining plans of homes in a late magazine." *National Archives.*

Original Caption: "Company commander and subaltern inspecting barracks. Waterville, Washington camp, Soil Conservation Service, June 1941." *National Archives.*

Dashiell Hammett

The Detective as Hero

While many responded to the trauma of the Great Depression politically and sought a remedy in Huey Long's Share Our Wealth movement, the Communist party's Unemployed Councils, or Franklin
Roosevelt's New Deal, others—often the same people—found a curious kind of comfort and security in a literary form that was rapidly
increasing in popularity. The period between the wars was the
golden age of the detective novel.

Dashiell Hammett's *Maltese Falcon,* excerpted below, is a classic
of the genre. Although written in the late 1920s, the story achieved
its phenomenal fame in the next decade. Warner Brothers filmed
three versions: in 1931, in 1936, and in 1941—John Huston's classic,
starring Humphrey Bogart.

Examine the selection (from the last pages of the novel) from
the perspective of Sam Spade, the protagonist and hero. What in
Spade—what values, what characteristics of behavior and personality—made him so popular a figure with American readers? What, for
example, is so special about Spade's tie to Miles Archer? What alternatives—perhaps represented by the woman in the scene—does Spade
reject? Many Americans believed that the Great Depression required
an increased reliance on government. Does the detective, as a social
type, speak to that question?

From the selection and from your general knowledge of detective fiction (the Sherlock Holmes stories of Arthur Conan Doyle,
while mostly written between 1890 and 1920, were widely read in the
interwar years), speculate on the reasons for the vogue of the detective story and the rise of the detective as a heroic type.

"You told him he was being shadowed," Spade said confidently. "Miles
hadn't many brains, but he wasn't clumsy enough to be spotted the first
night."

"I told him, yes. When we went out for a walk that night I pretended
to discover Mr. [Miles] Archer following us and pointed him out to Floyd."
She sobbed. "But please believe, Sam, that I wouldn't have done it if I had
thought Floyd would kill him. I thought he'd be frightened into leaving the
city. I didn't for a minute think he'd shoot him like that."

Spade smiled wolfishly with his lips, but not at all with his eyes. He
said: "If you thought he wouldn't you were right, angel."

The girl's upraised face held utter astonishment.

Spade said: "Thursby didn't shoot him."

Incredulity joined astonishment in the girl's face.

Spade said: "Miles hadn't many brains, but, Christ! he had too many years' experience as a detective to be caught like that by the man he was shadowing. Up a blind alley with his gun tucked away on his hip and his overcoat buttoned? Not a chance. He was as dumb as any man ought to be, but he wasn't quite that dumb. The only two ways out of the alley could be watched from the edge of Bush Street over the tunnel. You'd told us Thursby was a bad actor. He couldn't have tricked Miles into the alley like that, and he couldn't have driven him in. He was dumb, but not dumb enough for that."

He ran his tongue over the inside of his lips and smiled affectionately at the girl. He said: "But he'd've gone up there with you, angel, if he was sure nobody else was up there. You were his client, so he would have had no reason for not dropping the shadow on your say-so, and if you caught up with him and asked him to go up there he'd've gone. He was just dumb enough for that. He'd've looked you up and down and licked his lips and gone grinning from ear to ear—and then you could've stood as close to him as you liked in the dark and put a hole through him with the gun you had got from Thursby that evening." . . .

"Miles," Spade said hoarsely, "was a son of a bitch. I found that out the first week we were in business together and I meant to kick him out as soon as the year was up. You didn't do me a damned bit of harm by killing him."

"Then what?"

Spade pulled his hand out of hers. He no longer either smiled or grimaced. His wet yellow face was set hard and deeply lined. His eyes burned madly. He said: "Listen. This isn't a damned bit of good. You'll never understand me, but I'll try once more and then we'll give it up. Listen. When a man's partner is killed he's supposed to do something about it. It doesn't make any difference what you thought of him. He was your partner and you're supposed to do something about it. Then it happens we were in the detective business. Well, when one of your organization gets killed it's bad business to let the killer get away with it. It's bad all around—bad for that one organization, bad for every detective everywhere. Third, I'm a detective and expecting me to run criminals down and then let them go free is like asking a dog to catch a rabbit and let it go. It can be done, all right, and sometimes it is done, but it's not the natural thing. The only way I could have let you go was by letting Gutman and Cairo and the kid go. That's—"

"You're not serious," she said. "You don't expect me to think that these things you're saying are sufficient reason for sending me to the—"

"Wait till I'm through and then you can talk. Fourth, no matter what I wanted to do now it would be absolutely impossible for me to let you go without having myself dragged to the gallows with the others. Next, I've no reason in God's world to think I can trust you and if I did this and got away with it you'd have something on me that you could use whenever you happened to want to. That's five of them. The sixth would be that, since I've also got something on you, I couldn't be sure you wouldn't decide to shoot a hole in *me* some day. Seventh, I don't even like the idea of thinking that there might be one chance in a hundred that you'd played me for a sucker. And eighth—but that's enough. All those on one side. Maybe some of them are unimportant. I won't argue about that. But look at the number of them. Now on the other side we've got what? All we've got is the fact that maybe you love me and maybe I love you." . . .

"And you didn't know then that Gutman was here hunting for you. You didn't suspect that or you wouldn't have shaken your gunman. You knew Gutman was here as soon as you heard Thursby had been shot. Then you knew you needed another protector, so you came back to me. Right?"

"Yes, but—oh, sweetheart!—it wasn't only that. I would have come back to you sooner or later. From the first instant I saw you I knew—"

Spade said tenderly: "You angel! Well, if you get a good break you'll be out of San Quentin in twenty years and you can come back to me then."

She took her cheek away from his, drawing her head far back to stare without comprehension at him.

He was pale. He said tenderly: "I hope to Christ they don't hang you, precious, by that sweet neck." He slid his hands up to caress her throat.

In an instant she was out of his arms, back against the table, crouching, both hands spread over her throat. Her face was wild-eyed, haggard. Her dry mouth opened and closed. She said in a small parched voice: "You're not—" She could get no other words out.

Spade's face was yellow-white now. His mouth smiled and there were smile-wrinkles around his glittering eyes. His voice was soft, gentle. He said: "I'm going to send you over. The chances are you'll get off with life. That means you'll be out again in twenty years. You're an angel. I'll wait for you." He cleared his throat. "If they hang you I'll always remember you." . . .

She took a long trembling breath. "You've been playing with me? Only pretending you cared—to trap me like this? You didn't—care at all? You didn't—don't—l-love me?"

"I think I do," Spade said. "What of it?" The muscles holding his smile in place stood out like wales. "I'm not Thursby. I'm not Jacobi. I won't play the sap for you." . . .

Caste and Class

One of the paradoxes of the Great Depression was the persistence with which Americans—many of them, at least—continued to be fascinated by the doings of the rich and the sophisticated. Part of Franklin Roosevelt's appeal may have been his "aristocratic" back-

Original Caption: "New York City, December 7, 1931—The long-heralded contract bridge pair match between Sidney S. Lenz and Ely Culbertson got under way this evening in the Culbertsons' suite at the Hotel Chatham. The match is intended to test the relative merits of the approach-forcing bidding system favored by Mr. Culbertson and the 1–2–5 system sponsored by Mr. Lenz. Both rivals have agreed to play 150 rubbers. . . ." *National Archives.*

ground and manners. The photograph above is a rather remarkable scene, shot in 1931, which suggests something of the level of public attention that could still be focused on a game like bridge, played in formal dress in an elegant hotel suite in New York. (The fascination may have been the source of irritation, too, the kind of irritation that might have been tapped by a Huey Long.) What similarities does the game of bridge have to the "game" played by detectives? Might Americans have been attracted to these bridge "experts" for the same reason they were drawn to Sam Spade?

A Scene from *Modern Times* **(1936).** *National Archives.*

Above is a scene from one of Charlie Chaplin's most famous films, *Modern Times*, released in 1936. In it, he played a workingman caught in the factory system, suggested by the fantastic machinery in the background. What game is Chaplin imitating in the scene, and what is the effect of his pose? Can you draw any connection between this photograph and the one showing the bridge match at the Hotel Chatham? Had something changed in the five years since 1931? What attitudes toward work and wealth are suggested by Chaplin's manner and dress?

The Movies

Walker Evans of the Farm Security Administration took the 1936 photograph of billboards and frame houses in Atlanta, Georgia, that appears below. What do you think was Evans's purpose in making this photograph? What did he want to convey to the viewer? On another level, what might the subject of the center billboard, and Carole Lombard's black eye, tell us about how average people survived the Great Depression?

Billboards and Frame Houses, Atlanta, Georgia, March 1936. Photograph by Walker Evans for the Farm Security Administration. *Library of Congress.*

Enter the dreamhouse, brothers and sisters, leaving
Your debts asleep, your history at the door:
This is the time for heroes, and this loving
Darkness a fur you can afford.

From C. Day Lewis, "Newsreel," in *Short Is the Time: Poems 1936–43* (1938). Reprinted by permission of A. D. Peters & Co. Ltd.

9

From a New Deal to a New World War

As the shadows lengthened on the decade of the 1930s and on Franklin Roosevelt's second term, those who had expected the president's New Deal to alter profoundly the conditions of economic and social life must have wondered whether anything of the kind had taken place. Maldistribution of income—so critical in restricting purchasing power and bringing on the crash of 1929—had not been significantly remedied. The "soak-the-rich" Revenue Act of 1935, presumably a response to the challenge of Huey Long and other self-proclaimed economic reformers, did very little to redistribute wealth. Of more obvious benefit was the Fair Labor Standards Act of 1938, the major piece of social legislation in the second, or post-1935, New Deal. The act placed a floor under wages and a ceiling on hours, and it prohibited interstate shipment of goods made under "oppressive" conditions of child labor. Unfortunately, the wage and hour provisions of the act left millions of workers uncovered; the minimum wage (40 cents per hour after seven years) failed to provide a reasonable standard of living; and the child-labor sections, like old-age security, had been enacted in part to prevent the participation of a group of workers in a crowded labor market.

The doubts that many felt about the senile New Deal would have seemed of less consequence had Roosevelt succeeded in reviving the economy. In fact, the opposite happened. Roosevelt's own failure to pursue vigorous deficit spending had in 1937 nipped a feeble recovery in the bud and produced levels of unemployment not seen since 1933. In one year, unemployment increased from 14.3 percent to 19 percent of the labor force. It was war, and the planning for it, that finally brought full employment.

The recession of 1937 also brought a decline in patriotism; in a country whose self-image was bound up with its economic performance, national pride and economic growth were closely linked. The idea of going to war, even against a state as nastily aggressive as Nazi Germany, evoked an ambivalent response. Ninety percent of the population wanted the country to stay out of war; but more than 80 percent wanted the Allies to win it. Certain actions and activities were designed to allow the nation to remain aloof from European concerns. In 1934, the Nye Committee of the Congress sought to ensure that economic ties to foreign nations would not, as in 1917, force abandonment of neutrality. In 1940, France was invaded, defeated, and occupied. Yet Roosevelt did not ask for a declaration of war, and Charles Lindbergh emerged as leader of a powerful isolationist group called the America First Committee.

On the other side of the ledger were actions that seemed certain to lead to war. Most of these were taken in the Pacific, where Americans were more likely to see their vital interests at stake. First, Roosevelt encouraged a boycott of Japanese goods with a speech suggesting that the peace could be preserved only through a "quarantine" of aggressors. Then, in September 1940, the president embargoed scrap iron and steel sales to Japan, a move protested as "unfriendly." At home, as Hitler launched the battle of France, a presidential request to Congress for 50,000 planes brought thunderous approval. In an atmosphere beginning to resemble the Hundred Days of 1933, a nation eager to resolve its contradictions and doubts and to end a decade of depression submerged its differences and passed a peacetime Selective Service Act.

The Japanese attack on Pearl Harbor in December 1941 brought a flush of patriotism that temporarily buried any remaining doubts. Popular economics writer Stuart Chase argued that the two decades since the last war had found Americans living in a fairyland of advertising and consumer goods. "Our job in 1942," he emphasized, "is not to out-talk the enemy. Our job is to outshoot him. We are up against two-ton bombs, fifty-ton tanks and sixteen-inch shells. There is no publicity man in heaven, earth or hell who can tell us how to sell our way through them. We are being drawn back relentlessly to our foundations." A Virginia politician announced that "we needed a Pearl Harbor—a Golgotha—to arouse us from our self-sufficient complacency, to make us rise above greed and hate." Vice President Henry Wallace was one of many who revived Wilsonian idealism. "This is a fight," he wrote in 1943, "between a slave world and a free world. Just as the United States in 1862 could not remain half slave and half free, so in 1942 the world must make its decision for a complete victory one way or the other."

In many ways, the war justified idealism, for it accomplished what the New Deal had not. Organized labor prospered. The name "Rosie the Riveter" described the new American woman who found war-related opportunities in the factories and shipyards. Black people—segregated by New Deal housing programs, injured as tenant farmers by New Deal farm policies, and never singled out as a group worthy of special aid—found skilled jobs in the wartime economy. They also received presidential assistance—in the form of the Fair Employment Practices Committee—in their struggle to end racially discriminatory hiring practices. A growing military budget in 1941 produced the nation's first genuinely progressive income tax legislation. The ever-present threat of a postwar depression allowed liberals to dream, at least, of legislation that would commit the national government to regular support of a full-employment economy. Many, such as Rexford Tugwell, an economist who served on Roosevelt's brain trust, found in the wartime requirements of efficiency and unity an opportunity to turn from the tyranny of competition to a planned economy.

Yet liberals remained uneasy about the war and its impact on reform. By mid-1943, the conflict had brought an end to the Civilian Conservation Corps, the Justice Department's antitrust program, the Works Projects Administration, and the Home Owners' Loan Corporation. Literary critic Malcolm Cowley suggested another and more serious problem: that the bureaucracy created to implement the New Deal could be easily turned to other uses. "A fascist state," he wrote, "could be instituted here without many changes in government personnel, and some of these changes have been made already." Others wondered whether a viable democracy could be maintained under conditions of conflict—especially physical conflict with totalitarian states. Must a democracy take on the characteristics of fascism in order to possess its strengths and efficiencies? The problem was not unique to wartime. The nation had faced it in 1939, when Roosevelt sought congressional authorization for a major reorganization of the executive branch. Many thought the legislation would make Roosevelt a "dictator." As a result of such fears, the decade after 1935 found Americans engaged in a delicate balancing act, trying, on the one hand, to preserve the essence of democratic decision making and, on the other, to ensure that democratic methods would not interfere with the struggle at hand. Whether this balancing act was a success or a failure is the subject of most of the selections in this chapter.

Interpretive Essay

Roger Daniels

Concentration Camps, U.S.A.: Japanese Americans and World War II

The beginning of the war in the Pacific in 1941 confronted millions of Americans—many of them born in Japan or the children of Japanese immigrants—with a curious and tragic problem. What was to be the fate of the Japanese Americans who lived on the Pacific Coast? And if the Japanese-born, the Issei, were to suffer, would the native-born generation, the Nisei, have the equal protection of the laws guaranteed them by the Constitution and the Fourteenth Amendment? In the following essay, historian Roger Daniels sketches in the background to the decision that was finally made: to "intern" the Japanese, citizen and noncitizen alike, for the "duration" in concentration camps. The episode is one of the most shameful in the history of the United States. As you read Daniels's essay, however, you should try to understand the complex of attitudes, the mixture of Rooseveltian liberalism and simple racism, and the complications of bureaucratic machinery that led to the outcome. In short, it may be instructive to examine this episode as the beginnings of another New Deal "program," unique in its pathos, but still in some ways revealing.

If the attack on Pearl Harbor came as a devastating shock to most Americans, for those of Japanese ancestry it was like a nightmare come true. Throughout the 1930s the Nisei generation dreaded the possibility of a war between the United States and Japan; although some in both the Japanese and American communities fostered the illusion that the emerging Nisei generation could help bridge the gap between the rival Pacific powers, most Nisei, at least, understood that this was a chimera. As early as 1937 Nisei gloom about the future predominated. One Nisei spoke prophetically about what might happen to Japanese Americans in a Pacific war. Rhetorically he asked his fellow Nisei students at the University of California:

From Roger Daniels, *Concentration Camps, North America* (Malabar, Fla., 1971), pp. 26–29, 31–41, 95–96, 104–105, 157. Copyright © 1971 Roger Daniels.

. . . what are we going to do if war does break out between United States and Japan? . . . In common language we can say "we're sunk." Even if the Nisei wanted to fight for America, what chances? Not a chance! . . . our properties would be confiscated and most likely [we would be] herded into prison camps—perhaps we would be slaughtered on the spot.

As tensions increased, so did Nisei anxieties; and in their anxiety some Nisei tried to accentuate their loyalty and Americanism by disparaging the generation of their fathers. Newspaper editor Togo Tanaka, for example, speaking to a college group in early 1941, insisted that the Nisei must face what he called "the question of loyalty" and assumed that since the Issei were "more or less tumbleweeds with one foot in America and one foot in Japan," real loyalty to America could be found only in his own generation. A Los Angeles Nisei jeweler expressed similar doubts later the same year. After explaining to a Los Angeles *Times* columnist that many if not most of the older generation were pro-Japanese rather than pro-American, he expressed his own generation's fears. "We talk of almost nothing but this great crisis. We don't know what's going to happen. Sometimes we only look for a concentration camp."

While the attention of Japanese Americans was focused on the Pacific, most other Americans gave primary consideration to Europe, where in September 1939 World War II had broken out. Hitler's amazing blitzkrieg against the west in the spring of 1940—which overran, in quick succession, Denmark and Norway and then Holland, Belgium, Luxembourg, and France—caused the United States to accelerate its defense program and institute the first peacetime draft in its history. Stories, now known to be wildly exaggerated, told of so-called fifth column and espionage activities, created much concern about the loyalty of aliens, particularly German-born aliens, some 40,000 of whom were organized into the overtly pro-Nazi German-American Bund. As a component part of the defense program, Congress passed, in 1940, an Alien Registration Act, which required the registration and fingerprinting of all aliens over fourteen years of age. In addition, as we now know, the Department of Justice, working through the Federal Bureau of Investigation, was compiling a relatively modest list of dangerous or subversive aliens—Germans, Italians, and Japanese—who were to be arrested or interned at the outbreak of war with their country. The commendable restraint of the Department of Justice's plans was due, first of all, to the liberal nature of the New Deal. The Attorney General, Francis Biddle, was clearly a civil libertarian, as befitted a former law clerk of Oliver Wendell Holmes, Jr.

Elsewhere in the government, however, misgivings about possible fifth column and sabotage activity, particularly by Japanese, were strongly felt. For example, one congressman, John D. Dingell (D-Mich.), wrote the President to suggest that Japanese in the United States and Hawaii be used as hostages to ensure good behavior by Japan. In August 1941, shortly after Japanese assets in the United States were frozen and the Japanese made it difficult for some one hundred Americans to leave Japan, Dingell suggested that as a reprisal the United States should "cause the forceful detention or imprisonment in a concentration camp of ten thousand alien Japanese in Hawaii. . . . It would be well to remind Japan," he continued, "that there are perhaps one hundred fifty thousand additional alien Japanese in the United States who [can] be held in a reprisal reserve."

And, in the White House itself, concern was evidenced. Franklin Roosevelt, highly distrustful of official reports and always anxious to have independent checks on the bureaucracy, set up an independent "intelligence" operation, run by John Franklin Carter. Carter, who as the "Unofficial Observer" and "Jay Franklin" had written some of the most brilliant New Deal journalism and would later serve as an adviser to President Harry S Truman and Governor Thomas E. Dewey, used newspapermen and personal friends to make special reports. In early November he received a report on the West Coast Japanese from Curtis B. Munson. His report stressed the loyalty of the overwhelming majority, and he understood that even most of the disloyal Japanese Americans hoped that "by remaining quiet they [could] avoid concentration camps or irresponsible mobs." Munson was, however, "horrified" to observe that

> dams, bridges, harbors, power stations, etc., are wholly unguarded. The harbor of San Pedro [Los Angeles's port] could be razed by fire completely by four men with hand grenades and a little study in one night. Dams could be blown and half of lower California could actually die of thirst. . . . One railway bridge at the exit from the mountains in some cases could tie up three or four main railroads.

Munson felt that despite the loyalty or quiescence of the majority, this situation represented a real threat because "there are still Japanese in the United States who will tie dynamite around their waist and make a human bomb out of themselves." This imaginary threat apparently worried the President too, for he immediately sent the memo to Secretary of War Henry L. Stimson, specifically calling his attention to Munson's warnings about sabotage. In early December, Army Intelligence drafted a reply (which in the confusion following Pearl Harbor was never sent) arguing, quite correctly as it turned out, that "widespread sabotage by Japanese is not expected . . . identification of dangerous Japanese on the West Coast is reasonably complete." Although neither of these nor other similar proposals and warnings was acted upon before the attack on Pearl Harbor, the mere fact that they were suggested and received consideration in the very highest governmental circles indicates the degree to which Americans were willing to believe almost anything about the Japanese. This belief, in turn, can be understood only if one takes into account the half century of agitation and prophecy about the coming American-Japanese war and the dangers of the United States being overwhelmed by waves of yellow soldiers aided by alien enemies within the gates. . . .

It seems clear that well before the actual coming of war a considerable proportion of the American public had been conditioned not only to the probability of a Pacific war with Japan—that was, after all, a geopolitical fact of twentieth-century civilization—but also to the proposition that this war would involve an invasion of the continental United States in which Japanese residents and secret agents would provide the spearhead of the attack. After war came at Pearl Harbor and for years thereafter many Japanophobes insisted that, to use [H. G.] Wells's phrase, "the Yellow Peril was a peril after all," but this is to misunderstand completely Japan's intentions and capabilities during the Great Pacific War. The Japanese military planners never contemplated an invasion of the continental United States, and, even had they done so, the logistical problems were obviously beyond Japan's capacity as a nation. But, often in history, what men believe to be true is more important than the truth itself because the mistaken belief becomes a basis for action. These two factors—the long racist and anti-Oriental tradition plus the widely believed "yellow peril" fantasy—when triggered by the traumatic mechanism provided by the attack on Pearl Harbor, were the necessary preconditions for America's concentration camps. But beliefs, even widely held beliefs, are not always translated into action. We must now discover how this particular set of beliefs—the inherent and genetic disloyalty of individual Japanese plus the threat of an imminent Japanese invasion—produced public policy and action, the mass removal and incarceration of the West Coast Japanese Americans.

As is well known, despite decades of propaganda and apprehension about a Pacific war, the reality, the dawn attack at Pearl Harbor on Sunday, December 7, 1941, came as a stunning surprise to most Americans. Throughout the nation the typical reaction was disbelief, followed by a determination to close ranks and avenge a disastrous defeat. Faced with the fact of attack, the American people entered the war with perhaps more unity than has existed before or since. But if a calm determination to get on with the job typified the national mood, the mood of the Pacific Coast was nervous and trigger-happy, if not hysterical. . . .

Day after day, throughout December, January, February, and March, almost the entire Pacific Coast press . . . spewed forth racial venom against all Japanese. The term Jap, of course, was standard usage. Japanese, alien and native-born, were also "Nips," "yellow men," "Mad dogs," and "yellow vermin," to name only a few of the choicer epithets. *Times* columnist Ed Ainsworth cautioned his readers "to be careful to differentiate between races. The Chinese and Koreans both hate the Japs more than we do. . . . Be sure of nationality before you are rude to anybody." (*Life* Magazine soon rang some changes on this theme for a national audience with an article—illustrated by comic strip artist Milton Caniff, creator of *Terry and the Pirates* and, later, *Steve Canyon*—which purported to explain how to tell "Japs" from other Asian nationalities.) The sports pages, too, furnished their share of abuse. Just after a series of murderous and sometimes fatal attacks on Japanese residents by Filipinos, one sports page feature was headlined FILIPINO BOXERS NOTED FOR COURAGE, VALOR.

Newspaper columnists, as always, were quick to suggest what public policy should be. Lee Shippey, a Los Angeles writer who often stressed that *some* Japanese were all right, prophetically suggested a solution to California's Japanese problem. He proposed the establishment of "a number of big, closely guarded, closely watched truck farms on which Japanese-Americans could earn a living and assure us a steady supply of vegetables." If a Nazi had suggested doing this with Poles, Shippey, a liberal, undoubtedly would have called it a slave labor camp. But the palm for *shrecklichkeit* must go to Westbrook Pegler, a major outlet of what Oswald Garrison Villard once called "the sewer system of American journalism." Taking time off from his vendettas with Eleanor Roosevelt and the American labor movement, Pegler proposed, on December 9, that every time the Axis murdered hostages, the United States should retaliate by raising them "100 victims selected out of [our] concentration camps," which Pegler assumed would be set up for subversive Germans and Italians and "alien Japanese."

Examples of newspaper incitement to racial violence appeared daily (some radio commentators were even worse). In addition, during the period that the Japanese Americans were still at large, the press literally abounded with stories, and, above all, headlines, which made the already nervous general public believe that military or paramilitary Japanese activists were all around them. None of these stories had any basis in fact; amazingly, there was not one demonstrable incident of sabotage committed by a Japanese American, alien or native-born, during the entire war. Here are a few representative headlines.

JAP BOAT FLASHES MESSAGE ASHORE

ENEMY PLANES SIGHTED OVER CALIFORNIA COAST

TWO JAPANESE WITH MAPS AND ALIEN LITERATURE SEIZED

JAP AND CAMERA HELD IN BAY CITY

VEGETABLES FOUND FREE OF POISON

CAPS ON JAPANESE TOMATO PLANTS POINT TO AIR BASE

JAPANESE HERE SENT VITAL DATA TO TOKYO

CHINESE ABLE TO SPOT JAP

MAP REVEALS JAP MENACE

NETWORK OF ALIEN FARMS COVERS STRATEGIC DEFENSE AREAS OVER SOUTHLAND

JAPS PLAN COAST ATTACK IN APRIL WARNS CHIEF OF KOREAN SPY BAND

In short, any reading of the wartime Pacific Coast press—or for that matter viewing the wartime movies that still pollute our television channels—shows clearly that, although a distinction was continually being made between "good" and "bad" Germans (a welcome change from World War I), few distinctions were ever made between Japanese. . . .

The Department of Justice, working through the FBI and calling on local law enforcement officials for assistance and detention, began roundups of what it considered "dangerous" enemy aliens. Throughout the nation this initial roundup involved about 3000 persons, half of whom were Japanese. (All but a handful of these lived on the Pacific Coast.) In other words the federal officials responsible for counterespionage thought that some 1500 persons of Japanese ancestry, slightly more than 1 percent of the nation's Japanese population, constituted some kind of threat to the nation. Those arrested, often in the dead of night, were almost universally of the immigrant, or Issei, generation, and thus, no matter how long they had lived here, "enemy aliens" in law. (It must be kept in mind that American law prohibited the naturalization of Asians.) Those arrested were community leaders, since the government, acting as it so often does on the theory of guilt by association, automatically hauled in the officers and leading lights of a number of Japanese organizations and religious groups. Many of these people were surely "rooting" for the Emperor rather than the President and thus technically subversive, but most of them were rather elderly and inoffensive gentlemen and not a threat to anything. This limited internment, however, was a not too discreditable performance for a government security agency, but it must be noted that even at this restrained level the government acted much more harshly, in terms of numbers interned, toward Japanese nationals than toward German nationals (most known members of the German-American Bund were left at liberty), and more harshly toward Germans than to Italians. It should also be noted, however, that more than a few young Nisei leaders applauded this early roundup and contrasted their own loyalty to the presumed disloyalty of many of the leaders of the older generation.

In addition to the selective roundup of enemy aliens, the Justice Department almost immediately announced the sealing off of the Mexican and Canadian borders to "all persons of Japanese ancestry, whether citizen or alien." Thus, by December 8, that branch of the federal government particularly charged with protecting the rights of citizens was willing to single out one ethnic group for invidious treatment. Other national civilian officials discriminated in other ways. Fiorello La Guardia, an outstanding liberal who was for a time director of the Office of Civilian Defense as well as mayor of New York, pointedly omitted mention of the Japanese in two public statements calling for decent treatment for enemy aliens and suggesting that alien Germans and Italians be presumed loyal until proved otherwise. By implication, at least, Japanese were to be presumed disloyal. Seventeen years earlier La Guardia had been one of three congressmen who dared to speak in favor of continuing Japanese immigration, but in December 1941 he could find nothing good to say about any Japanese.

Even more damaging were the mendacious statements of Frank Knox, Roosevelt's Republican Secretary of the Navy. On December 15 Secretary

Knox held a press conference in Los Angeles on his return from a quick inspection of the damage at Pearl Harbor. As this was the first detailed report of the damage there, his remarks were front-page news all across the nation. Knox spoke of "treachery" in Hawaii and insisted that much of the disaster was caused by "the most effective fifth column work that's come out of this war, except in Norway." The disaster at Pearl Harbor, as is now generally acknowledged, was caused largely by the unpreparedness and incompetence of the local military commanders, as Knox already knew. (The orders for the relief of Admiral Kimmel were already being drawn up.) But the secretary, who, as we shall see, harbored deep-felt anti-Japanese prejudices, probably did not want the people to lose faith in their Navy, so the Japanese population of Hawaii—and indirectly all Japanese Americans—was made the scapegoat on which to hang the big lie. (Knox, it should be remarked, as a Chicago newspaper publisher in civilian life, had a professional understanding of these matters.)

But the truly crucial role was played by the other service, the United States Army. The key individual, initially, at least, was John L. De Witt, in 1941 a lieutenant general and commander of the Western Defense Command and the 4th Army, both headquartered at San Francisco's Presidio. Despite these warlike titles, De Witt, who was sixty-one years old and would be retired before the war's end, was essentially an administrator in uniform, a staff officer who had specialized in supply and had practically nothing to do with combat during his whole Army career. Even before Pearl Harbor, De Witt had shown himself to be prejudiced against Japanese Americans. In March 1941, for example, he found it necessary to complain to Major General William G. Bryden, the Army's Deputy Chief of Staff, that "a couple of Japs" who had been drafted into the Army were "going around taking pictures." He and Bryden agreed to "just have it happen naturally that Japs are sent to Infantry units," rather than to sensitive headquarters or coast defense installations. De Witt's prejudices, in fact, extended all along the color line. When he discovered that some of the troops being sent to him as reinforcements after Pearl Harbor were Negro, he protested to the Army's chief of classification and assignment that

> you're filling too many colored troops up on the West Coast. . . . there will be a great deal of public reaction out here due to the Jap situation. They feel they've got enough black skinned people around them as it is. Filipinos and Japanese. . . . I'd rather have a white regiment. . . .

Serving under De Witt, in December 1941, as the corps commander in charge of the defense of Southern California, was a real fighting man, the then Major General Joseph W. Stilwell, the famed "Vinegar Joe" of the heartbreaking Burma campaigns. His diary of those days, kept in pencil in a shirt-pocket notebook, gives an accurate and pungent picture of the hysteria and indecisiveness that prevailed at De Witt's headquarters and on the Coast generally.

Dec. 8

Sunday night "air raid" at San Francisco . . . Fourth Army kind of jittery.

Dec. 9

. . . Fleet of thirty-four [Japanese] ships between San Francisco and Los Angeles. Later—not authentic.

Dec. 11

[Phone call from 4th Army] "The main Japanese fleet is 164 miles off San Francisco." I believed it, like a damn fool . . .

Of course [4th Army] passed the buck on this report. They had it from a "usually reliable source," but they should never have put it out without check.

Dec. 13

Not content with the above blah, [4th] Army pulled another at ten-thirty today. "Reliable information that attack on Los Angeles is imminent. A general alarm being considered. . . ." What jackass would send a general alarm [which would have meant warning all civilians to leave the area, including the workers in the vital southern California aircraft industry] under the circumstances. The [4th] Army G-2 [Intelligence] is just another amateur, like all the rest of the staff. Rule: the higher the headquarters, the more important is *calm*.

Stilwell's low opinion of General De Witt was apparently shared by others within the Army; shortly after Vinegar Joe's transfer to Washington just before Christmas, he noted that Lieutenant General Lesley J. McNair, Deputy Commander, Army Ground Force, had told him that "De Witt has gone crazy and requires ten refusals before he realizes it is 'No.'" . . .

It was in this panic-ridden, amateurish Western Defense Command atmosphere that some of the most crucial decisions about the evacuation of the Japanese Americans were made. Before examining them, however, it should be made clear that the nearest Japanese aircraft during most of December were attacking Wake Island, more than 5000 miles west of San Francisco, and any major Japanese surface vessels or troops were even farther away. In fact, elements of the Luftwaffe over the North Atlantic were actually closer to California than any Japanese planes. California and the West Coast of the continental United States were in no way seriously threatened by the Japanese military. This finding does not represent just the hindsight of the military historian; the high command of the American army realized it at the time. Official estimates of Japanese capabilities made late in December concluded correctly that a large-scale invasion was beyond the capacity of the Japanese military but that a hit-and-run raid somewhere along the West Coast was possible. . . .

The first proposal by the Army for any kind of mass evacuation of Japanese Americans was brought forward at a De Witt staff conference in San Francisco on the evening of December 10. In the language of a staff memo, the meeting considered "certain questions relative to the problem of apprehension, segregation and detention of Japanese in the San Francisco Bay Area." The initial cause of the meeting seems to have been a report from an unidentified Treasury Department official asserting that 20,000 Japanese in the Bay Area were ready for organized action. Apparently plans for a mass roundup were drawn up locally, and approved by General Benedict, the commander of the area, but the whole thing was squelched by Nat Pieper, head of the San Francisco office of the FBI, who laughed it off as "the wild imaginings" of a former FBI man whom he had fired. The imaginings were pretty wild; the figure of 20,000 slightly exceeded the total number of Japanese men, women, and children in the Bay Area. But wild or not, De Witt's subordinate reported the matter to Washington with the recommendation that "plans be made for large-scale internment." Then on December 19 General De Witt officially recommended "that action be initiated at the earliest practicable date to collect all alien subjects fourteen years of age and over, of enemy nations and remove them" to the interior of the United States and hold them "under restraint after removal" to prevent their surreptitious return. (The age limit was apparently derived from the federal statutes on wartime internment, but those statutes, it should be noted, specified males only.)

De Witt was soon in touch with the Army's Provost Marshal General, Allen W. Gullion, who would prove to be a key figure in the decision to relocate the Japanese Americans. Gullion, the Army's top cop, had previously served as Judge Advocate General, the highest legal office within the Army. He was a service intellectual who had once read a paper to an International Congress of Judicial Experts on the "present state of international law regarding the protection of civilians from the new war technics." But, since at least mid-1940, he had been concerned with the problem of legally exercising military control over civilians in wartime. Shortly after the fall of France, Army Intelligence took the position that fifth column activities had been so successful in the European war in creating an internal as well as an external military front that the military "will actually have to control, through their Provost Marshal Generals, local forces, largely police" and that "the Military would certainly have to provide for the arrest and temporary holding of a large number of suspects," alien and citizen.

Gullion, as Judge Advocate General, gave his official opinion that within the United States, outside any zone of actual combat and where the civil courts were functioning, the "Military . . . does not have any jurisdiction to participate in the arrest and temporary holding of civilians who are citizens of the United States." He did indicate, however, that if federal troops were in actual control (he had martial law in mind), jurisdiction over citizen civilians might be exercised. Although martial law was never declared on the Pacific Coast, Chief of Staff George C. Marshall did declare the region a "Theater of Operations" on December 11. This declaration, which was not made with the Japanese Americans in mind, created the legal fiction that the Coast was a war zone and would provide first the Army and then the courts with an excuse for placing entirely blameless civilian citizens under military control.

By December 22 Provost Marshal General Gullion, like any good bureaucrat, began a campaign to enlarge the scope of his own activities, an activity usually known as empire building. He formally requested the Secretary of War to press for the transfer of responsibility for conduct of the enemy alien program from the Department of Justice to the War Department. This recommendation found no positive response in Stimson's office, and four days later Gullion was on the telephone trying to get General De Witt to recommend a mass roundup of all Japanese, alien and citizen. Gullion told the Western Defense commander that he had just been visited by a representative of the Los Angeles Chamber of Commerce urging that all Japanese in the Los Angeles area be incarcerated. De Witt, who would blow hot and cold, was, on December 26, opposed. He told Gullion that

> I'm very doubtful that it would be common sense procedure to try and intern 117,000 Japanese in this theater. . . . An American citizen, after all, is an American citizen. And while they all may not be loyal, I think we can weed the disloyal out of the loyal and lock them up if necessary.

De Witt was also opposed, on December 26, to military, as opposed to civilian, control over enemy aliens. "It would be better," he told Gullion, if "this thing worked through the civil channels."

While these discussions and speculations were going on all about them, the West Coast Japanese in general and the citizen Nisei in particular were desperately trying to establish their loyalty. Many Japanese communities on the Coast were so demoralized by the coming of war that little collective action was taken, especially in the first weeks after Pearl Harbor. But in Los Angeles, the major mainland center of Japanese population, frantic and often pitiful activity took place. Most of this activity revolved around the Japanese American Citizens League, an organization, by definition, closed to Issei, except for the handful who achieved citizenship because of their service in the United States armed forces during World War I. Immediately following Pearl Harbor the Japanese American Citizens League (JACL) wired the President, affirming their loyalty; the White House had the State Department, the arm of government usually used to communicate with foreigners, coolly respond by letter that "your desire to cooperate has been carefully noted." On December 9 the JACL Anti-Axis Committee decided to take no contribution, in either time or money, from noncitizens, and later, when special travel regulations inhibited the movement of aliens, it decided not to help Issei "in securing travel permits or [giving] information in that regard." In addition, Nisei leaders repeatedly called on one generation to inform on the other.

On the very evening of Pearl Harbor, editor Togo Tanaka went on station KHTR, Los Angeles, and told his fellow Nisei:

> As Americans we now function as counterespionage. Any act or word prejudicial to the United States committed by any Japanese must be warned and reported to the F.B.I., Naval Intelligence, Sheriff's Office, and local police. . . .

Before the end of the week the Los Angeles Nisei had set up a formal Committee on Intelligence and had regular liaison established with the FBI. These patriotic activities never uncovered any real sabotage or espionage, because there was none to uncover. Nor did it provide the protective coloration that the Nisei had hoped it would; race, not loyalty or citizenship, was the criterion for evacuation. It did, however, widen the gap between the generations, and would be a major cause of bitterness and violence after the evacuation took place.

Eight months after Pearl Harbor, on August 7, 1942, all the West Coast Japanese Americans had been rounded up, one way or another, and were either in Wartime Civil Control Administration (WCCA) Assembly Centers or War Relocation Authority (WRA) camps. By November 3 the transfer to WRA was complete; altogether 119,803 men, women, and children were confined behind barbed wire. Almost six thousand new American citizens would be born in the concentration camps and some eleven hundred were sent in from the Hawaiian Islands. The rest—112,704 people—were West Coast Japanese. Of these, almost two-thirds—64.9 percent—were American-born, most of them under 21 and 77.4 percent under 25. Their foreign-born parents presented a quite different demographic profile. More than half of them—57.2 percent—were over 50. The camps, then, were primarily places of confinement for the young and the old, and since young adults of the second generation were, in the main, the first to be released, the unnatural age distribution within these artificial communities became more and more disparate as time went by. . . .

After the [Salt Lake City] conference [in April 1942] WRA policy was clear: the relocation camps would be semipermanent establishments, sur-rounded with barbed wire and guarded by small detachments of military police. Rather than the large guard force envisioned by Gullion, the military manpower involved would be minimal. At Heart Mountain, Wyoming, for example, the guard contingent for about 10,000 evacuees numbered only 3 officers and 124 enlisted men. Two of the ten eventual concentration camps—Manzanar and Poston—had been selected and construction begun under WCCA—that is, essentially military—auspices. The other eight were selected by the WRA between April and June. All ten sites can only be called godfor-saken. They were in places where nobody had lived before and no one has lived since. The Army insisted that all camps be "at a safe distance" from strategic installations, and the WRA decided that, for a number of reasons, th: sites should be on federal property. Three of the eight WRA-selected sites—Tule Lake, California; Minidoka, Idaho; and Heart Mountain, Wyo-ming—were located on undeveloped federal reclamation projects. Gila River, Arizona, like Poston, was on an Indian reservation. Granada (Amache), in southeastern Colorado, was purchased by the Army for the WRA, and Topaz, the central Utah camp, involved some public domain, some tracts that had reverted to local authority for nonpayment of taxes, and several parcels pur-chased from private individuals. The two Arkansas centers, Jerome and Roh-wer, were on lands originally purchased by Rex Tugwell's Farm Security Administration as future subsistence homesteads for low-income southern families. That land originally intended to fulfill the promise of American life for some of its most disadvantaged citizens should, under the stress of war, be used as a place of confinement for other Americans is just one of the smaller ironies of the whole program. . . .

Life in these places was not generally brutal; there were no torture chambers, firing squads, or gas ovens waiting for the evacuated people. The American concentration camps should not be compared, in that sense, to Auschwitz or Vorkuta. They were, in fact, much more like a century-old American institution, the Indian reservation, than like the institutions that flourished in totalitarian Europe. They were, however, places of confinement ringed with barbed wire and armed sentries. Despite WRA propaganda about community control, there was an unbridgeable gap between the Caucasian custodians and their Oriental charges; even the mess halls were segregated by race. Although some of the staff, particularly those in the upper echelons of the WRA, disapproved of the racist policy that brought the camps into being, the majority of the camp personnel, recruited from the local labor force, shared the contempt of the general population for "Japs." . . .

By mid-1944, whatever remote possibilities there had been of a Japanese attack on the West Coast were past. Yet the restrictions remained in force until almost the end of the year. Roosevelt was reelected in November, and by December the Court was ready to hand down *Korematsu,* and more important, *Endo.* After the cases had been argued but before decisions were announced, the easing of exclusion from the West Coast was in the works. I have discovered no evidence that the War Department or the White House knew in advance what the Court would do but, as O. W. Holmes, Jr., used to say, "there is such a thing as presumptive evidence."

Five days before *Endo* made continued confinement for "loyal" citizens unconstitutional, War Secretary Stimson sent a secret message to the White House in which he admitted that "mass exclusion from the West Coast of persons of Japanese ancestry is no longer a matter of military necessity." There had been no military developments that month; if exclusion was unnecessary in mid-December 1944, it had been unnecessary for some time. He did claim that "face saving" raids from Japan were still possible. Then came the real reason:

> The matter is now the subject of litigation in the Federal Courts and in view of the fact that military necessity no longer requires the continuation of mass exclusion it seems unlikely that it can be continued in effect for any considerable period.

The War Secretary speculated that there might be some trouble from whites, but was confident that

> the common sense and good citizenship of the people of the Coast is such that the inauguration of this program will not be marred by serious incidents or disorders.

Just four days after Stimson's secret memorandum and only one day before the Court handed down *Endo,* Major General Henry C. Pratt, who had just taken over Western Defense Command from General Emmons, publicly announced that total exclusion from the West Coast of loyal Japanese American civilians was terminated, effective January 2, 1945.

Sources

Order and Unity

The Photographer's Record

The photographs on the next two pages belong chronologically to the New Deal era, rather than to the World War II years. They are included here because they demonstrate so forcefully that the cul-

Cutting Hay, Vermont. Photograph by Arthur Rothstein for the Farm Security Administration. *Library of Congress.*

FSA Clients at Home, Hidalgo, Texas, 1939. Photograph by Russell Lee for the
Farm Security Administration. *Library of Congress.*

tural pressures toward unity and discipline were significant *before* the
United States went to war in 1941. The harmony and cooperation
suggested in Arthur Rothstein's photograph of the hay cutters was
transferable to wartime factories; the values suggested in Russell
Lee's photograph—order, religion, division of labor, a willingness to
respond to the mass media—were essential ingredients in the war effort.

Uniforms

In wartime, the military uniform assumes added significance,
and even nonmilitary clothing takes on symbolic functions. The two
documents that follow—one a teenager's reminiscence, the other a
photograph of Los Angeles zoot-suiters—demonstrate the importance of one's wartime "uniform."

Virginia Rasmussen

The Dark Side of Rosie the Riveter

Virginia Rasmussen's account can be read as one person's encounter with the wartime mystique of the uniform and, perhaps, as part of a larger, cultural failure to separate the Hollywood image of soldiering from the reality of being a soldier and a soldier's girlfriend. But it should also remind us that the time-honored image of Rosie the Riveter—called on during a national emergency to "man" the nation's factories, learning to cope in a man's world—is by itself an unsatisfactory image of the war's impact on women.

I was a high-school junior in South Bend, Indiana, in 1941. Uniforms were everywhere. It was thrilling and glamorous, and I got caught up in all of it.

In my senior year I was dating a midshipman who was taking his training at the University of Notre Dame. When he graduated and went back to Pittsburgh, which was his hometown, we had one of these scenes at the airport that you always saw in the movies. He would walk a few steps and turn around and wave to me and I'd wave back. Then he'd go a few more steps and turn and wave again. It went like that until he finally entered the airplane and the door closed. That night I sat out on my back doorstep (there was a full moon, of course), and I listened to records—the ballads of the time said the things that you were feeling—and I wept all night long. It was a very dramatic experience, but it kept recurring with the various uniforms.

In 1943 I went to college at Indiana University and fell in love with another serviceman. He was in the Army Specialized Training Program, where you completed your college education and then went into officer candidate school. After OCS he was sent overseas, but before that, in early '44, we were engaged.

Then, as the time dragged on, and with all that distance between us, I began to wonder if I was really ready to be engaged. At the same time I met another serviceman in midshipman training at Notre Dame, and I fell in love again. So I became engaged to this fellow too, and I was ready to send the ring back to the first one when he arrived on the doorstep at the sorority house at college, unexpectedly. He had been wounded in France and been sent home for bone grafts. I hadn't even known that he was injured, and here he was with his arm in a cast and his ribbons, and very gaunt, and my heart went out to him. Of course I couldn't bring myself to break the engagement then. After all, he was a wounded war hero and I felt very sorry for him. I think this was one of the feelings that most people had at that time: Here is a wounded war hero, and we must treat him with respect and care.

So we began dating, and I never did get around to giving back his ring. Instead, I sent the ring back to the midshipman, and I married the war hero.

My parents advised me to wait a little longer until I was sure, but I was determined to go ahead and get married, so I did. He was hit in September of '44 and came back in February of '45, and we were married that July. Even as I was walking down the aisle I had reservations about the marriage, but it was a large wedding, and I felt what could I do? I couldn't stop things that were in motion. It was very difficult for me to make decisions at that time.

The romanticism of the uniform was very powerful. Being an officer was very important, too. My husband went over as a second lieutenant and came back as a captain. The second fellow that I was engaged to was an ensign. They were so very handsome in their officer's uniforms. Very gallant. It was the picture that you had seen in the movies, and they played it up very big.

Many things took place then because the men were being shipped overseas. There were a lot of girls I knew in college who got caught in that—let's make his last days here happy, just in case he never comes back. I don't know how many had illegitimate children as a result of that, but I do know that there were some in my sorority who had relationships simply because they felt they owed it to this man because this might be the last he'd ever have.

You were definitely caught up in that kind of feeling. They're going over to save us, let's do our part and make them happy before they go. I think it was a very bad time for women, in particular, because they had been taught these values of "nice girls don't do that," and then they're torn because here's this man who's going to give up his life for me. And, of course, the soldiers appealed to you like that.

The result was a number of hasty marriages to servicemen during the war and a number of divorces afterwards. My husband and I were both very immature; we were both groping for someone who cared. My parents, my father in particular, were very strict disciplinarians and held me in very tight control. My husband was an only child whose mother had died when he was in high school, and he and his father were not on the best of terms. So this was an escape for both of us, a glamorous escape. In addition, there were his injuries and feeling sorry for him. It was a combination of those emotions, not really love as I would define it today, and it quickly disintegrated.

The Zoot-Suit Riots

A different sort of uniform—a costume that included flared trousers, a broad felt hat, and a key chain with a pocket knife—was at the center of a series of wartime confrontations known as the Zoot-Suit Riots. The word "riot" may be a misnomer. No one was killed or even seriously injured. Still, sailors at the Chavez Ravine Naval Base did invade the Mexican section of Los Angeles in search of "zooters," and the "riots" of 1943 remain an important part of American history precisely because they seem to have been so patently symbolic.

Can you connect the riots to the treatment of Japanese Americans on the West Coast? How might Virginia Rasmussen have responded to the zoot-suiters?

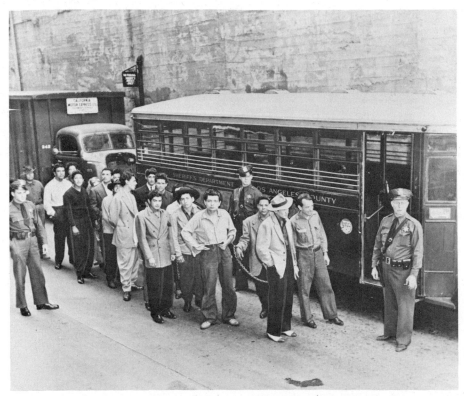

Original Caption: "Zoot suiters leave jail to make court appearance. Chains were in fashion, but they wore them on their wrists." *Library of Congress.*

Ernie Pyle

Word Images of War: The Beach at Normandy

Americans experienced World War II in a bewildering variety of ways, most of them firsthand and intense. But for those denied the experience of combat, this all-important facet of the war could be felt and measured only indirectly. Many Americans learned what war was really about by reading newspaper accounts by war correspondents.

Ernie Pyle was the most popular of the American correspondents who covered World War II. His experience was real enough; he was killed by Japanese machine-gun fire on a small Pacific island in April 1945.

In this selection, Pyle describes the beach at Normandy on the day after the Allied invasion of western Europe—D-Day. What was Pyle trying to say about the war? Would the sailors involved in the Zoot-Suit Riots have appreciated Pyle's account?

Beach landings are always planned to a schedule that is set far ahead of time. They all have to be timed, in order for everything to mesh and for the following waves of troops to be standing off the beach and ready to land at the right moment. Some elements of the assault force are to break through quickly, push on inland, and attack the most obvious enemy strong points. It is usually the plan for units to be inland, attacking gun positions from behind, within a matter of minutes after the first men hit the beach.

I have always been amazed at the speed called for in these plans. Schedules will call for engineers to land at H-hour plus 2 minutes, and service troops at H-hour plus 30 minutes, and even for press censors to land at H-hour plus 75 minutes. But in the attack on my special portion of the beach—the toughest spot of all, incidentally—the schedule didn't hold.

Our men simply could not get past the beach. They were pinned down right on the water's edge by an inhuman wall of fire from the bluff. Our first waves were on that beach for hours, instead of a few minutes, before they could begin working inland.

The foxholes were still there—dug at the very edge of the water, in the sand and the small jumbled rocks that formed parts of the beach.

Medical corpsmen attended the wounded as best they could. Men were killed as they stepped out of landing craft. An officer whom I knew got a bullet through the head just as the door of his landing craft was let down. Some men were drowned.

The first crack in the beach defenses was finally accomplished by terrific and wonderful naval gunfire, which knocked out the big emplacements. Epic stories have been told of destroyers that ran right up into shallow water and had it out point-blank with the big guns in those concrete emplacements ashore.

When the heavy fire stopped, our men were organized by their officers and pushed on inland, circling machine-gun nests and taking them from the rear.

As one officer said, the only way to take a beach is to face it and keep going. It is costly at first, but it's the only way. If the men are pinned down on the beach, dug in and out of action, they might as well not be there at all. They hold up the waves behind them, and nothing is being gained.

Our men were pinned down for a while, but finally they stood up and went through, and so we took that beach and accomplished our landing. In the light of a couple of days of retrospection, we sat and talked and called it a miracle that our men ever got on at all or were able to stay on.

They suffered casualties. And yet considering the entire beachhead assault, including other units that had a much easier time, our total casualties in driving that wedge into the Continent of Europe were remarkably low— only a fraction, in fact, of what our commanders had been prepared to accept.

And those units that were so battered and went through such hell pushed on inland without rest, their spirits high, their egotism in victory almost reaching the smart-alecky stage.

Their tails were up. "We've done it again," they said. They figured that the rest of the Army wasn't needed at all. Which proves that, while their judgment in this respect was bad, they certainly had the spirit that wins battles, and eventually wars. . . .

I took a walk along the historic coast of Normandy in the country of France. It was a lovely day for strolling along the seashore. Men were sleeping on the sand, some of them sleeping forever. Men were floating in the water, but they didn't know they were in the water, for they were dead.

The water was full of squishy little jellyfish about the size of a man's hand. Millions of them. In the center of each of them was a green design exactly like a four-leafed clover. The good-luck emblem. Sure. Hell, yes.

I walked for a mile and a half along the water's edge of our many-miled invasion beach. I walked slowly, for the detail on that beach was infinite.

The wreckage was vast and startling. The awful waste and destruction of war, even aside from the loss of human life, has always been one of its outstanding features to those who are in it. Anything and everything is expendable. And we did expend on our beachhead in Normandy during those first few hours.

For a mile out from the beach there were scores of tanks and trucks and boats that were not visible, for they were at the bottom of the water—

swamped by overloading, or hit by shells, or sunk by mines. Most of their crews were lost.

There were trucks tipped half over and swamped, partly sunken barges, and the angled-up corners of jeeps, and small landing craft half submerged. And at low tide you could still see those vicious six-pronged iron snares that helped snag and wreck them.

On the beach itself, high and dry, were all kinds of wrecked vehicles. There were tanks that had only just made the beach before being knocked out. There were jeeps that had burned to a dull gray. There were big derricks on caterpillar treads that didn't quite make it. There were half-tracks carrying office equipment that had been made into a shambles by a single shell hit, their interiors still holding the useless equipage of smashed typewriters, telephones, office files.

There were LCTs turned completely upside down, and lying on their backs, and how they got that way I don't know. There were boats stacked on top of each other, their sides caved in, their suspension doors knocked off.

In this shore-line museum of carnage there were abandoned rolls of barbed wire and smashed bulldozers and big stacks of thrown-away life belts and piles of shells still waiting to be moved. In the water floated empty life rafts and soldiers' packs and ration boxes, and mysterious oranges. On the beach lay snarled rolls of telephone wire and big rolls of steel matting and stacks of broken, rusting rifles.

On the beach lay, expended, sufficient men and mechanism for a small war. They were gone forever now. And yet we could afford it.

We could afford it because we were on, we had our toe hold, and behind us there were such enormous replacements for this wreckage on the beach that you could hardly conceive of the sum total. Men and equipment were flowing from England in such a gigantic stream that it made the waste on the beachhead seem like nothing at all, really nothing at all.

But there was another and more human litter. It extended in a thin little line, just like a high-water mark, for miles along the beach. This was the strewn personal gear, gear that would never be needed again by those who fought and died to give us our entrance into Europe.

There in a jumbled row for mile on mile were soldiers' packs. There were socks and shoe polish, sewing kits, diaries, Bibles, hand grenades. There were the latest letters from home, with the address on each one neatly razored out—one of the security precautions enforced before the boys embarked.

There were toothbrushes and razors, and snapshots of families back home staring up at you from the sand. There were pocketbooks, metal mirrors, extra trousers, and bloody, abandoned shoes. There were broken-handled shovels, and portable radios smashed almost beyond recognition, and mine detectors twisted and ruined.

There were torn pistol belts and canvas water buckets, first-aid kits, and jumbled heaps of life belts. I picked up a pocket Bible with a soldier's name in it, and put it in my jacket. I carried it half a mile or so and then put it back down on the beach. I don't know why I picked it up, or why I put it down again.

Soldiers carry strange things ashore with them. In every invasion there is at least one soldier hitting the beach at H-hour with a banjo slung over his shoulder. The most ironic piece of equipment marking our beach—this beach first of despair, then of victory—was a tennis racket that some soldier had brought along. It lay lonesomely on the sand, clamped in its press, not a string broken.

Two of the most dominant items in the beach refuse were cigarettes and writing paper. Each soldier was issued a carton of cigarettes just before he started. That day those cartons by the thousand, water-soaked and spilled out, marked the line of our first savage blow.

Writing paper and air-mail envelopes came second. The boys had intended to do a lot of writing in France. The letters—now forever incapable of being written—that might have filled those blank abandoned pages!

Always there are dogs in every invasion. There was a dog still on the beach, still pitifully looking for his masters.

He stayed at the water's edge, near a boat that lay twisted and half sunk at the waterline. He barked appealingly to every soldier who approached, trotted eagerly along with him for a few feet, and then, sensing himself unwanted in all the haste, he would run back to wait in vain for his own people at his own empty boat.

Over and around this long thin line of personal anguish, fresh men were rushing vast supplies to keep our armies pushing on into France. Other squads of men picked amidst the wreckage to salvage ammunition and equipment that was still usable.

Men worked and slept on the beach for days before the last D-day victim was taken away for burial.

I stepped over the form of one youngster whom I thought dead. But when I looked down I saw he was only sleeping. He was very young, and very tired. He lay on one elbow, his hand suspended in the air about six inches from the ground. And in the palm of his hand he held a large, smooth rock.

I stood and looked at him a long time. He seemed in his sleep to hold that rock lovingly, as though it were his last link with a vanishing world. I have no idea at all why he went to sleep with the rock in his hand, or what kept him from dropping it once he was asleep. It was just one of those little things without explanation that a person remembers for a long time.

The strong, swirling tides of the Normandy coast line shifted the contours of the sandy beach as they moved in and out. They carried soldiers' bodies out to sea, and later they returned them. They covered the corpses of heroes with sand, and then in their whims they uncovered them.

As I plowed out over the wet sand, I walked around what seemed to be a couple of pieces of driftwood sticking out of the sand. But they weren't driftwood. They were a soldier's two feet. He was completely covered except for his feet; the toes of his GI shoes pointed toward the land he had come so far to see, and which he saw so briefly.

A few hundred yards back on the beach was a high bluff. Up there we had a tent hospital, and a barbed-wire enclosure for prisoners of war. From up there you could see far up and down the beach, in a spectacular crow's-nest view, and far out to sea.

And standing out there on the water beyond all this wreckage was the greatest armada man has ever seen. You simply could not believe the gigantic collection of ships that lay out there waiting to unload. Looking from the bluff, it lay thick and clear to the far horizon of the sea and on beyond, and it spread out to the sides and was miles wide.

As I stood up there I noticed a group of freshly taken German prisoners standing nearby. They had not yet been put in the prison cage. They were just standing there, a couple of doughboys leisurely guarding them with tommy guns.

The prisoners too were looking out to sea—the same bit of sea that for months and years had been so safely empty before their gaze. Now they stood staring almost as if in a trance. They didn't say a word to each other. They didn't need to. The expression on their faces was something forever unforgettable. In it was the final, horrified acceptance of their doom.

10

Cold War and Containment

Some Americans looked to the postwar world for a new birth of international order and domestic progress, expecting to live, as *Life* publisher Henry Luce had forecast in 1941, in the "American Century" and expecting to participate in the great work of reconstructing the world in the American image. Others expected only another return to normalcy. What happened was neither. Instead, there was a new emergency to replace the Great Depression and World War II. This new crisis took shape within months of the surrenders of 1945 and very soon had a name: the cold war. The phrase was used to describe a state of continued hostility between the United States and the Soviet Union—a hostility short of war, and therefore "cold," but a war nonetheless.

The cold war can be understood neither as a great misunderstanding nor as a righteous American crusade against communist aggression and tyranny. The United States and the Soviet Union had very different ideas about the shape of the postwar world. The Soviets, who had once again been forced to wage a devastating campaign on their own soil, wanted immunity from future aggression. For Joseph Stalin, this meant friendly governments in Eastern Europe and weak states on his country's other frontiers. The American vision of the postwar world was inseparably tied to an ideal world economic order, based on free trade and consistent with its own needs for security from depression. At Bretton Woods in 1944, the United States had helped create several institutions—including the International Monetary Fund, the World Bank, and a system of currency exchange—thought essential to free-flowing trade and investment. Soviet domination of Eastern Europe had already closed off a substantial trading area; further "aggression" could seriously restrict markets and access to raw materials.

   The cold war came to maturity in a series of crises that took place between 1947 and 1950. In Greece, communist guerrillas threatened to unseat a corrupt, unpopular, and conservative government. President Harry Truman couched a request to Congress for funds to provide economic and military assistance to Greece in words that would become known as the Truman Doctrine. "I believe," Truman said, "that it must be the policy of the United States to support free peoples who are resisting attempted subjugation by armed minorities or by outside pressures." The same year, following a communist coup in Czechoslovakia, the United States began a comprehensive aid program for Western Europe. Known as the Marshall Plan, the program was designed to restrict communist influence and preserve American markets by stimulating economic recovery. Both the Marshall Plan and the Truman Doctrine were part of a general policy called "containment." As developed by George F. Kennan, our Moscow chargé d'affaires, in an influential article in the journal *Foreign Affairs,* containment was a policy of resistance. According to Kennan, the Soviets were "impervious to logic of reason," but "highly sensitive to logic of force." Soviet aggression could be effectively countered, but only if it were resisted at every point, and with the threat of physical force.

   The administration of Dwight Eisenhower adopted Truman's concept of a bipolar world while reshaping the policy of containment. Perhaps the least bellicose of all postwar presidents, Eisenhower sought to modulate conflict with the Soviets through summit conferences, ended the war in Korea, and managed to avoid direct military intervention in Vietnam. But John Foster Dulles, Eisenhower's able but militant secretary of state, redefined Kennan's containment policy into the more aggressive stance known as "brinkmanship" (defined by Dulles as "the ability to get to the verge without getting into the war"). Another rhetorical escalation, the Dulles doctrine of "massive retaliation," shifted conflict into an arms race and made events like the Soviet launching of the *Sputnik* satellite in 1957 into traumatic moments of political and military import.

   The victory over the Axis and a monopoly of atomic weapons had led Americans to believe that the postwar world could be shaped to suit their needs and desires. Three events made this assumption questionable. Early in 1949, China's incompetent American-supported Nationalist government withdrew to the island of Formosa, leaving the mainland in the hands of communists under the leadership of Mao Tse-tung. Soon thereafter, Americans learned that the Soviet Union had exploded a nuclear device, ending the American monopoly. And in June 1950, communist North Korea attacked

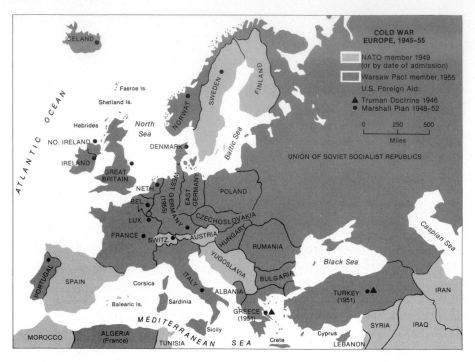

Cold War Europe, 1945–1955. *From Allen Weinstein and Frank Otto Gatell,* Freedom and Crisis: An American History, *3rd. edition., vol. 2 (New York: Random House, 1981), p. 812.*

South Korea and began a war that would end in a stalemate more than three years later.

But rather than acknowledge their own helplessness in the face of events beyond their control, Americans defended their unrealistic expectations by ferreting out the "real" causes of American weakness. For example: the Soviets had not developed the bomb; they had been given the secrets of atomic energy. Such reasoning led in June 1953 to the death of Julius and Ethel Rosenberg, the first Americans executed specifically for peacetime espionage. Another example: China had not suffered a revolution; State Department representatives, claimed Senator Robert Taft, had "promoted the communist cause in China." Finally, Alger Hiss, convicted of perjury in 1950, served as a scapegoat for the inability of the West to assert control over Eastern Europe as well as a symbol of the New Deal. Scholars still disagree about the actual guilt of the Rosenbergs and Hiss. What is clear is that cold war insecurities made impartial proceedings impossible.

The old dividing lines between questions that were foreign and questions that were domestic dissolved. Internal politics at every level, even down to town and county races, became focused on the question of "communism" and "free enterprise." Almost everything Americans did, from producing washing machines to teaching history, became ideologically tied to the cold war. Government agencies, business, and colleges became concerned with rooting out individuals who had ever displayed any sympathy for the communist movement. And political candidates competed with each other to see who could adopt the most vigorous stance of opposition to the Soviet "threat." The decades after 1945 were as dominated by the cold war as the 1930s had been by the emergency of the Great Depression.

The materials in this chapter are related to both the foreign-policy and the domestic aspects of the cold war. Taken together, they illustrate what amounts to a new consciousness among Americans, a consciousness of their society as an embattled stronghold of "capitalist" or "free-enterprise" values, threatened on every side and needing all its energies and resources to stand against its enemies, foreign and domestic.

Interpretive Essay

George C. Herring

A Dead-End Alley: War in Indochina, 1950–1954

No single event captures the demise of the idea of an "American Century" quite as well as the Vietnam War. For more than two decades, the United States tried, and failed, to create a Vietnam suitable to its own vision of the postwar world. This failure became most apparent in the 1960s, when the fighting of the war divided Americans into bitter factions. Apologists for John Kennedy believed that he would have avoided full-scale involvement. But Kennedy had remarked that a withdrawal from Vietnam would mean collapse in Southeast Asia; and by 1963 he had sent 15,000 advisers to the country, more than fifteen times Dwight Eisenhower's commitment. Lyndon Johnson also believed in the domino theory and defined the Vietnam problem as simple communist aggression, and in 1964, he inaugurated systematic air attacks on North Vietnam. But neither the air war nor an additional half-million American troops were sufficient to bring anything resembling victory. Even before the January 1968 Tet offensive, when Viet Cong and North Vietnamese attacks on major South Vietnamese cities made clear that the American claim to be winning the war was a sham, many Americans had come to question the war in moral terms. Over 200,000 marched against the war in Washington, D.C., in 1967. When Richard Nixon in 1970 moved ground troops into Cambodia, students closed down many colleges and universities in protest. By 1973, as Nixon withdrew the last of the nation's ground troops, the American Century (as well as the Eisenhower equilibrium—see Chapter 11) was a relic of another era.

What went wrong? The answer to that question lies as much in the seedtime of the cold war as it does in later decades, when defeat and frustration were more apparent. As George Herring makes clear in this essay, early American interest in Vietnam was inseparable from the larger issues of the cold war—the war in Korea, Soviet domination of Eastern Europe, the fall of China. How did American policy makers translate cold-war phenomena into a quarter-century of involvement in an obscure nation in Southeast Asia? Was the national interest at stake in Vietnam? Was our failure in Vietnam predictable, even in 1954?

When Ho Chi Minh proclaimed the independence of Vietnam from French rule on September 2, 1945, he borrowed liberally from Thomas Jefferson, opening with the words "We hold these truths to be self-evident. That all men are created equal." During independence celebrations in Hanoi later in the day, American warplanes flew over the city, U.S. Army officers stood on the reviewing stand with Vo Nguyen Giap and other leaders, and a Vietnamese band played the "Star-Spangled Banner." Toward the end of the festivities, Giap spoke warmly of Vietnam's "particularly intimate relations" with the United States, something, he noted, "which it is a pleasant duty to dwell upon." The prominent role played by Americans at the birth of modern Vietnam appears in retrospect one of history's most bitter ironies. Despite the glowing professions of friendship on September 2, the United States acquiesced in the return of France to Vietnam and from 1950 to 1954 actively supported French efforts to suppress Ho's revolution, the first phase of a quarter-century American struggle to control the destiny of Vietnam.

The Vietnamese revolution was in many ways the personal creation of the charismatic patriot Ho Chi Minh. Born in the province of Nghe An, the cradle of Vietnamese revolutionaries, Ho inherited from his mandarin father a sturdy patriotism and an adventurous spirit. Departing Vietnam in 1912 as a cabin boy aboard a merchant steamer, he eventually settled in France with a colony of Vietnamese nationalists, and when the Paris Peace Conference

From George C. Herring, *America's Longest War: The United States and Vietnam, 1950–1975* (New York: Wiley, 1979), pp. 1–42 as edited. Copyright © 1979 by Newbery Award Records, Inc. Reprinted by permission of Alfred A. Knopf, Inc.

rejected his petition for Vietnamese independence, he joined the French Communist party. Then known as Nguyen Ai Quoc (Nguyen the Patriot), he
worked for more than two decades as a party functionary and revolutionary
organizer in the Soviet Union, China, Thailand, and Vietnam. In 1930, he
organized the Indochinese Communist party and incited a series of revolts
which were brutally suppressed by the French. When Hitler conquered France
in 1940 and Japan began to move southward into Vietnam, Ho returned to
his homeland. A frail and gentle man who radiated warmth and serenity, he
was also a master organizer and determined revolutionary who was willing
to employ the most cold-blooded methods in the cause to which he dedicated
his life. Establishing headquarters in the caves of Pac Bo, by a mountain he
named Karl Marx and a river he named Lenin, Ho conceived the strategy
and founded the political organization, the Vietminh, that would eventually
drive the French from Vietnam.

The Vietminh capitalized on the uniquely favorable circumstances of
World War II to establish itself as the voice of Vietnamese nationalism. The
Japanese permitted the French colonial authorities to retain nominal power
throughout most of the war, but the ease with which Japan had established
its position discredited the French in the eyes of the Vietnamese, and the
hardships imposed by the Japanese and their French puppets fanned popular
discontent. The Vietminh leadership, composed primarily of Communists,
adopted a broad nationalist platform, stressing independence and the establishment of "democratic" freedoms. It enticed some rival nationalists into joining
it and ruthlessly eliminated some who refused. By the spring of 1945, Ho
had mobilized a base of mass support in northern Vietnam, and with the
assistance of Giap, a former professor of history, had raised an army of some
5,000 men. When the Japanese deposed the puppet French government in
March 1945, the Vietminh, working closely with an American intelligence
unit (hence the American presence on September 2), waged an intensive and
effective guerrilla war against their new colonial masters. When Japan surrendered in August 1945, the Vietminh quickly stepped into the vacuum, occupy-
ing government headquarters in Hanoi and proclaiming the independence of
Vietnam.

Independence would not come without a struggle, however, for the
French were determined to regain the empire they had ruled for more than
half a century. Conscious of their nation's declining position in world affairs,
many French politicians felt that France could "only be a great power so
long as our flag continues to fly in all the overseas territory." French Indochina,
comprising Cambodia, Laos, and the three Vietnamese colonies of Annam,
Tonkin, and Cochin China, was among the richest and most prestigious of
France's colonial possessions. The Vietminh had been unable to establish a
firm power base in southern Vietnam, and with the assistance of British
occupation forces, who had been given responsibility for accepting the Japanese surrender south of the seventeenth parallel, the French were able to
expel the Vietminh from Saigon and reestablish control over the southern
part of the country.

French Indochina.

For more than a year, France and the Vietminh attempted to negotiate an agreement, but their goals were irreconcilable. French colonial policy had always stressed assimilation, full French citizenship, rather than independence or dominion status, and France hedged on the Vietminh's demand for immediate self-government and eventual independence. For the Vietminh, unification of their country not only represented fulfillment of the centuries-old dream of Vietnamese nationalists but was also an economic necessity since the south produced the food surplus necessary to sustain the overpopulated, industrial north. The French were determined to keep Cochin China separate from Annam and Tonkin and to maintain absolute control in the southern colony where their economic interests were largest. Negotiations dragged on inconclusively, mutual suspicions increased, and outbreaks of violence became commonplace. The shelling of Haiphong by a French cruiser in November 1946, killing 6,000 civilians, set off a war which in its various phases would last nearly thirty years.

For a time during World War II, the United States actively opposed the return of Indochina to France. Before 1941, Americans had taken little interest in the area, but the Japanese takeover impressed upon them its importance as a source of foodstuffs and raw materials and as a strategic outpost guarding the major water routes of southern Asia. Some U.S. officials perceived the growth of nationalism in Vietnam during the war and feared that a French attempt to regain control of its colony might provoke a long and bloody war, bringing instability to an area of economic and strategic significance. Even if France should succeed, they reasoned, it would restore monopolistic controls which would deny the United States access to raw materials and naval bases. President Franklin D. Roosevelt seems instinctively to have recognized that colonialism was doomed and that the United States must identify with the forces of nationalism in Asia. Moreover, Roosevelt profoundly disliked France and its leader Charles de Gaulle, and regarded the French as "poor colonizers" who had "badly mismanaged" Indochina and exploited its people. Roosevelt therefore advocated placing Indochina under international trusteeship to be prepared for independence. . . .

After Roosevelt's death in April 1945, the United States adopted a policy even more favorable to France. Harry S. Truman did not share his predecessor's personal interest in Indochina or his concern about colonialism. American thinking about the postwar world also underwent a major reorientation in the spring of 1945. Military and civilian strategists perceived that the war had left the Soviet Union the most powerful nation in Europe and Asia, and the subjugation of Eastern Europe raised growing fears that Joseph Stalin had broader, perhaps global, designs. Assigning top priority to the promotion of stable, friendly governments in Western Europe that could stand as bulwarks against Russian expansion, the Truman administration concluded that the United States "had no interest" in "championing schemes of international trusteeship" that would weaken and alienate the "European states whose help we need to balance Soviet power in Europe." France assumed a rôle of special importance in the new scheme of things, and the State Department insisted that the United States must repair the rift that had opened under Roosevelt by cooperating "wholeheartedly" with France and allaying "her apprehensions that we are going to propose that territory be taken away from her." The Truman administration quickly scrapped what remained of Roosevelt's trusteeship plan and in the summer of 1945 gave de Gaulle firm assurances that it would not stand in the way of the restoration of French sovereignty in Indochina.

The United States viewed the outbreak of war in Indochina with concern. . . . The State Department's Asian experts warned of the dangers of identifying with French colonialism and pressed the administration to use its influence to force France to come to terms with Vietnamese nationalism.

American skepticism about French policy in Asia continued to be outweighed by European concerns, however. In the spring of 1947, the United States formally committed itself to the containment of Soviet expansion in Europe, and throughout the next two years American attention was riveted on France, where economic stagnation and political instability aroused grave fears of a possible Communist takeover. Warned by moderate French politicians that outside interference in colonial matters would play into the hands of the French Communist party, the United States left France to handle the Indochina question in its own way. An "immediate and vital interest" in keeping in power a "friendly government to assist in the furtherance of our aims in Europe," the State Department concluded, must "take precedence over active steps looking toward the realization of our objectives in Indochina."

By early 1947, moreover, the Truman administration had drawn conclusions about Ho's revolution that would determine American policy in Vietnam for the next two decades. On numerous occasions, Ho had openly appealed for American support, even indicating that Indochina would be a "fertile field for American capital and enterprise" and raising the possibility of an American naval base at Camranh Bay. U.S. diplomats in Vietnam insisted that they could find no evidence of direct Soviet contact with the Vietminh, and they stressed that, regardless of his ideology, Ho had established himself as the "symbol of nationalism and the struggle for freedom to the overwhelming majority of the population." But these arguments failed to persuade an administration increasingly obsessed with the Communist menace in Europe. Intelligence reports stressed that Ho had remained loyal to Moscow throughout his career, and the lack of close ties with the Soviet Union simply meant that he was trusted to carry out Stalin's plans without supervision. In the absence of irrefutable evidence to the contrary, the State Department concluded, the United States could not "afford to assume that Ho is anything but Moscow-directed." Unwilling, as Secretary of State George C. Marshall put it, to see "colonial empires and administrations supplanted by philosophies and political organizations emanating from the Kremlin," the administration refused to take any step which might facilitate a "Communist" triumph in Indochina. . . .

The possibility of a French defeat, along with the Communist victory in China, brought forth in early 1950 a decision to support France in Indochina, the first step toward direct American involvement in Vietnam. The French had launched the war in 1946 confident of victory, but Ho had predicted the nature and eventual outcome of the conflict more accurately. "If ever the tiger [Vietminh] pauses," he said, "the elephant [France] will impale him on his mighty tusks. But the tiger will not pause, and the elephant will die of exhaustion and loss of blood." The Vietminh retreated into the countryside, evading major engagements, mobilizing popular support, and harassing French outposts. France held the major towns and cities, but a series of unsuccessful and costly offensives and relentless hit-and-run raids by Vietminh guerrillas placed a growing strain on French manpower and resources and produced increasing war-weariness at home. The collapse of Chiang Kai-shek's government in China in 1949 and the southward advance of Mao Tse-tung's army raised the ominous possibility of Chinese Communist collaboration with the Vietminh. From late 1949 on, French officials issued increasingly urgent warnings that without direct American military aid they might be compelled to withdraw from Indochina.

The French appeals came at a time when Washington, already gripped by near panic, was frantically reassessing its global Cold War strategy. The fall of China and Russia's successful testing of a nuclear device persuaded many American officials that the Communist threat had assumed even more menacing proportions than that posed by the Axis a decade earlier. Any doubts about the direction of Stalin's foreign policy had long since been waved aside: the Soviet Union, "animated by a new fanatic faith," was determined to "impose its absolute authority on the rest of the world." Recent successes seemed to have spurred the Soviet leadership to a new level of confidence and militancy, and Communist expansion, in the eyes of American policymakers, had already reached a point beyond which it must not be permitted to go. Any further "extension of the area under the domination of the Kremlin," the National Security Council warned, "would raise the possibility that no coalition adequate to confront the Kremlin with greater strength could be assembled." Facing a world divided into two hostile blocs, a precarious balance of power, and the possibility, if not likelihood, of global war, the Truman administration initiated plans to increase American military capabilities, shore up the defense of Western Europe, and extend the containment policy to the Far East.

In the dramatically altered strategic context of 1950, support for France in Indochina was considered essential for the security of Western Europe. Massive expenditures for the war against the Vietminh had retarded France's economic recovery and the attainment of that level of political stability required to fend off the threat of Communism. Certain that Europe was more vulnerable than ever to the Soviet threat, American policymakers in early 1950 began to formulate plans to raise the military forces necessary to defend against the Red Army. Their preliminary proposals required France to contribute sizeable numbers of troops and provided for the rearmament of West Germany, measures the French were likely to resist. The administration thus feared that if it did not respond positively to its ally's appeals for aid in Indochina, France might refuse to cooperate with its strategic design for Western Europe. . . .

In the aftermath of the fall of China, American strategists concluded that Southeast Asia was vital to the security of the United States. Should the region be swept by Communism, the National Security Council warned, "we shall have suffered a major political rout the repercussions of which will be felt throughout the world." The loss of an area so large and populous would tip the balance of power against the United States. Recent Communist triumphs had already aroused nervousness in Europe, and another major victory might tempt the Europeans to reach an accommodation with the Soviet Union. The economic consequences could be equally profound. The United States and its European allies would be denied access to important markets. Southeast Asia was the world's largest producer of natural rubber and was an important source of oil, tin, tungsten, and other strategic commodities.

Should control of these vital raw materials suddenly change hands, the Soviet bloc would be enormously strengthened at the expense of the West.

American policymakers also feared that the loss of Southeast Asia would irreparably damage the nation's strategic position in the Far East. Control of the off-shore island chain extending from Japan to the Philippines, America's first line of defense in the Pacific, would be endangered. Air and sea routes between Australia and the Middle East and the United States and India could be cut, severely hampering military operations in the event of war. Japan, India, and Australia, those nations where the West retained predominant influence, would be cut off from each other and left vulnerable. The impact on Japan, America's major Far Eastern ally, could be disastrous. Denied access to the raw materials, rice, and markets upon which their economy depended, the Japanese might see no choice but to come to terms with the enemy.

American officials agreed that Indochina, and especially Vietnam, was the key to the defense of Southeast Asia. Soviet recognition of the Vietminh on January 30, 1950, confirmed long-standing beliefs about Ho's allegiance, revealing him, in Secretary of State Dean Acheson's words, in his "true colors as the mortal enemy of native independence in Indochina." It was also interpreted as a "significant and ominous" portent of Stalin's intention to "accelerate the revolutionary process" in Southeast Asia. Ho's well-organized guerrillas had already scored major gains against France, and with increased Soviet and Chinese backing might be able to force a French withdrawal, removing the last military bulwark between China and the rest of Southeast Asia. Indochina was in the "most immediate danger," the State Department concluded, and was therefore "the most strategically important area of Southeast Asia."

Indochina was considered intrinsically important for its raw materials, rice, and naval bases, but it was deemed far more significant for the presumed effect its loss would have on other areas. By early 1950, American policymakers had firmly embraced what would become known as the "domino theory," the belief that the fall of Indochina would bring about in rapid succession the collapse of the other nations of Southeast Asia. Acceptance of this concept reflects the perceived fragility of the region in 1950, as well as the experience of World War II, when Hitler had overrun Western Europe in three months and the Japanese had seized much of Southeast Asia in even less time. First employed to justify aid to Greece in 1947, the idea, once applied to Southeast Asia, quickly became an article of faith. Americans were certain that if Indochina fell the rest of Southeast Asia would be imperiled. The strategic reassessment of 1950 thus ended American "neutrality" and produced a commitment to furnish France military and economic assistance for the war against the Vietminh. It also established principles that would provide the basis for U.S. policy in Vietnam for years to come and would eventually lead to massive involvement.

The creation of nominally independent governments in Indochina made it easier for the United States to rationalize support of France. Unable to defeat the Vietminh militarily, the French had attempted to undercut it politically by forming native governments in Laos, Cambodia, and Vietnam, the latter headed by the former Emperor of Annam, Bao Dai, and according them the status of "free states" within the French Union. Many U.S. officials were skeptical of the so-called Bao Dai solution, warning that it was only a smoke-screen for continued French domination and had little chance of success. The State Department acknowledged the strength of these arguments, but Bao Dai seemed the only alternative to "Commie domination of Indochina," as Acheson put it, and while American support did not guarantee his success the lack of it seemed likely to ensure his failure. By backing Bao Dai, moreover, the United States would at least avoid the appearance of being an accomplice of French imperialism. In February 1950, the Truman administration formally recognized the Bao Dai government and the free states of Laos and Cambodia and initiated plans to support them with economic and technical assistance.

In retrospect the assumptions upon which American policymakers acted in 1950 appear misguided. The Southeast Asian revolutions were not inspired by Moscow and, although the Soviet Union and China at times sought to control them, their capacity to do so was limited by their lack of military and especially naval power and by the strength of local nationalism. The American assessment of the situation in Vietnam seems to have been well off the mark. Although a dedicated Communist, Ho was no mere tool of the Soviet Union, and while he was willing to accept help from the major Communist powers—indeed he had no choice but to do so—he was not prepared to subordinate Vietnamese independence to them. Vietnam's historic fears of its larger northern neighbor made submission to China especially unlikely. "It is better to sniff French dung for a while than eat China's all our life," Ho once said, graphically expressing a traditional principle of Vietnamese foreign policy. Perhaps most important, regardless of his ideology, Ho by 1950 had captured the standard of Vietnamese nationalism, and by supporting France, even under the guise of the Bao Dai solution, the United States was attaching itself to a losing cause.

American policymakers were not unaware of the pitfalls of intervention in Indochina. Should the United States commit itself to Bao Dai and should he turn out to be a French puppet, a State Department Asian specialist warned, "we must then follow blindly down a dead-end alley, expending our limited resources . . . in a fight that would be hopeless." Some Americans officials even dimly perceived that the United States might get sucked into direct involvement in Vietnam. But the initial commitment seemed limited and the risks seemed smaller than those of inaction. Caught up in a global struggle reminiscent of World War II, with Russia taking Germany's place in Europe and China Japan's place in Asia, U.S. officials were certain that if they did not back France and Bao Dai Southeast Asia might be lost, leaving the more awesome choice of making a "staggering investment" to recover the losses or falling back to a "much contracted" line of defense in the western Pacific.

By the time the United States committed itself to assist France, the Vietminh had gained the military initiative in Indochina. Ho Chi Minh controlled an estimated two-thirds of the countryside, and Vietminh regulars and guerrillas numbered in the hundreds of thousands. The Chinese were furnishing sanctuaries across the border and large stocks of weapons. By early 1950, Giap felt sufficiently confident of his strength to take the offensive for the first time. The French maintained tenuous control in the cities and the major production centers, but at a very high cost, suffering 1,000 casualties per month and in 1949 alone spending 167 million francs on the war. Even in the areas under nominal French control, the Vietminh spread terror after dark, sabotaging power plants and factories, tossing grenades into cafés and theaters, and brutally assassinating French officials. "Anyone with white skin caught outside protected areas after dark is courting horrible death," an American correspondent reported. . . .

Introverted and given to periodic moods of depression, Bao Dai was incapable of rallying popular support, and the reality of French dominance gave him nothing to work with. His government was composed largely of wealthy southern landowners who in no sense were representative of the people. Nationalists of stature refused to support him, and the masses either backed the resistance or remained aloof. Bao Dai's authority scarcely extended beyond the authority of the French army.

The onset of the Korean War in the summer of 1950 complicated an already difficult problem. The Truman administration perceived North Korea's invasion of South Korea as confirmation of its suspicion that the Soviet Union sought to conquer all of Asia, even at the risk of war, and the defense of Indochina assumed even greater importance in American eyes. By the end of the year, however, the United States and France had suffered major reversals. Chinese intervention in Korea forced General Douglas MacArthur into a head-long retreat from the Yalu. In the meantime, Giap had inflicted upon France its "greatest colonial defeat since Montcalm had died at Quebec," trapping an entire army at Cao Bang in northeastern Vietnam and costing the French more than 6,000 troops and enough equipment to stock an entire Vietminh division. Chinese intervention in Korea raised fears of a similar plunge across the border into Vietnam, and American policymakers were increasingly concerned that a growing defeatism in France would raise demands for withdrawal from Indochina.

Against this background of stunning defeat in the Far East, the Truman administration struggled to devise a workable policy for Indochina. With large numbers of American troops committed to Korea and Europe vulnerable to a possible Soviet invasion, the Joint Chiefs of Staff agreed that even should the Chinese invade Indochina the United States could not commit military forces to its defense. France must remain and bear primary responsibility for the war. More certain than ever that Indochina was essential to American security, the administration was forced to rely on military assistance to bolster French defenses. In late 1950, the United States committed more than $133 million for aid to Indochina and ordered immediate delivery of large quantities of arms and ammunition, naval vessels, aircraft, and military vehicles.

Most Americans agreed, however, that military equipment by itself would not be enough. As early as May, Acheson complained that the French seemed "paralyzed, in a state of moving neither forward or backward," and a fact-finding mission dispatched to Indochina *before* the Cao Bang disaster confirmed his fears. American observers reported that the French state of mind was "fatuous, even dangerous," and warned that unless France prosecuted the war with greater determination, made more effective use of native manpower, and moved boldly and generously to win over the Vietnamese, the United States and its ally might be "moving into a debacle which neither of us can afford." The Joint Chiefs of Staff proposed that the United States condition its military aid on French pledges to take drastic measures, including the promise of eventual independence.

The administration approached this question with great caution. Acheson conceded that if the United States supported France's "old-fashioned colonial attitudes," it might "lose out." But the French presence was essential to defend Indochina against Communism, he quickly added, and the United States could not press France to the point where it would say, "All right, take over the damned country. We don't want it." Admitting the inconsistency of American policy, he concluded that the only choice was to encourage the French to remain until the crisis had eased but at the same time persuade them to "play with the nationalist movement and give Bao Dai a chance really to get the nationalists on his side." Rejecting any form of pressure, the administration would go no further than gently urge France to make symbolic concessions and to build a Vietnamese army. The State Department, in the meantime, would hold Bao Dai's "feet to the fire" to get him to assert effective leadership under French tutelage.

To strengthen the governments of Indochina and increase their popular appeal, the United States established a program of economic and technical assistance in 1950 and over the next two years spent more than $50 million on various projects. American experts provided fertilizer and seeds to increase agricultural production, constructed dispensaries, developed malaria-control programs, and distributed food and clothing to refugees. . . .

The Truman policy brought only limited results. Their hopes of victory revived by the prospect of large-scale American assistance, the French in late 1950 appointed the flamboyant Jean de Lattre de Tassigny to command the armed forces in Indochina and instructed him to prosecute the war vigorously. A born crusader and practitioner of what he called *dynamisme,* de Lattre announced upon arriving in Vietnam that he would win the war within fifteen months, and under his inspired leadership French forces repulsed a major Vietminh offensive in the Red River Delta in early 1951. But when de Lattre attempted to follow up his success by attacking Vietminh strongholds just south of Hanoi, France suffered its worst defeat of the war. De Lattre himself would die of cancer in early 1952, and the French military position was more precarious at the time of his death than when he had come to Vietnam.

In other areas as well there was little progress. Desperately short of manpower, the French finally put aside their reluctance to arm the Vietnamese, and de Lattre made determined efforts to create a Vietnamese National Army (VNA). The Vietnamese were understandably reluctant to fight for what they regarded as a French cause, however, and by the end of 1951 the VNA numbered only 38,000 men, far short of its projected strength of 115,000. Responding to American entreaties, the French vaguely promised to "perfect" the independence of the Associated States, but the massive infusion of American supplies and de Lattre's early victories seemed to eliminate any compelling need for real concessions. The French were unwilling to fight for *Vietnamese* independence and never seriously considered the only sort of concession that would have satisfied the aspirations of Vietnamese nationalism. France transferred to the native governments some additional responsibilities, but they remained shadow governments lacking in real authority and in popular support. . . .

Deeply suspicious of American intrusion into their domain, the French expressed open resentment against the aid program and placed numerous obstacles in its ways. De Lattre bitterly complained that there were too many Americans in Vietnam spending too much money, that the American aid program was making France "look like a poor cousin in Vietnamese eyes," and that the Americans were "fanning the flames of extreme nationalism." French officials attempted to block projects which did not contribute directly to the war and encouraged Vietnamese suspicions by warning that American aid contained "hidden traps" to subvert their "independence." Largely as a result of French obstructionism, the aid program touched only a small number of people. American officials conceded that its "beneficial psychological results were largely negated because the United States at the same time was pursuing a program of [military] support to the French." America was looked upon "more as a supporter of colonialism than as a friend of the new nation."

While firmly resisting American influence in Indochina, France demanded larger military assistance and an expanded American commitment. Already facing the threat of a military and political collapse in Indochina, the French grew more concerned when American efforts to negotiate an end to the war in Korea raised the possibility that Chinese troops would be freed for a drive southward. In early 1952, France pressed Washington relentlessly for additional military aid, a collective security arrangement for the defense of Southeast Asia, and a firm commitment to provide American combat forces should Chinese troops cross the border into Vietnam.

Washington was extremely wary of expanding its commitments. The proposal for a collective security arrangement appeared to be a snare to draw the United States more deeply into the conflict, and the Truman administration promptly rejected it. The "line we took," Acheson later recalled, was that "in some places such as Europe and NATO, we had a common responsibility. In other places, one or the other of these nations had to take a leading part." The United States also refused to commit ground forces to Indochina under any circumstances. The administration had initiated a massive rearmament program, but progress had been slowed by the war in Korea and the National Security Council concluded that the nation faced the "continuing danger of global war, as well as local aggression in a situation of inadequate military strength." The drawn–out, costly stalemate in Korea had produced considerable frustration among the American people and had made abundantly clear the difficulties of fighting a land war in Asia. It would be "futile and a mistake to defend Indochina in Indochina," Acheson observed. We "could not have another Korea, we could not put ground forces into Indochina."

The administration was not prepared to abandon France, however. By early 1952, the domino theory was firmly rooted as a principle of American foreign policy. Policymakers agreed that Southeast Asia must not be permitted to "fall into the hands of the Communists like a ripe plum" and that a continued French presence in Indochina was essential to the defense of that critical region. . . .

America's Indochina policy continued to be a hostage of its policy in Europe, the area to which Truman and Acheson assigned the highest priority. Since 1951, the United States had been pressing for allied approval of the European Defense Community, a plan for the integration of French and German forces into a multinational army originally put forward by France to delay German rearmament. The French repeatedly warned that they could not furnish troops for European defense without generous American support in Indochina, a ploy Acheson accurately described as "blackmail." The European Defense Community had also become a volatile political issue in France, where there was strong nationalistic resistance to surrendering the identity of the French army and to collaborating with a recent, and still despised, enemy. With the question awaiting ratification by the French parliament, Acheson later recalled, no one "seriously advised" that it would be "wise to end, or threaten to end, aid to Indochina unless an American plan of military and political reform was carried out." NSC 124/2, a major policy statement on Indochina of June 1952, would go no further than state that the United States should use its "influence" to "promote positive political, military, economic, and social policies. . . ."

During the last half of 1952, Acheson did make a concerted effort to break through French secretiveness. The Secretary of State bluntly informed French officials in July that since the United States was paying about one-third of the cost of the war it did not seem "unreasonable" to expect some detailed information about its progress. The French did not dissent, Acheson later recalled, but "not much happened as a result." Following a long and heated session of the Council of Foreign Ministers in Paris in December, the French again requested additional military assistance. "At this point tired, hungry and exasperated," Acheson later wrote, "I ran out of patience." He complained forcefully that the United States was "thoroughly dissatisfied" with the information it was getting and warned that this situation "had to be remedied. We must know exactly what the situation was and what we were doing if, as and when we were to take any further step." Acheson's protest revealed the depth of American frustration with more than two years of partnership with France, but it came too late to have any effect. Within less than a month, the Truman administration would leave office, freeing it from further responsibility.

Despite a considerable investment in Indochina, Truman and Acheson left to their successors a problem infinitely more complex and dangerous than the one they had taken on in 1950. What had begun as a localized rebellion against French colonialism had expanded into an international conflict of major proportions. The United States was now bearing more than 40 percent of the cost of the war and had established a stake in its outcome. Chinese aid to the Vietminh had increased from 400 tons per month to more than 3,000, and as many as 4,000 Chinese "volunteers" assisted the Vietminh in various ways. The war had spilled over into neighboring Laos and Thailand where China and the Vietminh backed insurgencies against governments supported by the United States and France. In Vietnam itself, French control had been reduced to enclaves around Hanoi, Haiphong, and Saigon, and a narrow strip along the Cambodian border, and France faced a new and much more ominous type of military threat. "The enemy, once painted as a bomb-throwing terrorist or hill sniper lurking in night ambush," the veteran correspondent Theodore White observed, "has become a modern army, increasingly skillful, armed with artillery, organized into divisional groups." The French had naively hoped that American aid might be a substitute for increased sacrifice on their own part, but they had come to realize that it only required more of them. Fearful of their nation's growing dependence on the United States and aware that victory would require nothing short of an all-out effort, in late 1952 some French political leaders outside the Communist party began for the first time to recommend withdrawal from Indochina. The "real" problem, Acheson warned the incoming administration, was the "French will to carry on the . . . war."

The Republican administration of Dwight D. Eisenhower accepted without modification the principles of Indochina policy bequeathed by the Democrats. Eisenhower and his Secretary of State John Foster Dulles . . . were even more reluctant than Truman and Acheson to commit American combat forces to Southeast Asia and agreed that France must remain in Indochina and bear the burden of the conflict. . . .

The new administration set out zealously to correct the mistakes of its predecessor. Alarmed by growing signs of war-weariness in France, Eisenhower and Dulles gave firm assurances of continued assistance and promised that the nation's "tiredness" would "evaporate in the face of a positive and constructive program." The administration also made clear, however, that continued aid would be conditioned on detailed and specific information about French military operations and plans and on firm French pledges to expand the Vietnamese National Army and to develop a new, aggressive strategy with an explicit timetable for the defeat of the enemy's main forces. Eisenhower himself advised Ambassador Douglas Dillon in Paris to impress upon the French the importance of appointing a *"forceful and inspirational leader, empowered with the means and authority to win victory,"* and of making "clear and unequivocal public announcements, repeated as often as may be desireable," that complete independence would be granted "as soon as victory against the Communists had been won.". . .

Within six months after the United States and France had agreed upon the "end-the-war offensive," the military and political situation in Indochina had drastically deteriorated. . . .

By early 1954, both sides had committed major forces to the remote village of Dienbienphu in the northwest corner of Vietnam. Navarre* established a position at the intersection of several major roads near the Laotian border in hopes of cutting off the anticipated invasion and luring Vietminh main units into open battle. In a broad valley surrounded by hills as high as 1,000 feet, he constructed a garrison ringed with barbed wire and bunkers, and hastily dispatched twelve battalions of regulars supported by aircraft and heavy artillery. Giap took the "bait." After a quick strike into Laos, he retraced his steps and encircled the French garrison. Navarre now found 12,000 of his elite forces isolated in a far corner of Vietnam. Although increasingly uncertain that they could hold out against superior Vietminh numbers, in January he decided to remain. . . .

The political crisis of late 1953, along with an apparent shift in Soviet foreign policy, heightened French tendencies toward a negotiated settlement. Many French politicians concluded that Vietnamese association with the French Union, if only symbolic, was all that could be salvaged from the war and without this there was no reason to prolong the agony. The leaders who had assumed power in the Kremlin after Stalin's death in February had taken a conciliatory line on a number of major Cold War issues, Indochina included, and the French government hoped that Soviet influence would enable it to secure a favorable settlement. Over Dulles' vigorous opposition, France in early 1954 agreed to place Indochina on the agenda of an East–West conference scheduled to meet in Geneva to consider Far Eastern problems.

Eisenhower and Dulles could only acquiesce. Distrustful of the Soviet overtures and skeptical of the wisdom of the French decision, they were nevertheless unwilling to put the United States in the position of being the only great power to oppose peaceful settlement of a major international crisis.

In the spring of 1954, the United States for the first time faced the prospect of direct military intervention in Indochina. As late as mid-March, a special committee appointed by the President to review American policy concluded that the military situation, although dangerous, was not yet critical, and an American observer optimistically reported from Dienbienphu that the French fortress could "withstand any kind of attack the Vietminh are capable of launching." American officials feared, however, that French war-weariness would result in a surrender at Geneva. The special committee recommended that prior to the conference the United States should attempt to discourage defeatist tendencies in France and should use its influence at Geneva to ensure that no agreements were reached. If, despite American efforts, the French accepted a settlement which was unsatisfactory, the United States might have to arrange with the Associated States and other interested nations to continue the war without France.

While Eisenhower and his advisers pondered the long-range possibility

---

* General Henri Navarre commanded the French forces in Indochina.—*Ed.*

of American intervention in Indochina, Giap tightened the noose around Dienbienphu. On March 13, the Vietminh launched an all-out attack and within
twenty-four hours had seized hills Gabrielle and Beatrice, the outposts established by France to protect the fortress in the valley below. American and
French experts had predicted that it would be impossible to get artillery up
to the high ground surrounding the garrison. But the Vietminh formed "human ant-hills," carrying disassembled weapons up piece by piece, then reas-
sembling them and camouflaging them so effectively that they were impervious to artillery and strafing. The heavy Vietminh guns quickly knocked out
the airfield, making resupply impossible except by parachute drop and leaving
the garrison of 12,000 men isolated and vulnerable. . . .

Congressional opposition reinforced the administration's determination
to avoid unilateral intervention in support of France. In a speech that won
praise from both sides of the aisles, Democratic Senator John F. Kennedy of
Massachusetts warned that no amount of military aid could conquer "an
enemy of the people which has the support and covert appeal of the people,"
and that victory could not be attained in Indochina as long as France remained.
When a "high administration source," subsequently identified as Vice-President Richard M. Nixon, remarked "off the record" that if United Action
failed the United States might have to act alone, the reaction was immediate
and strong. Senate Democratic Leader Lyndon Johnson of Texas bitterly denounced the "Nixon war" and opposed "sending American G.I.s into the
mud and muck of Indochina on a blood-letting spree to perpetuate colonialism
and white man's exploitation in Asia."

Thus, even when France relented a bit, continued British opposition to
military intervention settled the fate of United Action.* . . . Eisenhower
informed Congressional leaders on April 26 that it would be a "tragic error
to go in alone as a partner of France" and made clear that the United States
would intervene only as part of a "grouping of interested nations." Three
days later, the National Security Council formally decided to "hold up for
the time any military action in IndoChina until we see how Geneva is coming
along."

The American decision sealed Dienbienphu's doom. Without American
air power, France had no means of saving the fortress. Subjected to merciless
pounding from Vietminh artillery and to a series of human-wave assaults,
the hopelessly outmanned defenders finally surrendered on May 7 after fifty-
five days of stubborn but futile resistance. The attention of belligerents and
interested outside parties immediately shifted to Geneva where the following
day the Indochina phase of the conference was set to begin. Buoyed by its
victory, the Vietminh confidently savored the prize for which it had been
fighting for more than seven years. Its influence in northern Vietnam now
reduced to a small pocket around Hanoi, France began preparations to abandon
the north and to salvage as much as possible in the area below the sixteenth

---

*A coalition including the United States, Great Britain, France, Australia, and New Zealand,
designed to guarantee the security of Southeast Asia.—*Ed.*

parallel. The French delegation came to Geneva, Bidault lamented, holding a "two of clubs and a three of diamonds."

The United States was a reluctant participant at Geneva. Negotiation with any Communist nation was anathema, but the presence of Communist China made the conference especially unpalatable. Dulles remained in Geneva only briefly and, in the words of his biographer, conducted himself like a "puritan in a house of ill repute." On one occasion, he remarked that the only way he and Chou En-lai, the top Chinese delegate, would meet was if their cars collided, and when they actually met face-to-face and Chou extended his hand, the Secretary reportedly turned his back. The administration had long feared that the conference would merely provide a fig leaf of respectability for the French surrender of Indochina, and the fall of Dienbienphu increased its concern. After departing Geneva, Dulles instructed the American delegation that it should participate in the conference only as an "interested nation," not as a "belligerent or a principal in the negotiations," and should not endorse an agreement which in any way impaired the territorial integrity of the Associated States. Given the military position of the Vietminh when the conference opened, Dulles was saying that the United States would approve no settlement at all. . . .

[In mid-June, when the Geneva conference was all but over,] the Eisenhower administration adopted a change of policy with momentous long-range implications. Recognizing that the war could not be prolonged without unacceptable risks and that part of Vietnam would probably be lost at Geneva, the administration began to lay plans for the defense of the rest of Indochina and Southeast Asia. Dulles informed Congressional leaders on June 24 that any agreement that emerged from Geneva would be "something we would have to gag about," but he nevertheless expressed optimism that the United States might still be able to "salvage something" in Southeast Asia "free of the taint of French colonialism." The United States would have to take over from France responsibility for defending Laos, Cambodia, and that part of Vietnam beneath the partition line. The first essential was to draw a line which the Communists would not cross and then to "hold this area and fight subversion within it with all the strength we have" by providing economic assistance and building a strong military force. The United States would also have to take the lead in forming a strong regional defense grouping "to keep alive freedom" in Southeast Asia.

Over the next few weeks, Dulles worked relentlessly to get the kind of settlement that would enable the United States to defend Indochina and Southeast Asia after Geneva. He secured British agreement to a set of principles that would constitute an "acceptable" settlement, including the freedom of Laos, Cambodia, and southern Vietnam to maintain "stable, non-communist regimes" and to accept foreign arms and advisers. He applied extreme pressure, even threatening to disassociate the United States entirely from Geneva, until [French Premier Pierre] Mendes-France accepted the so-called seven points as the basis for the French bargaining position. Although armed with firm British and French promises, Dulles still approached the last stages of the conference with great caution and with a determination to retain complete freedom of action. The United States should play no more than a passive role in the negotiations, he instructed the head of the American delegation, Walter Bedell Smith. If the agreement lived up to its standards, the administration would issue a unilateral statement of endorsement, but if it fell short the United States would reserve the freedom to "publicly disassociate itself." Under no circumstances would it be a "cosignatory with the Communists," and it would not be placed in a position of guaranteeing the results.

When the conference reconvened, pressures for a settlement had increased significantly. . . . Although the Vietminh's military position gave it strong claim for influence throughout Vietnam, both the Russians and Chinese exerted heavy pressure for a compromise peace. The Soviet Union had only limited interests in Southeast Asia and appears to have pursued a conciliatory line toward France in order to encourage French rejection of the European Defense Community. China sought to enhance its international prestige and to cultivate influence among the neutral nations of South and Southeast Asia by playing the role of peacemaker. Moreover, the Chinese apparently feared that a prolonged war ran serious risks of American intervention, and they may have felt that a partition arrangement would make the Vietminh more susceptible to their influence. For reasons of their own, the Russians and Chinese moderated Vietminh demands and played a crucial role in arranging the settlement.

The Geneva Accords of 1954 reflected these influences. Vietnam was to be partitioned along the seventeenth parallel to permit the regrouping of military forces from both sides. The agreements stressed that the division was to be only temporary and that it should not be "interpreted as constituting a political or territorial boundary." The country was to be reunified by elections scheduled for the summer of 1956 and to be supervised by an international commission composed of Canada, Poland, and India. To insulate Vietnam against a renewal of conflict during the transitional period, the agreements provided that forces should be withdrawn from the respective partition zones within 300 days, and they prohibited the introduction of new forces and equipment and the establishment of foreign military bases. Neither portion of Vietnam was to join a military alliance. The agreements also established cease-fire arrangements for Laos and Cambodia. The two nations' right to self-defense was explicitly recognized, but to assuage Chinese fears of American intervention, they were not to enter military alliances or permit foreign bases on their soil except in cases where their security was clearly threatened.

The Eisenhower administration viewed the Geneva Agreements with mixed feelings. As had been feared, the settlement produced some domestic political backlash; Republican Senate Leader William Knowland denounced it as the "greatest victory the Communists have won in twenty years." The administration itself regarded the loss of northern Vietnam—"the keystone to the arch of Southeast Asia"—with concern. Eisenhower and Dulles realized, as Smith put it, that "diplomacy has rarely been able to gain at the conference table what cannot be held on the battlefield." The administration protected itself against domestic criticism and retained its freedom of action by refusing to associate itself directly with the agreements. In a unilateral statement, Smith simply "took note" of the Geneva Accords and said that the United States would not "disturb them" by the "threat or the use of force."

The administration was not altogether displeased with the results, however. The agreements were better than had been anticipated when the conference opened, and they allowed sufficient latitude to proceed along the lines Dulles had already outlined. Partition was unpalatable, but it gave the United States the opportunity to build up non-Communist forces in southern Vietnam, a challenge Eisenhower and Dulles took up eagerly. The accords placed some limits on outside intervention, to be sure, but the administration did not view them as prohibitive. And some of the provisions seemed advantageous. Eisenhower and Dulles agreed, for example, that if elections were held immediately Ho Chi Minh would be an easy victor. But the two-year delay gave the United States "fairly good time" to get ready, and Canada's presence on the commission would enable it to "block things."

Eisenhower and Dulles viewed the apparent demise of French colonialism in Southeast Asia with equanimity, if not outright enthusiasm. From the start, the Franco-American partnership in Indochina had been marked by profound mutual suspicion and deep-seated tensions. From 1950 to 1954, the United States had provided France more than $2.6 billion in military aid, but its efforts to influence French policies by friendly persuasion and by attaching strings had failed, and the commitment to France had indeed turned out to be a "dead-end alley." Eisenhower and Dulles attributed France's failure primarily to its attempts to perpetuate colonialism in Indochina, and they were confident that without the problems posed by France the United States could build a viable non-Communist alternative to the Vietminh. "We must work with these people, and then they themselves will soon find out that we are their friends and that they can't live without us," Eisenhower observed. Conceding that the Geneva Accords contained "many features which we did not like" Dulles nevertheless insisted that they included many "good aspects," most important, the "truly independent status" of Laos, Cambodia, and southern Vietnam. The "important thing," he concluded, was "not to mourn the past but to seize the future opportunity to prevent the loss in Northern Vietnam from leading to the extension of communism throughout Southeast Asia and the Southwest Pacific."

Sources

The Second Red Scare

One consequence of the cold war was what came to be known as "McCarthyism," after Senator Joseph McCarthy, the most flamboyant and aggressive of the politicians whose careers were devoted to "rooting out" Communists and Communist "sympathizers" in American institutions. Although McCarthy did not create the second Red Scare—the Truman administration warrants this accolade for its

federal employee security program—it was the Wisconsin Republican who made anticommunism a crusade. From February 1950, when he charged that the State Department harbored more than 200 Communist sympathizers, until December 1954, when his colleagues in the Senate passed a resolution of censure, McCarthy held center stage. Bringing his campaign to television, McCarthy's investigations of the State Department, the United States Information Agency, and the army convinced many that communism had succeeded in corrupting our basic institutions of communication and defense. They also laid the groundwork for inquiries at all levels of government designed to cleanse American society—its films, libraries, labor unions, and schools, for example—of all vestiges of Communist party influence.

McCarthyism, Party, and Class

Many historians and political scientists believe that Joseph McCarthy was a kind of working-class hero. They argue that his straightforward, even boorish manner appealed to those who distrusted and disliked the stylish, elite products of the Ivy League colleges, and that his hard anticommunist line found a sympathetic ear among those with too little education to resist its simplistic appeal. The following materials are useful in evaluating the argument. First, make some as-

Party Sympathies and Voting Records of Those Favorable and Unfavorable to Senator J. McCarthy

Questions
  I. Did you vote for Eisenhower (Republican) or Stevenson (Democratic)?
 II. If the elections for Congress were being held today, which party would you like to see win in this state—the Republican Party or the Democratic Party?
III. (If undecided) As of today, do you lean more to the Republican Party or to the Democratic Party?
 IV. In politics, as of today, do you consider yourself a Democrat, Republican, or Independent?

Question	Favorable (%)				Unfavorable (%)			
	I	II	III	IV	I	II	III	IV
Republican	76	53	37	46	49	29	28	24
Democratic	21	29	23	30	49	57	38	58
Undecided	—	17	27	—	—	13	26	—
Other	3	1	13	24	2	1	8	24
	100	100	100	100	100	100	100	100
	(N = 350)	(N = 456)	(N = 77)	(N = 456)	(N = 560)	(N = 693)	(N = 88)	(N = 693)

From Gallup Survey 529 K, April 1954. Material reprinted in Nelson W. Polsby, "Towards an Explanation of McCarthyism," *Political Studies* 8 (October 1960): 262. Copyright, The Gallup Poll (American Institute of Public Opinion). Reprinted by permission.

sumptions about who usually votes Republican, and who, Democratic. Then, from the table, draw some conclusions about McCarthy's base of support. What does the map of Wisconsin—McCarthy's home state—tell us about those who elected him?

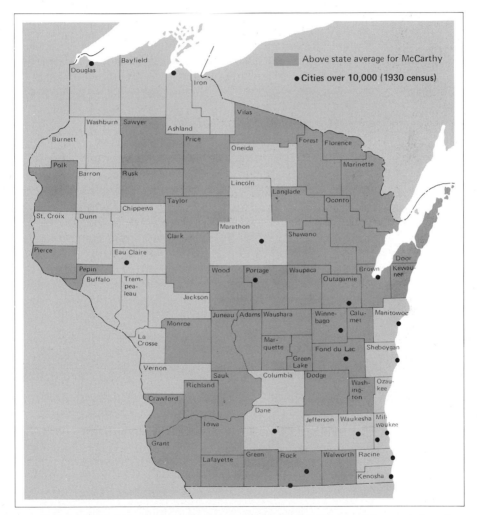

Support in Wisconsin for Senator Joseph McCarthy. *Reprinted by permission of the MIT Press from Michael Paul Rogin,* The Intellectuals and McCarthy: The Radical Specter *(Cambridge, Mass.: MIT Press, 1967), p. 87. Copyright © 1967 by the Massachusetts Institute of Technology.*

The Kitchen Debate, 1959

The "kitchen debate," a 1959 meeting between Soviet Premier Nikita Khrushchev and Vice President Richard Nixon, took place against a backdrop of more than a decade of conflict over the status of Berlin, a city deep inside East Germany that had been divided into Western and Soviet sectors.

The West had no legal claims to the city, whose Western sector had become a capitalist showcase and an embarrassment to the Soviets. In November 1958, Khrushchev threatened a separate peace with East Germany—meaning an end to Western influence in Berlin—if a "satisfactory settlement" were not reached within six months. As the deadline approached, fears grew that Berlin would finally bring a shooting war. But Khrushchev's deadline passed, and by the time the two leaders locked horns in the kitchen of the American National Exhibition in Moscow, it was not guns but butter that held center stage.

Khrushchev had emerged at the top of the Soviet hierarchy following the death of Joseph Stalin in 1953. His ascendancy presumably signaled a change in Soviet attitudes, for in 1956 Khrushchev denounced Stalin as a "distrustful man, sickly and suspicious."

The "kitchen debate" was widely interpreted in the United States as a moral victory for Nixon, who even at this date was actively campaigning for the presidency. Whether it was this or not, it was a unique event. Never before had two national leaders so freely and extemporaneously explored the relative merits of their respective economic and social systems. In the process, Nixon and Khrushchev bared national insecurities and demonstrated how subjects as different as free speech and color television had become part of the cold war.

Was the "kitchen debate" light entertainment, or did the participants come to grips with basic differences between the United States and the Soviet Union? In fact, does the debate reveal difference or suggest likeness? Why was there so much talk of consumer goods and living standards? Who was the more effective spokesman? Was Nixon engaged in a form of verbal containment?

Following is an account of the informal exchanges in Moscow yesterday between Vice President Richard M. Nixon and Premier Nikita S. Khrushchev. It was compiled from dispatches of the *New York Times*, the Associated Press, United Press International and Reuters. . . .

From "The Two-Worlds: A Day-Long Debate," *New York Times*, July 25, 1959, pp. 1, 3. Copyright © 1959 by The New York Times Company. Reprinted by permission.

A Trade of Gibes About Trade

On arriving at the gate of the American National Exhibition later in the morning, Mr. Khrushchev voiced a gibe about the United States ban on the shipment of strategic goods to the Soviet Union.

Khrushchev: "Americans have lost their ability to trade. Now you have grown older and you don't trade the way you used to. You need to be invigorated."

Nixon: "You need to have goods to trade."

The statesmen went on to look at equipment for playing back recordings. Mr. Nixon took a cue from it.

Nixon: "There must be a free exchange of ideas."

Mr. Khrushchev responded with a remark touching on the reporting of his speeches on his recent Polish tour.

Mr. Nixon said he was certain that Mr. Khrushchev's speeches and those of Frol R. Kozlov, a First Deputy Premier, had been fully reported in the West.

Khrushchev (indicating cameras, recording the scene on video tape): "Then what about this tape?" (smiling). "If it is shown in the United States it will be shown in English and I would like a guarantee that there will be a full translation of my remarks."

Mr. Nixon said there would be an English translation of Mr. Khrushchev's remarks and added his hope that all his own remarks in the Soviet Union would be given with full translations in that country.

Khrushchev: "We want to live in peace and friendship with Americans because we are the two most powerful countries, and if we live in friendship then other countries will also live in friendship. But if there is a country that is too war-minded we could pull its ears a little and say: Don't you dare; fighting is not allowed now; this is a period of atomic armament; some foolish one could start a war and then even a wise one couldn't finish the war. Therefore, we are governed by this idea in our policy—internal and foreign. How long has America existed? Three hundreds years?"

Nixon: "One hundred and fifty years."

They Will Wave as They Pass U.S.

Khrushchev: "One hundred and fifty years? Well, then, we will say America has been in existence for 150 years and this is the level she has reached.

We have existed not quite forty-two years and in another seven years we will be on the same level as America.

"When we catch you up, in passing you by, we will wave to you. Then if you wish we can stop and say: Please follow up. Plainly speaking, if you want capitalism you can live that way. That is your own affair and doesn't concern us. We can still feel sorry for you but since you don't understand us—live as you do understand.

"We are all glad to be here at the exhibition with Vice President Nixon. . . . I think you will be satisfied with your visit and if—I cannot go without saying it—if you would not take such a decision [proclamation by the United States Government of Captive Nations Week, a week of prayer for peoples enslaved by the Soviet Union] which has not been thought out thoroughly, as was approved by Congress, your trip would be excellent. But you have churned the water yourselves—why this was necessary God only knows.

"What happened? What black cat crossed your path and confused you? But that is your affair, we do not interfere with your problems. [Wrapping his arms about a Soviet workman] Does this man look like a slave laborer? [Waving at others] With men with such spirit how can we lose?"

Exchange of Ideas Urged by Nixon

Nixon (*Pointing to American workmen*): "With men like that we are strong. But these men, Soviet and American, work together well for peace, even as they have worked together in building this exhibition. This is the way it should be.

"Your remarks are in the tradition of what we have come to expect—sweeping and extemporaneous. Later on we will both have an opportunity to speak and consequently I will not comment on the various points that you raised, except to say this—this color television is one of the most advanced developments in communications that we have.

"I can only say that if this competition in which you plan to outstrip us is to do the best for both of our peoples and for peoples everywhere there must be exchange of ideas. After all, you don't know everything—"

Khrushchev: "If I don't know everything, you don't know anything about communism except fear of it."

Nixon: "There are some instances where you may be ahead of us, for example in the development of the thrust of your rockets for the investigation of outer space; there may be some instances in which we are ahead of you—in color television, for instance."

Khrushchev: "No, we are up with you on this, too. We have bested you in one technique and also in the other."

Nixon: "You see, you never concede anything."

Khrushchev: "I do not give up."

Appearances on TV Are Suggested

Nixon: "Wait till you see the picture. Let's have far more communication and exchange in this very area that we speak of. We should hear you more on our television. You should hear us more on yours."

Khrushchev: "That's a good idea. Let's do it like this. You appear before our people. We will appear before your people. People will see and appreciate this."

Nixon: "There is not a day in the United States when we cannot read what you say. When Kozlov was speaking in California about peace, you were talking here in somewhat different terms. This was reported extensively in the American press. Never make a statement here if you don't want it to be read in the United States. I can promise you every word you say will be translated into English."

Khrushchev: "I doubt it. I want you to give your word that this speech of mine will heard by the American people."

Nixon (shaking hands on it): "By the same token, everything I say will be translated and heard all over the Soviet Union?"

Khrushchev: "That's agreed."

Nixon: "You must not be afraid of ideas."

Khrushchev: "We are telling you not to be afraid of ideas. We have no reason to be afraid. We have already broken free from such a situation."

Nixon: "Well, then, let's have more exchange of them. We are all agreed on that. All right? All right?"

Khrushchev: "Fine. [Aside] Agree to what? All right, I am in agreement. But I want to stress what I am in agreement with. I know that I am dealing with a very good lawyer, I also want to uphold my own miner's flag so that the coal miners can say, 'Our man does not concede.'"

Nixon: "No question about that."

Khrushchev: "You are a lawyer for capitalism and I am a lawyer for communism. Let's compete."

Vice President Protests Filibuster

Nixon: "The way you dominate the conversation you would make a good lawyer yourself. If you were in the United States Senate you would be accused of filibustering."

Nixon (halting Khrushchev at model kitchen in model house): "You had a very nice house in your exhibition in New York. My wife and I saw and enjoyed it very much. I want to show you this kitchen. It is like those of our houses in California."

*Khrushchev (after Nixon called attention to a built-in panel-controlled washing ma-
    chine):* "We have such things."
Nixon: "This is the newest model. This is the kind which is built in thousands
    of units for direct installation in the houses."

He added that Americans were interested in making life easier for their
women. Mr. Khrushchev remarked that in the Soviet Union they did not
have "the capitalist attitude toward women."

Nixon: "I think that this attitude toward women is universal. What we want
    to do is make easier the life of our housewives."

He explained that the house could be built for $14,000 and that most
veterans had bought houses for between $10,000 and $15,000.

Nixon: "Let me give you an example you can appreciate. Our steel workers,
    as you know, are on strike. But any steel worker could buy this house.
    They earn $3 an hour. This house costs about $100 a month to buy on
    a contract running twenty-five to thirty years."
Khrushchev: "We have steel workers and we have peasants who also can afford
    to spend $14,000 for a house." He said American houses were built to
    last only twenty years, so builders could sell new houses at the end of
    that period. "We build firmly. We build for our children and grandchil-
    dren."

Mr. Nixon said he thought American houses would last more than twenty
years, but even so, after twenty years many Americans want a new home
or a new kitchen, which would be obsolete then. The American system is
designed to take advantage of new inventions and new techniques, he said.

Khrushchev: "This theory does not hold water."

He said some things never got out of date—furniture and furnishings,
perhaps, but not houses. He said he did not think that what Americans had
written about their houses was all strictly accurate.

Gadgetry Derided by Khrushchev

Nixon (pointing to television screen): "We can see here what is happening in
    other parts of the home."
Khrushchev: "This is probably always out of order."
Nixon: "Da [yes]."
Khrushchev: "Don't you have a machine that puts food into the mouth and
    pushes it down? Many things you've shown us are interesting but they

are not needed in life. They have no useful purpose. They are merely gadgets. We have a saying, if you have bedbugs you have to catch one and pour boiling water into the ear.". . .

Nixon (hearing jazz music): "I don't like jazz music."

Khrushchev: "I don't like it either."

Nixon: "But my girls like it.". . .

Russians Have It Too, Premier Asserts

Khrushchev: "The Americans have created their own image of the Soviet man and think he is as you want him to be. But he is not as you think. You think the Russian people will be dumbfounded to see these things, but the fact is that newly built Russian houses have all this equipment right now. Moreover, all you have to do to get a house is to be born in the Soviet Union. You are entitled to housing. I was born in the Soviet Union. So I have a right to a house. In America if you don't have a dollar—you have the right to choose between sleeping in a house or on the pavement. Yet you say that we are slaves of communism.". . .

Nixon: "To us, diversity, the right to choose, the fact that we have 1,000 builders building 1,000 different houses, is the most important thing. We don't have one decision made at the top by one government official. This is the difference.". . .

U.S. Models Stop the Debate, Briefly

Khrushchev (noting Nixon gazing admiringly at young women modeling bathing suits and sports clothes): "You are for the girls too."

Nixon (indicating a floor sweeper that works by itself and other appliances): "You don't need a wife."

Khrushchev chuckled.

Nixon: "We do not claim to astonish the Russian people. We hope to show our diversity and our right to choose. We do not wish to have decisions made at the top by government officials who say that all homes should be built in the same way. Would it not be better to compete in the relative merits of washing machines than in the strength of rockets? Is this the kind of competition you want?"

Khrushchev: "Yes, that's the kind of competition we want. But your generals say: 'Let's compete in rockets. We are strong and we can beat you.' But in this respect we can also show you something."

Nixon: "To me you are strong and we are strong. In some ways, you are stronger than we are. In others, we are stronger. We are both strong not only from the standpoint of weapons but from the standpoint of will and spirit. Neither should use that strength to put the other in a position where he in effect has an ultimatum. In this day and age that misses the point. With modern weapons it does not make any difference if war comes. We both have had it."

Khrushchev: "For the fourth time I have to say I cannot recognize my friend Mr. Nixon. If all Americans agree with you, then who don't we agree [with]? This is what we want."

Nixon: "Anyone who believes the American Government does not reflect the people is not an accurate observer of the American scene. I hope the Prime Minister understands all the implications of what I have just said. Whether you place either one of the powerful nations or any other in a position so that they have no choice but to accept dictation or fight, then you are playing with the most destructive force in the world.

"This is very important in the present world context. It is very dangerous. When we sit down at a conference table it cannot all be one way. One side cannot put an ultimatum to another. It is impossible. But I shall talk to you about this later."

Premier Insists That's a Threat

Khrushchev: "Who is raising an ultimatum?"

Nixon: "We will discuss that later."

Khrushchev: "If you have raised the question, why not go on with it now while the people are listening? We know something about politics, too. Let your correspondents compare watches and see who is filibustering. You put great emphasis on 'diktat' [dictation]. Our country has never been guided by 'diktat.' 'Diktat' is a foolish policy."

Nixon: "I am talking about it in the international sense."

Khrushchev: "It sounds to me like a threat. We, too, are giants. You want to threaten—we will answer threats with threats."

Nixon: "That's not my point. We will never engage in threats."

Khrushchev: "You wanted indirectly to threaten me. But we have the means to threaten too."

Nixon: "Who wants to threaten?"

Khrushchev: "You are talking about implications. I have not been. We have the means at our disposal. Ours are better than yours. It is you who want to compete, Da Da Da."

Nixon: "We are well aware of that. To me who is best is not material. . . . I see that you want to build a good life. But I don't think that the cause of peace is helped by reminders that you have greater strength than us because that is a threat, too."

Khrushchev: "I was answering your words. You challenged me. Let's argue fairly."

Nixon: "My point was that in today's world it is immaterial which of the two great countries at any particular moment has the advantage. In war these advantages are illusory. Can we agree on that?"

Khrushchev: "Not quite. Let's not beat around the bush."

Nixon: "I like the way he talks."

Peace to Russian Means: End Bases

Khrushchev: "We want to liquidate all bases from foreign lands. Until that happens we will speak different languages. One who is for putting an end to bases on foreign lands is for peace. One who is against it is for war. We have liquidated our bases, reduced our forces and offered to make a peace treaty and eliminate the point of friction in Berlin. Until we settle that question, we will talk different languages."

Nixon: "Do you think it can be settled at Geneva?"

Khrushchev: "If we considered it otherwise, we would not have incurred the expense of sending our foreign minister to Geneva. [Foreign Minister Andrei A.] Gromyko is not an idler. He is a very good man."

Nixon: "We have great respect for Mr. Gromyko. Some people say he looks like me. I think he is better looking. I hope it [the Geneva conference] will be successful."

Khrushchev: "It does not depend on us."

Nixon: "It takes two to make an agreement. You cannot have it all your own way."

Khrushchev: "These are questions that have the same aim. To put an end to the vestiges of war, to make a peace treaty with Germany—that is what we want. It is very bad that we quarrel over the question of war and peace."

Nixon: "There is no question but that your people and you want the Government of the United States being for peace—anyone who thinks that it is not for peace is not an accurate observer of America. In order to have peace, Mr. Prime Minister, even in an argument between friends, there must be sitting down around a round table. There must be discussion. Each side must find areas where it looks at the other's point of view. The world looks to you today with regard to Geneva. I believe it would be a grave mistake and a blow to peace if it were allowed to fail."

Khrushchev: "This is our understanding as well."

Nixon: "So this is something. The present position is stalemate. Ways must be found to discuss it."

Khrushchev: "The two sides must seek ways of agreement."

In the evening, after formal speeches, Mr. Khrushchev and Mr. Nixon, in departing, stopped by a table laden with glasses of wine. Mr. Khrushchev proposed a toast to "elimination of all military bases in foreign lands." Mr. Nixon sidestepped, suggested they drink to peace instead.

A Friendly Toast Set Off New Round

Khrushchev: "We stand for peace and elimination of bases. Those are our words and they do not conflict with our deeds. If you are not willing to eliminate bases then I won't drink this toast."

Nixon: "I don't like this wine."

Khrushchev: "I like this wine but not the policy."

Nixon: "I have always heard that the Prime Minister is a vigorous defender of his policy, not only officially but unofficially."

Khrushchev: "I defend the real policy, which is to assure peace. How can peace be assured when we are surrounded by military bases?"

Nixon: "We will talk about that later. Let's drink to talking—as long as we are talking we are not fighting."

Khrushchev (indicating a waitress): "Let's drink to the ladies."

Nixon: "We can all drink to the ladies."

A waiter: "A hundred years of life to Mr. Khrushchev."

Nixon: "I will drink to that. We may disagree but we want you to be in good health."

Khrushchev: "We accept your hundred years' proposal. But when I reach 99 we will discuss it further—why should we be in haste?"

Nixon: "You mean that in ninety-nine years you will still be in power—no election?"

Mr. Khrushchev drank. Then, leaving, he remarked that usually when foreign guests said good-by they mistakenly used the Russian words for "How do you do."

Khrushchev: "They say just the opposite of what they want to say."

Nixon: "I know a few things and when I see you again I'll know more. At least four words more—about bases."

Khrushchev (bidding farewell): "That's a very difficult thing to learn."

Selling America

The two photographs that follow are idealizations of American life, created by the United States Information Agency, the international propaganda arm of the American government. In a sense, they were weapons in the cold war. As you look at them, try to think of connections between them and the "kitchen debate" between Richard Nixon and Nikita Khrushchev. You may also want to compare them with the two Farm Security Administration photographs in Chapter 9. What continuities suggest themselves? what differences? According to the first photograph, what apparent relationship exists between technology and domestic bliss and harmony? What idealized notions of youth culture are present in the second photograph? Is there some connection between this photograph and Nixon's and Khrushchev's disavowal of jazz in the "kitchen debate"? between the photograph and the emergence of rock 'n' roll (Chapter 11)?

Original caption: "Takoma Park, Maryland—In the living room of their home, the A. Jackson Cory family and some friends watch a television program. Some sociologists claim the growing popularity of television will tend to make family life stronger and make the home the center of the family's recreation. 1950." *United States Information Agency photo, National Archives.*

Original Caption: "Washington, D.C.— Brennan Jacques, a typical American teenager, has his own orchestra, the 'Fabulous Esquires,' composed of youngsters aware of what their schoolmates like and do not like in current music. Here, young Jacques plays the piano for a group of young people, who have gathered around him. 1957." *United States Information Agency photo, National Archives.*

11

The Eisenhower Equilibrium

Reason, objectivity, dispassion—these were the qualities and values that twice elected Dwight Eisenhower to the presidency. His appeal was bipartisan. In 1948 and 1952, politicians of both major parties sought to nominate this man with the "leaping and effortless smile" who promised the electorate a "constitutional presidency"— immune from the ideological harangues of European dictators, American demagogues, and New Deal presidents—and a secure economy—immune from major dislocations. In effect, he offered Americans (a certain class of them at least) a "New Equilibrium" to replace the disjointed and unpredictable insecurity of depression and war.

By 1960, it was clear that Eisenhower—and the nation at large— had not sought to gain these ends through any radical departures from the past. The cold war, anticommunism, the welfare state—all inherited from his Democratic predecessor, Harry Truman—were not so much thrown aside as modulated, or refined, or brought into balance.

Joseph McCarthy would cease to be a factor after 1954, but otherwise, anticommunism was almost as much a part of the Eisenhower years as it had been of Truman's. The purges that cleansed most labor unions of communist influence were completed when Ike took office, but cold-war attitudes permeated the labor movement throughout the decade. The Committee on Un-American Activities of the House of Representatives (HUAC) would never know the acclaim it had mustered in the late 1940s, but each year it received more money from Congress and continued to function. In 1959, the Supreme Court refused to declare HUAC in violation of the First Amendment. New organizations—Robert Welch's John Birch Society and the Christian Anti-Communist Crusade, for example—

emerged to carry on the struggle against internal subversion. Welch labeled Eisenhower a "dedicated, conscious agent of the communist conspiracy."

Those who feared that the first Republican president since Herbert Hoover would grasp the opportunity to dismantle the welfare state had misunderstood both Eisenhower and the function of government at mid-century. If only intuitively, Eisenhower knew that what was left of the New Deal could not be eliminated without risking serious social and economic disruption. Countercyclical programs like old-age insurance and unemployment insurance were maintained or expanded; the Council of Economic Advisers, created in the Employment Act of 1946 to provide the president with his own planning staff, remained; spending for military hardware and interstate highways was expected to create jobs. Republicans did manage a rollback of New Deal policies in the areas of taxation and agriculture.

There was in much of this a pervasive element of acceptance—acceptance of American institutions as they were or as Americans wished they were. The power of the large corporation was accepted, its influence invited. Many agreed with General Motors president Charles E. Wilson, who during Senate hearings to confirm his nomination as secretary of defense said, "I thought what was good for our country was good for General Motors, and vice versa." Effective government was often conceptualized as the product of big business, big labor, and big government, each checking and balancing the others. The antitrust emphasis of the later New Deal was all but forgotten. Instead, Americans took comfort in John Kenneth Galbraith's theory of countervailing power, which postulated a self-regulating economy in which some big businesses (such as Sears, Roebuck) countervailed others (such as General Electric), leaving government the limited task of fine-tuning an economic system whose basic structure was virtually guaranteed to be competitive.

It followed that a wide variety of social problems—racism, unemployment, poverty, urban life, and the cult of domesticity, which suffocated women—were ignored, denied, accepted, or left in abeyance to be handled by some future generation. Throughout the 1950s, social commentators affirmed that America's central problems were ones of boredom, affluence, and classlessness. *The Midas Plague,* a science-fiction novel, described a world in which goods were so easily produced and so widely available that consuming had become a personal duty, a social responsibility, and an enormous and endless burden. David Riesman's *Lonely Crowd,* an influential study published in 1950, argued that the age of scarcity had ended; Americans would henceforth be concerned with leisure, play, and the "art of living." For many analysts of American society, the new conditions of life had eliminated the old conflicts between capital and labor and ushered in the "end of ideology." Economic growth—so the theory went—would increase the size of the total product to be distributed and soon result in a society consisting mainly of white-collar workers.

Beneath this surface of calm equilibrium, there were some currents that disturbed many Americans. Despite a landmark Supreme Court decision in 1954 ordering the eventual racial integration of public schools, black Americans remained outside the American system, gathering energies for a spectacular assault on the traditions of prejudice and exploitation. Intellectuals were worried about "conformity," and everyone was concerned about an apparent alienation among many young people, an alienation that expressed itself sometimes frighteningly as juvenile delinquency, sometimes just as a mystifying lack of energetic affirmation, most often in an affinity for a new music called rock 'n' roll. Following the launch of the Soviet satellite *Sputnik* in 1957, Americans began to ask whether this technological defeat reflected a general withering of national purpose (a theme taken up by Eisenhower's successor, John Kennedy). As the decade wore on, it became obvious, too, that millions of Americans were not participating in the prosperity the administration proclaimed. Eisenhower's farewell address would be silent on most of these issues; but its discussion of the military-industrial complex was perhaps Eisenhower's way of acknowledging that the equilibrium he had tried so hard to preserve—indeed, to create—was fundamentally unstable. If so, the next decade would prove him right.

Interpretive Essay

Henry F. Bedford

Boycott in Montgomery, 1955

More than three decades later, the boycott of buses by blacks in Montgomery, Alabama, remains an event of almost mythic importance. It has this quality not because the buses were boycotted or because the event dramatically changed race relations in Montgomery, but because it began in a single, dramatic, unplanned act. It seemed

then, and it seems today, as though Rosa Parks, in refusing to surrender her seat to a white man, had somehow stepped outside history—outside a century of segregation ordinances and black submission—to single-handedly launch the modern civil-rights movement.

Parks was not, of course, all that independent from history. She
had seen President Harry Truman, in 1946, appoint the Committee
on Civil Rights and then, in 1948, issue an executive order that
would begin the process of desegregating the armed forces. Just the
year before the trouble started in Montgomery, she had learned of
the Supreme Court's decision in *Brown* v. *Board of Education of
Topeka* (1954), in which segregated schools were held to be in violation of the Fourteenth Amendment to the Constitution. She may
also have followed the efforts of grass-roots civil-rights organizations that had been pressing for reforms in many southern communities.

Nonetheless, the Montgomery bus boycott was not a culmina-
tion, but a beginning. In style, mood, and tactics, it prefigured the
civil-rights movement of the late 1950s and early 1960s. One can see
the hand of Montgomery in the lunch-counter sit-ins at Greensboro,
North Carolina, in 1960; in the "freedom rides" of the early 1960s, in
which blacks and whites sought to end segregation in interstate
travel; in the great March on Washington in the summer of 1963; and
in the voter-registration drives of 1964. Soon thereafter, the civil-
rights movement would become something altogether different, but
until then, it bore the stamp of Rosa Parks, the bus boycott, and, of
course, Martin Luther King, Jr.

Consider the Montgomery bus boycott as just such a "typical"
episode in the civil-rights movement. What qualities did it have—
what mood and what tactics, for example? It is also important to remember that the events in Montgomery took place in the mid-1950s,
in the context of the Eisenhower equilibrium. Did the boycott upset
that equilibrium in any substantial way, or did the whole complex of
events take place without altering the balance of the era? To the extent that the boycott in Montgomery *was* a successful social movement, who or what made it so? Rosa Parks? Martin Luther King, Jr.?
the unity of the black community? the Supreme Court?

Martin Luther King, Jr., did not always arise with the sun. But Monday,
December 5, 1955, was a special day, and the excited young minister could
not sleep. Impatiently he paced the house, waiting for the first bus of the
day to reach its stop near his front porch. The vehicle was usually crowded
with black domestics on their way to the kitchens and yards of the white
employers of Montgomery, Alabama; it would be a good test of the boycott
he and others had urged local blacks to undertake. King had prepared himself
for disappointment and hoped to be cheered by partial success. But the first

bus was empty, and the second, and the third. The exhilarated pastor under-took a wider investigation in his car.

In another part of the city, a young white reporter was conducting his own investigation. Joe Azbell, city editor of the *Montgomery Advertiser,* stood on Court Square in the dim dawn. The city's Christmas decorations caught the early sun and tinkled when they stirred. A banner proclaiming PEACE ON EARTH cast a shadow, through which an erect, middle-aged black man walked as he crossed the street. At the corner a bus stopped, and the driver opened the door. When the man did not move, the driver asked "Are you gettin' on?" "I ain't gettin' on," the black returned, " 'till Jim Crow gets off." Jim Crow—the personification of racial segregation—was a perpet-ual passenger, so the driver closed the door and drove off.

The struggle to get Jim Crow off the buses and out of American life was one of the central themes of the nation's history after the Second World War. In retrospect, the early stages of the civil rights movement may seem idealistic and naive, and the participation of Northern whites patronizing and hypocritical. The progress they celebrated seems trivial now that Ameri-cans have a somewhat better sense of the detours on their pilgrimage to equality. Yet President Harry Truman's order in 1948 ending segregation in the armed forces was no minor matter when much of the nation's male youth expected a tour of military duty. And the Supreme Court's unanimous ruling in 1954 against segregated schooling in the case of *Oliver Brown et al.* v. *Board of Education of Topeka, Kansas* was even more inclusive.

President Dwight Eisenhower subordinated racial reform to his primary concern with domestic calm. He hoped to heal social divisions that derived from Truman's controversial domestic and foreign policies, to end the frustrat-ing Korean War, to take the passion out of the nation's obsession with subver-sion. Eisenhower soothed the country by his evident and sincere affirmation of traditional verities—patriotism, public service, personal courtesy, free enter-prise. Southern whites found his stance in the middle of the political road as congenial as his silent acceptance of continued segregation. Temperamentally, the President was neither a bigot nor a crusader, and his administration needed the political help of Southerners who dominated Congress. Pressure to carry out the *Brown* decision had to come from outside Washington.

And not, in most instances, from whites, since any affirmation of racial equality tended to provoke a noisy defense of white supremacy that forced moderates to choose between black and white. Even well-intentioned whites ordinarily kept a prudent silence in order to maintain their standing in the white community. When cornered, Southern officials declared that the *Brown* ruling applied only to the schools of Topeka and required no change in local laws or habits. This do-nothing strategy of whites gave the initiative to South-ern blacks, who began to ask admission to schools and all the other places from which they had always been excluded.

It became customary to identify the leaders of these efforts as "new Negroes," a phrase that often implied Northern education, Northern resi-dence, or extensive contact with whites through military service or another profession. This identification betrayed, slightly more subtly, the same condescension white Southerners expressed when they damned "outside agitators" for racial friction. Both explanations assumed that Southern blacks could not themselves conceive and execute a strategy for integration without assistance from whites, from an "enlightened" organization like the National Association for the Advancement of Colored People (NAACP), or from a subversive one such as the Communist party. A black mailman in Montgomery knew better:

> New Negro? It's just us old Negroes, the same old folks. It's not the "new Negro"—it's the new times.

In many respects, the postwar years were in fact "new times" in the Old South. Diversified and mechanized agriculture reduced the region's dependence on cotton and sharecropping. Displaced tenant farmers had to seek new jobs in cities—in Detroit or Chicago or Los Angeles, or in the industries and service trades of expanding Southern cities. Urban blacks gradually discovered that concentration gave them an independence that rural isolation never bestowed. In cities, blacks could support and encourage one another, gain the leverage of their combined economic power, and bring pressure to conform on those who were ready to sell out too soon.

Most urban whites retained their sentimental attachment to the Old South; the Stars and Bars, the flag of the Confederacy, still flew over the state capitol in Montgomery, for instance, and the city proudly billed itself as "the cradle of the Confederacy." But economically, Montgomery had rejoined the Union, for national defense was the chief industry. More important than the marketing of beef or lumber, and more important than the production of fertilizer for Alabama's farms were the air bases located just out of town. One in seven families in the region depended upon the sixty million federal dollars that flowed through Maxwell Field. Except for a few local peculiarities, wrote a visitor from the North in 1956, Montgomery could pass for Hartford or Des Moines.

One of those peculiarities, of course, was Montgomery's race relations. However rigid the segregation of Hartford or Des Moines, the pattern was not frozen in law. Even the federal government's insistence on the integration of Maxwell Field had almost no impact on Montgomery. A municipal ordinance, for example, prescribed separate taxis for black and white, and drivers who brought servicemen of both races from the base to the city were arrested and fined. Commanders at the base made no effort to modify off-post segregation and ordered air force personnel to avoid involvement when the boycott created racial tension in Montgomery.

Statistics indicate the persistence of injustice. The median white worker earned almost twice the $970 annual wage of the median black in 1950. Almost two-thirds of the employed black women were domestic servants, and almost half the black men were unskilled laborers or domestic handymen; there were two black lawyers in Alabama's capital city, where white lawyers abounded.

Two of three black families lacked flush toilets, a statistic that would have chagrined the city fathers of Lawrence forty years earlier. Systematic discrimination kept about fourteen of fifteen potential black voters unregistered and prevented any political expression of discontent.

The habits of segregation lingered in the decade after the Second World War, and the absence of new modes of race relations sometimes made social contact awkward. If black policemen were appointed, could they arrest white people? Should the white sales attendant say "thank you, sir" to a black customer? Could any step be taken that would not lead to integrated schools and to "race-mixing"? One of Montgomery's Episcopal clergymen explained the dilemma in terms of broken communication. Although we know the blacks we live with, Thomas R. Thrasher wrote, "we are aware that we know them not." "They speak," he continued; "we do not understand."

Many white moderates, like Thomas Thrasher, acknowledged the need to modify segregated ways. But most whites reserved the right to specify both kind and quantity of reform. "You'll be surprised at all the things we're planning for you people," Montgomery's mayor remarked to the young black lawyer who sought desegregation of the city's parks. The mayor probably meant well, but he could neither give blacks what they asked nor concede their ability to plan for themselves.

Actually, there were blacks in Montgomery who were entirely capable of planning for themselves. E. D. Nixon, a scarred veteran of the civil rights struggle, had registered to vote, run for municipal office, held virtually every office in the local NAACP, and served as president of the Alabama chapter. Mrs. Jo Ann Robinson, a teacher at the local black college and head of the Women's Political Caucus, had planned a bus boycott once before and cancelled it because the unmarried, pregnant, fifteen-year-old who had been arrested seemed an unsuitable symbol of racial discrimination. Ralph Abernathy, the sensible pastor of the First Baptist Church, counseled his friend Martin Luther King, Jr., and sometimes helped stiffen his determination.

King himself had some of the qualifications of an "outside agitator." Educated in the North and recently arrived in Montgomery, King's roots were nonetheless in the South. The son and grandson of Atlanta ministers, King had been reared in relative comfort among proud, educated blacks. His mother's father had sparked a black boycott that contributed to the failure of the Hearst paper in Atlanta. Martin Luther King, Sr., did not let success obscure his origin on a sharecropper's patch, his struggle for education, or his anger over Georgia's segregation statutes. He insulated his son from some of the ugliest manifestations of racism and encouraged the youngster's bookishness. Young Martin entered Morehouse College at fifteen and, after graduation, went to theological school in Pennsylvania and then sought further graduate study at Boston University. King could have made his career in the North, but the South was home and in 1954 he and his wife moved into the parsonage of Montgomery's Dexter Avenue Baptist Church.

In his first year in Montgomery, King attended to his pastoral chores and completed his doctoral dissertation. Although he declined to become president of the local chapter of the NAACP, justifiably pleading inadequate time, he hoped to persuade his parish to support programs for social and political change.

While King learned his calling and his community, the people of Alabama began to assimilate the Supreme Court's ruling on desegregation. A federal judge ordered the state university to admit two black women whose request had been in the courts for years. Parents in several communities, including Montgomery, petitioned school boards to assign black children to white schools. E. D. Nixon, head of the NAACP's committee on education, suggested a biracial committee to plan desegregation. The school board denied the petition and authorized, but did not appoint, the committee. Although the superintendent thought a great deal of study would be required, he did not indicate when it might begin. The *Montgomery Advertiser* approved evasion as the only possible course. The city would maintain segregation "pending, of course, a committee report and perhaps two or three exhaustive subcommittee reports."

White supremacists found the *Advertiser*'s support for segregation too tepid. The paper reported formation of die-hard White Citizens' Councils (WCC) in Mississippi and elsewhere in Alabama, but frowned editorially at the old-fashioned racism of these "manicured Ku Kluxers." An Alabama state senator suggested that a refusal to subscribe and to advertise might persuade the editors to reenlist in "this fight to preserve our heritage of segregation." A correspondent picked up the suggestion of economic coercion and carried it several steps further: all employers should fire their black employees and all businesses deny blacks credit.

Economic pressure was the tactic White Citizens' Councils advocated, and the *Advertiser* assigned a reporter to ask Montgomery's whites their opinion of the organization. The reporter found cautious support for the WCC's purpose, but not much for economic coercion, a conclusion confirmed in October when disappointed sponsors conceded that only 300 of Montgomery's 70,000 whites had attended the WCC's organizational rally. The audience, the *Advertiser* noted editorially, was not only pathetically tiny but also unrepresentative of the community: there were "no face cards"—"no bankers, doctors, lawyers, merchants, insurance executives, contractors, architects, PTA officers, preachers, auto dealers, gasoline distributors or—conspicuously—politicians . . . within a mile of the meeting." And what the audience heard were tired clichés about "mongrelizing our race."

The rejoinder was measured and literate. A letter to the editor corrected the *Advertiser*'s mistaken report that no clergymen had attended the WCC meeting. But Chester E. Johnson accepted the *Advertiser*'s general thesis that the community's leaders disdained the WCC, a circumstance that he thought augured well for the organization. Leaders, Johnson argued, had failed effectively to uphold the nation's principles during negotiations with Stalin at Yalta and in the United Nations; leaders had reduced the nation to its present sorry state. The WCC wanted no leaders and relied instead on the ordinary people who were the country's greatest resource.

Foremost among the leaders Alabama's WCC distrusted was Governor James E. Folsom. Called "Big Jim" because of his stature and "Kissing Jim" because of his campaign technique, Folsom had been the state's governor from 1947–1951 and easily won a second term in 1954. He was, the editor of the *Advertiser* wrote, "the only major southern demagogue in our history, with the short-time exception of Tom Watson of Georgia, who has . . . been able to harness the so-called red necks and the colored voters." Keeping those discordant factions "very happily in the same vest pocket," Grover Hall continued, was "an extraordinary performance in American politics." Folsom sustained the alliance with a revamped populism that combined progressive economic policy with hillbilly music and backwoods mannerisms.

If Folsom's stump tactics were conventional, his views on race relations were not. He had found blacks to be "good citizens," he said, "and if they had been making a living for me like they have for [whites in] the Black Belt, I'd be proud of them instead of kicking them and cussing them all the time." He openly supported the efforts of Alabama blacks to regain the right to vote, and he appointed people who shared that view to positions where they could influence registration. He watched with amusement as the Alabama legislature, with all the subtlety, grace, and effect of "a hound dog baying at the moon," found ways to record its disapproval of integration. He vetoed legislative attempts to cripple the NAACP and intimidate its members, although the legislature predictably overrode most of those vetoes. When a bill passed permitting local officials to consider the general welfare of the community and several other superficially nonracial factors in assigning children to schools, Folsom let the measure become law without his signature. This pupil-placement law had so much legislative support that a veto would have served only a symbolic purpose anyway.

Folsom's failure to champion segregation was a sin of omission that he soon compounded. Adam Clayton Powell, the Harlem congressman who stood for everything the WCC abominated, visited Montgomery in November 1955 for a speech at Alabama State College. The governor had a cocktail with the visiting congressman—the alcohol alone disturbed many Southern Baptists—discussed the pace of Southern integration, and placed a limousine at Powell's disposal. Powell told his audience that Folsom had said integration was inevitable: "it is here now." The governor later protested that he had been misquoted, and that his reference had been to the nation, not to Alabama. He might have saved his effort, for he had bet on the wrong horse. Integration and black political participation would not come to Alabama soon enough to save Folsom's career. George Wallace, one of Folsom's ablest political lieutenants, carefully disassociated himself from the governor's increasingly unpopular views, a decision that indicated the force of the political gale. Three months after Powell's visit, Folsom admitted he "couldn't be elected dog-catcher." There were simply too few whites for whom segregation was personally inconvenient or morally offensive to sustain Folsom's moderation.

Boycott

Rosa Parks had had a hard day. As usual, she had fussed over fit and pinned and stitched hems at the Montgomery Fair, a department store where she worked. She had done a little shopping herself. The crowds were abnormally large with Christmas less than a month away, so Mrs. Parks hoped there would be a seat that evening on the bus that would take her home to Cleveland Avenue. She paid her fare and then stepped off to board in the rear, as local custom required. Because the rear section was full, she sat in one of the middle seats that blacks might occupy when whites did not.

The bus made slow progress around Court Square and stopped at the Empire Theater, where several white passengers boarded. In accordance with a municipal ordinance, the driver asked four blacks, including Mrs. Parks, to stand in order to seat the additional white passengers. Three blacks promptly complied. Mrs. Parks refused. "I don't really know why I wouldn't move," she said later.

> There was no plot or plan at all. I was just tired from shopping. I had my sacks and all, and my feet hurt.

The driver found two policemen, who charged Mrs. Parks with violation of the city's segregation ordinance and ordered her to appear in court on Monday morning, December 5. Once booked, she called E. D. Nixon, for whom she had worked as a volunteer in the local office of the NAACP. Nixon spread the word.

Jo Ann Robinson reminded Nixon that plans to boycott the bus company had been shelved some months earlier. Both agreed that Mrs. Parks, who was well known and widely respected among Montgomery's blacks, presented an ideal symbol of the injustice of segregation. Dignified and diligent, forty-two years old, with coiled, braided hair and spectacles, Mrs. Parks was no pushy adolescent. After a momentary hesitation, Martin Luther King, Jr., volunteered his church for a planning session, to which Nixon and Mrs. Robinson invited leaders of the black community. Before the group could assemble, mimeographed leaflets proposing a boycott began to appear on the street.

The chance inquiry of an illiterate maid, unable to decipher one of those leaflets, alerted the *Montgomery Advertiser* to plans for a boycott. Or rather that was the explanation Joe Azbell used to protect his source, E. D. Nixon, who wanted a report in the Sunday paper to alert blacks who might not otherwise be informed. Although Azbell knew Ralph Abernathy and had other contacts in the black community, his first story left some loose ends: he did not specify the "unidentified Negro leaders" who were organizing the protest; he knew that Rosa Parks' arrest was a critical event, but he had not interviewed her; he had no hint of the agenda for a "top secret" meeting scheduled for Monday evening at the Holt Street Baptist Church. Azbell did reach an official of Montgomery City Lines, who told him that the company and its drivers had "to obey laws just like any other citizen," as if that explained everything.

Joe Azbell thought the city unnaturally quiet as he moved about on Monday. Even the throngs that surrounded the Holt Street Baptist Church seemed subdued when he arrived that evening. Inside, however, there was no hush, from the rousing initial chorus of "Onward Christian Soldiers" to the final shouted approval of a resolution to stay off the buses until the company agreed to hire black drivers, to guarantee courteous treatment of black passengers, and to permit first-come, first-served seating, whites from the front of the bus and blacks from the rear. Between the hymn and the business, speakers arrived and departed without introduction. One of them, an intense young man, reached for history to add significance to the moment: "And the history book will write of us as a race of people who in Montgomery County, State of Alabama, Country of the United States, stood up for and fought for their rights as American citizens, as citizens of democracy."

Martin Luther King, Jr., later remembered his peroration somewhat differently, but the exact words do not matter. Both the reporter and the unidentified (and to Azbell unknown) speaker sensed that the occasion was emotionally and historically important. King wanted to link moderation and militance in his speech, to inspire action and control it. He hoped his audience would extend their day-long boycott without becoming vindictive or violent. Azbell's account suggested that King had made his point:

> The meeting was much like an old-fashioned revival with loud applause added. It proved beyond any doubt there was a discipline among Negroes that many whites had doubted. It was almost a military discipline combined with emotion.

Montgomery's police commissioner thought the discipline came from systematic abuse by "Negro 'goon squads' " that kept nine of ten ordinary passengers off the buses. He assigned police to bus stops to prevent violence and ordered motorcycle policemen to convoy buses in the first days of the boycott. Ironically, this unusual protection may have increased participation, for some blacks apparently assumed they would be arrested for taking a bus.

All those policemen made one arrest—a nineteen-year-old charged with preventing an elderly woman from riding a bus. A few days later, a judge threw the case out of court when the woman testified that the thoughtful young man had been assisting her through a busy intersection. The absence of evidence did not prevent whites from regularly attributing the boycott's success to intimidation. That explanation held blacks at fault, exonerated segregation, and suggested that only terror could achieve black unity. Black spokesmen responded that conscience, not force, sustained the boycott. King later wrote that no wholly secular explanation would do; divine inspiration, he said, produced the dignified resistance of Montgomery's blacks. If not divine inspiration, Joe Azbell thought, at least forty-odd inspired preachers who presided at twice-weekly prayer meetings where audiences joyously re-dedicated themselves to the cause.

The dedication of Montgomery blacks was almost universal. Prominent "big Negroes" drove their big cars to take maids and handymen to work in white neighborhoods. Black owners of taxicabs charged their patrons bus fare. Hundreds of blacks insisted on walking to make their participation completely visible. J. H. Bagley, the bus company's local manager, estimated that the boycott was 90 percent effective and that "thousands" of riders had stayed off the buses. The *Advertiser* printed a photograph showing a solitary black figure in front of benches where ordinarily, the caption read, "several hundred Negroes" would be waiting. Yet most blacks somehow went where they wanted to go. Many attended the routine five-minute trial of Rosa Parks; she did not testify, was fined $10 and $4 costs, and filed a notice of appeal.

From the outset, the Montgomery Improvement Association (MIA), which represented boycotting blacks, offered to negotiate with the bus company and with the city. Jack Crenshaw, counsel for the bus line and the person who appears to have controlled the company's policy, may have misinterpreted that openness as a sign of weakness. The company held franchises from several Southern cities, and Crenshaw may have thought that any willing retreat from segregation would endanger every Southern contract. In any case, he apparently decided to do nothing without a court order. He would trade the permanent good will of Southern whites for the temporary loss of patronage by Montgomery's blacks. Until the threats and the violence ceased, Crenshaw said, the company would not even meet representatives of the MIA. (His reference to violence rested on reports by drivers of a few rocks thrown and fewer bullets fired at buses; Crenshaw assumed blacks were responsible.)

Suspecting that positions would soon become rigid, the executive director of the Alabama Council on Human Relations invited representatives of the MIA to meet with the city commissioners and officials of the company. The parley did not go well. As president of the MIA, King deplored violence, offered to report to police any offenders the organization discovered, and restated the black community's terms for ending the boycott. Crenshaw replied that the company could not permit first-come, first-served seating without a change in the city's segregation ordinance. Police Commissioner Clyde Sellers and Mayor W. A. ("Tacky") Gayle wanted no part of that hot potato and seemed to King to become "more and more intransigent" after Crenshaw had argued that point. The company would not consider hiring black drivers, but Crenshaw promised that white drivers would in the future be more courteous. Martin Luther King, Jr., among others, had heard that before. He suggested that the fruitless discussion end.

Apparently hoping a less charged atmosphere would have a better result, Mayor Gayle asked King and a few other MIA members to remain for informal conversation. Commissioner Frank A. Parks, an interior decorator at the beginning of his first term in public office, seemed ready to accept the MIA's seating proposal. "We can work it within our segregation laws," Parks said, indicating his agreement with a legal contention of the MIA. Crenshaw firmly contradicted him, and Parks soon backed down. Besides, Crenshaw went on, "If we granted the Negroes these demands, . . . they would go about boasting of a victory they had won over the white people; and this we will not stand for."

That aside helps explain the inflexible response of white supremacists to the most trivial request for changed racial practice. Any concession made under pressure would indicate both white weakness and black strength, and thereby subvert racist mythology: white men could make no concession without endangering white women. Subsequent meetings discovered no way around the impasse and both sides prepared for a siege instead of a settlement.

Indeed the company began these preparations so promptly that they were probably intended to force the MIA to a settlement. On the second day of the boycott, the local manager linked reduced revenue and reduced service. On the third day, curtailment began. Before the week was out, service to most of the city's black neighborhoods had been suspended, a step that certainly assisted advocates of the boycott. The emotional pitch in the black community dropped as the week wore on. One drenched student at Alabama State College announced that his principles would not survive one more day of rain. But when the determination of the black community faltered, there were no buses to board.

King and the MIA ran into official hostility as they improvised to provide other means of transportation. A letter from the city comptroller reminded owners of taxis that the standard fee schedule had the force of a municipal ordinance; he had heard, he continued, that some black operators were charging bus fare instead. The police chief reported "numerous complaints" about overloaded vehicles and ordered the force to be especially vigilant in checking car pools. As the weeks became months and the boycott drew national attention and support, the MIA set up regular assembly and dispatch points, raised money and purchased new station wagons, and hired full-time drivers. When somebody dumped acid on those shiny station wagons, the police were baffled.

Although transportation became readily available, some blacks continued to walk. The protest was for them a spiritual odyssey and the hardship a price they willingly paid for equality. King used the remarks of several anonymous walking blacks to illustrate for national audiences the dignified faith with which blacks met white oppression. An older woman overcame her obvious fatigue and declined a ride from one of the MIA's drivers: "I'm not walking for myself," she explained. "I'm walking for my children and grandchildren." Another woman made the same point: "My feet is tired, but my soul is at rest."

This resigned, Christian resistance to injustice was soon associated with the leadership of Martin Luther King, Jr., although his synthesis of ideology and tactic was neither original nor fully developed when the boycott commenced in December 1955. King brought no preconceived formula to events in Montgomery; indeed he did some prayerful rationalization to differentiate the MIA's boycott from unjust economic coercion of the sort advocated by White Citizens' Councils. As the boycott progressed, King gradually fused elements of Christian idealism, Gandhian nonviolence, and civil disobedience into a creed that inspired others and gave him a moral assurance that compensated for youthful inexperience, temper, and doubt.

He had some help from a gentle, sheltered, white librarian, who wrote a remarkable letter to the *Montgomery Advertiser* a week after the boycott began. "Not since the first battle of the Marne has the taxi been put to as good use as it has been this past week in Montgomery," Juliette Morgan began. Yet the city's blacks, she thought, owed more to the example of Gandhi's Salt March and to Thoreau's work on civil disobedience than to the inspiration of French troops. Montgomery's blacks faced greater obstacles than had Gandhi, for Southern whites held their prejudices more tenaciously than Great Britain had held the empire. Yet "passive resistance combined with freedom from hate" might be sufficient to the task. She dismissed as absurd the moral equation of the bus boycott with the economic coercion of the WCC; compare the speeches of white supremacists with those Joe Azbell reported from the meeting at the Holt Street Church, she urged, "and blush."

Miss Morgan borrowed the ingratiating device of white supremacists who prefaced their prejudice with protests of affection for blacks. She had ridden Montgomery's buses for fourteen years, she wrote, and she named several considerate drivers. Others, by contrast, used "the tone and manners of mule drivers in their treatment of Negro passengers." Several times she had herself left buses in indignation at discourtesy toward black passengers. For years, they had paid "full fare for fourth class service," and Miss Morgan could muster no sympathy for the economic plight of Montgomery City Lines. She summarized Crenshaw's argument as "Ye rebels! Disperse!" and punctured his pompous pretense of law and order. "I find it ironical," she wrote, "to hear men in authority . . . speak piously of law enforcement" while they are "openly flouting" the Supreme Court's interpretation of the Constitution. The incidence of violence, about which municipal authorities pretended disquiet, was trivial in comparison to the riots that greeted the abolition of fraternities and sororities at Montgomery's Lanier High School.

The United States of America, Miss Morgan reminded Montgomery, had been "founded upon a boycott" of British tea. And now, she felt,

> history is being made in Montgomery. . . . It is hard to imagine a soul so dead, a heart so hard, a vision so blinded and provincial as not to be moved with admiration at the quiet dignity, discipline, and dedication with which the Negroes have conducted their boycott. . . . Their cause and their conduct have filled me with great sympathy, pride, humility, and envy. I envy their unity, their good humor, their fortitude, and their willingness to suffer for great Christian and democratic principles, or [for] just plain decent treatment.

"This may be a minority report," she concluded, "but a number of Montgomerians not entirely inconsequential agree with my point of view."

Juliette Morgan may well have estimated accurately the support for integration among Montgomery's whites, but she overestimated their courage and perhaps even her own, for she became a pariah among whites and took her life in the summer of 1957. In the first days of the boycott, however, Juliette Morgan was not alone. Mrs. I. B. Rutledge had conducted an unscientific survey without finding "one white person who feels that it is right that a Negro be made to stand that a white person may sit." "Isn't it time," she asked, for "those of us who really believe in Christian and democratic principles . . . to speak out and help create a public opinion" that will permit a compromise?

Several other letter writers—almost exclusively women—agreed that, as one woman wrote, "the treatment of Negroes in our city buses has caused us to bow our heads in shame." Another had had enough of the defensive fantasy of white supremacists: "I am afraid," she wrote, "that the Negro is not now, nor has ever been, as happy and content with his place as we southern whites have believed." Grover Hall, the *Advertiser*'s editor, concurred. The white community, he said, had "kidded itself into believing" that terror explained the boycott and that "Negroes were happy in their state." Hall's initial editorial response suggested that first-come, first-served seating was not unthinkable, "if the grievance is confined to that."

But many whites quickly decided, as Jack Crenshaw had, that the grievance was not confined to that. Whatever the MIA said, many whites apparently believed the demand reached beyond equal, if separate, seats on buses to integration everywhere. Crenshaw's fear of any concession crept through the white community, as Grover Hall later confirmed: "The whites . . . are persuaded that they cannot allow themselves to be overcome on this terrain, ill-chosen . . . though it is, lest they be routed in the schools." Hall himself had first commended the city's "admirable coolness," but he soon lost his. Perhaps he was unconscious of his military metaphor, but the mask of moderation slipped when he warned Negro leaders to "reckon with two realities."

> The white man's economic artillery is far better emplaced, and commanded by more experienced gunners.
>
> Second, the white man holds all the offices of government. . . . There will be white rule as far as the eye can see. . . . Does any Negro leader doubt that the resistance to . . . Negro voting has . . . increased?

Hall held out the prospect of future suffrage (which the Fifteenth Amendment had guaranteed more than eighty years before) in response to a request for a seat on the bus. And he suggested that refusal of that unresponsive offer meant war.

But Hall did not blame black activism on Communists as other Southern whites sometimes did. Black unity in Montgomery, a correspondent of the *Advertiser* observed, derived from organization across the entire South, a circumstance that "must be a delight to Communists everywhere." Hall scoffed at the notion that the NAACP was a Communist front and assured his readers that racial agitation would continue even if Alabama's politicians succeeded in their effort to banish the NAACP. The editor asked one persistent woman how she knew that Communists were managing the boycott. "It just stands to reason," was her earnest reply.

It just stood to reason, from her perspective, because it was happening all over the South. While Montgomery's blacks stayed off the buses, other blacks in other places began to use public facilities. In Tuscaloosa, a black graduate student enrolled at the University of Alabama, where her brief appearance caused a riot, her suspension, readmission, and expulsion—with more court appearances and large headlines at each step. Almost every meeting of every state legislature and city council was preoccupied with the search for new devices to protect segregation. Although state courts usually proved reliable allies, federal courts did not, and informal enforcement through custom and subtle intimidation began to break down.

In this atmosphere, as Jack Crenshaw had perceived at the outset of the boycott, any black request was an entering wedge, any white concession an acceptance of "race-mixing." A seat in the front of the bus would lead to "a seat at the white lunch counter and [to] colored sales girls." Whites might responsibly encourage blacks to raise their standard of living, so long as changes did "not lay the foundation for ultimate intermarriage [and] the disintegration of the white race." A boycott was "a strike against the white people to gain superiority." The MIA advertised both its limited objective and its willingness to negotiate. But whites did not take the organization at its word, and the continuing success of the boycott undoubtedly checked the readiness of black leaders to make concessions.

In spite of stiffening resolve on both sides, Mayor Gayle at last found the elusive compromise. On Sunday, January 22, he announced that the city commission, the bus company, and a group of "prominent Negro ministers . . . representing the Negroes of Montgomery" had settled the dispute, and that bus service in the black neighborhoods would resume promptly. The negotiators had agreed, Gayle went on, that the company had complete authority to hire drivers and must obey applicable regulations requiring segregation. The company promised "uniform courtesy" to all patrons, and first-come, first-served seating in the middle section of the buses; whites would fill that section from the front, where ten seats were to be reserved, and blacks from the rear. Gayle had somehow induced black representatives to accept terms Jack Crenshaw would have offered weeks before and which blacks had subsequently rejected several times. It was a spectacular triumph.

But the mayor had made it up. The MIA disavowed the unidentified "prominent Negro ministers," who protested that they had been "hoodwinked," and whose version of the conference differed from the one Gayle gave the press. King and other members of the MIA visited taverns and other Saturday-night haunts to be sure that early reports did not deceive blacks who might not be in church on Sunday. By Monday morning, Gayle's settlement looked like a called bluff.

And the mayor was angry. "We have pussyfooted around on this boycott long enough," Gayle told Joe Azbell. Apparently the city's blacks had become convinced "that they have the white people hemmed up in a corner," Gayle continued, and that they need not "give an inch until they force the white people . . . to submit to their demands—in fact to swallow all of them." The blacks were mistaken, the mayor said, for most whites did not "care whether a Negro ever rides a bus again," especially if that act endangered "the social fabric of our community." Make no mistake, Gayle repeated; the goal was nothing less than the "destruction of our social fabric." To save it, he said, he and Commissioner Parks had joined the White Citizens' Council, as Commissioner Sellers had done some weeks before. Martin Luther King, Jr., Grover Hall observed, had managed to make the WCC respectable; "the Southern Moderate," Hall continued, "is as nearly extinct as the whooping crane."

Certainly the white people of Montgomery appeared to approve Gayle's outburst and the city's new "get-tough" policy. The switchboard at city hall handled "hundreds of telephone calls praising the mayor and the commissioners." Commissioner Parks reported that "dozens" of businessmen would institute a counterboycott and fire their black employees. Commissioner Sellers instructed police to disperse groups waiting for car pools. Mayor Gayle loosed a tirade against timid whites who paid cab fare or otherwise subsidized the boycott and thereby encouraged black radicalism. "The Negroes have made their own bed," Gayle said, "and the whites should let them sleep in it."

A plague of legal difficulties beset black leaders. Pending the outcome of cases the boycott had set in motion, Rosa Parks declined to pay her $10 fine; the judge offered her jail instead. Martin Luther King, Jr., spent a few anxious hours in the Montgomery jail on a charge of speeding. Four times insurers cancelled liability coverage for automobiles in the MIA's car pool. The local draft board abruptly revoked the occupational deferment of the young black attorney who had charted the MIA's course in the courts. Fred Gray was reclassified and available for immediate induction. His appeal moved like a yo-yo through the Selective Service hierarchy until officials in Washington reversed the Montgomery County board, an affront that triggered several resignations and a temporary refusal to provide any draftees from Alabama.

Of course somebody decided that legal harassment accomplished too little, too slowly. Martin Luther King, Jr., was preaching at one of the regular prayer meetings when the bomb thumped on the front porch of his house. Startled by the noise, Coretta Scott King moved toward their infant daughter, who was asleep at the rear of the residence. The bomb shattered the front window, tore a hole in the porch, and battered a column, but injured no one. By the time King reached the house, several hundred blacks had gathered in the area. The crowd's ugly mood frightened Joe Azbell, Mayor Gayle, Commissioner Sellers, and the white policemen who had rushed to the scene. "I was terrified," one officer recalled. "I owe my life to that nigger preacher, and so do all the other white people who were there."

King could not resist pointing out the logical consequences of "get-tough" public statements when Sellers and Gayle privately deplored violence. But King had swallowed his resentment by the time all three men went out on the blasted porch to try to calm the crowd. As he began, the young minister must have been speaking as much to himself as to the black faces in the darkness:

> We believe in law and order. Don't get panicky. Don't do anything panicky at all. Don't get your weapons. He who lives by the sword shall perish by the sword. . . . We are not advocating violence. We want to love our enemies.

He shifted to the first person singular as he regained his confidence:

> I want you to love your enemies. Be good to them. . . . I did not start this boycott. I was asked by you to serve as your spokesman. I want it to be known the length and breadth of this land that if I am stopped this movement will not be stopped. For what we are doing is right. What we are doing is just. And God is with us.

King's touch with the crowd was perfect. Back came a chorus of "Amens" and "God bless yous" that turned to jeers when Gayle and Sellers promised an unstinting search for the bomber and protection for King and his family. King spoke the benediction:

> Go home and don't worry. Be calm as I and my family are. We are not hurt, and remember that if anything happens to me, there will be others to take my place.

King's words did not end the sporadic violence; a few days later, a small bomb missed Nixon's house and smashed the fence in his yard. But both sides took steps to transfer the quarrel to the courts. On behalf of five black women, Fred Gray filed a suit in federal court asking that local and state regulations requiring segregated seating be declared unconstitutional. About the same time, a county grand jury, which included one black member, began weighing the prosecutor's evidence that the boycott was an illegal conspiracy against the bus company. No one could be compelled to patronize a business, Judge Eugene Carter explained to the jurors. On the other hand, "the right to conduct one's business without wrongful interference" was "a valuable property right" that merited legal protection. If the jurors found the boycott illegal, they could indict the leaders. On February 21, 1956, the second day of Brotherhood Week, the grand jury identified and indicted 115 leaders. It was, Grover Hall said later, "the dumbest act that was ever done in Montgomery."

The grand jury's list, which contained some duplications and several unaccountable omissions, lamented the "exemplary race relations" the boycott had impaired. The jurors exhorted "leaders of both races"—including presumably most of those under indictment—"to take a long and thoughtful look into the future." The grand jury then looked itself and saw no end to segregation:

> In this state we are committed to segregation by custom and by law; we intend to maintain it. The settlement of differences over school attendance, public transportation and other public facilities must be made within these laws which reflect our way of life.

Bombs and indictments indicated the "growing tension" and spreading "hate" that the grand jury noted during the third month of the boycott. Reverend Thomas Thrasher, one of the white clergymen on the Alabama Council on Human Relations, wrote of the "universal . . . fear" that gripped the community:

> The businessman's fear lest his business be destroyed by some false move or baseless rumor. The Negro's fear for his safety and his job. The clergy's fear that their congregations may be divided. . . . The politician's fear that he may do something disapproved by a majority of voters. And finally the whole community's fear that we may be torn asunder by a single rash act precipitating racial violence.

It did not matter, Joe Azbell asserted, who caused the violence. What did matter was that

> bombs are being tossed in a good city where good people live. What does matter is that none of this racial strife, this bomb throwing, and this harsh bickering is adding to the solution of the community's ticklish racial problem. It is adding to the problem.

Azbell doubted that more argument would change minds or leave a legacy of brotherhood. "All of us," he urged, must "tone down our feelings" lest a "full-scale racial war" sweep Montgomery. Blacks could reduce that danger immediately, he suggested, by ending their boycott. Tactical retreat would cost almost nothing, since they would surely win the court case that would require whites to make the final concessions. In fact, King may have considered the course Azbell recommended, but it did not gain wide acceptance and the moment passed.

Conciliators made no headway because both sides had handed the dispute to the courts. Conviction of the boycott's hundred-odd leaders, whites believed, would end the social pressure that kept blacks off the buses. Blacks, on the other hand, confident that their suit doomed segregated buses in Montgomery, turned the arrest of their leaders into a holiday. Sheriff's deputies brought in and booked Ralph Abernathy and others whose names headed the list. As word spread, blacks stopped at the station to find out if they were included; those omitted seemed more downcast than those indicted.

Corridors filled with joking blacks, who helped the deputies with unfamiliar names and addresses. The atmosphere, Joe Azbell wrote, was "much like 'old home week.' " Martin Luther King, Jr., was out of town and could not surrender until the following day.

King was the first defendant called a month later to the drab courtroom where Judge Carter heard the case without a jury. The state had little difficulty demonstrating that there was a boycott and that King had had a good deal to do with it. Intimidation and violence, the prosecution contended, meant that the conspirators had not merely, and legally, withheld their patronage, but had violated the law. Two witnesses testified that their refusal to observe the boycott had led to harassment and harm; the state might have selected more credible witnesses, however, than an employee of the county and the maid who worked for Mayor Gayle's mother-in-law. To connect King to the violence during the boycott, the prosecutor asked Joe Azbell if King's speeches had been inflammatory. No, Azbell replied, undermining the state's case; King had consistently counseled nonviolence.

In spite of his own anticlimactic testimony, Azbell thought the prosecution had made a reasonable presentation. King's defense rested on his contention that the boycott (if there was a boycott, which his lawyers did not concede) had "just cause" within the meaning of the Alabama statute. This contention permitted King's lawyers to call witness after witness who told of degrading discourtesy and physical mistreatment at the hands of callous drivers. King's own testimony was not heroic, but convenient lapses of memory did not prevent his conviction. Judge Carter offered King a choice of a fine of $500 or 386 days at hard labor. The penalty was low, Carter said, because King had earnestly tried to keep the protest peaceful. Unmoved by the judge's compassion, King posted bond and appealed.

The arrests and the trial put the boycott on the front page of the *New York Times* and the editorial page of the *Washington Post,* brought a *Life* photographer to Montgomery, and stimulated requests for presidential intervention from Adam Clayton Powell and the bishops of the African Methodist Episcopal Church. While the trial was in progress, a reporter asked for Eisenhower's reaction. Well, the President replied, he was not much of a lawyer. The rest of his answer was vintage Eisenhowerese, both in style and in content:

> I do believe that it is incumbent on all the South to show some progress. . . .
> I believe we should not stagnate, but again I plead for understanding, for really sympathetic consideration of a problem that is far larger, both in its emotional and even in its physical aspects than most of us realize.

The President summarized: "As far as I am concerned, I am for moderation, but I am for progress; that is exactly what I am for in this thing."

However fuzzy, the President was entitled to his opinion. But Joe Azbell and Grover Hall wearied of the opinions of out-of-town journalists who visited Montgomery briefly and filed stories based more on preconception than investigation. The Montgomery Azbell and Hall knew was not be-

nighted, and they bristled when simplistic self-righteousness passed for journalism. They began interviewing their professional guests about race relations
where they came from. The resulting articles sounded like the pot calling
the kettle names, but the *Advertiser*'s point that prejudice was no local phenomenon deserved a hearing.

By the spring of 1956, the boycott was no local phenomenon either.
White supremacists, arguing that compromise in Montgomery would bring
race-mixing elsewhere, enlisted national assistance. Those of both races who
favored integration provided the financial and legal support that kept the
MIA's station wagons on the streets and its lawyers in the courts. Local
leaders—especially Martin Luther King, Jr.—had made out-of-town promises
and had built national constituencies that had to be satisfied. The case pending
in the federal courts effectively removed legal issues from local control, even
if local leaders had been able to arrange a settlement. There was not much
to do but wait.

Municipal officials did pull one last string. They alleged that the MIA's
car pool was an unlicensed form of public transportation and went back to
Judge Carter for an injunction. Martin Luther King, Jr., wondered why they
had waited so long. The proceeding did not require a legal defense of segregation and would be difficult for the MIA to appeal to the federal courts. And
an injunction, which King expected, might undermine the morale of the
black community to the point that the boycott could not be sustained. Those
polished station wagons were rolling symbols of success, a constant source
of pride to blacks and of irritation for white supremacists. Even blacks who
chose to walk drew inspiration and comfort from the knowledge that they
could ride if they wished.

So King was apprehensive as he returned to Judge Carter's courtroom
in mid-November 1956. He heard attorneys outline the city's case and then,
in an entirely different mood, watched the charade play out to the injunction
he had once feared. For by the time Judge Carter issued his ruling, it was
irrelevant; as proceedings began in Montgomery, the Supreme Court of the
United States ruled that ordinances requiring segregated seating violated the
Fourteenth Amendment. The MIA could abandon the car pool and comply
with Carter's injunction because Montgomery City Lines had to abandon
segregation and comply with the order of the Supreme Court. The decision
seemed almost providential: "God Almighty has spoken from Washington,
D.C.," remarked a spectator in the Montgomery courthouse.

It took nearly a month for the official word to reach Montgomery. In
the interim, a solemn march of the Ku Klux Klan roused derision rather
than terror among Montgomery's newly confident blacks, and the city commissioners did nothing to prepare the community for the "tremendous impact" they warned that the decision would have. Instead they clung to their
get-tough policy:

> The City Commission, and we know our people are with us in this determination,
> will not yield one inch, but will do all in its power to oppose the integration of

the Negro race with the white race in Montgomery, and will forever stand like a rock against social equality, intermarriage, and mixing of the races under God's creation and plan.

King and the MIA used the interval to instruct blacks in courtesy that bordered on deference and in nonviolent response to provocation. On the morning of December 21, as he had done more than a year earlier, King got up to meet the first bus of the day. With Nixon, Abernathy, and a host of journalists and photographers, he waited for the vehicle to pull to the curb. "I believe you are the Reverend King, aren't you?" the driver asked. "We are glad to have you this morning." Later that day, a disgruntled rider looked around another bus and remarked emphatically, "I see this isn't going to be a white Christmas." One of the black passengers replied gently, "Yes, sir, that's right." "Suddenly, astonishingly," a reporter noted, "everybody on the bus was smiling."

There were, of course, sullen people on other buses. And there were shots, one of which hit a black passenger in the leg, and bombs, which damaged the homes and churches of several clergymen identified with the boycott, including Abernathy. A grand jury indicted seven white men for the bombings, but the two brought to trial were not convicted. Charges against the other five, and the still-pending indictments of black leaders for violating the antiboycott law, were dropped simultaneously. When legal technicalities jeopardized his appeal, King quietly paid his $500 fine. The cases were closed, the boycott concluded.

Christianity and Community

In spite of tension, temper, get-tough statements, bigotry, and bombs, no one had been killed. In part, Montgomery's good fortune was simply good fortune: dynamite and bullets and boycott-connected automobile accidents might have been fatal. More important than luck, however, was the strategy Montgomery's blacks had adopted. Unlike the sit-ins, protest marches, and demonstrations that came later in the civil rights crusade, a boycott kept the races apart and prevented the confrontation that led to violence. Furthermore, Montgomery in 1955 was no anonymous metropolis. If there was less interracial contact than white people thought, at least white people knew one another, had attended school together, belonged to the same clubs, read the same newspapers. Civic leaders had roots in the region, contact with their constituents, and pride in the city's growth. When the *Advertiser* or a group of business leaders preached patience and peace, people listened, and most of them heeded.

That same sense of community among blacks made the boycott effective and suppressed potential violence. In particular, black pastors knew one another and effectively led their congregations. Christian nonviolence was a familiar concept, spiritually nourishing as well as tactically promising, partly because many whites were earnest Christians too. Although Montgomery's churches were racially separate and differed on doctrinal details, the whole community at least outwardly respected Christian teaching. A great many had an inner commitment as well.

That Christian commitment was not so universal as it had once been in the United States. Secularization had gradually diminished the moral force of Christianity among both blacks and whites. Martin Luther King, Jr., would have to learn, a skeptic remarked, that the world was not just one big Baptist church, and that Christian nonviolence would not open every heart and every door. Neither Christianity nor nonviolence, for instance, inspired Northern ghettoes, where Muslims and other militants would in the coming decade counter King's ideas with black separatism. And the NAACP, the institutional expression of black aspirations for more than a generation, relied more heavily on the Constitution and the courts than on Christianity.

The leaders of the NAACP recognized King's charisma and acknowledged the tactical usefulness of nonviolence. But the NAACP had pointedly not endorsed the boycott at the outset, partly because an endorsement might have undermined the MIA's reiterated contention that the boycott was a local movement with specific objectives, and partly because those objectives, in the view of the NAACP, were too limited. Only when the boycott reached the courts, where for the first time the MIA broadened its challenge to segregation as a system, did the NAACP offer assistance. King's methods, leaders of the NAACP held, derived more from local circumstance than some of his enthusiastic followers recognized. Nonviolence and passive resistance did in fact attract the spotlight of national publicity and aroused the nation's liberal sympathy. But the media and liberal sentiment, however important, contributed less to the success of the boycott, the NAACP argued, than court orders and economic power. The loss of three-quarters of its revenue captured the attention of Montgomery City Lines in a way no ideology could. And the city fathers found a court order more compelling than conscience.

That view of events did not hold that King was mistaken, but only that his methods were not universally applicable and were not in themselves sufficient to achieve racial justice. The Southern Christian Leadership Conference (SCLC), which became his organizational expression in the years after Montgomery, did not directly integrate many schools, register many black voters, or modify economic institutions that discriminated on the basis of race. Indeed the SCLC sometimes seemed an organization in search of a cause, although King himself was perpetually leading a march or a demonstration. Because of the errors of whites, or the economic and political leverage of blacks, or the legal result of local circumstance, or the persuasive power of Christian nonviolence, some of those demonstrations accomplished their purpose. And win or lose, in a sense, King accomplished his purpose. For if he never narrowed his effort to one objective, he did focus on principles. And his statement of those principles lifted the aspirations of millions of Americans of both races and helped make the nation's racial practice slightly more congruent with its equalitarian ideal.

Suburbia: A Photo Essay

Suburbs were not new to the 1950s, but in no previous decade had suburban growth and development been so dramatic. Some suburbs, such as Park Forest, Illinois, and the several Levittowns, became well-known symbols of a new style of life. There was little agreement, however, on just what that new style of life was, or on why people had chosen to live in the suburbs rather than in the inner cities. Newly established suburbanites usually emphasized the advantages of home ownership and the quality of life possible in the new suburban homes. Scholars were more cynical. "The suburb," wrote sociologist David Riesman in 1958, "is like a fraternity house at a small college in which like-mindedness reverberates upon itself."

The photographs on the following pages provide a few hints about the causes of postwar suburbanization and the meaning of suburbia. Besides the evidence in the photos, we might also consider whether the events in Montgomery were in any way related to the migration to the suburbs. It is well to remember, too, that suburbanization continued apace in the 1960s and 1970s.

Fast Food: McDonald's

Students should examine the McDonald's phenomenon from two perspectives. The first perspective involves Ray Kroc's clientele. Who did he wish to serve and who to exclude? And what did his choice have to do with the Eisenhower equilibrium? The second perspective involves the *employees* at McDonald's. Assume that employment patterns present in McDonald's were increasingly typical of the economy. If so, was it reasonable to conclude that the old blue-collar society was disappearing, and with it many of the stresses of social and economic class? In short, wasn't McDonald's evidence that a classless society was just around the corner?

The first of Ray Kroc's McDonald's opened in the Chicago suburb of Des Plaines, Illinois, in June 1955. *Reproduced courtesy of Golin Communications, Inc.*

"Another judgment I made early in the game," writes Kroc, "was that there would be no pay telephones, no juke boxes, no vending machine of any kind in McDonald's restaurants. Many times operators have been tempted by the side income some of these machines offer, and they have questioned my decision. But I've stood firm. All of those things create unproductive traffic in a store and encourage loitering that can disrupt your customers. This would downgrade the family image we wanted to create for McDonald's. (*Quotation from Ray Kroc, with Robert Anderson,* Grinding It Out: The Making of McDonald's (*New York: Berkley, 1977*), p. 84.)

Filling Up: 1941, 1960

Important cultural changes are often reflected in our most familiar
institutions. The following photographs chronicle a modification in
gas-station design that presumably reflected more basic changes in
the role of the automobile in American life. Were Americans more
comfortable with the automobile in 1941 or in 1960? What conflicting
needs was the Shell station designed to bring into balance?

**Mobilgas Service Station, Washington and Flower streets, Los Angeles,
California, 1941.** *Reproduced by permission of Mobil Oil Corporation.*

Two-Bay Ranch-Style Service Station, 1960. *Courtesy, Shell Oil Company.*

Levittown, Long Island

Levittown, Long Island, named after the builder, consisted of 17,500 homes built within five and a half years in the 1950s.

UPI.

Challenges to Equilibrium

The equilibrium of the 1950s was maintained only with difficulty, if at all. One could theorize about the "American character," as many scholars did in the 1950s, but it was all too obvious that the blacks of Montgomery were in some important sense outside America. One could make the American family into a bastion of strength and stability (see the photograph on p. 269), but that would not make the new American working woman disappear. One could write, as John Kenneth Galbraith did, about a self-regulating economy of countervailing powers, but even Dwight Eisenhower could see that what he called the "military-industrial complex" was not self-regulating. The documents that follow—a selection about the beats, a photograph dealing with women, and some rock 'n' lyrics—represent three challenges to the equilibrium of the 1950s.

Joyce Johnson

The Beats

The beat phenomenon goes back to the late 1940s, when Jack Kerouac and Allen Ginsberg were students at Columbia University, and it reached its peak a decade later, when Ginsberg's poetry and Kerouac's novels (*On the Road* was published in 1957) brought the movement to the attention of the mass media. Even then, the beats, or "beatniks" as they were sometimes called, were always a tiny minority of the population, with much less presence and influence as a group than the hippies of the 1960s.

In the following passage, Joyce Johnson, a self-styled "minor character" in the story, describes something of the spirit of the Beat Generation and recalls her first encounter with Kerouac. How, and to what extent, did the beats challenge the dominant culture? In what sense could this challenge be described as "political"? Looking specifically at the role of women, what connections can you make between Johnson's account and the "Woman Citizen" in the photograph on page 303?

Jack Kerouac went on the road in the summer of 1947—from Ozone Park, Queens, of all places, to the Pacific, stopping off in Denver to see a new friend, Neal Cassady. As the saying goes, he was traveling light. None of the specialized equipment of latterday hitchhikers and wanderers. He had about fifty dollars in his pocket saved from veteran's benefits, a canvas bag "in which a few fundamental things were packed," and was wearing the wrong shoes—Mexican *huaraches,* the mark of the New York Bohemian intellectual back then.

It seems to have been a journey undertaken empirically, in mingled hope and desperation—an attempt to seek out a brand-new reality to match fantasy. He was looking, he said, for "girls, visions, everything; somewhere along the line the pearl would be handed to me."

It's strange, come to think of it, to go looking for visions. It seems more in the nature of visions to come upon you, seizing you unawares. If you look for them, they tend to recede, lead you a little further on. As for girls, there was uneasy flippancy in putting them at the head of his list—although looking for girls, in that sense, is not so much looking for love as for experience. The "everything," of course, was not to be found. Jack would find something out there, though. Sheer, joyous movement. If it had been possible to remain in motion forever, never tiring, speeding away from each new encounter while it was still unsullied by the flagging of the first excitement, he might have been happy. As happy as Neal Cassady,* who'd recently blown through the dragged-out end of the Columbia scene like a fresh wind from the West. A joy-riding car thief, a yea-saying delinquent, a guiltless, ravenous consumer of philosophy, literature, women—all varieties of sexuality, in fact. An undecadent alter ego, Neal seemed. He even uncannily looked like Jack—Jack the dark one, Neal golden like Lucien, but so different from him or any of the Columbia crowd. He seemed as familiar to Jack as the boys he'd grown up with in Lowell before he ever came to the city: "I heard again the voices of old companions and brothers under the bridge, among the motorcycles, along the wash-lined neighborhood and drowsy doorsteps of afternoon where boys played guitar while their older brothers worked in the mills."

Jack spent the months preceding his departure holed up in his mother's house—a retreat foreshadowing other retreats to come, in other houses to which he'd move Memere and all her pots and pans and furniture, as if home could be pitched like a tent—in Denver, Colorado; Orlando, Florida; Rocky Mount, North Carolina; Berkeley, California; Northport, Long Island; even Lowell again. In Ozone Park, the evenings were as drowsy as his memories of boyhood. In the eternal, spotless order of his mother's kitchen, a long subway ride from the all-night haunts of Times Square, he spread maps out on the table after the dishes were cleared, and like a navigator plotted the route of his contemplated journey. The western place names were magic words of incantation. Cimarron, Council Bluffs, Platte, Cheyenne. Thoughts of Neal stirred in him, merged with romantic images of plainsmen and pioneers. Cassady loomed in Jack's mind as archetypal, both his long-lost brother and the very spirit of the West in his rootlessness and energy. . . .

---

* Neal Cassady would reappear in the 1960s as the bus driver for the Merry Pranksters, a colorful and bizarre collection of antiauthoritarian performance-oriented California hippies, led (or not led) by novelist Ken Kesey.—*Ed.*

Fifteen years later kids went on the road in droves, in the context Kerouac and others had supplied for them. But in 1947, to be a college-educated hitchhiker was to be anachronistic. The Depression decade, when millions of the hungry, homeless, and unemployed had roamed the U.S. landscape, hopped freights, slept in open fields, was still grimly, unnostalgically alive in people's memories. Status and security had been so recently won and still seemed tenuously held. People did not walk the highways unless the cars they drove—preferably the latest models—had flats or ran out of gas. In Council Bluffs, where great wagon trains had gathered in the nineteenth century, Jack came upon a depressing vista of "cute cottages of one damn kind and another." In Cheyenne, he found Wild West Week being celebrated by "fat businessmen in boots and ten-gallon hats," in whose eyes it would have been an act of incomprehensible perversity for a young man to become deliberately classless if he had other options; in another few years, they would see it as positively un-American.

Already what was left of the true West, as envisioned by Jack in Ozone Park, could no longer be found in the places with the legendary names, but in the open, empty spaces in between—a spirit to be grasped fleetingly from the back of a truck filled with migrant workers speeding across the prairies at midnight.

In the fall of '56, having narrowly survived my twentieth year, I was just turning twenty-one. My crash course in the depths of human experience sometimes made me feel extremely old. This was not entirely an unpleasant feeling but new and strange, like walking around in an exotic garment that suddenly made you impervious to everything but didn't connect you to most of the people you knew in your everyday life. Once you'd touched bottom, what was there to be afraid of anymore? I was continually lonely, but very fearless. Life seemed grey but not impossible.

I found a new job at another literary agency and got a little more money. I moved into a new apartment of my own that happened to be around the corner from Alex's. I worked on the novel about Barnard I'd begun in Hiram Haydn's workshop. Elise and Alex were characters in it. By making Alex into a character, I took away his power to hurt me. Just like me, my heroine would have an affair with the Alex character and end up alone. But in my fictional rearrangement of life, it was she who was going to leave him after their one and only night together. I rewarded her with a trip to Paris. I typed forty letters a day and dreamed of taking off myself.

"Hello. I'm Jack. Allen [Ginsberg] tells me you're very nice. Would you like to come down to Howard Johnson's on Eighth Street? I'll be sitting at the counter. I have black hair and I'll be wearing a red and black checked shirt."

I'm standing in Elise's kitchen, holding the phone Allen has just handed me. It's a Saturday night shortly after New Year's.

"Sure," I say.

I put on a lot of eye shadow and my coat and take the subway down to Astor Place and begin walking westward, cross-town, passing under the bridge between the two buildings of Wanamaker's Department Store and the eye of the giant illuminated clock. It's a dark, bitter January night with ice all over the pavements, so you have to be careful, but I'm flying along, it's an adventure as opposed to a misadventure—under which category so far I've had to put most of the risky occurrences in my life.

The windows of Howard Johnson's are running with steam so you can't see in. I push open the heavy glass door, and there is, sure enough, a black-haired man at the counter in a flannel lumberjack shirt slightly the worse for wear. He looks up and stares at me hard with blue eyes, amazingly blue. And the skin of his face is so brown. He's the only person in Howard Johnson's in color. I feel a little scared as I walk up to him. "Jack?" I say.

There's an empty stool next to his. I sit down on it and he asks me whether I want anything. "Just coffee." He's awfully quiet. We both lack conversation, but then we don't know each other, so what can we say? He asks after Allen, Lafcadio, that kind of thing. I'd like to tell him I've read his book, if that wouldn't sound gauche, obvious and uncool.

When the coffee arrives, Jack looks glum. He can't pay for it. He has no money, none at all. That morning he'd handed his last ten dollars to a cashier in a grocery store and received change for a five. He's waiting for a check from a publisher, he says angrily.

I say, "Look, that's all right. I have money. Do you want me to buy you something to eat?"

"Yeah," he says. "Frankfurters. I'll pay you back. I always pay people back, you know."

I've never bought a man dinner before. It makes me feel very competent and womanly.

He has frankfurters, home fries, and baked beans with Heinz ketchup on them. I keep stealing looks at him because he's beautiful. You're not supposed to say a man is beautiful, but he is. He catches me at it and grins, then mugs it up, putting on one goofy face after another; a whole succession of old-time ridiculous movie-comedian faces flashes before me until I'm laughing too at the absurdity of this blind date Allen has arranged. (The notion of Allen Ginsberg arranging blind dates will crack people up years later when they ask me how on earth I met Kerouac.). . . .

I see the blue, bruised eye of Kerouac and construe his melancholy as the look of a man needing love because I'm, among other things, twenty-one years old. I believe in the curative powers of love as the English believe in tea or Catholics believe in the Miracle of Lourdes.

He tells me he's spent sixty-three days on a mountaintop without anyone. He made pea soup and wrote in his journal and sang Sinatra songs to keep himself company.

Some warning to me in all this. "You really liked being alone like that?" I ask.

"I wish I was there now. I should've stayed up there."

He could somehow cancel you out and make you feel sad for him at the same time. But I'm sure any mountaintop would be preferable to where he's staying—the Marlton Hotel on Eighth Street, with the dirty shades over the windows and the winos lounging on the steps.

"And where do you live?" Jack asks. He likes it that it's up near Columbia and the West End Bar where he used to hang out. Was Johnny the bartender still there? Johnny the bartender would remember him from the days he was a football hero at Columbia but he broke his leg in his sophomore year and stayed in his room reading Céline and Shakespeare and never went back to football again—thus losing his scholarship at Columbia, but he's always had affection for the neighborhood. "Why don't you let me stay at your place?" he says.

"If you wish," I say in *Desolation Angels,* deciding fast. And I know how I said it, too. As if it was of no great moment, as if I had no wishes of my own—in keeping with my current philosophy of nothing-to-lose, try anything. . . .

When we got in the door, he didn't ask to see my manuscript. He pulled me against him and kissed me before I even turned on the light. I kissed him back, and he acted surprised. He said I was even quieter than he was, he had no idea quiet girls liked kissing so much, and he undid the buttons of my coat and put both his hands up my back under my sweater. "The trouble is," Jack said with his voice against my ear, "I don't . . . like . . . blondes."

I remember laughing and saying, "Well, in that case I'll just dye my hair"—wondering all the same if it was true.

In the morning Jack left to get his stuff out of the Marlton. He returned with a sleeping bag and a knapsack in which there were jeans and a few old shirts like the one he was already wearing and some notebooks he'd bought in Mexico City. That was all he owned. Not even a typewriter—he'd been borrowing other people's typewriters, he said. I'd never seen such foreign-looking notebooks, long and narrow with shiny black covers and thin, bluish paper on which Jack's slanted penciled printing sped across page after page, interrupted here and there by little sketches. One notebook was just for dreams. He wrote in it every morning.

There was something heartbreakingly attractive in these few essentials to which Jack had reduced his needs. He reminded me of a sailor—not that I knew any sailors—something too about the way he looked coming out of the shower, gleaming and vigorous and ruddy with a white towel around his neck.

Very quickly it didn't seem strange to have him with me, we were somehow like very old friends—"buddies," Jack said, squeezing me affectionately, making me feel both proud and a little disappointed. Crazy as it was, I sometimes really wished I was dark—like this Virginia I felt jealous of for making him so wild. Or the girl named Esmeralda who lived in Mexico City and whom he'd loved tragically for a long time and written an entire novel about in one of his notebooks, calling her Tristessa. But he'd slept with her only once. She was a whore and a saint, so beautiful and lost—one of his mysterious *fellaheen* women, primeval and of the earth.

I was unprimeval and distinctly of the city. I was everydayness, bacon and eggs in the morning or the middle of the night, which I learned to cook just the way he liked—sunny-side up in the black iron frying pan. I'd buy slab bacon in the grocery store, like he'd always had in Lowell—not the skinny kind in packages—and add canned applesauce (a refinement I'd learned from Bickford's Cafeteria), which Jack had never thought of as anything that might enhance eggs. He took extraordinary pleasure in small things like that.

As a lover he wasn't fierce but oddly brotherly and somewhat reticent. I'd listen in amazement to his stories of Berkeley parties where everyone was naked and men and women engaged in some exotic Japanese practice called *yabyum* (but Jack, fully clothed, had sat apart brooding over his bottle of port, something he didn't tell me). In my memories of Jack in the good times we had together, I'm lying with my head on his chest, his heart pulsing against my ear. His smooth hard powerful arms are around me and I'm burying my face into them because I like them so much, making him laugh, "What are you doing there, Joycey?" And there's always music on the radio. Symphony Sid, whom he taught me to find on the dial, who always comes on at the stroke of midnight, bringing you the sounds of Charlie Parker, Lester Young, Miles Davis, and Stan Getz, and who, according to Jack, is a subterranean himself—you can hear it in his gravel voice smoked down to a rasp by innumerable weird cigarettes. "And now—after a few words about that fan-tastic Mo-gen David wine—the great Lady Day . . ." In the darkness of the room we drift together as Billie Holiday bewails lost loves . . .

But then Jack leaves me. He goes into the small back bedroom where I never sleep because there's no radiator there. He pulls the window all the way up, closes the door, and lies down on the floor in his sleeping bag alone. This is the cure for the cough he brought with him from Mexico City. In the morning he'll do headstands with his feet against the wall, to reverse the flow of blood in his body. He tells me a frightening thing about himself. He's known for eight years that a blood clot could finish him off at any minute.

How can you bear living, I wonder, knowing death could be so close? Little by little I'm letting go of what I learned on the abortionist's table in the white upstairs room in Canarsie.

I'm good for him, Jack tells me. I don't mind anything he does. I don't mind about the sleeping bag, do I?

I didn't really mind, that was the strange part. Everything seemed so odd, so charmed, so transformed. . . .

I hate Jack's woman-hatred, hate it, mourn it, understand, and finally forgive.

Women

In the two decades after World War II, growing percentages of American women worked outside the home. Yet this "liberation" was limited. Most women could find work only in factories or in traditionally feminine occupations—as teachers, nurses, secretaries, and telephone operators, for example. And working women were expected to add work outside the home to their duties within it. Even so, this movement of women into the paid labor force produced tensions in the rather rigid social order of the postwar equilibrium. The photograph below, of a display celebrating the one hundredth anniversary of the Women's Rights Convention at Seneca Falls, New York, reflects the ambivalence of women's position at mid-century. What points of view were represented in the display?

National Archives, Women's Bureau.

Rock 'n' Roll

The musical style called "rock 'n' roll" dates from the early 1950s. It is usually considered a sign of revolt, musical evidence that the generational rebellion that would sweep the 1960s was already under way even as Dwight Eisenhower was serving his first term. It was this. But rock 'n' roll was also essentially a white music, and a white music that was developed almost entirely from black musical styles.

The verses below—from the rock 'n' roll classic "Shake, Rattle and Roll" (1954)—allow us to inquire into the historical meaning of this new music. The verses on the left are from the original version, written by Charles Calhoun and recorded by Joe Turner for the black market. The verses on the right are from the more popular "cover" version by Bill Haley and the Comets. Both versions were hits in 1954.

Why did Haley change the words? Was rock 'n' roll part of the Eisenhower equilibrium or its antithesis?

"Shake, Rattle and Roll" (1954)

The Charles Calhoun/ Joe Turner version

The Bill Haley version

Get out of that bed,
And wash your face and hands. (twice)

Get out in that kitchen,
And rattle those pots and pans. (twice)

Get into the kitchen
Make some noise with the pots and pans.

Roll my breakfast
'Cause I'm a hungry man.

Well you wear those dresses,
The sun comes shinin' through. (twice)

You wear those dresses,
Your hair done up so nice. (twice)

I can't believe my eyes,
That all of this belongs to you.

You look so warm,
But your heart is cold as ice.

I said over the hill,
And way down underneath. (twice)

(the third verse of the Calhoun/Turner version is not part of the Haley version)

You make me roll my eyes,
And then you make me grit my teeth.

12

Coming Apart:
The 1960s

For a time, the decade of the 1960s looked very much like its predecessor. John F. Kennedy, elected by a narrow margin over Richard Nixon in 1960, sought to pump up the nation with rhetoric while practicing a brand of consensus politics designed to avoid overt conflict. The problems of the 1960s, said Kennedy at Yale University's commencement in 1962, presented "subtle challenges, for which technical answers, not political answers, must be provided." Because he believed that basic problems of adequate food, clothing, and employment had been solved through economic growth and the evolution of the welfare state, Kennedy was not the reform activist that many expected him to be. Several of his policies and programs—the commitment to space exploration, the Peace Corps, the rollback of prices in the steel industry—were essentially symbolic gestures. In foreign affairs, Kennedy carried on the cold war in grand fashion—deeper involvement in Vietnam; a CIA-sponsored invasion of Cuba in an attempt to depose Fidel Castro; a blockade to force the Soviets to remove their missiles from Cuba, when less bellicose but less satisfying alternatives were available.

There were signs of change and portents of turmoil in the early years of the decade—the Berkeley Free Speech Movement in 1964, the assassination of John F. Kennedy, the assertive youth culture fostered by the English rock band the Beatles. Yet the Eisenhower equilibrium was not irrevocably shattered until mid-decade. The cause was race. During the 1950s, black efforts to achieve integration had followed, in the main, legal channels. Gradually, though, black leaders like Martin Luther King, Jr., adopted the tactics of direct action: boycotts, picketing, sit-ins, and other methods of confrontation. Then, in 1965, a minor summer incident involving police in Watts, a black section of Los Angeles, set off five days of looting and rioting that left thirty-four people dead. Within two years, there were over a hundred major urban riots, all centered in black ghettos in cities like Newark and Detroit. It was in this setting that young black leaders began to question whether integration was an appropriate goal. They began to talk of black power. It was in this setting, too, that two of the most charismatic black leaders, Malcolm X and Martin Luther King, Jr., were shot to death.

The urban ghetto riots of the mid-1960s occurred during times of relatively low national rates of unemployment and inflation and within the context of Lyndon Johnson's Great Society—a liberal reform program that included the Voting Rights Act of 1965 and the war on poverty. While the voting-rights legislation had immediate results that went well beyond what the civil-rights movement had been able to accomplish in the early 1960s, the war on poverty as well as other Johnson programs were severely limited by a growing backlash against social unrest and the president's own policy of escalation in Vietnam. When Kennedy was killed in late 1963, there were fewer than 20,000 American personnel in Vietnam; in 1968, there were more than 500,000. For Johnson, each new American commitment was absolutely necessary. Defeat or withdrawal, he believed, would bring only more aggression, new tests of the national and presidential will. Others, however, saw the conflict in Vietnam largely as a civil war and American involvement as an immoral and/or unlawful interference in a domestic dispute.

Protests against the war, centered on the college campuses and utilizing the tactics of the civil-rights movement, began in earnest in early 1965 and grew in number and intensity through the decade. Almost every major campus in the United States was torn by rallies, teach-ins, and riots. One climax of the youth revolt was the massive demonstration—and the violent police response to it—centered on the Democratic National Convention in Chicago in 1968. The "protesters," as they had come to be called, could not prevent the nomination of the party's establishment candidate, Hubert Humphrey, but the event so clouded his candidacy that it almost ensured his defeat by Richard Nixon.

Nixon's widening of the Vietnam War in 1970, with an invasion of Cambodia, touched off the last major round of protest on the campuses. On May 4, panicky National Guardsmen, sent to quell a protest at Kent State University in Ohio, killed four students. Ten days later, two black youths were shot by police at Jackson State College in Mississippi.

By the end of the decade, the antiwar and civil-rights movements had been joined and fueled by women seeking liberation from confining social roles and by a new group of environmental and consumer activists who saw that the nation had pursued economic growth at great cost to the quantity and quality of its remaining resources and the health of its citizens. Portions of this counterculture of protest were nonpolitical (Ken Kesey's San Francisco–based Merry Pranksters, for example, painted their faces with Day-Glo and inveigled protesters to "drop acid" and simply turn their backs on the war). But protest movements of the 1960s were by and large committed to making existing political frameworks responsive. Many believed that the Great Society could reconstruct the nation's cities, force corporations to clean up the air and water, provide for genuine equality of opportunity for all races, and even eliminate poverty. Others had faith that Ralph Nader and his "raiders" could mount and sustain a meaningful consumer movement and that Common Cause, an extensive liberal lobby established by former Department of Health, Education, and Welfare secretary John Gardner, would significantly redress the balance in Congress. Not since the 1930s had Americans believed so mightily in the possibilities of change.

Interpretive Essay

Allen J. Matusow

The New Left

On the eve of the 1960s, college life was much like it is today. Concerned with preparing themselves for jobs and with making money, students gravitated to the sciences and to business courses or signed up for ROTC (Reserve Officer Training Corps) programs. As in the 1920s, fraternities and sororities prospered, as campus social life and intercollegiate athletics absorbed much of the time and energy of students. Protest—against anything except, perhaps, social restrictions and regulations—was rare.

In the following essay, historian Allen J. Matusow examines how and why this quiescent campus of the 1950s became the staging ground for the most powerful and active radical movement of the postwar era—the New Left. What were the movement's origins? What was its relationship to the Vietnam War? Was the campus a reasonable place from which to begin a profound reconstruction of American society? Had you been leading the SDS (Students for a

Democratic Society) in the late 1960s, what counsel would you have offered the organization?

While some young radicals in the 1960s rebelled against liberal culture, others forged a movement—called the "new left"—against liberal politics. New leftists were not dropouts questing after Dionysian ecstasies but, in the main, college students committed to reconstructing the social order. What was wrong with the old one? their baffled elders inquired, and how could a generation so pampered be so ungrateful?—questions that became ever more insistent as the new left moved through the decade from mere disaffection with liberalism to guerrilla warfare against "Amerika."

The phenomenon of the new left could be illumined from a variety of perspectives. The campus perspective focused on the explosive growth in enrollments in institutions of higher learning (from 2 million in 1946 to nearly 8 million in 1970). Here was a vast and volatile population that was largely segregated from the rest of society, freed of adult responsibility, encouraged to think critically, and often hostile to impersonal university bureaucracy—a mix of circumstances volcanic in possibility. The sociological perspective stressed the unprecedented affluence of the era and the upper-middle-class backgrounds of typical protesters. With parents disproportionately employed in well-paying professions, many students could afford the luxury of being political idealists, even utopians. The psychological perspective emphasized the early family life characteristic of new leftists—the permissive discipline, the democratic personal relations, the child-centered ethos. Having known equality at home, the students demanded instant gratification of their desire for its realization in society. And finally the religious perspective pointed up the overrepresentation of Jews in new left ranks. Heirs of a socialist tradition imported from the ghettos of Eastern Europe, conditioned to distrust authority by the historical memory of centuries of persecution, brought up by parents respectful of serious ideas, Jewish students played a conspicuous role in the campus left of the 1960s, just as their fathers had played a conspicuous role in the radical movements of the 1930s. Taken together, these various perspectives went far to answer the question—why the new left? A minority of an idealistic and privileged generation confronted the contradiction between American principles and American realities and would not abide it.

Accurate as far as it went, this view of the matter neglected a crucial feature of the new left—namely, the specific ideas in the heads of its adherents, their ever-changing conception of the world. Shaped by encounter with concrete historical circumstances, those ideas provided the best perspective from which to view the new left's development. Like any radical movement, this one, too, required a coherent body of ideas—call them an ideology—that located the source of current evils and proposed a way out. But formulation of an ideology for a new American left proved a task fraught with perplexities. What was the nature of the discrepancy between American principles and American realities? Who were the exploited peoples—the poor, the black, and maybe Third World peasants? Or did they also include middle-class students somehow thwarted by existing social arrangements from achieving happiness? Was the reconstruction of America to be undertaken for others or for the students themselves? The new left would answer these crucial questions in different ways at different times, but it would never answer them successfully. Without an adequate ideological framework to support its actions, the movement would become increasingly irresponsible, lose touch with social realities, and fade away with the decade.

I

The new left was wholly innocent of ideology when it spontaneously erupted in 1960, bringing to an end years of political torpor on campus. As would be true throughout the decade, blacks set the example. In February four students from North Carolina Agricultural and Technical College touched off a mass sit-in movement in the upper South by refusing to leave a segregated lunch counter at a Woolworth's in Greensboro. In the following months Bay Area students braved fire hoses to protest the appearance of the House Committee on Un-American Activities in San Francisco. Harvard students sponsored a peace walk that attracted a thousand people. The newly formed Student Peace Union sparked demonstrations against ROTC, nuclear testing, and the arms race at Michigan, Chicago, Dartmouth, and Oberlin. And students in a number of northern communities engaged in sympathy picketing to support black students on the front lines of the southern freedom struggle. If anything united the protesters, it was their insistence on "speaking truth to power," on calling America to redeem her democratic values. On May 1 a few hundred opponents of capital punishment, including Berkeley student Abbie Hoffman, stood vigil outside a prison in San Rafael, California, where author and convicted rapist Caryl Chessman was about to lose his twelve-year battle against the executioner. Hoffman recalled that one demonstrator, on the sad ride back to Berkeley after both the governor and the warden had expressed regrets, mused aloud, "How does that work? In a democracy, I mean, no one wants to see him die and the state kills him?"

Sensing they were something new in American politics, the intellectuals among the protesters began immediately to define their distinguishing characteristics. New leftists, they emphasized, were not liberals. Liberals, for example, saw politics as a means to resolve conflicts; early new leftists, as a way to achieve a moral society. Liberals had unlimited faith in the electoral process; new leftists were moving beyond elections to direct action, both as a tactic to achieve justice and as a way to testify to principle. Liberals still believed in America's anti-Communist world mission; most new leftists were trying to detach themselves from the Cold War, and a few were moving with the leadership of the Student Peace Union into a third camp that blamed both great powers for current tensions. And, beyond issues, the early protesters shared a vague feeling, entirely lacking in contemporary liberalism, that some-how the form of existing institutions discouraged authentic personal rela-tions. . . .

The group that undertook the task of comprehending the new student movement and providing it an ideology was Students for a Democratic Society (SDS). SDS was the student arm of the League for Industrial Democracy, which traced its origins back to 1905, when Jack London, Upton Sinclair, and Clarence Darrow had founded a socialist discussion group. By the 1950s the League was a feeble collection of liberals and social democrats subsisting on the charity of a few unions, and its student affiliate, then called the Student League for Industrial Democracy, was a handful of dissenters huddling to-gether for intellectual warmth in the dark days of McCarthyism. But in 1960 the Student League changed its name and acquired vigorous leadership in the person of Robert "Al" Haber, then twenty-four years old and a graduate student at the University of Michigan. A self-described radical, Haber criti-cized the 1960 student demonstrations for "isolation, narrowness, and shallow-ness." There was, he said, "no recognition that the various objects of protest are not *sui generis* but are symptomatic of institutional forces with which the movement must ultimately deal." Haber intended to make SDS a radical think-tank that would uncover the interconnection of the issues and formulate "radical alternatives to the inadequate society of today."

In the spring of 1960 Haber looked up a twenty-year-old junior at Michi-gan named Tom Hayden, then a rising reporter on the student paper. Reared by his Catholic family in a Detroit suburb, Hayden had been a teenage rebel with beat tendencies but no politics, until Haber persuaded him to participate in a sit-in. That summer Hayden hung around with some radicals at Berkeley and then went to Los Angeles to picket the Democratic convention with Martin Luther King. By the fall of 1960, he was hooked on radicalism, dividing his time between the *Michigan Daily,* which he edited, and a new campus political party called VOICE, which he founded. After graduation, Haber hired Hayden to help him transform SDS from an obscure organization of five hundred members into the acknowledged voice of the emerging student movement.

In the fall of 1961 Hayden went south to become SDS's liaison with SNCC. There he got a quick taste of life in the civil rights movement. The Klan beat him up in the streets of McComb, Mississippi, and in Albany, Georgia, the police charged him with Freedom Riding and threw him in jail. In a letter smuggled out of his cell, he wrote that he was glad for the semidarkness because there was much he would rather not see. "For instance, the stained seatless toilet and the rusted tin cup by the water spigot. . . . For instance, the wet patches of water, excretion and spittle that cover the floor where I sleep." Hayden's tribulations in the South and the dispatches he sent from the front lines helped advertise SDS and enhance its reputation on northern campuses.

But his greatest contribution to SDS was a paper he wrote for the organization's 1962 annual convention at a labor resort in Port Huron, Michigan. Revised and released to the world by the fifty-nine persons in attendance, the *Port Huron Statement* seriously attempted to provide the infant new left with an ideology that would analyze the causes of current evils, offer a vision of a better future, and locate the agent of change to effect the social transformation.

The *Port Huron Statement,* which gave form to what hitherto had been mere mood, little resembled radical manifestos of the past. There was in it no analysis of class exploitation or material deprivation. The sickness of America, Hayden maintained, stemmed from the contradiction between democratic principles and actual practice—a sickness that brought spiritual, not economic, misery to the mass of Americans, including students. Elites had perverted democracy by assuming control of major institutions and rendering average citizens isolated, apathetic, and bereft of community. Giant corporations controlled the economy, excluding people from "basic decisions affecting the nature and organization of work." Labor unions were so mired in organizational routine that they were failing the unorganized and the unemployed. The existing system of government thwarted the popular will and permitted business interests to manipulate the state. And universities were run by cumbersome bureaucracies that contributed "to the sense of outer complexity and inner powerlessness that transforms the honest searching of many students to a ratification of convention."

If powerlessness was the evil to be purged, then Hayden's vision of a better future was a society in which the people would take control over their own lives, a society governed by something he called "participatory democracy." This was a concept he only vaguely explained but that was obviously similar to the anarchist dream of inherently good men and women liberated from hierarchic institutions and living in decentralized communities where the individual counted. If students, for example, could manage their own education in true academic communities built by themselves, their alienation would be overcome and their spiritual health restored. Brilliantly expressive of SDS's gut rejection of the form of contemporary institutions, participatory democracy would become the slogan, the rallying cry, and the myth that fused the inchoate protests into a purposive movement.

How would the transformation from corporate to decentralized society be accomplished? Who would be the agent of change? The *Port Huron Statement* nominated students themselves for a crucial role. In complex industrial societies, after all, universities occupied "a permanent position of social influence." If students and faculty would "wrest control of the educational process from the administrative bureaucracy," they could build bridges to other centers of dissidence—in the civil rights movement, in the peace movement, and among disenchanted liberals in the Democratic party. The result would be a radical movement devoted to nothing less than the reconstruction of American democracy. . . .

In the school year 1965–1966 the new left began to assume the dimensions of a mass movement. It was, of course, primarily the war that turned college students against their government and made recruits by the thousands for the radical cause. One symptom of the deepening radical impulse was the spurt in SDS membership—from 2,500 in December 1964 to 10,000 the following October. Henceforth, SDS would cease to be a group of comrades in a close community and would become a collection of autonomous campus chapters with only the loosest connections among themselves and with the national office in Chicago. This arrangement conformed to the anarchist tendency of the movement but was unlikely to contribute to its political effectiveness.

The new militance found expression in the new left's evolving protest tactics. On October 15, 1965, for example, during the so-called International Days of Protest, 10,000 students marched from Berkeley to close down the Army's induction center in nearby Oakland. At the Oakland city limits march leaders disappointed the crowd by voting 5 to 4 to turn back rather than challenge cops armed with clubs, dogs, and tear gas. Jerry Rubin, a leader who had wanted to plunge on, drew the moral for the militants. "A movement that isn't willing to risk injuries, even deaths, isn't worth shit," he said. In the spring of 1966 radical students at a number of schools staged sit-ins against universities for acts of complicity in the war—especially furnishing draft boards with class rankings for the purpose of determining deferments.

Another sign of the movement's rapid radicalization in 1965–1966 was its interest in alternative or counter institutions. SNCC as usual had pointed the way by creating, in the previous year, an alternative political party called the Mississippi Freedom Democratic party. Equating Mississippi with America, the new left now decided to build a new society, with its own institutions, inside the shell of the old. "Free" universities sprang up at mid-decade to offer students radical instruction, experimental pedagogy, and participatory democracy. Soon the radicals would have their own newspapers, radio stations, theaters, community organizations, and co-ops. In a particularly utopian flight of fancy, Tom Hayden even envisioned a Continental Congress called by excluded peoples—"a kind of second government, receiving taxes from its supporters, establishing contact with other nations . . . dramatizing the plight of all groups that suffer from the American system." Whatever else they meant, counter institutions meant at least this: young people in alarming numbers were withdrawing allegiance from the United States of America.

Vietnam, which created the favorable climate for radical growth, posed problems as well. The hordes of converts created by the war knew that the government was evil and liberals the enemy, but quite often they knew little else. Denied the years of gradual disillusionment that had educated the new left's founding generation, most of the newcomers were radicals by emotion rather than by reason and possessed an alarming potential for mindless activism. Though there could be no doubt of their alienation, the real source of that alienation remained unclear. Were they alienated primarily because America bombed Vietnam, or because America was a gilded cage in which middle-class students were among the prisoners? Were the radical thousands fighting against the oppression of others or against the oppression of themselves?

II

In the year 1966–1967 leading movement intellectuals made a serious effort to root the radicalism of the student mass in its own grievances. . . .

Borrowing ideas from European Marxists as well as from [Herbert] Marcuse, [SDS national secretary Greg] Calvert tried his own hand at sketching an ideology for middle-class liberation. His attempt was in the tradition of the *Port Huron Statement,* though far more radical and sympathetic to Marxism. The oppressed group that could make the revolution, he said, was "the new working class." Old leftists had erred in equating the working class with blue-collar workers. In fact, said Calvert, white-collar employees were no less workers in the classical Marxist sense since they "sell their labor power in order to live and have no control whatsoever over the means of production." Materially prosperous, members of the new working class—teachers, engineers, salaried professionals, and other highly trained technical workers— were manipulated, repressed, bureaucratic men, spiritually choking on waste production for false needs. Here was the subsection of the working class that might lead the whole in a revolutionary struggle. Here were workers strategically located to sabotage the system and intellectually equipped to grasp their own unfreedom. The historic task confronting the new left was to help white-collar slaves pierce the mystification of abundance and perceive their slavery.

New working-class theory provided a convenient rationale for the program and tactics of the movement in 1966–1967. At the Iowa convention in August 1966, newly elected vice president Carl Davidson, a twenty-three-year-old philosophy instructor at the University of Nebraska, led SDS back to campus under the slogan "student power." Students were victims, Davidson argued. Acting at the behest of their corporate masters, universities trained them for membership in the working class, reproducing on campus "all the conditions and relations of production in the factories of advanced corporate capitalism—isolation, manipulation, and alienation." Students fighting for control of the universities would soon see that the issues of dorm hours and Vietnam were connected and that corporate liberalism was the system responsible for both. More important, they would be preparing for the postgraduate struggle in the workplace against their corporate oppressors. That year, in the name of student power, SDS chapters coast to coast used a variety of tactics, including civil disobedience, to attack dorm regulations, ROTC, university cooperation with draft boards, and on-campus recruitment by the military and by the Dow Chemical Company, maker of napalm.

New working-class theory also meshed neatly with SDS's new antiwar program. At its December 1966 National Council meeting, SDS denounced the war as genocidal and summoned its chapters to organize draft-resistance unions. As Peter Henig ingeniously demonstrated the following month in the SDS paper *New Left Notes,* students fighting the draft were fighting not only for the Vietnamese but for themselves. This was true even though most students enjoyed the privilege of draft deferment. Quoting from Selective Service documents, Henig showed how the draft was designed to channel young men into school and from there into occupations deemed worthy by the government. Either they conformed to society's wishes—by becoming trainees for the new working class—and were deferred, or they were drafted into the army. "The psychology of granting wide choice under pressure . . . is the American or indirect way of achieving what is done by direction in foreign countries where choice is not permitted," the Selective Service wrote in one of the documents from which Henig gleefully quoted. The draft, then, was not merely an antiwar issue but SDS's perfect illustration of the totalitarian reality behind America's liberal façade. . . .

III

In the following school year, 1967–1968, the concept of the new working class was consigned to the new left's junk heap of discarded theories. Traditional Marxists skillfully attacked it as a verbal phenomenon lacking in analytic rigor, and most of the movement's rank and file proved uninterested in ideologies of self-liberation. If not for themselves, then for whom would the young radicals fight? If not for themselves, Greg Calvert had predicted, the young radicals would end up fighting out of guilt for the liberation of Third World peoples. This is precisely what happened.

The prophet of the new direction was Carl Oglesby, whose *Containment and Change* (written with Richard Shaull and published in the spring of 1967) provided the movement with an ideological perspective it really wanted. A year and a half before, Oglesby had not dared to use the word "imperialism" to describe American policy. Now he marshaled evidence to prove that America was a greedy imperialist power, driven by the requirements of capitalism to feed on the resources and exploit the markets of Third World nations. For the new left, the image of America the bloodsucker organized the data of politics in a compelling and persuasive new way. But it also deflected the movement onto a disastrous course by fostering a romantic sense of identification with Third World guerrillas, by bringing old left Marxism back into fashion, and by undermining the movement's commitment to democratic values. . . .

The ascendance of the imperialist perspective in the summer of 1967 owed as much to ghetto rebellions at home as to the Vietcong. While Detroit and Newark burned, black power ideologues offered a powerful metaphor of explanation. Black ghettos, they said, were internal colonies victimized by American imperialism precisely as were the colonies of Africa, Asia, and Latin America. It followed that black rioters were no less revolutionary guerrillas than the Vietcong—urban guerrillas waging war in the belly of the beast. SNCC chairman H. Rap Brown selected August 18, 1965, as the independence day of the internal colony because on that day "the blacks of Watts picked up their guns to fight for their freedom. That was our Declaration of Independence, and we signed it with Molotov cocktails and rifles." In August 1967 Stokely Carmichael, past SNCC chairman, joined revolutionaries from twenty-seven Latin American countries for a conference in Havana to discuss ways of implementing Che's recent call for "two, three, many Vietnams." Carmichael declared the solidarity of American blacks with revolutionary movements everywhere, and the conference passed a resolution calling on "the Negro people of the U.S. to answer the racist violence of the U.S. imperialist government by increasing direct revolutionary action and strengthening their fraternal relations with the people of Africa, Asia, and Latin America that fight against the same hated enemy: U.S. imperialism." Said Huey Newton of the Black Panther party, "We can stop the machinery. We can stop the imperialists from using it against black people all over the world. We are in a strategic position in this country, and we won't be the only group rebelling against the oppressor here."

As usual, whites in the movement let blacks set the style. Tom Hayden, who had witnessed the 1967 Newark riot first-hand, welcomed the emergence of the "conscious guerrilla," capable of keeping alien authority in the ghetto on the defensive, capable in riots of diverting the police from looters, capable— when appropriate—of carrying the torch to white neighborhoods and business districts. "If necessary," he said, in a line that revealed how far the movement had traveled since Port Huron, "he can successfully shoot to kill." If black radicals could use violence against imperialism, then, some asked, why not white radicals? "Do what John Brown did—," Rap Brown advised the movement, "pick up a gun and go out and shoot our enemy."

The white left took the decisive step toward acting out its guerrilla fantasy during two spectacular demonstrations in the third week of October 1967. The first, called Stop the Draft Week, occurred in Oakland, California, where Bay Area radicals again attempted to close down the Army's induction center. In the planning stage the Resistance argued for nonviolent civil disobedience, even in the face of arrest. But SDS-ers and other militants flatly rejected nonviolence, hoping to move the antiwar movement "from the level of moral protest to a show of power." In the end, no compromise was possible; so it was agreed that the factions would demonstrate on different days of the week.

Monday, October 16, 1967, belonged to the Resistance, 124 of whose supporters were arrested at the doors of the induction center in a classic example of moral witness. Tuesday belonged to the militants. Three thousand showed up, and were charged by police, gassed, and routed. Enraged, the militants waited for the pacifists to sit in again on Wednesday and Thursday, and then on Friday returned ten thousand strong. The battle that ensued was the Bastille Day of the new left. Blockading intersections with parked cars, trash cans, parking meters, and potted trees, the crowd ringed twenty-five square blocks, declared them a liberated area, and attempted to hold them with improvised guerrilla tactics. When police charged, the protesters broke into small groups, retreated, and then reformed elsewhere to set up new barricades. At two intersections demonstrators found themselves superior in force and retook lost positions. After holding the streets for a few hours, the students retreated rather than engage the National Guard and marched in triumph back to Berkeley.

That next day, October 21, 1967, across the country in Washington, D.C., there occurred one of the most remarkable events in American history. After listening to the usual speeches at the Lincoln Memorial, fifty thousand American citizens made their contribution to Stop the Draft Week by marching into Virginia to close down the Pentagon. "We're now in the business of wholesale disruption and widespread resistance and dislocation of the American society," project director Jerry Rubin had declared on the march's eve. Once on the Pentagon grounds, approximately one thousand demonstrators disregarded the agreements their leaders had negotiated with the government on permissible forms of civil disobedience and immediately headed for forbidden areas, some of them shoving through a line of U.S. marshals to establish an illegal beachhead on the asphalt plaza leading to the Pentagon's main entrance. A handful even briefly made it past guards through a side door. Thousands more crowded menacingly onto the steps leading to the plaza and on the grassy mall below. This was resistance, and to direct it SDS leaders, including Greg Calvert, materialized with bullhorns at strategic locations.

There followed several hours of revolutionary theater—girls putting flowers into the gun barrels of soldiers, hippies attempting to levitate the Pentagon, forays across the plaza to break an occasional window, eloquent pleas to the soldiers to "join us," ugly taunting of MPs, bloody encounters with the troops, and early in the evening small bursts of flame as demonstrators burned draft cards. Past midnight, after the press went home, the authorities struck back in force. Forming a wedge, soldiers and marshals proceeded to clear the plaza, which the protesters held in violation of their permit, and the steps, which legally were theirs. And here a curious thing happened. Though the marshals performed their work brutally, the demonstrators locked arms and passively resisted, waiting their turn to be beaten and arrested. Movement tacticians disapproved. "One is misreading Che Guevara," a new left writer said, "by concluding that a guerrilla fighter confronts a superior military force in positional combat. That just doesn't make sense."

Reaction on the new left to the October demonstrations was euphoric. Underground papers exulted over the tactical brilliance of the protestors, the barriers of fear they demolished, their ability to contest the enemy on battlefields of their own choosing. Cathy Wilkerson, editor of *New Left Notes* and one of those who provided leadership at the Pentagon, wrote, "The success of the Pentagon siege lay fundamentally in our determination to finally demand a serious response from the power structure in America and our ability to withstand that response, learn from it and strengthen ourselves to proceed further." Jeff Segal, a West Coast SDS leader, regarded the Oakland demonstration as a watershed in movement history. The action had not been actual guerrilla warfare, he conceded, but it "carried within itself the seeds for all the elements that we will need when, indeed, our time does come." Commented another participant, "imperialism cannot be defeated by cardboard signs and flowers."

With the onset of the guerrilla fantasy, the corruption of the new left commenced. In the early years movement people tried to live their values by practicing participatory democracy in their organizations, cultivating open relationships, and creating their own community. But even as real guerrillas employed inhumane means to achieve the humane ends of revolution so now new leftists began to wonder whether, given their new seriousness, they could any longer afford to indulge their values. Democracy was the first casualty. Shortly after the siege of the Pentagon, Calvert dismissed participatory democracy because it fostered manipulation by elites, "long, formless mass meetings," and sloppy strategic thinking. He favored "responsible collective leadership which can be held accountable to its constituency." In retrospect, this was the first step toward creation of a party based on the Leninist principle of "democratic centralism." In an even more dangerous departure, Carl Davidson explicitly rejected the very norms of democracy itself. The social order we fight against is "totalitarian, manipulative, repressive, and anti-democratic," he said. Since its institutions "are without legitimacy in our eyes, they are without rights." To accord them civil liberties, to debate rather than immobilize them, was to play by the very bourgeois rules designed to enslave us. As a result, "it is the duty of a revolutionary not only to be intolerant of, but to actually suppress the anti-democratic activities of the dominant order." This argument would become a staple of the new left as it descended into its own form of totalitarianism.

Post-Pentagon, young radicals readily conceded that their liberation fight was not for themselves—beneficiaries of American imperialism—but for imperialism's victims, especially American blacks. SNCC's James Forman found a receptive audience among white leftists in February 1968, when he explained what black radicals expected of them. "Since black people in this country are engaged in a protracted warfare against their colonial domination by the United States," he said, black people must lead the struggle. The tasks of white radicals were to fight fascist tendencies in the working class, combat the power structure, and above all commit themselves to defending blacks from government repression. "White America must begin to formulate its plans to deal with the 101st Airborne Cavalry and all other divisions when they occupy the ghettos of the United States trying to exterminate black people," Forman said. When "the Man" kills "uppity niggers" like himself, whites must retaliate. "And," concluded Forman, "I will tell you what I will expect from white revolutionaries for my assassination:

> 10 war factories destroyed.
> 15 police stations blown up.
> 30 power plants demolished.
> No flowers.
> 1 Southern governor, 2 mayors, and 500 racist
>   white cops dead."

At Columbia University in the spring of 1968 the implications of the anti-imperialist tendency in the new left became clearer. The crisis at Columbia began in March when the so-called "action-faction" captured control of the local SDS chapter and set out to polarize the university on radical issues, forcing the students to choose sides. The leading spokesman for action was Mark Rudd, newly elected chapter president. A twenty-year-old junior barely known on his own campus when the year began, Rudd would emerge within months as an international celebrity—mainly because the news media chose him as the symbol of the radical student movement now rapidly attaining mass dimension.

It was not a bad choice. A third-generation Jewish American whose grandparents had immigrated from Eastern Europe (the family name had been Rudnitsky), Rudd was reared in comfortable and secure surroundings in the suburb of Maplewood, New Jersey, not far from Newark. His father, a retired Army officer in the real-estate business, supported Mark's extracurricular radicalism, and his doting mother spoke proudly of my son "the rebel." On Mother's Day 1968, while Mark was busy paralyzing Columbia, Mrs. Rudd prepared a home-cooked meal and drove with the family to the campus so he could eat it. "I was a member of the depressed generation, and my greatest concern has always been making a living," his father remarked. "Mark doesn't have to worry about that so much and we're glad he has time to spend on activities like politics. He never cared about material things anyway." Mark himself traced the origins of his radicalism to his early perception of some ugly American realities. "I lived in a middle-class home and I could see the contrast between the environment I grew up in and the slums. My grandmother owned a candy store in the Central Ward of Newark, and I used to visit her all the time. The area was turning black and I was stunned by the poverty." Why did this young man—former Boy Scout, good student—come to rage against America? Perhaps he screamed "motherfuckers" at the authorities because he was conducting some unconscious Freudian vendetta against his father. Or perhaps, more plausibly, he entered Columbia a naïve and idealistic adolescent and discovered there, in the fashionable radicalism of the time, an explanation of the world so compelling that he gave himself to it utterly.

Rudd's real education had little to do with his formal classes. In his sophomore year he became friends with Herbert Marcuse's stepson Mike Neumann, who introduced him to SDS activists as well as to the works of the new left's favorite philosopher. Though Rudd claimed to have been influenced by Marcuse, the real tendency of his thought was better indicated by his March 1968 trip to Cuba, where he confirmed his admiration for Castro's revolution, his hero worship of the martyred Che, and his affinity for the seductive Third World Marxist perspective. Meanwhile, he was emerging as a leader of the tiny Columbia left. Lanky and stoop-shouldered, with black hair, strong jaw, and piercing blue eyes, he had the power to stir people by the passion of his radical commitment. He was not a deep thinker, merely quick; not a notably informed speaker, but one in command of the facile categories of his radicalism. Rather soon he evinced characteristics hardly unknown to revolutionaries of the past—abrasiveness, intolerance, and a capacity to be ruthless. Like others in SDS, he was mastering that fear of violence and of bad manners that was the affliction of the children of his class. Under Rudd's leadership SDS members pushed a lemon meringue pie into the face of a Selective Service officer, disrupted the university's memorial service for Martin Luther King, and in Rudd's name sent a letter to Columbia president Grayson Kirk that concluded, "There is only one thing left to say. It may sound nihilistic to you since it is the opening shot in a war of liberation. I'll use the words of Le Roi Jones, whom I'm sure you don't like a whole lot: 'Up against the wall, motherfucker, this is a stick-up.'"

In the end the university gave Rudd the issue he needed to vindicate the action faction. Brushing aside years of protest by black community groups, the Columbia administration had begun construction of a new gymnasium in Morningside Park, a sloping hill that separates Columbia above from Harlem below. At noon, Tuesday, April 23, 1968, supported for a change by the Students Afro-American Society, SDS called a meeting at the Sundial in the center of the campus to protest the gym and other issues. At one point, part of the assembled crowd of five hundred charged Low Library, only to be repulsed by a line of conservative students. While Rudd stood on a trash can pondering aloud what to do next, the crowd suddenly dashed toward the gym site, where some of its members ripped down a fence, tussled briefly with police, then retreated to campus. Back at the Sundial Rudd was again immobilized by uncertainty—until a black student, William Sales, made a speech that uncannily caught the developing mood of the new left.

> I thought up until this stage of the game, white people weren't ready, but I saw something today that suggests that this is not true. . . . Because when the deal hit the fan you were there. . . . If you're talking about revolution, if you're talking about identifying with the Vietnamese struggle, you don't need to go to Rockefeller Center, dig? There's one oppressor—in the White House, in Low Library, in Albany, New York. You strike a blow at the gym, you strike a blow for the Vietnamese people. You strike a blow at Low Library, you strike a blow for the freedom fighters in Angola, Mozambique, Portuguese Guinea, Zimbabwe, South Africa. . . . All we need is some sophistication. . . . Next time we go down there, [the police] will be waiting. An incoherent mob will not be able to deal with them. So we have to be more sophisticated. Need I say more? I don't want to get arrested for sedition.

Galvanized by this expression of the imperialist hypothesis and the guerrilla fantasy, Rudd shouted, "Let's go to Hamilton," a classroom and administration building nearby. Four hundred and fifty people marched into the building, hung a picture of Che over a doorway, and took a dean prisoner. It was great fun at first—live rock, red balloons, Chinese takeout food—until black militants from Harlem, rumored to be carrying guns, began filtering in. At 5:30 A.M., blacks ordered the whites to pick up their blankets and go, which, disappointed and chagrined, they did. Nevertheless, Rudd would say afterward, "We were spurred on by a tremendous push from history, if you will, embodied in the militant black students of Columbia."

Resilient, the whites decided to occupy a building of their own, choosing Low Library, where Grayson Kirk had his offices. Soon students were smoking Kirk's cigars and rifling his files. In the past SDS's antics had left most Columbia students cold, but this time SDS had the right issues. Over the next week, a thousand Columbia students participated in the takeover of three more buildings, including Mathematics Hall, where Tom Hayden himself turned up to provide leadership. At Columbia, as Mark Rudd explained later, the movement learned "that racism and imperialism really are issues that affect people's lives. And it was these things that people moved on, not dorm rules, or democratizing university governance or any of that bullshit." So far had the movement come since Berkeley!

Inside the buildings the students created communes governed by participatory democracy and devoted to the creation of the "new man." Many communards who entered the buildings only vaguely sympathetic to SDS left them convinced radicals. Unfortunately, they did not leave voluntarily. SDS would not compromise its demands, and the administration would not grant amnesty to the demonstrators. The cops came, as they had to, and behaved as Rudd knew they would, wantonly and with violence. Police brutality furthered the radicalization of the student mass, and the inevitable strike received overwhelming undergraduate support. Classes virtually ceased in Columbia College and final exams were canceled. SDS had, in effect, closed down a great American university.

Rudd was not one who saw Columbia as a victory. After the police bust, SDS argued for a radical strike that would destroy the university and replace it with one that was truly free. But the mass of the students, demanding "student power," wanted only to restructure the existing institution. Rudd finally concluded that there could be no free university until revolution put an end to unfree society. Soon a major figure in national SDS, he became a strident voice urging the movement to look away from the campus for allies in the revolutionary task of bringing down the empire.

That spring the slogan "two, three, many Columbias" sounded on campuses across America, and as it did, dozens of colleges and universities experienced various forms of militant protest. The movement had forced its way to center stage, and its possibilities suddenly seemed limitless. Writing in *Ramparts,* Hayden proclaimed Columbia to be "a new tactical stage in the resistance movement that began last fall: from the overnight occupation of buildings to permanent occupations; from mill-ins to the creation of revolutionary committees; from symbolic civil disobedience to barricaded resis-

tance." As support for the movement developed in the cities, Hayden continued, "A crisis is forseeable that would be too massive for police to handle."
One thing was certain: "We are moving toward power—the power to stop
the machine if it cannot be made to serve humane ends."

In truth, Columbia began the new left's decline into madness. Greg Calvert had once advocated resistance as a way to build revolutionary consciousness. After Columbia, revolutionary consciousness rapidly took hold, and
the goal of the movement became the seizure of power. Events worldwide
conspired that spring to create the illusion of a revolutionary situation ready
for exploitation by the sons of Che. In Vietnam the Tet Offensive seemed
to signal the American defeat. In the black ghettos of American cities Martin
Luther King's assassination touched off a new wave of bloody rioting. In
world money markets the American dollar was taking a beating, and the
international monetary system was edging toward collapse. Above all, in
France students and workers paralyzed the country in May 1968, by striking
against the universities and factories, nearly toppling the regime. Totally mis-
conceiving reality, the new left concluded that the empire was nearing collapse
and that the time had come to assist blacks at home and peasants abroad in
finishing it off.

IV

The death of SDS in 1969 did not immediately finish the movement. Radicals
continued to paralyze campuses, blow up buildings, and trash stores. And
in May 1970, in the wake of Nixon's invasion of Cambodia, a wave of
strikes—unprecedented in size and militance—swept the universities, including
Kent State, where National Guardsmen shot and killed four young Americans,
fatalities in the new American Civil War. Protests flared intermittently for
another year and then, as suddenly and unexpectedly as it had emerged, the
new left was gone.

Reasons for the collapse were not hard to find: government repression,
de-escalation of the Vietnam War, loss of moral authority as a consequence
of movement violence, inability to find off-campus allies, commitment to
revolution in a nonrevolutionary situation. More fundamental than any of
these was the failure of the movement to fashion an ideology for a native
American radicalism. Such an ideology would have accounted for the alienation of the new left's student base and offered a persuasive analysis of the
oppressive character of American institutions. In truth, the new left never
found a solution to the ideological problem because none was possible. There
is no doubt that the young radicals despised mass culture, the competitive
ethic, and "plastic" American civilization. But their critique was more aesthetic
than political, and—Marcuse notwithstanding—few could long sustain a self-
image as technology's slaves, impoverished by abundance. The young knew
that they enjoyed more freedom, more privileges, more options—more Eros—
by far than did poor people, peasants, their parents, or past generations of

the young. Grievances they possessed, but none so crushing as to validate Marcuse's Great Refusal.

Among the sources of sixties radicalism none was more important than disillusionment with liberalism. A generation reared to believe in America as the land of the free and the home of the brave was forced by events to confront the facts of American racism, poverty, and imperialism. The same liberals who promised to abolish these evils, new leftists came to believe, played politics with race, fought a phony poverty war, and napalmed Vietnamese. Beneficiaries of a system that seemed to do evil, guilt-ridden students committed themselves to liberate those whom America oppressed. Moral outrage, then, not self-liberation, was the principal fuel of this radicalism, which went far to explain both the movement's militance and its brevity. Moral outrage could not long be sustained at high levels of intensity and eventually exhausted those whose actions depended upon it. By the early seventies, movement veterans were burned out, students entering college had heard too much too long about racism and imperialism to be shocked by either, and hard times fostered the ascendance of personal over social values. Idealists may become revolutionaries, but cynics never.

Ephemeral though it was, the movement had significant consequences. It brought the war home and so helped force de-escalation. It attacked the form and the values of the contemporary university, making it less authoritarian and more responsive to students. It helped demystify authority and contributed, therefore, to its decline. And its insistent challenge threw mainstream liberals on the defensive. Confronted by the rage of their own children, mainstream liberals moved left. Those who did not—the Johnsonian liberals of the Democratic party, the corporate liberals of new left demonology— lost their capacity to shape events. The young Americans throwing rocks at the Pentagon and chanting, "Hey, hey, LBJ. How many kids did you kill today?" were one reason why Lyndon Johnson, as he entered the election year of 1968, was staggering toward political extinction.

Sources

Vietnam

Orville Schell

Cage for the Innocents

In 1969, the United States had more than 500,000 troops in Vietnam and was spending more than $20 billion on the war in Indochina. Nonetheless, there are many who believe that the United States and

South Vietnam could have won the war had the military been given free rein and additional men and supplies. There can be no easy resolution of this debate; indeed, there are those who would argue the immorality of posing the problem in terms of victory and defeat.

Writing for *The Atlantic Monthly,* journalist Orville Schell described a prisoner interrogation he witnessed in January 1968. If one assumes that this account accurately reflects the nature of the conflict, what lessons does it contain? How would Schell stand on the question of victory and defeat, framed in the paragraph above?

Nguyen Luc, who is seventy-seven years old, came from Phuctien village, in Tienphuc District, Quangtin Province. He had also been designated an Innocent Civilian and was waiting to be shipped out. He was probably the oldest inmate in the Chulai camp. Although his hair was not completely gray, he was hunched over from years of bending down working in the rice paddies. He walked extremely slowly and finally had to be helped up the steps of the interrogation hut. I reached down to give him a hand. His wiry body could not have weighed more than eighty pounds. A major from the Press Information Office thrust out a glad hand in welcome. But Nguyen did not know the significance of shaking hands. Instead he placed both hands together in front of him in a prayer-like motion, which is the traditional form of Vietnamese greeting. The major gave a nervous laugh and then tried to clasp him around the back like a public relations man squiring a big client into his office. But Luc had already begun to sit down. His eyes were riveted to the ground the whole time. He wore an oversize pair of sawed-off army fatigues, and sat quietly on a small wood stool. He seemed neither nervous nor scared, just weary. I had the feeling that even if I had wished to, I could have done nothing which would have elicited any emotional response from him.

Q. How long have you been here?
A. Six days.
Q. How were you captured?
A. I was captured in the morning while out in the rice fields working. The Americans and the ARVN's[*] came and ordered me to go with them.
Q. Did they allow you to return home and talk to your family or bring any possessions?
A. No, they were in a very big hurry. They pointed guns at me and I just went.
Q. Had your fields been planted?
A. Yes.

---

[*] Army of the Republic of Vietnam—the South Vietnamese army.—*Ed.*
Orville Schell, "Cage for the Innocents," *The Atlantic Monthly,* January 1968, pp. 33–34. Reprinted with permission of the author.

Q. What will happen to them now?
A. I don't know who will harvest the rice. I would like to go back because now there are very few people in the village. They all live underground. All our houses have been bombed and destroyed. The bombs have made big holes in our rice fields.
Q. When did the bombing start?
A. [He paused.] It started three years ago—but then not as much as now.
Q. Did the people fear the V.C. or the bombing more in your village?
A. We don't like the Viet Cong because they take our rice and sometimes make us work.
Q. But which do you fear the most?
A. We fear the bombing because we don't know when it will come and we can't see it. [At this point Luc began fidgeting with his pants. I asked why, but he did not respond.]
Q. Who are the Americans?
A. [Pause.] The Americans are like the French. The French were very cruel.
Q. Are the Americans cruel?
A. The French beat the people.
Q. Do the Americans beat the people?
A. [Luc glanced over at the agitated but silent PIO officer.] Sometimes the Americans give candy. [Again he started tugging at his baggy fatigue shorts, which I noticed were missing most of the buttons on the fly.]
Q. Why are you fidgeting? Are you hurt?
A. [A long pause during which time Luc stared at his feet.] I want some underwear. I am embarrassed because my pants will not fasten.
Q. Have you asked the Americans for some new clothes? You know that they give clothes to inmates, don't you?
A. Yes.
Q. Have you asked them? [The PIO major interrupted here to assure me that all prisoners received all the clothing and medical attention that they needed.]
A. Yes, once.
Q. What happened?
A. I asked the Americans, but they did not understand me. They just laughed at me, and one struck me. He slapped me on my face. I was very scared. I didn't dare ask again.
Q. Why do you ask now? I have explained that I am not in the army.
A. The atmosphere is good. [The PIO major acted shocked and assured me that this "oversight" would be corrected. After the interview he hurried to the office to launch his protest.]
Q. Do you know why your village was bombed?
A. The people said that it was because of the Communists.
Q. What is a Communist? Who are they?
A. [Long pause.] They are . . . I don't know.
Q. Have you ever heard of Nguyen Cao Ky or Nguyen Van Thieu?
A. No, I do not know them.

Q. Have you ever heard of Ho Chi Minh?
A. Yes, he sent troops from the North. He is well known.
Q. Why were you detained?
A. I don't know why. They just brought me in.
Q. But has anyone explained to you the reason for detaining you?
A. No. They do not speak Vietnamese. We cannot understand one another.
Q. What did they tell you in the interrogation?
A. They asked me questions. They asked me if I was a Viet Cong and if I
    knew where the Viet Cong were hiding. They just asked me questions.
Q. Do you know that you have been designated an Innocent Civilian?
A. What is that? [The PIO major moved forward on his chair ready to give
    an explanation.]
Q. Where are you going when you leave here?
A. I don't know what they are going to do with us. Will I be able to go
    back to my village? I am very worried because no one is there to look
    after our ancestral tombs.
Q. Do you have a family?
A. Yes, a wife, two sons, and some grandchildren.
Q. Where are they now?
A. I don't know. I am very sad because I don't know what has happened
    to them. Maybe they are worrying about me also.
Q. Perhaps they are in refugee camps. Do you know anything about the
    resettlement program?
A. No.
Q. Have the Americans ever dropped leaflets on your village explaining the
    refugee program and warning you to leave your village because it will
    be bombed?
A. Yes, sometimes they drop leaflets. But I can't read. Many people can't
    read. Now there are no schools in the countryside. They are all destroyed.
Q. Do you know what is going to happen to you?
A. No, I don't know. I need someone to help me. I am very scared here all
    alone.

James Fallows

"What Did You Do in the Class War, Daddy?"

**Resistance to the draft and to military service was widespread in the
1960s. According to one estimate, some 250,000 draft-age men failed
to register for the draft in the Vietnam era, and about 17,500 young
men became fugitives rather than serve in the military. Thousands**

more, including the author of the following selection, fulfilled the
letter of the law but managed to stay out of the military.

James Fallows, who would later serve in the Carter administration, was a student at Harvard University when he was drafted in the
fall of 1969 under the Nixon administration's new lottery system. In
this system, birthdates were drawn at random once each year, and
those, like Fallows, whose birthdates came up early in the drawing
were assured of being called to serve.

The Nixon administration was also responsible for the system
now being used to provide the armed forces with manpower: a "volunteer" army, buttressed by a system of monetary rewards for those
choosing military service. Does this system correct the inequities described by Fallows?

Many people think that the worst scars of the war years have healed. I
don't. Vietnam has left us with a heritage rich in possibilities for class warfare,
and I would like to start telling about it with this story:

In the fall of 1969, I was beginning my final year in college. As the
months went by, the rock on which I had unthinkingly anchored my hopes—
the certainty that the war in Vietnam would be over before I could possibly
fight—began to crumble. It shattered altogether on Thanksgiving weekend
when, while riding back to Boston from a visit with my relatives, I heard
that the draft lottery had been held and my birthdate had come up number
45. I recognized for the first time that, inflexibly, I must either be drafted
or consciously find a way to prevent it.

In the atmosphere of that time, each possible choice came equipped with
barbs. To answer the call was unthinkable, not only because, in my heart, I
was desperately afraid of being killed, but also because, among my friends,
it was axiomatic that one should not be "complicit" in the immoral war
effort. Draft resistance, the course chosen by a few noble heroes of the movement, meant going to prison or leaving the country. With much the same
intensity with which I wanted to stay alive, I did not want those things
either. What I wanted was to go to graduate school, to get married, and to
enjoy those bright prospects I had been taught that life owed me.

I learned quickly enough that there was only one way to get what I
wanted. A physical deferment would restore things to the happy state I had
known during four undergraduate years. The barbed alternatives would be
put off. By the impartial dictates of public policy I would be free to pursue
the better side of life.

Like many of my friends whose numbers had come up wrong in the
lottery, I set about securing my salvation. When I was not participating in
anti-war rallies, I was poring over the Army's code of physical regulations.

From James Fallows, "What Did You Do in the Class War, Daddy?" *The Washington Monthly,*
October 1975, pp. 5–7. Reprinted with permission from *The Washington Monthly.* Copyright
by the Washington Monthly Co., 1711 Connecticut Avenue, NW, Washington, D.C. 20009.

During the winter and early spring, seminars were held in the college common rooms. There, sympathetic medical students helped us search for disqualifying conditions that we, in our many years of good health, might have overlooked. Although, on the doctors' advice, I made a half-hearted try at fainting spells, my only real possibility was beating the height and weight regulations. My normal weight was close to the cut-off point for an "underweight" disqualification, and, with a diligence born of panic, I made sure I would have a margin. I was six-feet-one-inch tall at the time. On the morning of the draft physical I weighed 120 pounds.

Before sunrise that morning I rode the subway to the Cambridge city hall, where we had been told to gather for shipment to the examination at the Boston Navy Yard. The examinations were administered on a rotating basis, one or two days each month for each of the draft boards in the area. Virtually everyone who showed up on Cambridge day at the Navy Yard was a student from Harvard or MIT.

There was no mistaking the political temperament of our group. Many of my friends wore red arm bands and stop-the-war buttons. Most chanted the familiar words, "Ho, Ho, Ho Chi Minh/NLF is Gonna Win." One of the things we had learned from the draft counselors was that disruptive behavior at the examination was a worthwhile political goal, not only because it obstructed the smooth operation of the criminal war machine, but also because it might impress the examiners with our undesirable character traits. As we climbed into the buses and as they rolled toward the Navy Yard, about half of the young men brought the chants to a crescendo. The rest of us sat rigid and silent, clutching x-rays and letters from our doctors at home.

Inside the Navy Yard, we were first confronted by a young sergeant from Long Beach, a former surfer boy no older than the rest of us and seemingly unaware that he had an unusual situation on his hands. He started reading out instructions for the intelligence tests when he was hooted down. He went out to collect his lieutenant, who clearly had been through a Cambridge day before. "We've got all the time in the world," he said, and let the chanting go on for two or three minutes. "When we're finished with you, you can go, and not a minute before."

From that point on the disruption became more purposeful and individual, largely confined to those whose deferment strategies were based on anti-authoritarian psychiatric traits. Twice I saw students walk up to young orderlies—whose hands were extended to receive the required cup of urine—and throw the vial in the orderlies' faces. The orderlies looked up, initially more astonished than angry, and went back to towel themselves off. Most of the rest of us trod quietly through the paces, waiting for the moment of confrontation when the final examiner would give his verdict. I had stepped on the scales at the very beginning of the examination. Desperate at seeing the orderly write down 122 pounds, I hopped back on and made sure that he lowered it to 120. I walked in a trance through the rest of the examination, until the final meeting with the fatherly physician who ruled on marginal cases such as mine. I stood there in socks and underwear, arms wrapped around me in the chilly building. I knew as I looked at the doctor's face that he understood exactly what I was doing.

"Have you ever contemplated suicide?" he asked after he finished looking over my chart. My eyes darted up to his. "Oh, suicide—yes, I've been feeling very unstable and unreliable recently." He looked at me, staring until I returned my eyes to the ground. He wrote "unqualified" on my folder, turned on his heel, and left. I was overcome by a wave of relief, which for the first time revealed to me how great my terror had been, and by the beginning of the sense of shame which remains with me to this day.

It was, initially, a generalized shame at having gotten away with my deception, but it came into sharper focus later in the day. Even as the last of the Cambridge contingent was throwing its urine and deliberately failing its color-blindness tests, buses from the next board began to arrive. These bore the boys from Chelsea, thick, dark-haired young men, the white proles of Boston. Most of them were younger than us, since they had just left high school, and it had clearly never occurred to them that there might be a way around the draft. They walked through the examination lines like so many cattle off to slaughter. I tried to avoid noticing, but the results were inescapable. While perhaps four out of five of my friends from Harvard were being deferred, just the opposite was happening to the Chelsea boys.

We returned to Cambridge that afternoon, not in government buses but as free individuals, liberated and victorious. The talk was high-spirited, but there was something close to the surface that none of us wanted to mention. We knew now who would be killed. . . .

We have not, however, learned the lesson of the day at the Navy Yard, or the thousands of similar scenes all across the country through all the years of the war. Five years later, two questions have yet to be faced, let alone answered. The first is why, when so many of the bright young college men opposed the war, so few were willing to resist the draft, rather than simply evade it. The second is why all the well-educated presumably humane young men, whether they opposed the war or were thinking fondly of A-bombs on Hanoi, so willingly took advantage of this most brutal form of class discrimination—what it signifies that we let the boys from Chelsea be sent off to die.

Legacies: The Monument Controversy

A decade after the last American soldiers left Vietnam in 1973, Americans quarreled again over Vietnam—this time over the shape of a monument to commemorate the war dead. The two most prominent proposals were for a sunken wall, inscribed with the

names of the dead, and a statue of combat soldiers. The upshot was a memorial incorporating both designs; the statue is positioned a short distance from the wall. What was at stake in the monument controversy? What, in your opinion, is the message or theme of each design, and how might each represent a distinct understanding of the war?

The Wall Portion of the Vietnam Memorial. The design by Yale University architecture student Maya Ying Lin was the winning entry in an open competition. *National Park Service.*

The Statue Portion of the Vietnam Memorial. Sculpted by Frederick Hart.
National Park Service.

From Montgomery to Watts

Compare and contrast these photographs, representative of a decade
of black protest and resistance. What do the photographs tell us
about the participants in each decade's protests? about the goals of
protest activity? What is the relationship between the activity shown
in the Watts photograph and the slogan "black power"?

1955. Walking to work during the Montgomery bus boycott. *Grey Villet,* Life *Magazine,* © *Time, Inc.*

1965. A decade later, blacks in Watts, a section of Los Angeles, are in the streets with a different purpose—transporting goods taken from ghetto stores. *AP—Wide World Photos.*

Greil Marcus

Apocalypse at Altamont

The New Left and the counterculture were not synonymous. The New Left was a political phenomenon, rooted in such organizations as SDS and SNCC (Student Nonviolent Coordinating Committee), which sought change through politics. The counterculture was defined by dress, drugs, music, and general life style. After the famous Woodstock concert of August 1969, many Americans believed that the burden of social change would be borne by the counterculture-as-community: the Woodstock generation.

That euphoric vision was shattered only months later, at Altamont raceway near San Francisco, where the Rolling Stones gathered the countercultural multitudes for a free concert (which would result in a profitable film). There, the spirit of the 1960s died, as it had in Memphis, My Lai, and a dozen other places. What happened? What was it that was "coming apart"?

I had seen the naked woman perhaps a dozen times during the day. Repeatedly she would choose a male, run toward him, throw her arms around his neck, and rub her body up and down his. The comeback was predictable: "Hey, baby, wanna fuck?" At this, the woman would commence a series of psychotic screams and run blindly into the crowd. After a few minutes she would calm down sufficiently to begin the game all over again. Eventually people began to keep their distance.

But now, in the dark, behind the stage, with only a little yellow light filtering through to where I was standing, waiting for the Stones to begin their first tune, the woman looked different. As she passed by, her head on her chest, I realized her body was covered with dried blood. Her face was almost black with it. Someone had given her a blanket to cover herself with—it was very cold by now—but she didn't wear it. She held on to a corner, as if she'd simply forgotten to throw it away, and it trailed behind her as she walked.

Then I saw the fat man. Hours before—it seemed like days—he had leaped to his feet to dance naked to Santana as they kicked off the day. All good times, let it loose, don't hang me up, uh-huh. The huge man seemed full of the Woodstock spirit, but those sitting near the stage, as I was, noticed that in fact he used the excuse of his dance to stomp and trample the people around him, particularly several young blacks. After a short time the Hell's Angels, who had been placed in charge of crowd and stage "security," got sick of the sight of him; they came off the stage swinging weighted pool cues and beat the fat man to the ground. He didn't seem to understand what was happening; again and again, he got up and continued his dance-stomp. Ultimately the Angels got him out of the area and took him behind the stage, where they could continue their work with greater efficiency.

Like the naked woman, the fat man was now brown with blood. His teeth had been knocked out, and his mouth still bled. He wandered across the enclosure, waiting, like me, for the music.

As the Stones began, the mood tensed and the gloomy light took on a lurid cast. The stage was jammed with sound people, Angels, writers, hangers-on. There wasn't an extra square foot. Kids began to climb the enormous sound trucks that ringed the back of the stage, and men threw them off. Some fell ten and fifteen feet to the ground; others landed on other trucks. I climbed to the top of a VW bus, where I had a slight view of the band. Several other people clambered up with me, waving tape recorder mikes in the hopes of capturing the sound. Every few minutes, it seemed, the music was broken up by waves of terrified screams from the crowd: wild ululations that went on for thirty, forty seconds at a time. We couldn't see the screamers, but with their sound, the packed mass on the stage would cringe backward, shoving the last line of people off the stage and onto the ground. As the fallen climbed back, small fights would break out.

By this time it was impossible even to guess what the screams meant. All day long people had speculated on who would be killed, on when the killing would take place. There were few doubts that the Angels would do the job. A certain inevitability had settled over the event. The crowd had been ugly, selfish, territorialist, throughout the day. People held their space. They made no room for anyone. Periodically the Angels had attacked the crowd or the musicians. It was a gray day, and the California hills were bare, cold and dead. A full beer bottle had been thrown into the crowd, striking a woman on the head, nearly killing her. Fantasies of the 300,000 turning back toward Berkeley to take People's Park back from the fence that surrounded it shifted by midafternoon to fantasies of the War Machine eliminating 300,000 enemies with nerve gas as they sat immobilized by the prospect of the Rolling Stones.

Behind the stage I could hear Keith Richard cut off the music and berate the Angels. I heard an Angel seize the mike from Keith. The screams were almost constant by this time. People on the stage were rushing forward now, then scurrying back. Two more kids made it onto the top of the VW, and it collapsed. They went right through the roof. Some of those who fell off proceeded to punch out the windows.

With all this, the music somehow picked up force. It was very strong. I turned my back on the stage and began to walk the half-mile or so to my car. Heading up the hill in the darkness, I tripped and fell head-first into the dirt, and for some reason I felt no need to get up. I lay there, intrigued by the blackness and by the sound of feet passing by me on either side and by the sound the Stones were making. I began to abstract the music from the events that surrounded it, that were by now part of it. The Stones were playing "Gimme Shelter." I tried to remember when I'd heard anything so powerful. I reveled in the song, and when it was over, I got up and went on to my car to wait for the friends from whom I'd been separated hours before, when the Angels first jumped off the stage and into our laps.

I didn't suffer at Altamont; like a lot of other people, I had a particularly bad time, but once home I was ready and eager to forget all about it. The murder of Meredith Hunter made that impossible; at the same time, the murder crystallized the event. A young black man murdered in the midst of a white crowd by white thugs as white men played their version of black music—it was too much to kiss off as a mere unpleasantness. For the year that followed, not a day passed when I didn't think about Altamont. I stopped listening to rock and roll and bought a lot of country blues records. Somehow Robert Johnson's songs contained Altamont; those of the Stones deflected it, just as they had done in the moments before I finally left the place. Johnson's music was calming and ominous at the same time, and that was just what I wanted: a mood to get myself out of the past and into a future to which I was hardly looking forward.

In the middle of the day at Altamont, as a refugee from the front ranks of the crowd, I met Marvin Garson, the founder of San Francisco's finest underground newspaper, the *Express Times,* called by then the *Good Times,* reflecting a shift from politics to vibe-ism. Marvin had transformed himself into a Ranter some months previously (the Ranters were a loosely organized group of Antinomians who emerged in the middle of the seventeenth century in England, resurfacing 150 years later as a body of Primitive Methodists; their basic tactic consisted of shouting down priests and other pillars of the established order). Marvin was very good at Ranting, and this day, he was crowing: "What an ending! What an ending!" "To what?" I asked. "The Sixties?" "No, no!" he cried. *"To my book!"*

In terms of cause and effect there was little more to Altamont than that. It did not in and of itself "end" anything. Rather, as Robert Christgau has said, it provided an extraordinarily complex and visceral metaphor for the *way* things of the Sixties ended. All the symbols were marshaled, and the crowd turned out, less to have a good time than to help make counterculture history. The result was that the counterculture, in the form of rock and roll, Hell's Angels ("our outlaw brothers," as many liked to call them), and thousands of politicized and unaffiliated young people, turned back upon itself. No one knew how to deal with a spectacle that from the moment it began contradicted every assumption on which it had been based, producing violence instead of fraternity, selfishness instead of generosity, ugliness instead of beauty, a bad trip instead of a high. Only the music kept its shape—in fact, driven on by the fear and danger of the day and the moment, the music, as the Stones played it, achieved a shape more perfect than it had ever taken on before. Take that for what it's worth.

13

America Under Siege

By the mid-1980s, it had become obvious that the reform promise of the 1960s would not be fulfilled. Of the various "liberation" movements of that decade of protest, only a few—the campaigns for gay rights, for women's rights, and against age discrimination—remained vital through the 1970s. Then, in 1982, the women's movement was dealt a severe blow when it became clear that the Equal Rights Amendment would fail to receive the ratification of the thirty-eight states needed to make it the Twenty-seventh Amendment to the Constitution. Only the elderly, with the Retirement Act of 1978, could claim real legislative gains in the 1970s. Of the great liberal political initiatives of the 1960s—including the war on poverty, the rebuilding of the inner cities, and a variety of efforts to combat employment discrimination and other forms of racism, sexism, and ageism—only environmental issues proved able to generate an ongoing consensus for continued governmental action.

Another aspect of the 1970s was perfectly captured by President Jimmy Carter in a televised address delivered in July 1979. The address was the product of the most intense preparation. To Camp David, the presidential retreat, Carter invited economists, members of the clergy, mayors, labor leaders, psychiatrists—even historians—to discuss the state of the nation. Based on their counsel, Carter fashioned a vision of America. It was vision of America in "crisis"—a "nearly invisible" crisis, a crisis of confidence. Americans, Carter announced, had lost their faith in progress, their faith in the future, their faith in the ability to govern themselves.

Carter traced the new American malaise back to the shocks of the 1960s. "We were sure that ours was a nation of the ballot, not of the bullet," he said,

> until the murders of John Kennedy and Robert Kennedy and Martin Luther King, Jr. We were taught that our armies were always invincible and our causes were always just only to suffer the agony of Vietnam. We respected the Presidency

as a place of honor until the shock of Watergate. We remember when the phrase "sound as a dollar" was an expression of absolute dependability until 10 years of inflation began to shrink our dollar and our savings. We believed that our nation's resources were limitless until 1973, when we had to face a growing dependence on foreign oil.

It is not at all clear that any president—even one more politically adept than Carter—could have "solved" the problems he had described. The nation's economic difficulties had much to do with a declining ability to compete in international trade and with the irrevocable loss of control over the resources of the Third World. In any event, it was Carter's fate to preside over another "agony," this one in Iran, where less than six months after Carter's address on the national malaise, militant students seized the United States embassy and held Americans prisoner. Carter's patient handling of the hostage crisis (52 prisoners were not freed for 444 days) was applauded by some, but for many Americans, it was just the latest in a long line of national humiliations.

Ronald Reagan was elected to the presidency in 1980, and reelected in 1984, for two reasons. First, many Americans, among them millions who had been liberal Democrats all their voting lives, had come to believe that the welfare state was at the root of the nation's social and economic problems. Unlike Dwight Eisenhower's 1952 victory, Reagan's was a vote against a welfare-state tradition that included the New Deal and the Great Society. Second, Reagan seemed to offer, as had John Kennedy in 1960, the best hope of national escape from Carter's (partly self-made) slough of despond.

As Reagan completed six years in office, the voters' faith appeared to have been at least partially justified. The catastrophic inflation rates of the Carter years had been dramatically reduced. Unemployment, which had reached a post-World War II peak of 10 percent in the second year of Reagan's first term, had been reduced as well. The Reagan administration seemed to have found a remedy for "stagflation"—that combination of high unemployment and high inflation that had seemed so intractable in the 1970s.

Yet problems remained. In the midst of the prosperity of 1985 and 1986, unemployment stayed at a level more than twice that considered reasonable a generation earlier. A massive federal budget deficit, ballooned by Reagan's enthusiasm for military spending, threatened a return to double-digit inflation. Major industries, including machine tools, automobiles, and steel, remained at the mercy of foreign competition. The United States was losing its heavy industry, with consequences as yet unknown. In addition, the Reagan administration's ability to generate political solutions to these and other problems was severely damaged in late 1986, with revelations that the administration had been secretly selling arms to Iran and that some of the income from these sales had been illegally directed to forces seeking to undermine the Communist government of Nicaragua.

More serious for the long term was the pervasive sense that the bonds that held the nation together had been progressively weakened since the assassination in Dallas on November 22, 1963. Scholars from every field and of every political persuasion commented on this deterioration of nationhood and the rise of a new kind of self-interested consciousness based on ethnic group, gender, religion, race, age, on one's view of forced busing or abortion—indeed, on everything but some shared notion of what it meant to be an American. As the United States lurched toward the twenty-first century, no question seemed more important: Was this "Balkanization" of America a healthy sign of a new trend toward economic and social decentralization? Or did it point, in historian Andrew Hacker's phrase, toward "the end of the American era"?

Interpretive Essay

Samuel P. Hays

Environmental Politics

In the following essay, historian Samuel P. Hays outlines the transition from a turn-of-the-century "conservation" approach to natural resources, to a post-1960 "environmental era." This broad historical overview makes it possible to understand environmental concerns not just as another 1960s issue that happened to survive into the 1970s, but also as a product of major and ongoing changes in the lives of most Americans. Why, then, did environmental matters remain potent issues in the 1980s, whereas public housing, urban "renewal," and other ingredients of Lyndon Johnson's Great Society had virtually disappeared from the political agenda? What great historical forces underpinned the environmental era? In what other ways have those forces changed today's world?

From Samuel P. Hays, "From Conservation to Environment: Environmental Politics in the United States Since World War Two," *Environmental Review* 6, no. 2 (Fall 1982): 14–41. First published in *Environmental Review*. Reprinted with permission of the publisher.

The historical significance of the rise of environmental affairs in the United States in recent decades lies in the changes which have taken place in American society since World War II. Important antecedants of those changes, to be sure, can be identified in earlier years as "background" conditions on the order of historical forerunners. But the intensity and force, and most of the substantive direction of the new environmental social and political phenomenon can be understood only through the massive changes which occurred after the end of the War—and not just in the United States but throughout advanced industrial societies. . . .

The Conservation and Environmental Impulses

Prior to World War II, before the term "environment" was hardly used, the dominant theme in conservation emphasized physical resources, their more efficient use and development. The range of emphasis evolved from water and forests in the late 19th and early 20th centuries, to grass and soils and game in the 1930's. In all these fields of endeavor there was a common concern for the loss of physical productivity represented by waste. The threat to the future which that "misuse" implied could be corrected through "sound" or efficient management. Hence in each field there arose a management system which emphasized a balancing of immediate in favor of more long-run production, the coordination of factors of production under central management schemes for the greatest efficiency. All this is a chapter in the history of production rather than of consumption, and of the way in which managers organized production rather than the way in which consumers evolved ideas and action amid the general public.

Enough has already been written about the evolution of multiple-purpose river development and sustained-yield forestry to establish their role in this context of efficient management for commodity production. But perhaps a few more words could be added for those resources which came to public attention after World War I. Amid the concern about soil erosion, from both rain and wind, the major stress lay in warnings about the loss of agricultural productivity. What had taken years to build up over geologic time now was threatened with destruction by short-term practices. The soil conservation program inaugurated in 1933 gave rise to a full-scale attack on erosion problems which was carried out amid almost inspired religious fervor. . . .

Perhaps the most significant vantage point from which to observe the common processes at work in these varied resource affairs was the degree to which resource managers thought of themselves as engaged in a common venture. It was not difficult to bring into the overall concept of "natural resources" the management of forests and waters, of soils and grazing lands, and of game. State departments of natural resources emerged, such as in Michigan, Wisconsin and Minnesota, and some university departments of forestry became departments of natural resources—all this as the new emphases on soils and game were added to the older ones on forests and waters. By the time of World War II a complex of professionals had come into being, with a strong focus on management as their common task, on the organization of applied knowledge about physical resources so as to sustain output for given investments of input under centralized management direction. This entailed a common conception of "conservation" and a common focus on "renewable resources," often within the rubric of advocating "wise use" under the direction of professional experts.

During these years another and altogether different strand of activity also drew upon the term "conservation" to clash with the thrust of efficient commodity management. Today we frequently label it with the term "preservation" as we seek to distinguish between the themes of efficient development symbolized by Gifford Pinchot and natural environment management symbolized by John Muir. Those concerned with national parks and the later wilderness activities often used the term "conservation" to describe what they were about. In the Sierra Club the "conservation committees" took up the organization's political action in contrast with its outings. And those who formed the National Parks Association and later the Wilderness Society could readily think of themselves as conservationists, struggling to define the term quite differently than did those in the realm of efficient management. . . .

Prior to World War II the natural environment movement made some significant gains. One thinks especially of the way in which Pinchot was blocked from absorbing the national parks under his direction in the first decade of the century and then, over his objections, advocates of natural environment values succeeded in establishing the National Park Service in 1916. Then there was the ensuing struggle of several decades in which an aggressive Park Service was able to engage the Forest Service in a contest for control of land and on many occasions won. . . .

After the War a massive turnabout of historical forces took place. The complex of specialized fields of efficient management of physical resources increasingly came under attack amid a new "environmental" thrust. It contained varied components. One was the further elaboration of the outdoor recreation and natural environment movements of pre-War, as reflected in the Wilderness Act of 1964, the Wild and Scenic Rivers Act of 1968, and the National Trails Act of the same year, and further legislation and administrative action on through the 1970's. But there were other strands even less rooted in the past. The most extensive was the concern for environmental pollution, or "environmental protection" as it came to be called in technical and managerial circles. While smoldering in varied and diverse ways in this or that setting from many years before, this concern burst forth to national prominence in the mid-1960's and especially in air and water pollution. And there was the decentralist thrust, the search for technologies of smaller and more human scale which complement rather than dwarf the more immediate human setting. . . . The search for a "sense of place," for a context that is more manageable intellectually and emotionally amid the escalating pace of size and scale had not made its mark in earlier years as it did in the 1970's to shape broad patterns of human thought and action.

One of the most striking differences between these post-War environmental activities, in contrast with the earlier conservation affairs, was their social roots. Earlier one can find little in the way of broad popular support for the substantive objectives of conservation, little "movement" organization, and scanty evidence of broadly shared conservation values. The drive came from the top down, from technical and managerial leaders. . . . [I]n sharp contrast, the Environmental Era displayed demands from the grass-roots, demands that are well charted by the innumerable citizen organizations and studies of public attitudes. One of the major themes of these later years, in fact, was the tension that evolved between the environmental public and the environmental managers, as impulses arising from the public clashed with impulses arising from management. This was not a new stage of public activity per se, but of new values as well. The widespread expression of social values in environmental action marks off the environmental era from the conservation years.

It is useful to think about this as the interaction between two sets of historical forces, one older that was associated with large-scale management and technology, and the other newer that reflected new types of public values and demands. The term "environment" in contrast with the earlier term "conservation" reflects more precisely the innovations in values. The technologies with which those values clashed in the post-War years, however, were closely aligned in spirit and historical roots with earlier conservation tendencies, with new stages in the evolution from the earlier spirit of scientific management of which conservation had been an integral part. A significant element of the historical analysis, therefore, is to identify the points of tension in the Environmental Era between the new stages of conservation as efficient management as it became more highly elaborated, and the newly evolving environmental concerns which displayed an altogether different thrust. . . .

There was, for example, the changing public conception of the role and meaning of forests. The U.S. Forest Service, and the entire community of professional foresters, continued to elaborate the details of scientific management of wood production; it took the form of increasing input for higher yields, and came to emphasize especially even-aged management. But an increasing number of Americans thought of forests as environments for home, work and play, as an environmental rather than as a commodity resource, and hence to be protected from incompatible crop-oriented strategies. Many of them bought woodlands for their environmental rather than their wood production potential. But the forestry profession did not seem to be able to accept the new values. The Forest Service was never able to "get on top" of the wilderness movement to incorporate it in "leading edge" fashion into its own strategies. As the movement evolved from stage to stage the Service seemed to be trapped by its own internal value commitments and hence relegated to playing a rear-guard role to protect wood production. . . .

There was one notable exception to these almost irreconcilable tensions between the old and the new in which a far smoother transition occurred— the realm of wildlife. In this case the old emphasis on game was faced with a new one on nature observation or what came to be called a "non-game" or "appreciative" use of wildlife. Between these two impulses there were many potential arenas for deep controversy. But there was also common ground in their joint interest in wildlife habitat. The same forest which served as a place for hunting also served as a place for nature observation. . . . As a result of this shared interest in wildlife habitat it was relatively easy for many "game managers" to shift in their self-conceptions to become "wildlife managers." . . .

If we examine the values and ideas, then, the activities and programs, the directions of impulses in the political arena, we can observe a marked transition from the pre-World War II conservation themes of efficient management of physical resources, to the post-World War environmental themes of environmental amenities, environmental protection, and human scale technology. Something new was happening in American society, arising out of the social changes and transformation in human values in the post-War years. These were associated more with the advanced consumer society of those years than with the industrial manufacturing society of the late 19th and the first half of the 20th centuries. Let me now root these environmental values in these social and value changes.

The Roots of New Environmental Values

The most immediate image of the "environmental movement" consists of its "protests," its objections to the extent and manner of development and the shape of technology. From the media evidence one has a sense of environmentalists blocking "needed" energy projects, dams, highways and industrial plants, and of complaints of the environmental harm generated by pollution. Environmental action seems to be negative, a protest affair. This impression is also heavily shaped by the "environmental impact" mode of analysis which identifies the "adverse effects" of development and presumably seeks to avoid or mitigate them. The question is one of how development can proceed with the "least" adverse effect to the "environment." From this context of thinking about environmental affairs one is tempted to formulate an environmental history based upon the way in which technology and development have created "problems" for society to be followed by ways in which action has been taken to cope with those problems.

This is superficial analysis. For environmental impulses are rooted in deep seated changes in recent America which should be understood primarily in terms of new positive directions. We are at a stage in history when new values and new ways of looking at ourselves have emerged to give rise to new preferences. These are characteristic of advanced industrial societies throughout the world, not just in the United States. They reflect two major and widespread social changes. One is associated with the search for standards of living beyond necessities and conveniences to include amenities made possible by considerable increases in personal and social "real income." The other arises from advancing levels of education which have generated values associated with personal creativity and self-development, involvement with natural environments, physical and mental fitness and wellness and political autonomy and efficacy. Environmental values and objectives are an integral part of these changes. . . .

The "environmental impulse" . . . reflects a desire for a better "quality of life" which is another phase of the continual search by the American people throughout their history for a higher standard of living. Environmental values are widespread in American society, extending throughout income and occupational levels, areas of the nation and racial groups, somewhat stronger in the middle sectors and a bit weaker in the very high and very low groupings. There are identifiable "leading sectors" of change with which they are associated as well as "lagging sectors." They tend to be stronger with younger people and increasing levels of education and move into the larger society from those centers of innovation. They are also more associated with particular geographical regions such as New England, the Upper Lakes States, the Upper Rocky Mountain region and the Far West, while the South, the Plains States and the lower Rockies constitute "lagging" regions. Hence one can argue that environmental values have expanded steadily in American society, associated with demographic sectors which are growing rather than with those which are more stable or declining.

Within this general context one can identify several distinctive sets of environmental tendencies. One was the way in which an increasing portion of the American people came to value natural environments as an integral part of their rising standard of living. They sought out many types of such places to experience, to explore, enjoy and protect: high mountains and forests, wetlands, ocean shores, swamplands, wild and scenic rivers, deserts, pine barrens, remnants of the original prairies, places of relatively clean air and water, more limited "natural areas." Interest in such places was not a throwback to the primitive, but an integral part of the modern standard of living as people sought to add new "amenity" and "aesthetic" goals and desires to their earlier preoccupation with necessities and conveniences. These new consumer wants were closely associated with many others of a similar kind such as in the creative arts, recreation and leisure in general, crafts, indoor and household decoration, hi-fi sets, the care of yards and gardens as living space and amenity components of necessities and conveniences. Americans experienced natural environments both emotionally and intellectually, sought them out for direct personal experience in recreation, studied them as objects of scientific and intellectual interest and desired to have them within their community, their region and their nation as symbols of a society with a high degree of civic consciousness and pride.

A new view of health constituted an equally significant innovation in environmental values, health less as freedom from illness and more as physical and mental fitness, of feeling well, of optimal capability for exercising one's physical and mental powers. The control of infectious diseases by antibiotics brought to the fore new types of health problems associated with slow, cumulative changes in physical condition, symbolized most strikingly by cancer, but by the 1980's ranging into many other conditions such as genetic and reproductive problems, degenerative changes such as heart disease and deteriorating immune systems. All this put more emphasis on the non–bacterial environmental causes of illness but, more importantly, brought into health matters an emphasis on the positive conditions of wellness and fitness. There was an increasing tendency to adopt personal habits that promoted rather than threatened health, to engage in physical exercise, to quit smoking, to eat more nutritiously and to reduce environmental threats in the air and water that might also weaken one's wellness. [One] result of this concern [was] the rapid increase in the business of health food stores, reaching $1.5 billion in 1979. . . .

These new aesthetic and health values constituted much of the roots of environmental concern. They came into play in personal life and led to new types of consumption in the private market, but they also led to demands for public action both to enhance opportunities, such as to make natural environments more available and to ward off threats to values. The threats constituted some of the most celebrated environmental battles: power and petrochemical plant siting, hardrock mining and strip mining, chemicals in the workplace and in underground drinking water supplies, energy transmission lines and pipelines. Many a local community found itself faced with a threat imposed from the outside and sought to protect itself through "environmental action." But the incidence and intensity of reaction against these threats arose at a particular time in history because of the underlying changes in values and aspirations. People had new preferences and new personal and family values which they did not have before. . . .

Still another concern began to play a more significant role in environmental affairs in the 1970's—an assertion of the desirability of more personal family and community autonomy in the face of the larger institutional world of corporate industry and government, an affirmation of smaller in the face of larger contexts of organization and power. This constituted a "self-help" movement. It was reflected in numerous publications about the possibilities of self-reliance in production of food and clothing, design and construction of homes, recreation and leisure, recycling of wastes and materials, and use of energy through such decentralized forms as wind and solar. These tendencies were far more widespread than institutional and thought leaders of the nation recognized since their world of perception and management was far removed from community and grass-roots ideas and action. The debate between "soft" and "hard" energy paths seemed to focus much of the controversy over the possibilities of decentralization. But it should also be stressed that the American economy, while tending toward more centralized control and management, also generated products which made individual choices toward decentralized living more possible and hence stimulated this phase of environmental affairs. While radical change had produced large-scale systems of management it had also reinvigorated the more traditional Yankee tinkerer who now found a significant niche in the new environmental scheme of things.

Several significant historical tendencies are integral parts of these changes. One involves consumption and the role of environmental values as part of evolving consumer values. At one time, perhaps as late as 1900, the primary focus in consumption was on necessities. By the 1920's a new stage had emerged which emphasized conveniences in which the emerging consumer durables, such as the automobile and household appliances were the most visible elements. This change meant that a larger portion of personal income, and hence of social income and production facilities were now being devoted to a new type of demand and supply. By the late 1940's a new stage in the history of consumption had come into view. Many began to find that both their necessities and conveniences had been met and an increasing share of their income could be devoted to amenities. The shorter work week and increasing availability of vacations provided opportunities for more leisure and recreation. Hence personal and family time and income could be spent on amenities. Economists were inclined to describe this as "discretionary income." The implications of this observation about the larger context of environmental values is that it is a part of the history of consumption rather than of production. That in itself involves a departure from traditional emphases in historical analysis.

Another way of looking at these historical changes is to observe the shift in focus in daily living from a preoccupation with work in earlier years to a greater role for home, family and leisure in the post-War period. Public opinion surveys indicate a persistent shift in which of these activities respondents felt were more important, a steady decline in a dominant emphasis on work and a steady rise in those activities associated with home, family and leisure. One of the most significant aspects of this shift was a divorce in the physical location of work and home. For most people in the rapidly developing manufacturing cities of the 19th century the location of home was dictated by the location of work. But the widespread use of the automobile, beginning in the 1920's, enabled an increasing number of people, factory workers as well as white collar workers, to live in one place and to work in another. The environmental context of home, therefore, came to be an increasingly separate and distinctive focus for their choices. Much of the environmental movement arose from this physical separation of the environments of home and work.

One can identify in all this an historical shift in the wider realm of politics as well. Prior to World War II the most persistent larger context of national political debate involved the balance among sectors of production. From the late 19th century on the evolution of organized extra-party political activity, in the form of "interest groups," was overwhelmingly devoted to occupational affairs, and the persistent policy issues involved the balance of the shares of production which were to be received by business, agriculture and labor, and sub-sectors within them. Against this array of political forces consumer objectives were woefully weak. But the evolution of new types of consumption in recreation, leisure and amenities generated a quite different setting. By providing new focal points of organized activity in common leisure and recreational interest groups, and by emphasizing community organization to protect community environmental values against threats from external developmental pressures, consumer impulses went through a degree of mobilization and activity which they had not previously enjoyed. In many an instance they were able to confront developmentalists with considerable success. Hence environmental action reflects the emergence in American politics of a new effectiveness for consumer action not known in the years before the War.

One of the distinctive aspects of the history of consumption is the degree to which what once were luxuries, enjoyed by only a few, over the years became enjoyed by many—articles of mass consumption. . . . And so it was with environmental amenities. What only a few could enjoy in the 19th century came to be mass activities in the mid-20th, as many purchased homes with a higher level of amenities around them and could participate in outdoor recreation beyond the city. Amid the tendency for the more affluent to seek out and acquire as private property the more valued natural amenity sites, the public lands came to be places where the opportunity for such activities remained far more accessible to a wide segment of the social order.

A major element of the older, pre-World War II "conservation movement," efficiency in the use of resources, also became revived in the 1970's around the concern for energy supply. It led to a restatement of rather traditional options, as to whether or not natural resources were limited, and hence one had to emphasize efficiency and frugality, or whether or not they were unlimited and could be developed with unabated vigor. Environmentalists stressed the former. It was especially clear that the "natural environments" of air, water and land were finite, and that increasing demand for these amid a fixed supply led to considerable inflation in price for those that were bought and sold in the private market. Pressures of growing demand on limited supply of material resources appeared to most people initially in the form of inflation; this trend of affairs in energy was the major cause of inflation in the entire economy. The great energy debates of the 1970's gave special focus to a wide range of issues pertaining to the "limits to growth." Environmentalists stressed the possibilities of "conservation supplies" through greater energy productivity and while energy producing companies objected to this as a major policy alternative, industrial consumers of energy joined with household consumers in taking up efficiency as the major alternative. In the short run the "least cost" option in energy supply in the private market enabled the nation greatly to reduce its energy use and carried out the environmental option.

In accounting for the historical timing of the environmental movement one should emphasize changes in the "threats" as well as in the values. Much of the shape and timing of environmental debate arose from changes in the magnitude and form of these threats from modern technology. That technology was applied in increasing scale and scope, from enormous drag-lines in strip mining, to 1000-megawatt electric generating plants and "energy parks," to superports and large-scale petrochemical plants, to 765-kilovolt energy transmission lines. And there was the vast increase in the use and release into the environment of chemicals, relatively contained and generating a chemical "sea around us" which many people considered to be a long-run hazard that was out of control. The view of these technological changes as threats seemed to come primarily from their size and scale, the enormity of their range of impact, in contrast with the more human scale of daily affairs. New technologies appeared to constitute radical influences, disruptive of settled community and personal life, of a scope that was often beyond comprehension, and promoted and carried through by influences "out there" from the wider corporate and governmental world. All this brought to environmental issues the problem of "control," of how one could shape more limited personal and community circumstance in the face of large-scale and radical change impinging from afar upon daily life.

Stages in the Evolution of Environmental Action

Emerging environmental values did not make themselves felt all in the same way or at the same time. Within the context of our concern here for patterns of historical change, therefore, it might be well to secure some sense of stages of development within the post-World War II years. The most prevalent notion is to identify Earth Day in 1970 as the dividing line. There are other candidate events, such as the publication of Rachel Carson's *Silent Spring* in 1962, and the Santa Barbara oil blowout in 1969. But in any event definition of change in these matters seems to be inadequate. Earth Day was as much a result as a cause. It came after a decade or more of underlying evolution in attitudes and action without which it would not have been possible. Many environmental organizations, established earlier, experienced considerable growth in membership during the 1960's, reflecting an expanding concern. The regulatory mechanisms and issues in such fields as air and water pollution were shaped then; for example the Clean Air Act of 1967 established the character of the air quality program more than did that of 1970. General public awareness and interest were expressed extensively in a variety of public forums and in the mass media. Evolving public values could be observed in the growth of the outdoor recreation movement which reached back into the 1950's and the search for amenities in quieter and more natural settings, in the increasing number of people who engaged in hiking and camping or purchased recreational lands and homes on the seashore, by lakes and in woodlands. This is not to say that the entire scope of environmental concerns emerged fully in the 1960's. It did not. But one can observe a gradual evolution rather than a sudden outburst at the turn of the decade, a cumulative social and political change that came to be expressed vigorously even long before Earth Day.

We might identify three distinct stages of evolution. Each stage brought a new set of issues to the fore without eliminating the previous ones, in a set of historical layers. Old issues persisted to be joined by new ones, creating over the years an increasingly complex and varied world of environmental controversy and debate. The initial complex of issues which arrived on the scene of national politics emphasized natural environment values in such matters as outdoor recreation, wildlands and open space. These shaped debate between 1957 and 1965 and constituted the initial thrust of environmental action. After World War II the American people, with increased income and leisure time, sought out the nation's forests and parks, its wildlife refuges, its state and federal public lands, for recreation and enjoyment. Recognition of this growing interest and the demands upon public policy which it generated, led Congress in 1958 to establish the National Outdoor Recreation Review Commission which completed its report in 1962. Its recommendations heavily influenced public policy during the Johnson administration. . . .

During the 1950's many in urban areas had developed a concern for urban overdevelopment and the need for open space in their communities. . . . The concern for open space extended to regional as well as community projects, involving a host of natural environment areas ranging from pine barrens to wetlands to swamps to creeks and streams to remnants of the original prairies. Throughout the 1960's there were attempts to add to the national park system which gave rise to new parks such as Canyonlands in Utah, new national lakeshores and seashores and new national recreation areas.

These matters set the dominant tone of the initial phase of environmental concern until the mid-1960's. They did not decline in importance, but continued to shape administrative and legislative action as specific proposals for wilderness, scenic rivers or other natural areas emerged to be hotly debated. Such general measures as the Eastern Wilderness Act of 1974 . . . and the Alaska National Interest Lands Act of 1980 testified to the perennial public concern for natural environment areas. . . . One might argue that these were the most enduring and fundamental environmental issues throughout the two decades. While other citizen concerns might ebb and flow, interest in natural environment areas persisted steadily. That interest was the dominant reason for membership growth in the largest environmental organizations. The Nature Conservancy, a private group which emphasized acquisition of natural environment lands, grew in activity in the latter years of the 1970's and reached 100,000 members in 1981. . . .

Amid this initial stage of environmental politics there evolved a new and different concern for the adverse impact of industrial development with a special focus on air and water pollution. This had long evolved slowly on a local and piecemeal basis, but emerged with national force only in the mid-1960's. In the early part of the decade air and water pollution began to take on significance as national issues and by 1965 they had become highly visible. The first national public opinion poll on such questions was taken in that year, and the President's annual message in 1965 reflected, for the first time, a full fledged concern for pollution problems. Throughout the rest of the decade and on into the 1970's these issues evolved continually. Federal legislation to stimulate remedial action was shaped over the course of these seven years, from 1965 to 1972, a distinct period which constituted the second phase in the evolution of environmental politics, taking its place alongside the previously developing concern for natural environment areas.

The legislative results were manifold. Air pollution was the subject of new laws in 1967 and 1970; water pollution in 1965, 1970 and 1972. The evolving concern about pesticides led to revision of the existing law in the Pesticides Act of 1972. The growing public interest in natural environment values in the coastal zone, and threats to them by dredging and filling, industrial siting and offshore oil development first made its mark on Congress in 1965 and over the next few years shaped the course of legislation which finally emerged in the Coastal Zone Management Act of 1972. Earth Day in the spring of 1970 lay in the middle of this phase of historical development, both a result of the previous half-decade of activity and concern and a new influence to accelerate action. . . .

Yet this new phase was shaped heavily by the previous period in that it gave primary emphasis to the harmful impact of pollution on ecological systems rather than on human health—a concern which was to come later. In the years between 1965 and 1972 the interest in "ecology" came to the fore to indicate the intense public interest in potential harm to the natural environment and in protection against disruptive threats. The impacts of highway construction, electric power plants and industrial siting on wildlife, on aquatic ecosystems and on natural environments in general played a major role in the evolution of this concern. . . . The major concern for the adverse effect of nuclear energy generation in the late 1960's involved its potential disruption of aquatic ecosystems from thermal pollution rather than the effect of radiation on people. The rapidly growing ecological concern was an extension of the natural environment interests of the years 1957 to 1965 into the problem of the adverse impacts of industrial growth.

Beginning in the early 1970's still a third phase of environmental politics arose which brought three other sets of issues into public debate: toxic chemicals, energy and the possibilities of social, economic and political decentralization. These did not obliterate earlier issues, but as some natural environment matters and concern over the adverse effects of industrialization shifted from legislative to administrative politics, and thus became less visible to the general public, these new issues emerged often to dominate the scene. They were influenced heavily by the seemingly endless series of toxic chemical episodes, from PBB's in Michigan to kepone in Virginia to PCB's on the Hudson River, to the discovery of abandoned chemical dumps at Love Canal and near Louisville, Kentucky. These events, however, were only the more sensational aspects of a more deep-seated new twist in public concern for human health. Interest in personal health and especially in preventive health action took a major leap forward in the 1970's. It seemed to focus especially on such matters as cancer and environmental pollutants responsible for a variety of health problems, on food and diet on the one hand and exercise on the other. From these interests arose a central concern for toxic threats in the workplace, in the air and water, and in food and personal habits that came to shape some of the overriding issues of the 1970's on the environmental front. It shifted the earlier emphasis on the ecological effects of toxic pollutants to one more on human health effects. Thus, while proceedings against DDT in the late 1960's had emphasized adverse ecological impacts, similar proceedings in the 1970's focused primarily on human health.

The energy crisis of the winter of 1973–74 brought a new issue to the fore. Not that energy matters had gone unnoticed earlier, but their salience had been far more limited. After that winter they became more central. They shaped environmental politics in at least two ways. First energy problems brought material shortages more forcefully into the realm of substantive environmental concerns and emphasized more strongly the problem of limits which these shortages imposed upon material growth. The physical shortages of energy sources such as oil in the United States, the impact of shortages on rising prices, the continued emphasis on the need for energy conservation all helped to etch into the experience and thinking of Americans the "limits" to which human appetite for consumption could go. Second, the intense demand for development of new energy sources increased significantly the political influence of developmental advocates in governmental, corporate and technical institutions which had long chafed under both natural environment and pollution control programs. This greatly overweighted the balance of political forces so that environmental leaders had far greater difficulty in being heard. . . .

Lifestyle issues also injected a new dimension into environmental affairs during the course of the 1970's. They became especially visible in the energy debates, as the contrast emerged between highly centralized technologies on the one hand, and decentralized systems on the other. Behind these debates lay the evolution of new ideas about organizing one's daily life, one's home, community and leisure activities and even work—all of which had grown out of the changing lifestyles of younger Americans. It placed considerable emphasis on more personal, family and community autonomy in the face of the forces of larger social, economic and political organization. The impact and role of this change was not always clear, but it emerged forcefully in the energy debate as decentralized solar systems and conservation seemed to be appropriate to decisions made personally and locally—on a more human scale—contrasting markedly with high-technology systems which leaders of technical, corporate and governmental institutions seemed to prefer. Issues pertaining to the centralization of political control played an increasing role in environmental politics as the 1970's came to a close. . . .

From the beginning of [the Reagan] administration, the new governmental leaders made clear their conviction that the "environmental movement" had spent itself, was no longer viable, and could readily be dismissed and ignored. During the campaign the Reagan entourage had refused often to meet with citizen environmental groups, and in late November it made clear that it would not even accept the views of its own "transition team" which was made up of former Republican administration environmentalists who were thought to be far too extreme. Hence environmentalists of all these varied hues faced a hostile government that was not prone to be evasive or deceptive about that hostility. Its anti-environmental views were expressed with enormous vigor and clarity.

We can well look upon that challenge as an historical experiment which tested the extent and permanence of the changes in social values which lay at the root of environmental interest. By its opposition the Reagan administration could be thought of as challenging citizen environmental activity to prove itself. And the response, in turn, indicated a degree of depth and persistence which makes clear that environmental affairs stem from the extensive and deep-seated changes we have been describing. Most striking perhaps have been the public opinion polls during 1981 pertaining to revision of the Clean Air Act. On two occasions, in April and in September the Harris poll found that some 80% of the American people favor at least maintaining that Act or making it stricter, levels of positive environmental opinion on air quality higher than for polls in the 1960's or 1970. . . .

We might take this response to the Reagan administration challenge, therefore, as evidence of the degree to which we can assess the environmental activities of the past three decades as associated with fundamental and persistent change, not a temporary display of sentiment, which causes environmental values to be injected into public affairs continuously and even more vigorously in the face of political adversity. The most striking aspect of this for the historian lies in the way in which it identifies more sharply the social roots of environmental values, perception and action. Something is there, in a broad segment of the American people which shapes the course of public policy in these decades after World War II that was far different from the case earlier. One observes not rise and fall, but persistent evolution, changes rooted in personal circumstance which added up to broad social changes out of which "movements" and political action arise and are sustained. Environmental affairs take on meaning as integral parts of a "new society" that is an integral element of the advanced consumer and industrial order of the last half of the 20th century.

Sources

Watergate

The most compelling symbol of national decline was Richard Nixon, forced to resign the presidency in 1974 as a result of his participation in the Watergate "cover-up."

Although we normally associate this event with the 1970s, Watergate had its origins in the late 1960s, when members of the Nixon administration began wiretapping telephones in an effort to

plug information leaks about the secret bombing of Cambodia. Consumed by the need to control, the Nixon administration had by the fall of 1969 embarked on a campaign to isolate and discredit the peace movement and had brought Jeb Stuart Magruder to Washington to centralize White House public relations. May Day demonstrations against the American invasion of Cambodia in April 1970 and the leak of military documents (the so-called Pentagon Papers) by Pentagon employee Daniel Ellsberg in June 1971 brought increasing pressure on Magruder (who had moved to the Committee for the Reelection of the President [CREEP]) to engage in intelligence-gathering activities. As the 1972 election approached, Magruder and John Mitchell, former attorney general and then CREEP head, began to gather information on contenders for the Democratic presidential nomination and on Larry O'Brien, chairman of the Democratic National Committee. In June 1972, five CREEP operatives were apprehended at the Democratic National Committee headquarters in Washington's Watergate complex. When the president's own tape recordings revealed that he and a number of his advisers had conspired to conceal information about the break-in, a humiliated Nixon resigned.

What follows is a partial transcript of a conversation held in the Oval Office on March 21, 1973, between Nixon (P) and White House counsel John Dean (D), whose testimony before the Senate Select Committee on Presidential Campaign Activities would later prove the undoing of the administration. Among those mentioned are Donald Segretti, in charge of campaign "dirty tricks"; G. Gordon Liddy, counsel to CREEP; Gordon Strachan, assistant to H. R. Haldeman, the White House chief of staff; Senator Edmund Muskie, a contender for the 1972 Democratic presidential nomination; E. Howard Hunt, a former CIA agent who was one of those caught in the Watergate complex; Charles Colson, special counsel to Nixon; John Ehrlichman, Nixon's chief domestic-policy adviser; and Egil Krogh, Jr., chief assistant to Ehrlichman.

From this account, how would you evaluate Nixon's relationship to the Watergate burglary? How would you characterize his response to Dean's information? What conclusions were the American people entitled to draw from evidence such as this?

D I think that there is no doubt about the seriousness of the problem we've got. We have a cancer within, close to the Presidency, that is growing. It is growing daily. It's compounded, growing geometrically now, because it compounds itself. That will be clear if I, you know, explain some of the details of why it is. Basically, it is because (1) we are being blackmailed; (2) People are going to start perjuring themselves very

quickly that have not had to perjure themselves to protect other people
in the line. And there is no assurance—

P That that won't bust?

D That that won't bust. So let me give you the sort of basic facts, talking
first about the Watergate; and then about Segretti; and then about some
of the peripheral items that have come up. First of all on the Watergate:
how did it all start, where did it start? O.K.! It started with an instruction
to me from Bob Haldeman to see if we couldn't set up a perfectly legitimate campaign intelligence operation over at the Re-Election Committee.
Not being in this business, I turned to somebody who had been in this
business, Jack Caulfield. I don't remember whether you remember Jack
or not. He was your original bodyguard before they had the candidate
protection, an old city policeman.

P Yes, I know him.

D Jack worked for John and then was transferred to my office. I said Jack
come up with a plan that, you know—a normal infiltration, buying
information from secretaries and all that sort of thing. He did, he put
together a plan. It was kicked around. I went to Ehrlichman with it. I
went to Mitchell with it, and the consensus was that Caulfield was not
the man to do this. In retrospect, that might have been a bad call because
he is an incredibly cautious person and wouldn't have put the situation
where it is today. After rejecting that, they said we still need something
so I was told to look around for someone who could go over to 1701
and do this. That is when I came up with Gordon Liddy. They needed
a lawyer. Gordon had an intelligence background from his FBI service.
I was aware of the fact that he had done some extremely sensitive things
for the White House while he had been at the White House and he had
apparently done them well. Going out into Ellsberg's doctor's office—

P Oh, yeah.

D And things like this. He worked with leaks. He tracked these things down.
So the report that I got from Krogh was that he was a hell of a good
man and not only that a good lawyer and could set up a proper operation.
So we talked to Liddy. He was interested in doing it. I took Liddy
over to meet Mitchell. Mitchell thought highly of him because Mitchell
was partly involved in his coming to the White House to work for
Krogh. Liddy had been at Treasury before that. Then Liddy was told
to put together his plan, you know, how he would run an intelligence
operation. This was after he was hired over there at the Committee.
Magruder called me in January and said I would like to have you come
over and see Liddy's plan.

P January of '72?

D January of '72.

D "You come over to Mitchell's office and sit in a meeting where Liddy is
going to lay his plan out." I said I don't really know if I am the man,
but if you want me there I will be happy to. So I came over and Liddy
laid out a million dollar plan that was the most incredible thing I have

ever laid my eyes on: all in codes, and involved black bag operations, kidnapping, providing prostitutes to weaken the opposition, bugging, mugging teams. It was just an incredible thing.

P Tell me this: Did Mitchell go along—?

D No, no, not at all. Mitchell just sat there puffing and laughing. I could tell from—after Liddy left the office I said that is the most incredible thing I have ever seen. He said I agree. And so Liddy was told to go back to the drawingboard and come up with something realistic. So there was a second meeting. They asked me to come over to that. I came into the tail end of the meeting. I wasn't there for the first part. I don't know how long the meeting lasted. At this point, they were discussing again bugging, kidnapping and the like. At this point I said right in front of everybody, very clearly, I said, "These are not the sort of things (1) that are ever to be discussed in the office of the Attorney General of the United States—that was where he still was—and I am personally incensed." And I am trying to get Mitchell off the hook. He is a nice person and doesn't like to have to say no when he is talking with people he is going to have to work with.

P That's right.

D So I let it be known. I said "You all pack that stuff up and get it the hell out of here. You just can't talk this way in this office and you should re-examine your whole thinking."

P Who all was present?

D It was Magruder, Mitchell, Liddy and myself. I came back right after the meeting and told Bob, "Bob, we have a growing disaster on our hands if they are thinking this way," and I said, "The White House has got to stay out of this and I, frankly, am not going to be involved in it." He said, "I agree John." I thought at that point that the thing was turned off. That is the last I heard of it and I thought it was turned off because it was an absurd proposal.

P Yeah.

D Liddy—I did have dealings with him afterwards and we never talked about it. Now that would be hard to believe for some people, but we never did. That is the fact of the matter.

P Well, you were talking with him about other things.

D We had so many other things.

P He had some legal problems too. But you were his advisor, and I understand you had conversations about the campaign laws, etc. Haldeman told me that you were handling all of that for us. Go ahead.

D Now. So Liddy went back after that and was over at 1701, the Committee, and this is where I come into having put the pieces together after the fact as to what I can put together about what happened. Liddy sat over there and tried to come up with another plan that he could sell. (1) They were talking to him, telling him that he was putting too much money in it. I don't think they were discounting the illegal points. Jeb is not a lawyer. He did not know whether this is the way the game was played and what it was all about. They came up, apparently, with another plan, but they couldn't get it approved by anybody over there. So Liddy and Hunt apparently came to see Chuck Colson, and Chuck Colson picked up the telephone and called Magruder and said, "You all either fish or cut bait. This is absurd to have these guys over there and not using them. If you are not going to use them, I may use them." Things of this nature.

P When was this?

D This was apparently in February of '72.

P Did Colson know what they were talking about?

D I can only assume, because of his close relationship with Hunt, that he had a damn good idea what they were talking about, a damn good idea. He would probably deny it today and probably get away with denying it. But I still—unless Hunt blows on him—

P But then Hunt isn't enough. It takes two doesn't it?

D Probably. Probably. But Liddy was there also and if Liddy were to blow—

P Then you have a problem—I was saying as to the criminal liability in the White House. . . .

D Magruder gave the instructions to be back in the DNC.*

P He did?

D Yes.

P You know that?

D Yes.

P I see. O.K.

D I honestly believe that no one over here knew that. I know that as God is my maker, I had no knowledge that they were going to do this.

P Bob didn't either, or wouldn't have known that either. You are not the issue involved. Had Bob known, he would be.

D Bob—I don't believe specifically knew that they were going in there.

P I don't think so.

D I don't think he did. I think he knew that there was a capacity to do this but he was not given the specific direction. . . .

D Hunt has now made a direct threat against Ehrlichman. As a result of this, this is his blackmail. He says, "I will bring John Ehrlichman down to his knees and put him in jail. I have done enough seamy things for he and Krogh, they'll never survive it."

P Was he talking about Ellsberg?

D Ellsberg, and apparently some other things. I don't know the full extent of it.

P I don't know about anything else. . . .

P What in the (expletive deleted) caused this? (unintelligible)

D Mr. President, there have been a couple of things around here that I have gotten wind of. At one time there was a desire to do a second story

*Headquarters of the Democratic National Committee.—*Ed.*

job on the Brookings Institute where they had the Pentagon papers. Now I flew to California because I was told that John had instructed it and he said, "I really hadn't. It is a mis-impression, but for (expletive deleted), turn it off." . . .

D So that is it. That is the extent of the knowledge. So where are the soft spots on this? Well, first of all, there is the problem of the continued blackmail which will not only go on now, but it will go on while these people are in prison, and it will compound the obstruction of justice situation. It will cost money. It is dangerous. People around here are not pros at this sort of thing. This is the sort of thing Mafia people can do: washing money, getting clean money, and things like that. We just don't know about those things, because we are not criminals and not used to dealing in that business.

P That's right.

D It is a tough thing to know how to do.

P Maybe it takes a gang to do that.

D That's right. There is a real problem as to whether we could even do it. Plus there is a real problem in raising money. Mitchell has been working on raising some money. He is one of the ones with the most to lose. But there is no denying the fact that the White House, in Ehrlichman, Haldeman and Dean are involved in some of the early money decisions.

P How much money do you need?

D I would say these people are going to cost a million dollars over the next two years.

P We could get that. On the money, if you need the money you could get that. You could get a million dollars. You could get it in cash. I know where it could be gotten. It is not easy, but it could be done. But the question is who the hell would handle it? Any ideas on that?

D That's right. Well, I think that is something that Mitchell ought to be charged with.

P I would think so too.

D And get some pros to help him. . . .

P Who else do you think has—

D Potential criminal liability?

P Yeah.

D I think Ehrlichman does. I think that uh—

P Why?

D Because of this conspiracy to burglarize the Ellsberg doctors' office.

P That is, provided Hunt's breaks?

D Well, the funny—let me say something interesting about that. Within the files—

P Oh, I thought of it. The picture!

D Yes, sir. That is not all that buried. And while I think we've got it buried, there is no telling when it is going to pop up. Now the Cubans could start this whole thing. When the Ervin Committee starts running down

why this mysterious telephone was here in the White House listed in
the name of a secretary, some of these secretaries have a little idea about
this, and they can be broken down just so fast. That is another thing I
mentioned in the cycle—in the circle. Liddy's secretary, for example, is
knowledgeable. Magruder's secretary is knowledgeable.

P Sure. So Ehrlichman on the—

D What I am coming in today with is: I don't have a plan on how to solve
   it right now, but I think it is at the juncture that we should begin to
   think in terms of how to cut the losses; how to minimize the further
   growth of this thing, rather than further compound it by, you know,
   ultimately paying these guys forever. I think we've got to look—

P But at the moment, don't you agree it is better to get the Hunt thing
   that's where that—

D That is worth buying time on.

P That is buying time, I agree.

The Women's Movement

Robin Morgan

Rights of Passage

**When Kevin Phillips coined the term "Balkanization" to describe
the fragmentation of the American nation in the 1970s, he cited the
women's movement for its militance and for its contribution to di-
visive group categorization. The following manifesto, written in
1975 by radical feminist and poet Robin Morgan, may suggest another interpretation, one that might lead us to question whether
"Balkanization" should be used as a pejorative.**

I wanted to write a sort of "personal retrospective" on the Women's
Movement: where we've been, where we are, where we might be going—
all this in a classically theoretical style, preferably obscure, yea, unintelligible,
so that people would be unable to understand what in hell I was saying and
would label me, therefore, A Brilliant Thinker. But the risk-taking, subjective
voice of poetry is more honestly my style, and so, to look at the Women's
Movement, I go to the mirror—and gaze at myself. Everywoman? Surely a
staggering egotism, that! I hardly believe "Le Mouvement, c'est moi." I *do*
still believe, though, that the personal is political, and vice versa (the *politics*
of sex, the *politics* of housework, the *politics* of motherhood), and that this

insight into the necessary integration of exterior realities and interior impera-
tives is one of the themes of consciousness that makes the Women's Movement
unique, less abstract, and more functionally *possible* than previous movements
for social change.

So I must dare to begin with myself, my own experience.

Ten years ago I was a woman who believed in the reality of the vaginal
orgasm (and had become adept at faking spiffy ones). I felt legitimized by a
successful crown roast and was the fastest hand in the east at emptying ash-
trays. I never condemned pornography for fear of seeming unsophisticated
and prudish. My teenage rebellion against my mother had atrophied into a
permanent standoff. Despite hours of priming myself to reflect the acceptable
beauty standards, I was convinced that my body was lumpy, my face was
possessed of a caterpillar's bone structure, and my hair was resolutely unyielding to *any* flattering style. And ten years ago my poems quietly began muttering something about my personal pain as a woman—unconnected, of course,
to anyone else, since I saw this merely as my own inadequacy, my own
battle. . . .

There were the years in the New Left—the civil rights movement, the
student movement, the peace movement, and their more "militant" offspring
groups—until my inescapably intensifying woman's consciousness led me,
along with thousands of other women, to become a refugee from what I
came to call "the male-dominated left" and what I now refer to as "the
boys' movement." . . .

That was the period when I still could fake a convincing orgasm, still
wouldn't be caught dead confronting an issue like pornography (for fear,
this time, of being "a bad-vibes, up-tight, un-hip chick"). I could now afford
to reject my mother for a new, radical-chic reason: the generation gap. I
learned to pretend contempt for monogamy as both my husband and I ca-
reened (secretly grieving for each other) through the fake "sexual revolution"
of the sixties. Meanwhile, correctly Maoist beancurd and class-conscious rice
and beans filled our menus—and I *still* put in hours priming myself to reflect
the acceptable "beauty" standards, those of a tough-broad street fighter: uniform jeans, combat boots, long hair, and sunglasses worn even at night (which
didn't help one see better when running from rioting cops). And my poems
lurched forth guiltily, unevenly, while I developed a chronic case of Leningitis
and mostly churned out those "political" essays—although Donne and Dickin-
son, Kafka, Woolf, and James were still read in secret at our home (dangerous
intellectual tendencies), and television was surreptitiously watched (decadent
bourgeois privileges).

For years my essays implored, in escalating tones, the "brothers" of
the "revolution" to let us women in, to take more-than-lip-service notice of
what the women's caucuses were saying, especially since "they" (women)
constitute more than half the human species. Then, at a certain point, I began
to stop addressing such men as "brothers," and began (O language, thou
subtle Richter scale of attitudinal earthquakes!) to use the word "we" when
speaking of women. And there was no turning back.

The ensuing years can seem to me a blur of joy, misery, and daily surprise: my first consciousness-raising group and all the "daughter" groups I was in; the guerrilla theater, the marches, meetings, demonstrations, picketings, sit-ins, conferences, workshops, plenaries; the newspaper projects, the child-care collectives, the first anti-rape squads, the earliest seminars (some women now prefer the word "ovulars"—how lovely!) on women's health, women's legal rights, women's sexuality. And all the while, the profound "interior" changes: the transformation of my work—content, language, *and* form—released by this consciousness; the tears and shouts and laughter and despair and growth wrought in the struggle with my husband; the birth of our child (a radicalizing experience, to say the least); the detailed examinations of life experiences, of power, honesty, commitment, bravely explored through so many vulnerable hours with other women—the discovery of a shared suffering and of a shared determination to become whole.

During those years we felt a desperate urgency, arising partly from the barrage of brain-boggling "clicks" our consciousness encountered about our condition as females in a patriarchal world; but also, I must confess, arising from the leftover influence of the male movements, which were given to abstract rhetoric but "ejaculatory tactics." That is, if the revolution as they defined it didn't occur within the next week, month, five years at the minimum—then the hell with it. We wouldn't be alive, anyway, to see it, so we must die for it (this comfortably settled the necessity for any long range *planning*).

Today, my just-as-ever-urgent anger is tempered by a patience born of the recognition that the *process*, the *form of change itself, is everything:* the means and the goal justifying *each other.*

There are no easy victories, no pat answers—and anyone who purveys such solutions alarms me now. But when I look back from my still-militantly rocking chair, or sit at my ultimate weapon, the typewriter, I see the transformations spiraling upward so rapidly and so astonishingly that my heart swells with gratitude to have been a part of such changes.

We were an "American phenomenon," they said—an outgrowth of the neurosis and stridency of spoiled American women. ("They" were the patriarchal left, right, and middle, the media, most men, and some women.) They overlooked certain little facts: that women had been oppressed longer than any other group, this subjugation having stood as the model for all subsequent forms of oppression; that women were a *majority* of the world's population; that specific commonalities of biology, attitude, and certainly treatment potentially united us across all the patriarchally imposed barriers of race, age, class, sexual preference, superficial politics, and lifestyles. Now, as I write, this potential is vibrating throughout the globe—among Women's Movements in Senegal and Tanzania, Japan and Australia, China and South America, and all across Europe, New Zealand, Algeria, Canada, Israel, Egypt, and the Indian subcontinent.

We were "a white, middle-class, youth movement," they said. And even as some of us wrung our hands with guilt hand lotion, we knew otherwise.

Because there were from the beginning women involved who were of every class and race and age, even if the media did focus on a conveniently stereotyped "feminist image." . . . [D]omestic workers, secretaries, hospital employees, welfare mothers, waitresses, and hundreds of thousands of other women—too long a list to name here—are fighting for their/our rights.

They said we were "anti-housewife," though many of us *were* housewives, and it was not us, but society itself, as structured by men, which had contempt for life-sustenance tasks. Today, too many housewives are in open participation in the Women's Movement to be ignored—and many are talking of a housewives' union. (Not to speak of the phenomenon of "runaway wives," as the news media calls them in articles which puzzle over the "motivation" of women who simply have picked up one dirty sock too many from the living-room floor.)

They said we were "a lesbian plot," and the carefully implanted and fostered bigotry of many heterosexual feminists rose eagerly, destructively, to deny that, thereby driving many lesbian women out of the Movement, back into the arms of their gay "brothers," who promptly shoved mimeograph machines at them. What a choice. But the process did continue, and so the pendulum swung into its tactically tragic but expectable position, a reply-in-kind from some lesbian-feminists who created the politics of "dyke separatism," the refusal to work with or sometimes even speak to women who could not prove lesbian credentials. This was sometimes accompanied by the proclamation that lesbians were the only true feminists, or were the feminist "vanguard," and the accusation that all heterosexual women were forever "sold out" to men (leaving lesbian mothers, by the way, in a no-woman's-land). In some parts of the country it was called "the lesbian-straight split"—or even the "lesbian-feminist split"—with a terrifying antagonism on both sides. Yet most serious feminists continued to work together, across sexual-preference labeling, and the process endured (through many, many tears), and we survived. More and more, every day, that "split" is healing. . . .

They said we were "anti-motherhood"—and in the growing pains of certain periods, some of us were. There were times when I was made to feel guilty for having wanted and borne a child—let alone a male one, forgodsake. There were other times when we "collectivized" around children, and I found myself miffed at the temporary loss of that relationship unique to the specific mother and specific child. So much of the transition is understandable now. Since the patriarchy commanded women to be mothers (the thesis), we had to rebel with our own polarity and declare motherhood a reactionary cabal (antithesis). Today, a *new* synthesis is emerging: the concept of mother-right, the affirmation of child bearing and/or child rearing when it is a woman's *choice*. And while that synthesis itself will in turn become a new thesis (a dialectic, a process, a development), it is refreshing at last to be able to come out of my mother-closet and yell to the world that I love my dear wonderful delicious child—and am not one damned whit less the radical feminist for that.

None of the above-mentioned issues, or even "splits," among us as women is simple. None is "solved." Struggle, experimentation, and examination of each of these differences (and new ones yet to come) will continue, must continue, for years. And we can expect these divisions to be exploited as *diversions* by those who would love to see us fail. But that no longer scares or depresses me, despite the enormity of the job ahead. The only thing that does frighten me is the superficial treatment of any such issue, the simplifying of complexities out of intellectual laziness, fear of the unknown, or rigidified thinking. Yet despite the temptation to fall into such traps of "non-thought," the growth does continue and the motion cannot be stopped. There is no turning back. . . .

I've watched the bloody internecine warfare between groups, between individuals. All that fantastic energy going to fight each other instead of our oppression! (It is, after all, safer to attack "just women.") So much false excitement, self-righteousness and judgmental posturing! Gossip, accusations, counter-accusations, smears—all leapt to, spread, and sometimes believed without the impediments of such things as facts. I've come to think that we need a feminist code of ethics, that we need to create a new *women's* morality, an antidote of honor against this contagion by male supremacist values.

I've watched the rise of what I call "Failure Vanguardism"—the philosophy that . . . to succeed in the slightest is to be Impure. . . . Well, to such a transparently destructive message I say, with great dignity, "Fooey." I want to *win* for a change. I want us *all* to *win*. And I love, support, and honor the courage of every feminist who dares to try to *succeed,* whatever the realm of her attempt. . . .

I would say to those few dear "oldies" who are burned out or embittered: you have forgotten that women are not fools, not sheep. We know about the dangers of commercialism and tokenism from the male right, and the dangers of manipulation and cooptation from the male left (the boys' establishment and the boys' movement). We are, frankly, bored by correct lines and vanguards and failurism and particularly by that chronic disease—guilt. Those of us who choose to struggle with men we love, well, we demand respect and support for that, and an end to psychological torture which claims we made our choice only because of psychological torture. Those of us who choose to relate solely to other women demand respect and support for *that,* and an end to the legal persecution and attitudinal bigotry that condemns freedom of sexual choice. Those of us who choose to have or choose *not* to have children demand support and respect for *that.* We know that the emerging women's art and women's spirituality are life-blood for our survival—resilient cultures have kept oppressed groups alive even when economic analyses and revolutionary strategy have fizzled.

We know that serious, lasting change does not come about overnight, or simply, or without enormous pain and diligent examination and tireless, undramatic, every-day-a-bit-more-one-step-at-a-time work. We know that such change seems to move in cycles (thesis, antithesis, and synthesis—which itself in turn becomes a new thesis . . .), and we also know that those cycles are not merely going around in circles. They are, rather, an *upward spiral,* so that each time we reevaluate a position or place we've been before we do so from a new perspective. . . .

Housewives across the nation stage the largest consumer boycott ever known (the meat boycott) and while it may not seem, superficially, a feminist action, *women* are doing this, women who ten years ago, before this feminist movement, might have regarded such an action as unthinkable. The campaign for passage of the Equal Rights Amendment continues to gain supporters (like that fine closet-feminist Betty Ford) despite all the combined right *and* left forces of reaction against it. Consciousness-raising proliferates, in groups, in individuals, in new forms and with new structures. The lines of communication begin to center around content instead of geography, and to stretch from coast to coast, so that women in an anti-rape project, for example, may be more in touch with other anti-rape groups nationally than with every latest development in the Women's Movement in their own backyards. I think this is to the good; it's a widening of vision, an exercising of muscle. It's Thinking Big.

We Haven't Come a Long Way, and Don't Call Me Baby

What conclusions can you draw from this photograph about the woman's movement—about its strengths and weaknesses? Does the photograph anticipate some of the problems raised in Robin Morgan's essay?

A Rally in Washington, D.C., November 1971. *Photo by Dennis Brack from Black Star.*

High Culture

Against a background of Watergate, the energy crisis, and recession, the opening of the National Gallery's East Building in mid-1978 took on great symbolic importance. Although most of the funds for the project had been donated by Paul Mellon and Bunny Mellon, the building itself was interpreted by critics in the most public terms. "What a difference a little glory makes," wrote Henry Mitchell in the *Washington Post*.

> For the first time, many thought, the city has a building that does not so much interpret this century as give stature to it. Our daily lives—the snafu of airports, the botch of subways, the abrasion of petty concerns—all this is transformed. The building tells every citizen of the town that theirs is no mean city, and their lives are no mean lives, but fit for a fabric of astonishing richness and grace.

In analyzing the photographs, assume that the building was in some sense designed as an antithesis to Watergate or to what Watergate represented. In this light, what sort of statement does the East Building make? In your opinion, does the building deserve the praise it received?

Interior View of the East Building, National Gallery, Washington, D.C.
Designed by I. M. Pei, the building was opened in 1978. *National Gallery*.

Exterior View of the East Building, National Gallery, Washington, D.C.
National Gallery.

Mass Culture: The Television Age

In the 1950s, the new medium of television was, for the most part, received uncritically. It was, in fact, often celebrated as a kind of family and cultural adhesive—part of the Eisenhower equilibrium, in a sense (see the photograph on p. 269). The 1960s brought increasing awareness of the control of television by giant corporations and with that awareness, the development of public television. By the 1980s, critics of American television united in condemning the medium as stupid, boring, vacuous, and—perhaps most important—harmful to children. Among those who entered the debate were writer Neil Postman and cartoonist Tom Toles. Do their analyses of television's place in American culture differ from each other?

Neil Postman

Childhood's End

In order for me to get to the center of my argument as quickly as possible, I am going to resist the temptation to discuss some of the fairly obvious effects of television, such as its role in shortening our students' attention span, in eroding their capacity to handle linguistic and mathematical symbolism, and in causing them to become increasingly impatient with deferred gratification. The evidence for these effects exists in a variety of forms—from declining SAT scores to astronomical budgets for remedial writing classes to the everyday observations of teachers and parents. But I will not take the time to review any of the evidence for the intellectually incapacitating effects of television. Instead, I want to focus on what I regard as the most astonishing and serious effect of television. It is simply this: Television is causing the rapid decline of our concept of childhood. . . .

For the past 350 years we have been developing and refining our concept of childhood, this with particular intensity in the 18th, 19th, and 20th centuries. We have been developing and refining institutions for the nurturing of children; and we have conferred upon children a preferred status, reflected in the special ways we expect them to think, talk, dress, play, and learn.

All of this, I believe, is now coming to an end. And it is coming to an end because our communication environment has been radically altered once again—this time by electronic media, especially television. Television has a transforming power at least equal to that of the printing press and possibly as great as that of the alphabet itself. It is my contention that, with the assistance of other media such as radio, film, and records, television has the power to lead us to childhood's end.

Here is how the transformation is happening. To begin with, television presents information mostly in visual images. Although human speech is heard on TV and sometimes assumes importance, people mostly *watch* television. What they watch are rapidly changing visual images—as many as 1,200 different shots every hour. This requires very little conceptual thinking or analytic decoding. TV watching is almost wholly a matter of pattern recognition. The *symbolic form* of television does not require any special instruction or learning. In America, TV viewing begins at about the age of 18 months; by 30 months, according to studies by Daniel Anderson of the University of Massachusetts, children begin to understand and respond to TV imagery. Thus there is no need for any preparation or prerequisite training for watching TV. Television needs no analogue to the McGuffey *Reader*. And, as you must know, there is no such thing, in reality, as children's programming on

From Neil Postman, "The Day Our Children Disappear: Predictions of a Media Ecologist," *Phi Delta Kappan*, January 1981, pp. 382–386. Reprinted with permission of the author.

TV. Everything is for everybody. So far as symbolic form is concerned, "Charlie's Angels" is as sophisticated or as simple to grasp as "Sesame Street." Unlike books, which vary greatly in syntactical and lexical complexity and which may be scaled according to the ability of the reader, TV presents information in a form that is undifferentiated in its accessibility. And that is why adults and children tend to watch the same programs. I might add, in case you are thinking that children and adults at least watch at different times, that according to Frank Mankiewicz's *Remote Control,* approximately 600,000 children watch TV between midnight and two in the morning.

To summarize: TV erases the dividing line between childhood and adulthood for two reasons: first, because it requires no instruction to grasp its form; second, because it does not segregate its audience. It communicates the same information to everyone simultaneously, regardless of age, sex, race, or level of education.

But it erases the dividing line in other ways as well. One might say that the main difference between an adult and a child is that the adult knows about certain facets of life—its mysteries, its contradictions, its violence, its tragedies—that are not considered suitable for children to know. As children move toward adulthood we reveal these secrets to them in what we believe to be a psychologically assimilable way. But television makes this arrangement quite impossible. Because television operates virtually around the clock—it would not be economically feasible for it to do otherwise—it requires a constant supply of novel and interesting information. This means that all adult secrets—social, sexual, physical, and the like—must be revealed. Television forces the entire culture to come out of the closet. In its quest for new and sensational information to hold its audience, TV must tap every existing taboo in the culture: homosexuality, incest, divorce, promiscuity, corruption, adultery, sadism. Each is now merely a theme for one or another television show. In the process each loses its role as an exclusively adult secret. . . .

We are a nation of chronological grown-ups. But TV will have none of it. It is biased toward the behavior of the child-adult.

In this connection, I want to remind you of a TV commercial that sells hand lotion. In it we are shown a mother and daughter and challenged to tell which is which. I find this to be a revealing piece of sociological evidence, for it tells us that in our culture it is considered desirable that a mother should not look older than her daughter, or that a daughter should not look younger than her mother. Whether this means that childhood is gone or adulthood is gone amounts to the same thing, for if there is no clear concept of what it means to be an adult, there can be no concept of what it means to be a child.

In any case, however you wish to phrase the transformation that is taking place, it is clear that the behavior, attitudes, desires, and even physical appearance of adults and children are becoming increasingly indistinguishable. There is now virtually no difference, for example, between adult crimes and children's crimes; in many states the punishments are becoming the same. There is also very little difference in dress. The children's clothing industry has undergone a virtual revolution within the past 10 years, so that there no longer exists what we once unambiguously recognized as children's clothing. Eleven-year-olds wear three-piece suits to birthday parties; 61-year-old men wear jeans to birthday parties. Twelve-year-old girls wear high heels; 42-year-old men wear sneakers. . . .

In the 2 November 1980 *New York Times Magazine,* [historian Barbara] Tuchman offered still another example of the homogenization of childhood and adulthood. She spoke of the declining concept of quality—in literature, in art, in food, in work. Her point was that, with the emergence of egalitarianism as a political and social philosophy, there has followed a diminution of the idea of excellence in all human tasks and modes of expression. The point is that adults are *supposed* to have different tastes and standards from those of children, but through the agency of television and other modern media the differences have largely disappeared. Junk food, once suited only to the undiscriminating palates and iron stomachs of the young, is now common fare for adults. Junk literature, junk music, junk conversation are shared equally by children and adults, so that it is now difficult to find adults who can clarify and articulate for youth the differences between quality and schlock. . . .

This brings me to the final characteristic of TV that needs mentioning. The *idea* of children implies a vision of the future. They are the living messages we send to a time we will not see. But television cannot communicate a sense of the future or, for that matter, a sense of the past. It is a present-centered medium, a speed-of-light medium. Everything we see on television is experienced as happening *now,* which is why we must be told, in language, that a videotape we are seeing was made months before. The grammar of television has no analogue to the past and future tenses in language. Thus it amplifies the present out of all proportion and transforms the childish need for immediate gratification into a way of life. And we end up with what Christopher Lasch calls "the culture of narcissism"—no future, no children, everyone fixed at an age somewhere between 20 and 30. . . .

So my bad news essay comes down to these questions: In a world in which children are adults and adults children, what need is there for people like ourselves? Are the issues we are devoting our careers to solving being rendered irrelevant by the transforming power of our television culture? I devoutly hope your answers to these questions are more satisfactory than mine.

Reprinted with permission of Tom Toles and the Buffalo and Erie County Historical Society.

About the Editors

William Graebner is Professor of History at the State University of New York at Fredonia. He received the Frederick Jackson Turner Award from the Organization of American Historians for *Coal-Mining Safety in the Progressive Period: The Political Economy of Reform*. Another book, *A History of Retirement: The Meaning and Function of an American Institution, 1885–1978*, was published in 1980. He is also the author of *The Engineering of Consent: Democracy and Authority in Twentieth-Century America* (1987).

Leonard Richards is Professor of History at the University of Massachusetts at Amherst. He was awarded the 1970 Beveridge Prize by the American Historical Association for his book *"Gentlemen of Property and Standing": Anti-Abolition Mobs in Jacksonian America*. Professor Richards is also the author of *The Advent of American Democracy* and *The Life and Times of Congressman John Quincy Adams*. He is planning another book on the social history of industrial New England.

A Note on the Type

The text of this book has been set via computer-driven cathode-ray tube in a typeface named Bembo. The roman is a copy of a letter cut for the celebrated Venetian printer Aldus Manutius by Francesco Griffo and first used in Cardinal Bembo's *De Aetna* of 1495—hence the name of the revival. Griffo's type is now generally recognized, thanks to the researchers of Mr. Stanley Morison, to be the first of the old face group of types. The companion italic is an adaptation of the chancery script type designed by the Roman calligrapher and printer Lodovico degli Arrighi, called Vincentino, and used by him during the 1520s.

Composed by
Arcata Graphics/Kingsport
Kingsport, Tennessee

Printed and bound by
R. R. Donnelley
Harrisonburg, Virginia